1974

may be kept

AYS

THE NEWSMONGERS

Other Books by Robert A. Rutland

The Golden Hurricane (1953)
The Birth of the Bill of Rights (1955)
George Mason, Reluctant Statesman (1961)
The Ordeal of the Constitution (1966)
The Papers of George Mason (editor, 1970)

TWO CENTURIES OF AMERICAN LIFE:
A Bicentennial History
Harold M. Hyman and Leonard W. Levy, Editors

THE
NEWSMONGERS

Journalism in the
Life of the Nation
1690–1972

ROBERT A. RUTLAND

The Dial Press   New York   1973

Printed in the United States of America
Book design by Margaret McCutcheon Wagner
First Printing

Library of Congress Cataloging in Publication Data

Rutland, Robert Allen, 1922–
    The newsmongers.

    (Two centuries of American life)
    Includes bibliographical references.
    1. Journalism—United States—History.
I. Title.
PN4855.R8 1973   071'.3   72–10757

To Aubrey C. Land

who showed me the way

Table of Contents

Preface

Americans are often inclined to judge men and movements by a single standard: did they turn a profit or not? The so-called Sick Newspaper bill passed by Congress in 1971 follows this same line of reasoning, yet unprofitable newspapers have produced some of our best examples of crusading, informative journalism while many successful newspaper chains have a dull patina and duller word content. This criterion of success may boomerang, for in 1972 it was clear that the *New York Times* and several other excellent newspapers were faced with declining profit margins that will have to be arrested if excellence and stability are to be maintained. If a combination of forces, including the merchandising chain owner and the reckless union leader, succeed in strangling America's great newspapers one of the ironies will surely be that irresponsible capital and labor have joined an unholy alliance. The result would shake the faith of liberals and confirm the worst suspicions of the labor-baiters.

In the long run, history passes judgment on a people apart from their ability to make money. *The Newsmongers* is no conventional assessment of the failures or successes of the American press and its various offshoots. Rather, it is an effort to tell what happened when an invention from Europe was carried across the Atlantic and turned loose by a dynamic, restless, well-intentioned, and essentially conservative people who chose the path of independence. A contemporary historian of the Revolution, William Gordon, assumed that "In establishing American independence, the pen and press had merit equal to that of the sword. . . . To rouse and unite the inhabitants, and to persuade them to patience for several years . . . was effected in a great measure by the tongues and pens of the well informed citizens." In short, the press helped make America independent. Since then, the constant struggle has been to determine whether the many experiments launched by the American Revolution will have lasting value.

The term *journalism* has been variously interpreted. Journalism in the pre-radio days might consist only of a printed page issued on a regular schedule. In this volume the assumption is that journalism is a spoken, printed, or visual report of timely interest to a mass audience. Thus, while the town crier's messages were not recorded, they were a rudimentary form of journalism. Indeed, journalism, particularly before 1800, included not only newspapers and magazines but broadsides, almanacs, and pamphlets as well.

When we move from what constitutes journalism to what makes news, a different set of values must be faced. As Professor Wilbur Schramm has pointed out, news audiences have generally fitted into one of two categories. The "immediate reward" audience seeks immediate gratification of the senses, delights in scandal and small talk, and has no worries about what is news and what is entertainment—all are of a piece. Increasingly the leisure time of the immediate reward audience has been tilting away from the printed medium and toward the sight-and-sound choices offered in the twentieth century. On the other hand, the "delayed reward" audience is composed of merchants, professional men, scholars, and others who want information that may be put to use in buying stocks, renting homes, picking bargains, and learning how to use their time profitably.

Of course, the readers of the New York *Daily News* and the *New York Times* both want assurance that they are well informed. Not to be well informed is to be "out of it," and yet Dr. Samuel Johnson took a contrary view after the English learned the sad news about Saratoga in 1778. "Now the popular Clamour runs so high about our Disgraces in America, our Debt at home, our Terrors of a Bankruptcy, & Fears of a French war; what signifies all this Canting, says the Doctor? The World goes on just the same as it did; who eats the less, or who sleeps the less? Or where is all this Consternation you talk of . . . but in the News papers [?] nobody is thinking or feeling about the matter, otherwise than 'tis somewhat to talk about." Perhaps Dr. Johnson was right, and yet the heart of journalism beats because most citizens seek information about weather, wars, markets, politics, society, sports, business, and education.

In the present century, urbanization and leisure have also given journalism a unique role. Professors Paul Lazarsfeld and Robert Merton have concluded that many Americans seek information simply to be smugly well informed. They hint that many readers and viewers immerse themselves in information and delude themselves at the same time. These people read all they can find about a given topic—pollution, slum clearance, racial tension—and before long believe they are active in a viable movement. Actually they have only armchair knowledge of polluted streams, racism, slums, or whatever they learn about. This headlong plunge into the media produces what Lazarsfeld and Merton call a "narcotizing dysfunction." These readers and viewers are well informed, but otherwise almost socially inert. The Founding Fathers would have been impatient with such lethargy.

Probably the most striking feature of American journalism since 1776 has not been a remarkable stirring of ideas but instead the awesome technological progress made in gathering and distributing news to a mass audience. This positive gain has been in some degree counterbalanced by a side effect of technology—the increasingly impersonal and institutionalized journalism. For better or worse, American journalism achieved great political influence in the 1760s; two centuries later, it had declined to an auxiliary position with the average citizen commuting more and reading less than any Americans in our history. Clearly, the speed developed for reporting, printing, or otherwise disseminating the news had not been matched by a sophisticated effort to help citizens make wise social or political decisions. The point of a free press, as the Founding Fathers saw it, was to guarantee a free and helpful flow of information to active citizens. For reasons that are not altogether clear, American journalism has increasingly become a business with a secondary concern for the improvement of public men or policies. Still, there have always been men in American journalism who have believed in the people's enormous potential for proper conduct, provided they are well informed. These few crusaders, whether "muckrakers" or ink-stained do-gooders, may represent the noblest strain of American journalism.

Americans enter the Bicentennial era beset with difficulties of their own making. The verdict history will render on their nation as it passes through its two hundredth year of independence in part depends upon their willingness to reassess and realign their values. In journalism, a crucial test will come when the American people are asked to decide whether freedom of the press (and other civil liberties) is to be absolute, or whether public expression must inevitably conform to certain norms that in the long run impose restrictions. From the pages of history we can see that personal freedom, despite its great excesses, has meant a certain grandeur of the spirit. We are unsure, however, as to where the most permissive society in world history is headed. Yet nobody seems to have improved on Milton's plea: "Give me the liberty to know, to utter, and to argue freely according to conscience, above all other liberties." American journalism has been at its best when it has tried to be the nation's conscience, but a great deal of the newsmonger's energy has been spent in a desperate effort to avoid bankruptcy. After two hundred years, expensive technological changes in journalism have become in themselves revolutionary, but the basic product merely costs more, with a negligible improvement in quality. We enter the Bicentennial era with the same doubts that gripped our forebears.

THE NEWSMONGERS

In America, the impertinent eagerness for news should be scolded or laughed into moderation. The country gentleman, at peace on his farm, asks for translations from the Paris *Moniteur*, absurdly anxious for the welfare of Frenchmen, skipping over the carcass of their king and country. . . . Ye querists, ye quidnuncs, check your impertinent curiosity. Devote not life to hearing and telling new things. If ye have business, mind it; are you masters of families, stay at home. Your heads are too shallow to contain the myriads of novel ideas ye wish. Action, not tattle, is the business of life.

From "On Newsmongers," in Joseph Dennie, *The Lay Preacher* (1817)

I

Daring Men
and Their
Printing Machines

Newspapers and newsmen have been troublemakers in American history almost from the first creaking of a press in New England nearly three centuries ago. Those early printers had no sense of missionary zeal. They were merely businessmen with a special advantage—they created something—and an enormous disadvantage. The drawback was, and is, that a newspaper is somewhat akin to a loaded pistol: just about anybody can use it.

Troublesome devices carry awesome responsibility and involve great risks. The first American—really a transplanted Englishman—who tried to pretend otherwise was Benjamin Harris. Harris was a former resident of London, a printer, a businessman, and a traveler who had—by 1690—been around perhaps too much for his own good. He knew, for example, how it felt to be ridiculed in public with his hands and feet dangling out of heavy wooden stocks. He knew the taunts and the aching back and the humiliation of the mob when he tried to buck the Establishment. He became a victim of medieval justice when he published words the king's attorney believed improper. His experiences could have been disastrous, but

Harris came out alive and with enough capital for a fresh start in America. So he turned up in the unlikely town of Boston, where more than enough printers already plied their trade, and there Harris tried to make a better life for himself by bringing to New England the same kind of news sheet that was popular in the homeland.

Newspapers had been an accepted part of English commerce for a generation when Harris undertook his venture by imitating the size and style of newspapers then circulated in London. He called his sheet *Publick Occurrences Both Forreign and Domestick.* In its upper corner he implied that he was in business to stay as he labeled the issue "Numb. I." There was never to be a Number II, however, for Harris had asked for trouble. His wretched confinement in the stocks had not brought about the desired humility a libel conviction was supposed to impose on contrite printers.

Before Harris discovered that America was rather more like England than he had realized, the Boston emigrant took the traditional pathway of a printer whose press was too often idle. In a frontier town, he learned, there is more optimism about the future than present business. Thus, to make ends meet, he turned to selling books, running a coffeehouse, and offering the usual legal forms and other printer's merchandise to customers who dropped in at "The Sign of the Bible, over against the Blew-Anchor, Cornhill." However slow business might have been before Thursday, September 25, 1690, there must have been an upturn in activity during the next few days because, on September 29, the Establishment in Massachusetts Bay decreed the suspension of *Publick Occurrences.* Harris seems to have made the mistake of issuing his newspaper without first asking the governor and council what they thought of his idea. Their dignity offended, these early Americans found that Harris's brand of journalism "contained Reflections of a very high nature" and "also sundry doubtful and uncertain Reports." So Harris's promise to keep readers informed about public affairs and to cure "that Spirit of Lying, *which prevails amongst us,*" was not kept. Thereafter, would-be colonial newspaper publishers found it important to know where they stood with the community bosses.

Indeed, in England printing had been a risky venture from the days of Henry VIII onward.[1] Once the great religious controversy flared, there had been no end to the problems of churchmen and royal authorities in their efforts to fit all Englishmen into a single mold. The task proved impossible but dozens perished—for after Pope Alexander's bull of 1501 to print without a license was to court disaster. England recognized the danger of words on paper by a statute passed in the last year of Henry's reign which declared that printed works could be treasonable. And something akin to an underground press must have existed in London around 1570, when Elizabeth's Licensing Act was meant to bring every printed work before a royal censor "to stop the Presse from publishing anything that might discover the Corruption of Church or State." But somehow, in the aftermath of the Reformation, Englishmen inched slowly toward a less brutal and more open society. The first wave of English colonists was still battling the wilderness when Milton told his countrymen that intellectual freedom was to be treasured "above all other liberties."

Nonetheless, such ideals gained little ground amid the successive political crises of seventeenth-century England. The old system of heavy-handed repression gave way slowly. Stephen Day, the first printer in Boston, had been taken into custody in 1643 for an unspecified act (possibly akin to Harris's error) and placed under a £100 bond. Struggling communities on the Atlantic frontier had no immediate need for newspapers and could barely support a printer, but as Boston grew its citizens came to know that early cousin of the newspaper—the broadside—a small printed sheet concerned with a single news item. Even these attempts to circulate the news were to prove worrisome in Massachusetts. In 1662 the authorities cast an ever-suspicious eye toward printing presses and appointed censors. Nearly three decades of tranquility followed. Then, a year before Harris's fiasco, a Boston broadside provoked the colonial council to warn printers that because "many papers . . . tending to the disturbance of the peace" had recently appeared, the continued publication of "such like papers" would be met "with the uttermost severity." And, as Harris learned, the authorities were not bluffing.

These beginning attempts at journalism were made within earshot of Boston wharves where, after more than two generations of American experience, this growing seaport needed a printed record of events issued with some regularity. Some time before 1622 English printers had experimented with newsletters by imitating the one-page Dutch newssheets called *courantos*.* These earliest forms of modern journalism were linked to the ocean because the sea gave northern Europe a commercial highway that supported an expanding international trade. Profits in commerce were directly related to news. Merchants had seen this point demonstrated earlier by the exemplary Fugger house of Augsburg—news was a valuable commodity that often determined the flow of guilders and guineas. Before the newspaper was invented, Europeans had relied on private letters, rumors, alehouse gossip, court reports, ship captain's accounts, and town criers for their news. Methods were inefficient and quality varied. The church lost its monopoly on literacy as a demanding mercantile class took a secularized view of society that left no room for intolerance when profits hung in the balance. The prestige of landholding remained, but the real strength of the western economy was shifting to the marketplace. The merchants needed and would secularize and subsidize an invention that in its simplicity and impact has never been equaled in western history: the device for printing words from movable type.

In time the printing trade outgrew the medieval guild system, adapting to the needs of a mercantilist society that worked hand in

---

* The world's oldest newspaper is the *Nieuwe Haarlemsche Courant*, the lineal descendant of the *Weekelycke Courant* (1656). See Warren Chappell, *A Short History of the Printed Word* (New York, 1970), 127–31.

glove with the constituted authority. An imprimatur was still needed on certain printed works, but increasing secularization was evident, as in creative type designs that broke away from the old-style monastic lettering. Still, in an era notable for superstition and suspicion, there was a tendency to accept printed words as truth. The establishment in England of a Royal Stationer's office to censor printed works, Milton's *Areopagitica*, and John Lilburne's heroic protests and subsequent punishment—all were part of the American printers' heritage when a Virginia printer learned from harsh experience what Harris would know eight years later. John Buckner was reprimanded by Lord Culpeper and the Virginia council in February 1682, "for printing the laws of 1680, without his excellency's license." The reprimand of Buckner occurred less than a decade after crusty Sir William Berkeley lifted his thanks that Virginia had been spared from free schools and printing presses, and prayed: "God keep us from both."

Insecure authorities, before and since Berkeley's blessing of ignorance, have proved Berkeley a colonial official typical of his breed. In the same decade, the New York governor received royal instructions to "allow no printing press in the province," and William Bradford in Philadelphia had a run-in with the authorities because he printed a document without statehouse clearance. This censorship went against the grain of American experience, however. Nowhere else on earth were so many people being reared in a permissive climate that placed a premium on literacy, information, and freedom of movement. Surely the literacy rate in the northern colonies was much higher than in Europe, otherwise the surprised comments of visitors from the Continent are unaccountable. This was particularly true in New England, as La Rochefoucauld noticed, where the people "from the landlord down to the housemaid . . . all read two newspapers a day."

It would be wrong to assume that the misfortunes of Buckner and Bradford were typical of a society where printers were usually at odds with the authorities. Most printers preferred to make a decent living rather than pick a fight. In early America the people in power were close to the community as a whole, so that the local magistrate was able to identify his interests with the printers, merchants, and farmers through day-to-day contact. A society that began bustling with the cock's crow had little time to spare for socializing. But wherever a printing press rested there was a natural congregating place because news from the outside world was siphoned through mails, particularly newspapers, that came in weekly or bimonthly bundles. There was no more natural appointee for a postmastership than the printer, for he presided over the news pipeline his office afforded. As postmaster, the printer was more than conversant with the local authorities and might be a part of the power structure. Thus, the printer-postmaster tradition, born of expedience, became a fixture in small-town America that endured well into the nineteenth century. Few early printers ever prospered without a postmastership, and the most famous printer-postmaster—Benjamin Franklin— turned the job at Philadelphia into a stepping-stone for a useful and profitable public career.

The early American newspaper, then, was naturally imitative of the English product at outposts of the transatlantic culture wherever there was a cluster of topmasts and shipmasters. The ocean was the lifeblood of commerce, and commerce was to be the lifeblood of journalism. A newspaper changed from a printer's vision into reality when the seaport he served had sufficient trade in a mercantile community that would support a circulation of at least three hundred copies weekly. After Boston, the next American seaport to qualify was Philadelphia, with its *American Weekly Mercury* started in 1719. By 1725 New York's harbor had turned the former Dutch village into a thriving town ready for its own *Gazette*. The printers had to be subsidized by public printing orders, of course, but despite their feeble financing, the audacity of starting a newspaper was revealing. At that same time, long-established English cities such as Liverpool and Birmingham were still without a single local newspaper.

The first colonial newspapers could not have survived had they depended solely on the income provided by one-shilling advertisements and two-penny counter sales. The postmasterships and other patronage of colonial governors and legislatures who wanted council orders and provincial statutes printed kept newspapers alive when their subscription lists sagged. Moreover, the common practice of delivering newspapers on credit haunted printers for well over a century. Subscribers were notoriously tardy in their payments, but printers rarely were solvent enough to turn down new business even when a new subscriber often represented more risk. William Bradford complained in 1728 that he had lost £35 on his *New-York Gazette* after thirty months of operations because of delinquent subscribers. The printer immune to such hardships was rare, and there were hundreds of echoes of Thomas Fleet's doleful report from the Boston *Evening Post*:

> The Subscribers for this Paper, (especially those at a Distance) who are shamefully in Arrear for it, would do well (methinks) to remember those Apostolical Injunctions, Rom. xiii. 7, 8. *Render* therefore to all their dues; and Owe no man any thing. It is wonderful to observe, that while we hear so much about a great Revival of Religion in the Land; there is yet so little Regard had to Justice and Common Honesty!

The *Connecticut Journal & New-Haven Post Boy* printer told a similar story on April 12, 1773. "The Printers are sorry, they can with truth inform the public, that they have not, for this year past, received from all the customers for this Journal, so much money as they have expended for the blank paper, on which it has been printed." From the 1750s until the 1890s readers frequently encountered a printer-editor's testy notice that "unless the subscribers in arrears settle with the printer AT ONCE no more copies of this newspaper will be delivered." For all the potential power of his newspaper, the printer was usually the servant of his community rather than its master. The town was divided into two parts—people he owed, or the larger groups that owed him. Indeed, a leading authority on colonial printers held that they conducted "a reasonably profitable trade," but used the firm of Franklin & Hall for his model, which is akin to saying General Motors makes money. He added that most printers earned "a decent living if only rarely [rewarded] by large monetary return." [2]

The colonial printer was ordinarily a man of small means, with less than £200 invested in his shop and equipment. His types had been cast in Holland or England, where the metal parts of his cumbersome press also originated. There had not been much improvement since Gutenberg's day (ca. 1440) in the printer's craft, and indeed some of the type faces such as the long ſ were direct carryovers from the German trade. The whole operation rested on the availability of cheap labor. The usual route in the printing trade was for the beginner to start as either a devil or apprentice signed into long-term bondage (by his parents or a guardian) lasting seven years, or until his twenty-first birthday. He then became a journeyman printer, and could either hire out at piecework rates or take wages of around 10 shillings for a 75-hour work week. Earning about 20 cents an hour, he could never hope to become rich, but an ambitious journeyman yearned for his own business and the status of a master printer.

Unquestionably there were printers in the key cities of Boston, New York, and Philadelphia who had a sense of mission that sustained them when creditors had to be avoided by back alleys. For all his skirting the edge of poverty, however, the colonial printer of a newspaper was a man to be reckoned with. Authorities in the late seventeenth century, and throughout the eighteenth, were never able to cope with the power of newspapers because they did not fully understand what was happening. Ordinary men were not supposed to meddle in the business of government—that high calling was reserved for gentlemen. Yet here was the printer—a mere tradesman—attempting to affect public policy. His news items and anonymous essays spread before every literate person the inner workings of the system. Information once shared by only the privileged few was now out in the open, and often to be criticized rather than commended. To have town meetings where articulate men could sway the majority was bad enough, but worse by far was to have inconsequential printers turn out a weekly record of what was going on—taxes levied, turnpike routes proposed, ferry monopolies granted, privileges abused. Elected legislators were as sensitive as appointed councilors in their quick denunciation of an intrusion into what until recent times had been considered none of the people's business. But now the people were learning about government, and some of them had a vote. This new development gave the printer a place in the community far beyond economic appearances. Rich or poor, eccentric or levelheaded, the colonial printer could not be ignored in any alignment of a community's power structure.

The abrasive edge of journalism on entrenched authority cut two ways. Whenever the printer turned into an agent of protest, his newspaper became much more interesting. We know about James Franklin and John Peter Zenger primarily because they took on the Establishment. Fresh reports of faraway tensions were read for a vicarious thrill, but local battles carried their own stamp of immediacy and authenticity. Conflict stories made good reading—those about conflict under the reader's very nose made the best reading of all. At the same time, some printers believed they were promoting a healthy climate of protest against harmful situations. In order to report or comment on those circumstances, it was in the printer's self-interest to proclaim freedom of the press as a working community principle. Freedom of expression was to be no abstract right to them, but a matter of everyday concern. The gnawing question, when tension between authorities and insurgent printers became acute, was whether printers should operate with caution and anxiety, or should be free to act as were other purveyors of goods or services.

The amazing fact was that penurious printers were sometimes willing to take on entrenched authorities. To be popular was no guarantee of financial reward. Indeed, the crusading journalist in American history has rarely been well rewarded for his efforts. Even the venerable veteran printer Benjamin Edes of Boston, who was foremost in the patriot-printer ranks during the 1770s, confessed as the century closed that his Boston *Gazette* subscriber's list shrank from 2,000 to 500 customers after all the battles had been won. After forty-four years as editor-printer of the *Gazette*, Edes admitted that "the cause of LIBERTY is not always the channel of preferment or pecuniary reward." The *Gazette* went to an unmarked grave, though Edes struggled on as a job printer for five more years until his death in 1803. The complete patriot during the Revolution, Edes had been the ally but never the business partner of the merchant-lawyer class that needed his newspaper until the din of battle faded.

Except for Franklin, the Bradfords in New York, Thomas in New England, and perhaps a half dozen other printers with uncommon good luck and much business acumen, few colonial printers were prosperous. For every Franklin who made a fortune there were countless others who were witnesses and recorders of prosperity but rarely participants in it as they dunned delinquent subscribers for petty debts or patiently waited for a merchant to pay a Spanish milled dollar for a "Calicoes freshly arrived" advertisement long after the bolts of cloth had been sold.

Clearly the chief benefactors of early American newspapers were merchants and shippers who advertised their wares and services, sometimes using a single newspaper (as with the *Virginia Gazette* in Williamsburg) to cover a market area with several hundred thousand people. They were among the first "delayed reward" readers, whom Wilbur Schramm named with precision—men who used information to make money. The "immediate reward" readers were to have their day at a later time and must have constituted a relatively small band in the eighteenth century. Even the macabre accounts of suicides and murders in early journalism were printed with a moral purpose alien to their sensational tone. Colonial readers were more interested in making their way in the world than in being entertained through news channels. Life was a serious business, and journalism reflected this attitude by its emphasis on improvement—be it civic or self—for colonials always seem compelled to prove themselves as good as the home stock. Certainly this must have been true for readers of the

Boston *News-Letter* or New York *Weekly Post-Boy,* who read London news as a means of comparison with local conditions. They also must have enjoyed moral essays, delighted in what now seems incredibly bad poetry, and found it useful to study suggestions on the manuring of corn fields with river sand. The community shuddered when it read of a bastard infant found smothered in a nearby hayloft, or looked for stronger locks when warned that marauding bands of desperadoes had slaughtered whole families in isolated regions. Life was chronicled through the seasons, and the printer paid his bills by serving as a public bulletin board carrier, as his advertisements told of ships coming and going, goods arrived, services offered, legal actions pending, and gold watches found or lost. Then there were reports of runaway slaves or servants, frequent warnings ("My wife having left my bed and board"), and the evergreen hopes of lottery promoters. Dancing masters and actors, the exhibitors of wild animals, and the owners of lost or strayed cattle all needed the newspaper. In short, there was something in it for nearly everybody—except the printer.

Much evidence suggests that the colonial printer rested below a tombstone earlier than the merchant he served or that most numerous of all colonial citizens—the yeoman farmer. Isaiah Thomas attended too many funerals for fellow tradesmen not to know the toll, and Thomas's monumental *History of Printing in America* is replete with laconic entries for widows who maintained newspapers from Boston to Williamsburg long after their husbands had worked themselves to death in their late thirties or early forties.[3] Benjamin Franklin's brother, James, was thirty-eight when he died and left the *Rhode-Island Gazette* in his widow's hands. James Franklin, Jr., died in his early thirties, leaving the Newport *Mercury* to his widowed mother, who saw it fail in 1763. Ebenezer Watson's *Connecticut Courant* was inherited by his widow, who married another printer (as often happened) and kept the newspaper alive. John Peter Zenger died in 1746, leaving the *New-York Journal* in his widow's care until their son became the publisher in 1748. The widows of John Holt, Thomas Greenleaf, Andrew Bradford, Jonas Green, William Parks,

William Hunter, William Rind, Benjamin Franklin Bache, Lewis Timothy, Charles Crouch, and Richard Draper tried to maintain the newspapers founded or owned by their husbands between 1733 and 1798.

Lest the picture appear too bleak, recall that working conditions in the eighteenth century were probably no more healthy for cobblers, cordwainers, coopers, or other tradesmen than for printers. Close confinement, long working days, poor ventilation, and restricted diets took their toll among laboring men whose chief exercises were heavy lifting and hard tugging. Small wonder that "the cough" or "consumption" was often entered on a printer's death certificate. Longevity was the exception, not the rule, and the French visitor Moreau noted in 1797 that most Americans fell sick and died "between thirty-five and forty-five." [4]

There were exceptions, of course, and one lived on to become the patron saint of American printers. Benjamin Franklin set type before his thirteenth birthday on brother James Franklin's feisty *New-England Courant*, and through a stroke of bad luck for his older brother Benjamin Franklin escaped a long apprenticeship. James Franklin's paper bore no official seal of approval and the powerful Mather family despised his irreverent attitude, particularly after he spoke out against their campaign for smallpox inoculations. It was probably the venerable Cotton Mather who blasted the *Courant* as "a Notorious, Scandalous Paper . . . tending to Quarrels and Divisions, and to Debauch and Corrupt the Minds and Manners of New England." Jailed once for twitting colonial authorities, James Franklin overstepped their bounds a second time in 1722, was hailed before the council, interrogated, and hustled to the town jail. The council forbade him to print the *Courant* "Except it be first Supervised, by the Secretary of this Province." As a subterfuge, Benjamin Franklin's apprenticeship was ostensibly voided and his name inserted as publisher. The tricky maneuver kept the *Courant* alive, but Benjamin Franklin was clever enough to see that a secret contract he signed for James was really worthless. Freed from his bond, the younger Franklin eventually ran away to a new career in Philadelphia.

James Franklin nursed his grudges for three more years, but he had made a mark of sorts on American journalism with his anti-inoculation campaign. Although fought in a bad cause, this "first American newspaper crusade did what such campaigns still do: it won the attention of the town, gave a one-sided story, and built circulation, and it made the paper bitter enemies," historian Frank Luther Mott observed.[5] The teen-aged Franklin would remember the experience after he cut loose from his family ties, and eventually chose to settle in Philadelphia.

Well beyond the frontier stage, Philadelphia was on its way to becoming the second largest city in the British Empire—a bustling, thriving seaport ripe for a good printer who knew that the best way to conduct any business was with lots of black ink. By 1729 Franklin had brought his talents into play with the purchase of the stumbling *Universal Instructor in all Arts and Sciences; and Pennsylvania Gazette.* He shortened the name and lengthened the subscriber's list, thus turning the newspaper into a profitable and influential journal that dominated the field for the next sixty years. Later Franklin closed the circle of influence when he became (in 1737) the Philadelphia postmaster. His control over the sources of information doubtless was enhanced when Franklin became the deputy postmaster-general in 1753, while another printer (William Hunter in Williamsburg) took a similar title and responsibility for mail below the Potomac.

Franklin would have been a success in any endeavor, no doubt, for he had the midas touch. An excellent printer, he was an even more skilled writer. From 1732 until 1757 he peppered the pages of his profitable *Poor Richard's Almanack* with sprightly "Proverbs, which contained the Wisdom of many Ages and Nations." [6] There Franklin used the pseudonym "Richard Saunders" to ladle out large helpings of homespun advice for "the common People, who bought scarce any other Books." True to his New England upbringing,

Franklin counseled thrift to others as he lent capital to hard-working younger men so that they could set up printing shops in seaports. Typical among his debtors was Lewis Timothy of Charleston, who borrowed from Franklin to establish the *South Carolina Gazette*. After 1780, Timothy's widow and her sons, Peter and Benjamin Franklin Timothy, continued the *Gazette* until 1800.

Another New England printer whose career placed him in the forefront of the trade and also the resistance movement against England was Isaiah Thomas. Thomas's widowed mother apprenticed her seven-year-old son to Zechariah Fowle in 1756. Thomas escaped his bondage by running away from Fowle after a dozen years spent mastering every phase of the printing trade. Later venturing to the Carolinas, where he resisted offers to begin a newspaper, Thomas returned to Boston and founded the *Massachusetts Spy*. Thomas's masthead motto—Open to all Parties, but Influenced by None—was a familiar phrase in early American journalism when printers decried factionalism while they practiced it. An innovator, Thomas announced that the *Spy* was intended for "mechanics [workmen], and other classes of people who had not much time to spare from business" who would value a newspaper that could be "read at a leisure moment."

Thomas started with 200 customers and by 1772 claimed to have the largest circulation of any New England journal. In that time of great ferment the *Spy* was soon second only to Edes's Boston *Gazette* in providing the Whig spokesmen with a vehicle to condemn British policies and Tory leadership in the colony. Thomas was in league with Samuel Adams and other Boston radicals who had better things to do on Sunday than attend day-long church services. John Adams recalled that they spent Sabbath hours "cooking ..p paragraphs, articles, occurrences, &c., working the political engine!" Their burning prose stoked the *Gazette* and *Spy,* causing Tory officials to pray for the early demise of "those Miserable Pests of Society." Still a young man, Thomas threw himself headlong into the shaping battle and announced that the *Spy* would "assist in detecting, and exposing to public view, those miscreants who, for the sake of public or private advantage to themselves, would sacrifice both their King and Country." [7]

Once the fighting started in earnest Thomas removed the *Spy* to Worcester, where he carried on the enterprise with undiminished ardor. Thomas's shop proved a great training ground for young patriots as well as dedicated printers. Among his ablest pupils were Thomas Greenleaf and Benjamin Russell, and Thomas seems to have made loans to protégés who founded newspapers at Walpole, New Hampshire, and other New England villages. Not all of Thomas's ventures succeeded, and a most notable failure was his *Royal American Magazine* despite its instructive patriotic cartoons engraved by Paul Revere. After the Revolution Thomas expanded his printing business with a book shop, and became a wholesaler of printing supplies; and his wealth increased. In other ways, Thomas's life and times paralleled Franklin's. Franklin turned to scholarly investigations and helped found the American Philosophical Society. Thomas cultivated a love of books and founded the great repository of early American printing in his beloved Worcester, the American Antiquarian Society. And both men left notable literary contributions— Franklin through his *Autobiography* and other writings, and Thomas in his monumental *History of Printing in America*. Each died wealthy and heaped with honors—Franklin in 1790 (in his eighty-fourth year) and Thomas in 1831 (aged eighty-two).

These were the giants, however, ranking alongside Bennett, Greeley, and Pulitzer as major figures in American journalism. Most Americans read newspapers published by printers who were less distinguished but hard-working men whose influence in local affairs was part of the compensation of their back-breaking endeavors. In order to operate with any regularity the small-town printer had to meet paper bills with cash in good times or rely on the barter system in leaner days. Since there were no reporters, the printer had to be his own editor. He clipped stories from the productions of brother printers which arrived in the weekly mails and accepted essays turned in at the shop by townspeople (oftentimes anonymously slipped under the door at night). But whatever the means, his columns were filled without the taking of a single copper from his pocket. The so-called exchanges (borrowed clippings) were the root-and-branch of American journalism until after the Civil War, long aided by post-office subsidies in one form or another. Another major source of news were excerpts from private letters which a printer-postmaster passed on to readers without questioning the authenticity of their information. Hundreds of news reports began under the heading, "A Letter lately received here by a gentleman from a friend in London," wherein news and opinion were jumbled in random fashion. These reports dominated news columns until the Revolution as much of the newspapers' focus was on Europe or the West Indies. Besides the obvious heritage of a common language, English standards were adopted wholesale so that American tastes long ran to the clothes, customs, architecture, and journalism prevalent in the homeland.

England was still spoken of by homesick settlers and seasoned natives as home, while the newspapers they read often devoted long columns to English court gossip that was the dessert after generous helpings of reports from London coffeehouses. The American printers' magazines were so imitative of the home product that one historian has called them mere "British magazines published in the colonies." The Anglo-American magazines were pretentious efforts to give the colonies a literary stake they had no real claim to, and furnished evidence that a frontier is no healthy place for the roots of culture. Franklin's *General Magazine* was proof that not everything the clever postmaster touched turned to gold. Similarly, Andrew Bradford's *American Magazine,* begun a few days apart from Franklin's venture, also found the reading public apathetic. The small number of Americans genuinely interested in literary journals picked and chose from periodicals pouring from presses in London and Edinburgh. Even when the dispute with Britain became heated, the few magazines "exerted little influence because of their small circulation," as Arthur M. Schlesinger, Sr., observed.[8]

Almanacs were another matter. Though not a part of early American journalism in the ordinary sense, almanacs flourished because of price (threepence and up), versatility, and accessibility. Every printer had an edition of his own or sold a popular version from a fellow artisan's press. As Daniel Boorstin has pointed out, the almanac "offered an 18th-century American farmer the services now performed by agricultural extension, urban newspapers, magazines, radio, and television." Franklin's *Poor Richard's Almanack* was so popular in the middle colonies that the compiler sold nearly 250,000 copies between 1732 and 1757, spreading the gospel of "Industry and Frugality, as the Means of procuring Wealth and thereby securing Virtue." In New England the most successful compilers of almanacs were the father-son team of Nathaniel Ames, junior and senior, of Dedham, Massachusetts. Both were physicians and the older Ames also operated a tavern, but between times *An Astronomical Diary, or Almanack,* was compiled by the elder Ames from 1726 until 1764, and by his son until 1775.[9] They claimed their annual sales hovered around 10,000 copies as they furnished printer Bartholomew Green, Jr., and a long line of successors with details on the movements of heavenly bodies, aphorisms, medical and farming advice, moral essays, and an occasional woodcut illustration that was commendable only for the effort.

For forty years the almanacs eschewed political involvement, but the Stamp Act changed their course. An unauthorized 1766 edition of the Ameses' almanac announced the "Price before the Stamp Act takes Place, Half-a-Dollar per Dozen, and six coppers Single. After the Act takes place, more than double the Price." Nonenforcement of the act kept pamphlet printers from using the subterfuge practiced on newspapers, and the political tone of almanacs increased. Essays on "perspiration," a description of the twenty-two-inch-tall Miss Emma Leach (complete with a woodcut that might have been used to frighten naughty children), and court calendars were supplemented with remarks indicative of a prevailing shift in public opinion. After the Boston Massacre of 1770 the emphasis was on military prepared- ness as the colonists accumulated powder and weapons—ostensibly for their militia musters as provided by law. "Now my brave coun- trymen prepare for dire approaching civil wars!" Ames warned in his 1772 edition. A year later, Ames reflected his generation's belief that nothing could ruin a nation faster than an unjust monarch unless it was that effeminizing luxury "which viciates the morals of the peo- ple." Ames told perhaps 60,000 readers that "as too great authority intoxicates and poisons Kings, so luxury poisons a whole nation." Such advice buttressed the predilections of New England farmers and made the almanac a topical, timely, and persuasive part of pre- Revolutionary journalism. This judgment counters that of Philip Da- vidson, whose *Propaganda and the American Revolution* was a ground-breaking study of the effects of journalism upon eighteenth- century Americans. Davidson asserted that almanacs were "of little value to the propagandists" because they were issued only once a year. He goes on to say, a "six months' old appeal even that age had little value. *Yet the almanac reached the country people in a way that the newspaper, pamphlet, and broadside never did.*" [10]

Similarly, broadsides were an important form of eighteenth-cen- tury journalism, although their publication was irregular. Broadsides were printed on one side of a sheet, carried news reports or an- nouncements, and were intended for immediate distribution at low cost. Probably by 1750 printers used this familiar device to inform readers of extraordinary news—hence the word *extra* was attached to those issued as a supplement to regular newspapers and became part of the printer's jargon until electronic means supplanted the "extras" urgency. Broadsides told of the 1770 Boston Massacre, New York's Battle of Golden Hill, the town meetings that led to the Boston Tea Party, and during the Revolution reported every important battle from Lexington-Concord to Yorktown. These broadsides were passed from hand to hand, tacked on tavern doors, and gave an immediacy and importance to news that had been lacking before the Revolution began. A special kind of journalism, the "gale of broadsides reached hurricane proportions in the final years of the dispute" between America and Britain.[11]

Pamphlets were equally admissible, historian Merrill Jensen notes, with newspapers as "interchangeable tools" in the communications mechanism of the Revolution. They were cheap, available at every print shop, and full of topical opinions. Often pamphlets were reprints of essays first carried in newspapers or borrowed from English editions (there were no copyright laws to prevent unauthorized editions). The "Letters from a Farmer in Pennsylvania to the Inhabitants of the British Colonies" first appeared in the *Pennsylvania Chronicle* between December 1767 and February 1768, and were soon issued in pamphlet form. Before long the so-called farmer was revealed as John Dickinson, and the thousands of pamphlets sold marked him as the foremost member of the political *illuminati*. Dickinson's attack on the Townsend acts made him beloved by Whigs and notorious to Tories, who saw the farmer's letters as a warning that "Parliament may enact declaratory Acts as many as they please; but they must not expect any real obedience" from truculent colonists.

Along with the native productions, pamphlets favorable to the American position by Bishop Shipley, John Cartwright, Richard Price, and other English radicals were reprinted and eagerly purveyed by printers in Boston, Philadelphia, and New York. Their influence in sustaining American morale is beyond doubt. In the midst of the political crisis in England fostered by the Revolution it was a perceptive Englishman, Josiah Tucker, who reminded his fellow countrymen that "from the Days of Thucydides down to the present Time . . . it is the Nature of them all [i.e., colonies] to aspire after Independence, and to set up for themselves as soon as ever they find that they are able to subsist, without being beholden to the Mother-Country." [12] Such views encouraged colonial protests from Arthur Lee, Jefferson, and Paine when a military collision became inevitable.

The electrifying effect of Paine's *Common Sense* in the winter of 1775–1776, when it sold over 120,000 copies, made it the most popular piece of American journalism in its time. Persuasively, Paine's ridicule of George III demolished the affection Americans held for their monarch and made independence a compelling necessity. In all likelihood no other piece of propaganda has ever been as effective in American journalism, either in the magnitude of its coverage or its conversion of the readership. *Common Sense* was a verbal fortress for those already convinced that independence was necessary, while "the more timid delegates [in the Continental Congress] could use the reaction to *Common Sense* as a barometer of public opinion and guide themselves accordingly." From Benjamin Harris's time until the 1780s, American journalism was dependent on England for its news and a concept of what constituted news. There was, until the Revolution, no sense of urgency about the news except for the periodic interruption of wars (Queen Anne's, Jenkin's Ear, and French and Indian) when there were militia calls, travel interruptions, and the price fluctuations common to all wars. Otherwise the main business of America centered around domestic agricultural concerns—tobacco plantings, wheat, corn, indigo, rice—with more attention in New England to ships and fisheries. The news from Europe was often six weeks old but hardly considered stale since the freshness of reports was relative to conditions of the day. "When news is printed it leaves Sir to be news," as Ben Jonson had said, but until published a year-old story stayed as fresh as on the first day of its happening. (In later American journalism Jonson's aphorism became modernized: "News isn't news until it's printed.") Print turned rumor into fact, created a visible record of that fact, and became a salable item in a society on the periphery of mercantilist England.

In the face of small circulation, inefficient means for distribution, and considerable illiteracy, the colonial newspaper established a beachhead. By 1736 six seaports and the Virginia capital (a few miles inland) all had at least one newspaper. Boston, Philadelphia, and

New York had competing newspapers, and during the next generation all the colonies except New Jersey would have at least one (although Delaware's *Wilmington Chronicle* had a short life.) The pattern that prevailed everywhere except at the Virginia capital in Williamsburg was: seaport, mercantile community, printer, and a population of fifteen hundred or more. Given these conditions in the area northeast of the Susquehanna River, a newspaper was soon in the works. By the time of the Revolution about forty communities had qualified for at least one printer's risk, most of them in the populated area running northward from Philadelphia through New York to Boston. Apparently, the rudimentary school system in the middle and northern colonies formed a base of literacy that the South could not match. The population, North and South, was about evenly distributed, but there were three times as many newspapers in the North by 1735, and by 1765 the imbalance was five to one against the South.

These developments in America roughly followed by a generation the rapid growth of a more sophisticated kind of journalism in the mother country. By 1702 London had a daily newspaper, and in Samuel Buckley a new breed of printer. Buckley added a dateline to his news ("Paris, February 10, 1703") as a device to set readers on their guard. "Seeing from what Country a piece of News comes with the Allowance of that Government, [readers] may be better able to Judge of the Credibility and Fairness of the Relation." Within the same era the *Tatler* and *Spectator* also catapulted into English journalism, in newspaper form, and sold for a penny. Daniel Defoe, Jonathan Swift, and other English luminaries made England's journalism as colorful as it would ever be, and the lessons were not lost on Americans. Parliament, however, reacted to this flowering of English letters by clamping down on literary license through a stamp tax imposed in 1712 and retained for the rest of the century. The political leaders in England feared the effects of widespread newspaper readership and took steps to curb it. Meanwhile, Americans were beginning their own experiments, and learned their lessons from England well, where the pseudonym thwarted watchful officials and made *Tatler, Spectator,* and *Cato* household words.[13]

The English stamp act did not leap across the Atlantic, but the spirit of the times was undeniable. English printers had paid for their obstinancy since Henry VIII's reign, with slitted ears, and even the gibbet was in store for those who insisted on an untrammeled right of expression. Frederick Siebert found evidence of underground newspapers in London by 1572, and it was within the memory of living Americans that printers had been sent to the gallows for high treason. Yet in 1704 John Tutchin had published charges of bribery and corruption in the London *Observator* and though brought to trial and found guilty, Tutchin was never sentenced and the case was finally dropped. Loopholes were found in Parliament's stamp act and by 1715 England's sixty-seven newspapers showed signs of expansion. So it was in America within two decades.

From Massachusetts Bay southward the English-American newspaper gave the impression of great civility, but in fact there was a native strain of discord always lurking in the colonial print shop. Sixteen-year-old Benjamin Franklin said it well when he used his brother's *New-England Courant* to warn the authorities:

> I am . . . a mortal Enemy to arbitrary Government and unlimited power. I am naturally very jealous for the Rights and Liberties of my Country; and the least appearance of an Incroachment on those invaluable Priviledges, is apt to make my Blood boil exceedingly.[14]

Hiding behind the pseudonym of "Silence Dogood," Franklin carried off his masquerade well and must have heartened the Bostonians who were tired of the dominant oligarchy. The Mather family was one target of the iconoclastic Hellfire Club that eagerly sought a clash with the self-anointed. In a fury against the *Courant's* barbs, Cotton Mather confided to his diary that "Warnings are to be given

unto the wicked Printer, and his Accomplices, who every week publish a vile Paper to lessen and blacken the Ministers of the Town, and
render their Ministry ineffectual. A Wickedness never parall'd any
where upon the Face of the Earth."

Indeed, a few printers overstepped the bounds of propriety and
landed in jail, but the *Courant* and other obstreperous newspapers signaled the rise of a new kind of journalism in America that would not
truckle for long to any officialdom. This defiant breed of newspaper
would "penetrate the inland villages and slowly wear away their in-
sularity of temper and outlook, bringing fresh ideas to minds that had
long stagnated," Vernon Parrington once observed. "On the whole
it was not a liberal press, but its final effect was profoundly liberaliz-
ing."

2

Ink-Stained Revolutionaries

Crèvecoeur was not the first foreigner to notice that the American was "a new man, who acts upon new principles," but the Frenchman focused attention upon a unique characteristic of the Americans. What this observation glosses over is the English heritage of the American that was so pervasive it was a commonplace. Although his family connections in Sussex or Surrey became more and more remote, the colonial American kept an Englishman's set of values. By George II's time, that American would have been isolated indeed who did not dislike the pope, fear the French, love to own land, and believe that the British monarchy and constitution were the finest political instruments ever devised. But, as a colonial, the American also liked to dodge taxes rather than pay them, and because of lingering frontier conditions he usually owned a musket or two. This provincial man believed he had a God-given right to use those weapons to protect his property from either varmints or nosy customs collectors.

As with every colonial people, the eighteenth-century American resented controls from abroad but enjoyed the benefits of an imperial link. Not until he decided that the controlled status of a provincial was too costly was the American ready to rebel. When that decision came, it was reinforced by the newspapers that were the leading critics of transatlantic controls. Historian Carl Becker once suggested that the real American Revolution concerned not so much home rule, but the power struggle to determine who should rule at home. That fight was to end as it began, with the colonial opinion makers serving as bellwether revolutionaries. In the protest movement against restrictive English policies, the newspaper proved to be the ultimate weapon of American radicals.

The American colonial printer was never effectively muzzled because he shared vicariously in the English press' victories, while shaping a few of his own. Parliament had permitted the old licensing act to lapse in 1695 not because of a liberal sentiment, but because it was a decrepit anachronism in England's political climate when the Whigs and Tories began to square off. Although Parliament tried to find an answer in the stamp tax, ingenious Englishmen found ways and means of circumventing the successive acts in 1712, 1724, and 1757. Even the vindictive act of 1743, meant to forbid street sales of unstamped newspapers, had loopholes. Meanwhile, American printers had a few battle scars earned in the common cause.

The most notable incident in American journalism prior to the Stamp Act was John Peter Zenger's trial of 1734–1736. The facts were never in dispute. Zenger, a German-trained immigrant printer, was the pawn in a larger game being played in the rising city of New York between rival political factions. William Bradford, who had felt the lash of authority in Pennsylvania for printing without official sanction, had turned the other cheek in New York. Now he was on the opposite side, entrenched as the Crown printer and publisher of the *New-York Gazette*. All went well until the arrival of Governor William Cosby in 1732. Cosby fell out with a strong clique that was still more frustrated because the royal appointee had a newspaper to air his side of the controversy. To remedy matters, the anti-Cosby faction induced Zenger to set up his own newspaper, the *New-York*

Weekly Journal. From the first issue of November 3, 1733, Zenger was headed for trouble as the clever antiadministration party used the *Journal* columns for their veiled attacks on Cosby.[1]

Predictably, Cosby was furious, and he must have known that a young lawyer was the real author of the essays the governor regarded as the most scurrilous. Nonetheless, Cosby tried to use the law to squelch the *Journal* by shackling Zenger. The medieval notion that a piece of paper could be evil in itself was still the law, so the Cosbyites sought a common-law indictment against the hapless Zenger and not against the intellectual Alexander (who probably was delicately masked by such pseudonyms as "Cato" and "Thomas Standby").

It took Cosby and his legal aides a year to land Zenger in jail. The indictment on seditious libel came after tactics of intimidation, including a publicized burning of a copy of the *Journal* by the hangman, had failed to silence Cosby's critics. A hand-picked judge and jury awaited Zenger after six months in jail (where Zenger slipped messages in and out of a hole in the cell door, a façade that made continued printing of the *Journal* possible). The only point at issue, Judge Delancey insisted, was whether Zenger had printed the seditious article. If he were guilty of that, then the jury could leave the punishment to the judge's discretion. A month of delay was all Zenger's supporters could salvage from their first court skirmish.

During July 1735, the men who had backed Zenger proved their mettle. James Alexander, Zenger's logical defense counsel, had been disbarred along with William Smith, another anti-Cosby lawyer with a facile pen. Perhaps Benjamin Franklin took an interest in the case from Philadelphia, but for whatever reason, the city's best lawyer, old Andrew Hamilton, traveled North and on the day Zenger's trial began in earnest, Hamilton was there as his counsel. The preliminaries over, Hamilton readily admitted that his client had published the offending article, since its comments fell with "the right of every free born Subject." The issue, Hamilton said, was whether this publication was in fact criminally libelous "that is, *false, malicious, and seditious*—or else we are not guilty."

Hamilton was flying into the face of the Star Chamber pronouncement of 1606, *de Libellis Famasis,* which in effect said that truth was no defense in a libel case. Times had changed, and Hamilton knew it. It did not make sense to tell an American jury that a man was breaking the law by telling the truth.

This seemed to be impudence on Hamilton's part, but the judge let him get away with it. There was some argument as to exactly what power the jury had in the matter, but Hamilton insisted the twelve good men had the right "beyond all Dispute, to determine both the Laws and the Facts." The question, he continued, "is not of small nor private concern, it is not the cause of a poor printer, nor of New York alone, which you are now trying: No! It may in its consequence affect every freeman that lives under a British Government on the main[land] of America. It is the best cause. It is the Cause of Liberty."

When the trial ended, Hamilton had the jury eager to do his bidding. A gaping judge and Crown attorney heard the unbelievable verdict: not guilty.

Although a stunned legal profession soon denigrated the Zenger verdict, its meaning was clear. Americans could be convinced that laws that made no sense ought to be broken. They believed Hamilton when he said there was a natural right "of complaining or remonstrating" open to British Americans. The Crown attorneys and their superiors could not understand this kind of logic, and they promptly issued tracts denouncing the New York verdict as patent nonsense. But issues of Zenger's own newspaper carried the trial proceedings and these were later prepared as a pamphlet to spread the word. It was in all likelihood Alexander's triumphant message, far ahead of its time, that had really been vindicated.

It is indeed urged that the liberty of the press ought to be restrained because not only the actions of evil ministers may be exposed, but the character of good ones traduced. Admit it in the strongest light that calumny and lies would prevail and blast the character of a great and good minister; yet that is a less evil than the advantages we reap from the liberty of the press, as it is a curb, a bridle, a terror, a shame, and restraint to evil ministers; and it may be the only punishment, especially for a time.

Nor was the lesson lost despite the catcalls of English lawyers. In Boston and London, the *Brief Narrative* was reprinted in 1738, and six other Anglo-American editions appeared between 1745 and 1770. The Zenger case was more than a mere straw in the wind. It was a warning to the Establishment that the American was indeed "a new man, who acts upon new principles." [2]

The long-range effect of dramatic incidents such as the Zenger case can, of course, be overstated. Most of Zenger's contemporaries doubtless never heard his name, and whether the Palatinate native really understood the forces taking shape around him is uncertain. The point was that the printers were showing daring and doing so in the name of freedom of the press. Since John Lilburne's time, English printers had come a long way; but American printers caught up with and outdistanced them between Zenger's trial and 1773. After decades of insistence, on both sides of the Atlantic, that "LIBERTY *of the* PRESS [is] the palladium of OUR Liberties" public opinion was moving ahead of the law. Events in America between 1765 and 1775 made a shambles of Blackstone's dictum that liberty of the press was merely "the absence of prior restraint."

Public opinion had to be nurtured, however, and for the generation of colonists who sowed crops, laid bricks, or planed barrel staves during the years between Zenger's triumph and the imperial earthquake of 1765, there was much other business on their minds. Between the accession of Queen Anne in 1702 and the death of George II in 1760, England fought the Spanish and French while Parliament was consolidating its gains over weak and timid sovereigns. The mercantilist system, whereby Parliament passed laws to benefit English merchants and exploited the colonies for raw materials and markets, kept the economy in England and America spurting. American tobacco, fish, and lumber went eastward as English manufactured goods moved west in ships of ever-increasing tonnages. Under Robert Walpole's ministry, Parliament was concerned mainly with the external affairs of the colonies (trade and currency regulations, restrictions on manufacturing) while the reins dangled loosely on colonial assemblies' management of domestic affairs. Actually, a rather elaborate administrative system for the colonies was evolving, but the average American was unaware of it until his pocketbook was threatened.

Meanwhile, journalism expanded on the Atlantic seaboard. William Parks was enticed to Williamsburg by a public printer's job and supplemented his salary of two hundred pounds in tobacco by founding the *Virginia Gazette* in 1736. Parks also had started Maryland's first newspaper in 1727 at Annapolis, and claimed to have made arrangements on a trip to England in 1730 "by which upon all Occasions, I shall be furnished with the freshest Intelligence both from thence and other parts of Europe." More rival newspapers appeared in Boston, New York, and Philadelphia, while New London, Providence, and Charleston, South Carolina, welcomed venturesome printers willing to start a newspaper "from scratch." Jonas Green revived Annapolis's *Maryland Gazette* with the announcement that his newspaper would have "always a principal Regard to such Articles as nearest concern the American Plantations in general, and the Province of Maryland in particular; ever observing the strictest Justice and Truth in Relation of Facts." If news became scarce, Green promised, he would choose literary material with "a due Regard to whatever may conduce to the Promotion of Virtue and Learning, the Suppression of Vice and Immorality, and the Instruction as well as Entertainment of our Readers." Undoubtedly the entrepreneurial spirit which was to dominate American society was at work in journalism as in other forms of commerce, and the modest requirements of capital and talent left the field wide open for any printer possessed of £50 or a working press and job cases.

The American printer-editor was in fact an active businessman on several fronts. Besides his income from printing, Thomas Fleet of Boston depended on sales of "Books, Household goods, Wearing apparel, or any other Merchandize, by Vendue, or Auction," to keep his growing family warm and well fed. From his shop under "the sign of the Heart & Crown," Fleet probably operated a rather typical American printing establishment, and that included the printing of sermons by local divines as a source of income. Fleet was one of those indiscreet souls, however, who never knew how to keep his foot out of his mouth. In 1741 he printed one of John Wesley's sermons in his Boston *Evening Post,* and was promptly attacked by a Congregational minister for this affront. Fleet replied that he was a better judge of these matters than dull-witted preachers, and soon was involved with another clergyman who was advising his flock to avoid newspapers that printed religious quarrels. This implied censorship galled Fleet, who seems often to have itched for battle. "The next stroke [from the pulpit] may probably be at the *Liberty of the Press,*" Fleet fumed, "And what a fine introduction this will be to *Popery* we leave our readers to judge." Fleet, good New Englander that he was, never missed a chance to throw a bolt at the Roman church. In 1748, after the capture of several bails of papal indulgences from a Spanish ship, Fleet bought them and printed songs and ballads on the verso side. He advertised that he was selling "Choice Pennsylvania Tobacco Paper . . . also [to] be had the Bulls or Indulgences of the present Pope Urban VIII. either by the single Bull, Quire, or Ream, at a much cheaper Rate than they can be purchased of the *French* or *Spanish* priests. . . ."

Fleet's profits from such sources were doubtless meager, but he was constantly in search of ways to turn a shilling into a pound. An apocryphal story credits Fleet with assembling the bedtime verses composed by his mother-in-law, Mrs. Elizabeth Goose. Didactic books for young readers helped printers supplement their incomes, and Isaiah Thomas's editions of *The Little Pretty Pocket Book* and *The History of Little Goody Two-Shoes* became classics.

Children's books were of little concern to most colonists, however, as they were preoccupied with more serious matters as "the dogs of war" were unleashed and moved from Europe to the New World. A general European war broke out in 1740 over the Austrian succession, and in 1744 Britain declared war on France. The French threat was used to frighten New Englanders into active participation in the siege of Louisbourg, a key fortification above the fishing banks. News of the surrender thrilled New England readers and the war brought prosperity to the region's shippers and merchants. All in all, the period ushered in a modern concept of war with large armies, open-handed commissary agents, and a sense of global mission that was not lost on Yankee traders and ship captains.

This excitement had hardly passed when the "Bonny Prince," Charles Stuart, made his abortive move to seize the throne and was crushed at Culloden Moor in 1746. Taken together these events electrified both English and American readers, and the *Virginia Gazette's* essay "On the Rise and Utility of NEWSPAPERS" (borrowed from an English journal) noted that "intestine Broils" called young Englishmen "from their villages to assist their King and Country . . . hence the Parents became anxious to know the State of their young Adventurers; they caught with Eagerness the publick Papers, and read impatiently an Account of every Battle, while Fear foreboded that their Sons had fallen. It is from this Era that we may date the Universality of Newspapers in this Kingdom. They were at first the Vehicles of political Information only . . . but . . . they are now become the Vehicles of general information." [3]

By the middle of the eighteenth century, British America had settlements from the Maine country south to Georgia, and had penetrated to the Appalachian foothills in the west. For a population approaching 1.5 million people, most of them living on farms, there were scarcely a baker's dozen American newspapers with a total subscription list of 15,000. The readership was mainly in the seaports; it is only a guess as to how many citizens actually read each newspaper, but it may have reached as high as ten readers per journal. That would still mean that only about one American in a hundred was literate and interested enough, had access to, and could pay for a newspaper printed in America. Since these native productions were supplemented by printed material from England, Scotland, Ireland, and the British West Indies there appears to have been enough reading around to give Americans a collective feeling of being well informed. Moreover, until inland roads improved, it was probable that a New Englander knew more about the happenings in London or Paris than about those in Savannah. His Georgia counterpart must have had more information about the Bahamas and Barbados than about Boston. The Virginia planter had the Chesapeake for his highway and knew of Philadelphia and Annapolis, but little of Boston or Savannah. It took the Stamp Act to change all this.

Meanwhile, journalism in the colonies knew its dark moments as the colonial legislatures benefited from Walpole's policies while the homegrown assemblies' powers expanded. During the seventeenth century printing in America was a hazardous proposition with the reason for prosecutions or intimidation nearly always the same: insecure and arbitrary officials who feared and read into the printer's daily work a threat to their authority. By Zenger's time there was courage enough to fight back, but even in New York the lesson was not well learned. Hugh Gaine of the *New-York Mercury* was called before the provincial legislature for printed words the delegates considered, in 1753, an effrontery to their power. James Parker and William Weyman of the *New-York Gazette* were arrested in March 1756 on orders from the New York Assembly for printing a critical essay written anonymously by the Reverend Hezekiah Watkins. After the printers begged the house's pardon and informed the affronted delegates of Watkins's identity, they were released. At their next session, the delegates voted the minister in contempt and ordered him arrested. The clergyman paid his fine, begged forgiveness, and was finally released with a reprimand.

Printers in Boston had to be vigilant, not of the king's attorney but of their own elected representatives. Fleet complained in his *Evening Post* that "Every one, almost, thinks he has a Right to read News; but few find themselves inclined to pay for it." Fleet's complaints over delinquent subscribers were harmless enough, but when his barbs were more directly aimed at the General Assembly's affairs the law-makers moved swiftly to have Fleet arrested in 1741 and jailed until he was humbled into more proper conduct. Although printers liked to think they had a sacred duty to relay information to the public, legislators fixed on printer-editors full responsibility for whatever appeared in their journals. When an essay signed by a "Cato" or a "Brutus" was slipped under a print-shop door, the responsibility for using it or throwing it into the waste bin rested on the editor. Pseudonyms rarely aided those printers whose conduct was based on the assumption that the press was indeed free. Daniel Fowle of Boston incurred the wrath of the General Assembly in 1754 for recklessly allowing an offending item in his newspaper. Eventually Fowle was released and the charges dropped, although Fowle published a tract, *A Total Eclipse of Liberty*, which told his side of the controversy. In 1757–1758 the printers of the *Pennsylvania Gazette* and *Philadelphia Zeitung* were called before the provincial assembly and ordered to reveal an essayist's identity. The Reverend William Smith was exposed and found in contempt for refusing to answer the assembly's queries. He spoke with such indignation that the gallery reportedly broke into applause. Nevertheless, Smith lost some of his boldness after three nights in jail. The printers were spared further humiliation, but Smith was released only after paying a fine. He later appealed the case to the Privy Council in London and was exonerated on a technicality.

Isaiah Thomas took particular note of all such incidents, some of them occurring before his eyes. A catalog of printers' arrests helped fill his invaluable history of the era. Almost invariably, it was not a royal official but a legislative clique that would resort to intimidation as a weapon in efforts to curb overly zealous editors. As Leonard Levy has pointed out, these legislative controls formed a kind of censorship that does not square with the popular concept of an unfettered press in early America. The facts indicate that newspaper publishers ran articles or essays critical of provincial lawmaking bodies at their own risk and peril even after 1776. When we know a great deal more about these early legislatures perhaps we will understand better why they were so easily offended. Marshall McLuhan alludes to the respect held for the printed word from Gutenberg's time until our own. Surely by the middle of the eighteenth century newspapers were not only respected by readers but also feared by authorities, who thought the only way to keep the lid on things—to insure political conformity—was to squelch all printed criticism. It was one thing to be a critical tavern drunk but quite another for a local newspaper to intimate that the legislature had severe weaknesses. Most printers stayed in line either because they had vital business arrangements with the colony or because of community pressure that created a consensus judgment. The printer who was a troublemaker often stood alone, and this is one distinguishing feature of the Zenger case —the considerable support for an impecunious New York printer. The assistance rallied for Zenger was unique and explains not only why he won, but why other nonconformist printers in America between 1735 and 1765 lost.

In time, the suspicious legislators and the printers were forced into an alliance. The Stamp Act proved to be the catalytic agent that joined insubordinate assemblies with the owners of those vehicles of propaganda now needed to spread the alarm. Nothing was more indicative of the changed attitude than the decision of the Massachusetts House of Representatives in 1766 to open a spectator's gallery— a complete reversal of form that would have shocked most assemblymen a decade earlier. The difference, of course, was that the lawmakers decided they needed popular support in their argument with the Crown, and realized that only through publicity and public discussion could they make their protest movement succeed.

Most Americans must have long remained unaware of the sources of the mounting imperial tension. In the decade preceeding the Stamp Act, several provincial legislatures passed their own version of such a tax without provoking widespread resentment (the English stamp taxes, as with other legislation, were applicable only in Britain unless the law specifically included the colonies). In 1755 the Massachusetts General Assembly levied a halfpenny tax on every newspaper for a two-year period.[4] A replica of the red mark stamped on English-made sheets appeared in Boston in the form of a bird in flight. New York legislators imitated this act in late 1756 and the unperturbed printers merely passed the halfpenny charge on to their subscribers. The revenues thus raised were meant to cover expenses created by the French and Indian War, and were accepted in that light by nearly everyone except James Parker, who condemned the tax in his *New-York Gazette* as potentially ruinous, as did Edes and Gill in their Boston *Gazette*. The Bostonians reprinted English attacks on the British stamp tax and by implication suggested that the native levy was similarly intended to muzzle the press. But the majority of the printers and their patrons were unmoved by these assertions, since the taxes had been levied by their own representatives to pay for local government. Most Americans did not subscribe to a newspaper anyway, so it appeared to be a tax by the few on the few. There seemed no great harm in that.

Indeed, Americans in the 1750s and 1760s were not spoiling for a fight. The American was a bolder thinker perhaps than his European counterpart, but his concepts of sanitation, medicine, and disease were but shortly removed from the Middle Ages. Technologically there had been great improvement, but some of the best English magazines carried stories and pictures of mermaids reported not as hoaxes but as facts. The traditional celebration of Guy Fawkes day in New England gave vent to delirious notions of the pope and of Catholicism generally. And though the last witch had been hung outside Boston in 1692, superstition and ignorance abounded. The oncoming war with France and the French victory over Braddock in 1755 created panic on the frontier. Learned men insisted that a northwest passage to the Orient existed near Hudson Bay, and foolish men invested money trying to prove it. New Yorkers paid sixpence in 1756 to view "at the sign of the Golden Apple,"

a large snake-skin, 21 feet long and four feet one inch wide . . .
killed by some of Gen. Braddock's men by firing six balls into
him, close by the Allegheny Mountains, supposed to be coming
down to feed on dead men. When it was killed, there was found
in its belly a child, supposed to be four years old, together with a
live dog! It had a horn on its tail seven inches long, and it ran as
fast as a horse.[5]

The newspaper advertisement did not tell how many had fainted at
the sight, but clearly Barnum had a predecessor who respected the
power of the printed word. A sense of humor was rarely displayed in
colonial newspapers but surely readers who stomached the dragon-
snake story must have smiled when their neighbors went to a newspaper column to call each other to account. Portrait painter Charles
Willson Peale used the *Maryland Gazette* in 1774 to warn tardy debtors. "If a certain E.V. does not immediately pay for his family picture," one Peale advertisement cautioned, "his name shall be published at full length in the next paper." A week later, Peale inserted
his promised follow-up: MR. ELIE VALLETTE, PAY ME FOR PAINTING
YOUR FAMILY PICTURE. CHARLES PEALE. That drew a response that titillated Annapolis readers seven days later: MR. CHARLES WILLSON
PEALE, ALIAS CHARLES PEALE—YES, YOU SHALL BE PAID; BUT NOT
BEFORE YOU HAVE LEARNED TO BE LESS INSOLENT. ELIE VALLETTE.[6]

Such goings-on in newspapers provided a break in the routine of
colonial life that was splattered with disease and death, violence and
boredom. Drinking fountains, common sewers, outdoor privies, and
the dreaded "sickly season" were all of a piece in a society preoccupied with health as hardy men were widowers at twenty-five and
thrice-married by sixty, while childbearing girls died in their teens.
Yet, for all these terrors, it was a society that welcomed each day
with the expectation that tomorrow would bring improvement. One
man embodied the spirit of practicality and betterment. Benjamin
Franklin worked for free libraries and better streets, encouraged vol-
unteer firemen to mitigate the dangers of a holocaust, and tried to
give his fellow printers both a line of credit and improved postal serv-

ice. Indeed, the postal reforms of Franklin's day may have made local service as good as it would be two centuries later, with no more criticism and far less cost. His list of innovations included free exchanges between printers and a more systematic upkeep of post roads. Many printers, in their dual role as postmasters, applauded Franklin's changes for they had previously paid post riders a bonus. Now the "printer's exchange" was entrenched as the chief newsgathering method in the colonies. By 1765 there was regular postal service between Philadelphia and New York three times each week. The Boston-to-New York stages passed through New Haven, New London, and Providence on a weekly schedule. A traveler not in a great hurry could go overland from Falmouth (now Portland, Maine) in the north to Charleston, South Carolina, and within a decade makeshift roads reached Saint Augustine, Florida. Mail packets ranged the coastal waters and in perfect sailing weather ships had been known to reach Europe from American ports in less than thirty days.

Although thin fingers of settlement reached into the backlands, most Americans in the 1760s lived in regions lapped by tidewaters or near the deepest rivers. Philadelphia was the great metropolis, served by oceangoing vessels that brought goods to the wharves which served a population nearing 40,000—enough to make the city the second largest in the British Empire. New York had over 20,000 people, and Boston seemed to have leveled out at around 16,000 souls. In these three cities were concentrated the bulk of American journalism—four newspapers in Boston, five in both Philadelphia and New York. Events would soon prove that power and numbers do not always go together. When the storm of protest broke over the Stamp Act, newspapers became the propaganda vehicles for a small circle of opinion makers that widened until a whole region seemed alive with protest.

Samuel Adams, more persistently than any other American, tended the furnaces of dissent. Boston was his crucible, the town Committee of Correspondence and the Whig newspapers his devices for communicating with the rest of the colonies. "The influence of the propagandists was out of all proportion to their numbers," Davidson noted.[7] Adams, indefatigable and vindictive, declared his personal war on England in advance of most Americans, then gave all his energies to prove the wisdom of his decision. Closeted with Benjamin Edes and other radicals in the "Loyal Nine," Adams plotted a course calculated to infuriate the royal Establishment; by accident or design his incendiarism could only lead in one direction—toward independence. "Independence, it is true, was declared in Congress in 1776," Tory Peter Oliver recalled, "but it was settled in Boston, in 1768, by *Adams* and his Junto." [8]

Before independence was ever seriously discussed, however, a long barrage was needed to prepare Americans for the ultimate decision. The main artillerists in the war of words were New England men, prepared not for job-case careers but for the more genteel lives of lawyers. Fate made a strange turn when James Otis, more brilliant than Adams and a natural leader, dropped out of the radical movement after a tavern brawl left him disabled. Thereafter, Samuel Adams dominated the Boston scene and led the Caucus Club radicals in the planting of newspaper essays, in calling town meetings, and in printing broadsides or pamphlets—whatever came to hand and could carry a message—to attack Crown agents. First Governor Francis Bernard was set upon, then the Stamp Act came along to feed the flames of discord, and finally Thomas Hutchinson was the scapegoat who moved into oblivion while Adams, his cousin John, and other bold spirits persuaded Americans that George III's ministers were the conspirators in a plot to destroy American rights and liberties.

For all the skill of the Adamses and such other propagandists as Alexander McDougall and Thomas Jefferson, the patriot's cause probably would have failed without the overwhelming support of the printers. "Nothing has been done without the Approbation of the People, who have indeed out run their Leaders," George Mason recalled in surveying the events that took place between 1774 and 1776.[9] Public opinion assuredly favored the steps taken to weaken the imperial bonds, but it was the newspapers and the pamphlets that prepared public opinion for drastic measures and finally made it seem that thirty or thirty-five newspapers spoke the people's minds.

The bumbling of English politicians set the stage, when a timid ministry was frightened by the statistics of a national debt and began probing for ways to pay the interest. It seemed only fair to place a small tax on American newspapers, legal documents, playing cards, and other paper products that had long been taxed in Britain. The Stamp Act hardly caused a flutter when it passed Parliament, and even Benjamin Franklin prepared to accept the inevitable by laying in a paper supply "in the vain expectation of evading the full penny tax." What no one in England anticipated, of course, was the hastily contrived alliance between the legal profession and newspaper printers—the two groups most affected by the new law. As Arthur M. Schlesinger, Sr., observed, printers rapidly closed ranks because "the Stamp Act imposed hardships affecting every branch of their trade." Franklin wrote his partner in Philadelphia that the new law "will affect the Printers more than anybody, as a Sterling Halfpenny Stamp on every Half Sheet of a Newspaper, and Two Shillings on every Advertisement, will go near to knock up one Half of both." James Parker had turned his *New-York Gazette* over to John Holt and planned to start another newspaper in New Jersey, but arrival of the sad news "of the Killing Stamp, has struck a deadly Blow to all my Hopes on that Head," he moaned.[10]

Slightly chagrined that Patrick Henry's denunciation furnished the thunderclap, Samuel Adams probably lamented that southern radicals had "first asserted their Rights with *decent Firmness*" ahead of Boston malcontents. Adams' busy pen scratched far in the night—his cluttered desk became a factory for inflammatory essays written over a variety of pseudonyms that gave the appearance of not one embattled citizen, but a whole army of indignant sufferers, who were busily engaged in denouncing the departure from past British policy. Heretofore Parliament had used revenue acts to regulate trade but never taxed the colonies internally to raise money. It was Adams who saw the long-range implications of this change and kept up a drum-fire of alarums against British intentions. Using as a base the Virginia resolutions (that denied Parliament the right to impose internal taxes), Adams and his Caucus Club cronies fired paper salvos in the *Gazette* and *Spy* with a frenzy that Governor Francis Bernard could scarcely believe. "It is inconceivable how they [Virginia resolves] have roused up the Boston Politicians, & have been the Occasion of a fresh inundation of factious & insolent pieces in the popular Newspapers," he lamented.

For all the screeds printed attacking Parliament, not a single newspaper publisher was indicted by a grand jury despite the use of incendiary rhetoric which a generation earlier would have made a Crown attorney turn livid. Why the difference? The attacks were upon Parliament and the ministry of Lord Bute, but the king's appointees knew they would be powerless if they tried to persuade grand juries to bring in a seditious libel indictment. "Seldom in American history have the newspapers been so united behind a single cause as in 1765–66," Curtis Nettels has pointed out. In that unanimity the radical colonists found their strength. Thenceforth, the power of less than a hundred men and their printing-press allies could not be denied.

The last stamp-free day for printers fell on an ominous October 31, 1765. William Bradford of the *Pennsylvania Journal* defiantly placed a bold black border around his front page and topped it with a gravedigger's tool and death's head. Under the motto—EXPIRING: In Hopes of a Resurrection to LIFE Again—Bradford candidly explained that on the morrow he was suspending his newspaper "in order to deliberate, whether any Methods can be found to elude the chains forged for us, and escape the insupportable Slavery." Thanks to the propaganda barrage, a method of eluding the Stamp Act had been found—no one was brave enough to sell the stamped paper. Would-be stamp agents were everywhere intimidated by threats of tar and feathers or saw their effigies hung from a makeshift gibbet. A variety of stratagems was soon in use by the newspapers, ranging from publishing without a nameplate to issuing a claim (quite true) that stamped paper was impossible to find. A few newspapers suspended temporarily, but not a single one was ever issued bearing the detested stamps that their English cousins had been buying since 1712.

Englishmen were taken aback by the American onslaught against the Stamp Act to the point that threatened boycotts of British goods brought quick relief. A repeal act was passed but with a string attached—the Declaratory Act which reasserted Parliament's supreme rights over the colonies. After a committee of London merchants boasted that their claims brought the repeal but warned the colonies, in effect, "Don't let it happen again," the mood of Americans was truculent. Their patronizing letter was printed in American newspapers, George Mason commented, with the tone and "authoritative Style of a Master" sternly lecturing "a School-Boy." Mason sent his reply to the *London Public Ledger* with the warning: "Such another Experiment as the Stamp-Act wou'd produce a general Revolt in America." [12]

If Mason's admonition ever was printed in England, the right people failed to heed it. Charles Townshend easily whisked through Parliament bills which levied a new tax program aimed at American pocketbooks. Once again, printers were peculiarly hard hit by the inept English bureaucrats who included in their revenue-producing schemes one section that taxed sixty-seven grades of paper. As "Farmer" John Dickinson quickly noted, it was so much nonsense to draw a real distinction between "the rates mentioned in the *Stamp-Act*, on the *Use* of paper," and the new levies "on the *importation* of it." [13] Dickinson's calculated charges appeared in twenty-two of the twenty-six newspapers then serving American readers. His moderate, scholarly tone gave the precise answer Americans needed as a cudgel on their neighbors who still insisted Parliament had not overstepped its authority. Talk about "internal" or "external" taxes, one supposedly wrong and the other right, was so much poppycock to Dickinson. The point was that any tax from Parliament was made without the Americans' consent and "names will not change the nature of things."

Printers doted on Dickinson's words. Toasts to "the celebrated Farmer" were raised in defiance and in drunkenness. After the Stamp Act fiasco, the reception for Townshend's taxing scheme should have warned prudent men that the vapor pouring from American presses was evidence of a seething volcano. No longer was the protest movement a Boston-centered imbroglio, although it was in that haven of "foul-mouthed Trumpeters of Sedition" (as one loyalist put it) that the pressure was greatest on royal authority.

Americans struck back with solemn promises to support a boycott of English goods until the obnoxious duties were lifted. Vigilante committees were formed, charged with ferreting out backsliders and publishing their names in the newspapers to stigmatize them "as Enemys to their Country." John Mein, a tough Scot who had founded the *Boston Chronicle* in the midst of the turmoil, refused to be intimidated by John Hancock or the Boston Committee of Merchants. Instead, Mein published a certified list of importers that was deadly evidence against some of the sanctimonious Whig merchants. Mein's telltale list with its thinly veiled attack on the Boston radicals shook the confidence of printers and patriots elsewhere when Mein's exchanges reached them. Recognizing the setback, Boston radicals made no pretense at tolerance. "Mr. Mein at present is so obnoxious to the People on account of his Publishing the Manifests, that he's oblig'd to go Arm'd, and 'tis but a few Nights Since that two Persons who resembled him pretty much were attack'd in a narrow Alley with Clubs, and would in all probability have lost their Lives if the Mistake had not been timely discover'd," a sympathetic loyalist reported. When a mob finally caught up with the real Mein, the embattled Tory printer fired his pistol in the melee that followed and struck a bystander with a wild shot. Prudently, Mein caught the next ship for England, bearing all the ill wishes of the Boston radicals and the prayers of a friend who thought the incident proved Americans were "a Hypocritical, Canting Disaffected People, who I really believe wish for nothing more, than the overthrow of the Parent State." [14]

Running Mein out of town was an effective way to restrict the blessings of a free press to the Whig majority. Mein's cleverness had been intolerable, and the backroom politicians who were tired of his *Chronicle* harpoons made it clear that freedom of expression would be limited to those safely in the Whig fold. Then came the incident on March 5, 1770, which allowed them to tar native loyalists and Crown officials with the same brush. The Boston Massacre gave the patriots a fresh cause which Sam Adams exploited with a town meeting and great wailing and moaning in the press. Before Adams and his crew finished, the five-casualty street brawl had become a "horrid Massacre" with dogs "greedily licking human Blood in King-Street." It was not a pretty picture, and Paul Revere's engraving added alarm to the devastation of Adams' propaganda blows. The British soldiers were exonerated by a court, but Adams retried them in the Boston *Gazette* where, as "Vindex," he insisted that innocent American patriots had been wantonly butchered.

New York had been calm, by comparison, but it was only a matter of time until a combination of newspapers, broadsides, and pamphlets brought on a confrontation there with authorities. For a while the Manhattan Whigs seemed more worried about the threatened power of the Anglican church than of Parliament's tax program. The implication of the Whig writers was that England's policies were potentially a grave danger to American liberties—it was the threatening aspect rather than the present problem—and that was a connecting link between the most able patriot writers. As David Ramsay, the contemporary historian of the Revolution, discerned when the events were still fresh, this sense of urgency was the day-and-night message of most Whig newspapers. Jeremiads appeared in the leading vehicles of protest "to awaken the attention of the people . . . to a sense of their danger, and point out the fatal consequences of the late acts of Parliament. Every newspaper teemed with dissertations in favor of liberty—with debates of the members of Parliament, especially with the speeches of the favorers of America, and the protests of the dissenting Lords." [15] Indeed, the printers gleaned incoming English pamphlets and newspapers for news of men in high places who thought the American protests were reasonable. The names of Bishop Shipley and other English radicals became familiar to Americans after printers in Boston and Philadelphia reprinted their sympathetic essays as proof of the justice of the patriots' cause.

These Whig attacks, mainly directed at Parliamentary leadership, infuriated Crown authorities in the colonial Establishment who were unsure of how dissent should be suppressed. There was no getting around the traditional English belief that unless a man spoke sedition against the Crown, he was free to speak his piece. The trouble was, in the Tory mind, that the clear line of sedition was difficult to trace. Thus the Tory gentlemen privately denounced the newspapers as "sowers of sedition" but knew that seeking a grand jury indictment would be futile. So no printers were prosecuted and the ministry in London counseled a beneath-our-contempt policy that seemed to allow the protest virus to spread in every direction from the Boston hotbed.

The colonial essayists were not the country bumpkins the English politicians assumed them to be. To make their battle appear to be a fight on behalf of English liberties in the abstract, the names of John Wilkes, William Pitt, Isaac Barré, and other Whigs in good standing were hailed as among the staunch defenders of the British Constitution. Alexander McDougall, a blustering Whig merchant in New York, became famous as "the Wilkes of America" when his broadside message slapped the provincial assembly for voting an increase in subsidies to maintain British soldiers quartered on Manhattan. Although the message was signed by "A Son of Liberty," the assembly thought it knew who had breached their privileges and sent McDougall to jail early in 1770. McDougall became a pampered prisoner and continued to fire hot verbal bolts from his cell, but the indignant legislators kept him jailed for months, threatening a prosecution that never reached a court.

Running a print shop had become, by 1770, no mere business enterprise. In peaceful times printer Franklin had noted

> That the Business of Printing has chiefly to do with Men's Opin-
> ions [which led to] the peculiar Unhappiness of that Business,
> which other Callings are [in] no way liable to . . . the Smith, the
> Shoemaker, the Carpenter, or the Man of any other Trade, may
> work indifferently for People of all Persuasions, without offending
> any of them: and the Merchant may buy and sell with Jews,
> Turks, Hereticks and Infidels of all sorts, and get Money by every
> one of them, without giving Offence to the most orthodox . . . or
> suffering the least Censure or Ill-will.[16]

The truth was, Franklin went on, "That if all Printers were deter-
min'd not to print any thing till they were sure it would offend no
body, there would be very little printed." But what the militant
Whigs insisted upon by the 1770s was *absolute* conformity. As Mein
learned, the Whigs were not interested in hearing both sides of any
argument with England. The lukewarm *New-York Gazette* printer
had been warned in 1765 that if he did not continue his newspaper in
defiance of the law, "depend upon it, your House, Person and
Effects, will be in imminent Danger." Though loyalists railed at the
tactics of "Rash conceited Priggs & Printers," they rode an irresistible
tide that engulfed well-intentioned but timorous men whose chief
fault was that they were outnumbered.

What Americans were witnessing, was community censorship,
with the intolerant Whig-patriot groups ready to use whatever
means was needed to exercise control. Perhaps in numbers this band
was small, but if the majority found fault with what was going on
(and the evidence is to the contrary), it remained quiet. Printers
grew bolder as Whig essayists saw that in England the trenchant
"Junius" had convulsed Tories but still remained at liberty and unin-
dicted because his true identity was unknown. "Junius" in late 1769
had called upon George III to admit past mistakes and alter ministe-
rial policies or suffer the fate of Charles I. The effrontery of "Junius"
made English Whigs gasp (and Tories fume), but Americans saw in
the failure to find and prosecute "Junius" a clear implication. The
criticism of public measures that James Alexander had dreamed of in

1734 was now freely dispensed. Still, it was a one-sided freedom. Persistent pressure finally permitted the Tories but a few newspapers and these could operate only in Boston and New York. Suspected essayists for Tory newspapers were threatened with a hemp necklace, although in Boston a band of redcoated soldiers turned the tables by warning Isaiah Thomas that he would soon wear a coat of tar and feathers if his *Spy* did not call off its war against the king's authorities.

Thomas had no intention of seeking a truce. Instead he worked with Edes, Gill, and other Whig printers to keep the protest movement smoldering during the brief lull in 1771–1772, when Parliament turned to other problems and let America alone for the time. At Samuel Shed's grocery shop on Milk Street in Boston, the Whigs congregated and waited. A new tax bill with its slanted provision favoring East India Company tea gave them an opportunity to begin their propaganda mills afresh. After the uproarious Tea Party late in 1773 came the Intolerable Acts, which created unforeseen sympathy in the sister colonies for beleaguered Massachusetts Bay. No other colony had been seriously hampered, despite all the Whig noise about slavery and suppression. As the witness and historian Ramsay observed, however, the Whigs sought to convince all colonists that what affected Bostonians would eventually ruin twelve other provinces. This was the point of Whig propaganda, Ramsay explained, and they achieved their goal "in a great measure by means of the press."

That a handful of Whig newspapers guided such a powerful protest is testimony to the credibility of Americans. Thomas's motto was *Noscere res humanas est Hominis* (Knowledge of the World Is Necessary for Every Man) and a conviction grew among printers and writers that if the people were sufficiently informed they would do the right thing. Indeed, it is this strand that has held much of the web of American journalism together. In time of crisis a small band of writers has often started its crusade with the inner conviction that the people could be trusted, if they were sufficiently informed of the facts. As the tension in 1774 mounted, one observer found that

Americans were "a well-informed, reasoning commonality . . . their frequent and free elections . . . together with the freedom and general circulation of newspapers, and the eagerness and leisure of the people to read them or to listen to those who do" gave Whigs a weapon that the Crown could never wrest from them, and so it never tried.[17]

Finally, there was Lexington-Concord, with Isaiah Thomas's passionate account gathered from eye witnesses. "AMERICANS! forever bear in mind the BATTLE of LEXINGTON!—where British Troops, unmolested and unprovoked, wantonly, and in a most inhuman manner fired upon and killed a number of our countrymen, then robbed them of their provisions, ransacked, plundered and burnt their houses!" The report was in Thomas's transplanted *Spy*, moved from British-occupied Boston.

For the next eight years Whig newspapers fulfilled a historic role —they kept up morale, told citizens what was going on, trumpeted the precious few victories and played down the many defeats. All the while, Americans in the hinterlands, distant from the battlefields, carried on a relatively unhampered life of commerce and agriculture. To many Americans the only direct affect the war had was on the prices they paid or received for crops, and the kind or amount of taxes they paid. Meanwhile, their newspapers appealed for rags (needed to make paper), printed outrageous rumors (there was no censorship since outside of New York, and a few occupied towns, the Whigs were in complete control), and helped make Washington into a national hero and demigod.

From the earliest days of the Republic, heroes have been made by the newspapers. All societies seem to have developed some form of hero worship, and it was important to Americans after 1775 that they have at least one national hero. The newspapers gave them one in General Washington. Washington's force of character and other qualities sustained him throughout the war, but it was the repeated newspaper accounts of his exploits from Cambridge in 1775 onward that made Washington the most popular man in the country. Whatever hold Franklin or John Hancock had on the public's imagination certainly was transferred to Washington after the much-needed victory at Trenton in 1776. Thus newspapers not only helped sustain morale during the Revolution but also projected an image of national leadership that the thirteen widely separated seaboard states desperately needed for survival.

Printers with good Whig credentials learned that the safe way to avoid mob action was to keep their columns crammed with diatribes directed at the Tory elements in the community. It is difficult for us to understand how much hatred was stirred by the Americans who remained loyal to George III, but the intensity of Washington's epithet for them—"the abominable pests of society"—gives a clue. A newspaper printer with loyalist leanings ran incredible risks if he persisted in his Tory course. Economic coercion and personal insults must have worked wonders. On other occasions, a local "committee of tarring and feathering" was ready to take over, as in the case of Samuel Loudon, the Whig printer of the *New-York Packet* who made the mistake of believing that a liberal attitude meant that all parties were entitled to a public hearing. Loudon soon learned that what might be liberal in calm days became treason in stormy times. For printing Charles Inglis's rebuttal to *Common Sense,* Loudon was paid a midnight visit by a band of superpatriots in March 1776. The angry Whigs destroyed Loudon's stock of fifteen hundred pamphlets, pied his type forms, and forced him to hand over the offending manuscript.[18] As the war progressed, printers tended to flee when the military support retreated and to speak boldly when the threat of arms was remote. By the autumn of 1776 the loyalty of most printers had been so tested that the printer of a loyalist newspaper needed assurances that the king's regiments were within earshot.

The many-faceted role that printers played during the Revolution is further illustrated by the controversial part James Rivington of New York took in both the propaganda attacks and a murky cloak-and-dagger drama. The nature of the business has left Rivington's exact status in dispute, but it is clear that at one time he tried to pursue a neutral course and wound up with a wrecked printing shop for his trouble. Later, Rivington settled down to the comfortable life of a coffeehouse operator and Crown printer after the British occupied Manhattan. By 1777 the columns of Rivington's *New-York Gazette* became abusive in their anti-Whig bias, and British officers knew that intercepted and usually embarrassing letters would be printed there to the discomfort of rebel generals and congressmen. But Rivington, who apparently bore a grudge against Sir William Howe, also saw in time that the tide of war had turned. Isaiah Thomas hinted in his *History* at this secret role when he noted that Rivington "sent out of the city such communications as he knew would be interesting to the commanders of the American armies." [19]

Despite the skepticism of historians since Thomas's day, there is little doubt but that Rivington became an American agent by 1780 and that on the eve of Yorktown he procured and secretly sent to Washington the British fleet's signal book. After Washington led the Continental army back into New York, it seems likely that special measures were taken to protect Rivington from unruly citizens not privy to the whole story. The circumstances of Rivington's ability to remain on Manhattan Island when the rest of the British community was embarking, and the discovery of an American spy's manuscripts, combine to make it clear that Rivington was reviling Washington in his news columns and essays while actually sending helpful information inside the bindings of harmless-looking books. About £1,500 in cash, passed to him secretly, probably helped Rivington decide that America was going to win.

Philadelphian Benjamin Towne stood somewhere between Rivington and Isaiah Thomas. Towne had once worked with Goddard on the *Chronicle,* and early in 1775 had started the triweekly *Pennsylvania Evening Post* with some support from the more liberal commercial gentlemen of Philadelphia. When the British thought the war could be ended with one knockout blow and invaded the City of Brotherly Love, Towne decided not to flee with the alarmed Whigs but to stay and make his peace with the conquerors by claiming he was not a soldier but a tradesman. Proscribed by the Pennsylvania legislature, Towne remained in Philadelphia until Howe's army withdrew, then changed his loyalties (such as they were) back to the American cause. When questioned about this turnabout, Towne issued a personal manifesto of neutrality. "They are pleased to charge me with hypocrisy in pretending to be a Whig when I was none," Towne insisted. "This charge is false; I was neither Whig nor Tory but a Printer." [20]

Towne may have been excused as a harmless eccentric, for he was indeed no ordinary mortal. Yet Towne left his mark in the annals of journalism by converting the *Post* into America's first daily newspaper in 1783. His operation was doomed and Towne must have been a pitiful sight as he tried in desperation to peddle the *Post* on street corners, but he deserves credit for pushing an idea that was only slightly ahead of its time.

The year 1783 was, in fact, a period of anxiety and unsteadiness in America. The Republic was in its seventh year of independence and the first year of peace, but the new state walked into the family of nations on legs as shaky as a newborn colt's. Still, many of America's institutions were far from new and the Founding Fathers thought they had been treading a path to nationhood along classic Roman lines. Never before, on the other hand, had the newspapers of a country joined forces with revolutionaries to bring about a complete overthrow of the power structure. As an instrument in the battle for social and political change, the press had proved its mettle. Strident newspapers had helped bring off the most successful anti-imperial revolution in history.

Still to be determined was America's pathway in peace. Postwar unrest caused Benjamin Rush to react hysterically to the local scene when a small band of disgruntled veterans intimidated the Continental Congress. "The house is on fire—it is no matter *where* it kindled or *who* blew the flame. Buckets—buckets should be the cry of every good citizen," Rush sputtered.[21] In every community honest men shared Rush's anxiety and wondered aloud, as did David Humphreys, what could be done "to make the Revolution a blessing instead of a curse"? [22] Had Rush bothered to ask printer John Dunlap or his apprentice David Claypoole, his Philadelphia neighbors, he might have been buoyed by their confidence. Instead of sagging spirits, Dunlap and Claypoole saw a new era of peace and plenty ahead. They tested their faith in the marketplace by starting the new nation's first successful daily publication—the *Pennsylvania Packet and Daily Advertiser*—born on September 21, 1784. The *Packet* would be as lusty and swaggering as the readers it served for the next fifty-five years. Its lineal descendant survives in the Bicentennial era as the Philadelphia *Inquirer.* [23]

3

"The Dæmon of Faction" Triumphant

A postwar doldrums settled over parts of the new United States after the Treaty of Paris ended the fighting phase of the Revolution. Some of the anxieties expressed about independence proved well founded. Ocean commerce declined, but was partly offset by the freehand traders now exercised in world markets. Land speculators looked longingly across the Alleghenies to fertile valleys now within the jurisdiction of an impoverished Congress. Bought in depreciated currency or Continental loan paper, the Northwest Territory tracts beckoned to those farsighted citizens who sought "riches beyond the dreams of avarice." The Congress itself had never recovered from the shock sustained at the war's end when a small band of rum-swilling veterans in search of their back pay bullied their way into Philadelphia. The nail-biting congressmen scurried off to Princeton. Except for a post office and a foreign affairs section that hardly deserved the name, national government was almost at a standstill.

Yet, although the prestige of "the United States in Congress assembled" was low, the morale of the plain people was probably much higher than that of their leaders. There was a natural optimism in

eighteenth-century America that kept bobbing up in the newspapers
—in essays on canal systems or in the printed letters from Kentucky
that described the weather and soil. The perspective of many politicians was different; they were preoccupied with the need for a sound
credit system that would pay off wartime debts and stabilize the hel-
ter-skelter currency situation. Pelatiah Webster's essays in the *Pennsylvania Evening Post* had long warned of "the Danger of too much
Circulating Cash." Thirteen states and as many monetary systems,
with no courts to enforce contracts beyond state boundaries, made
commerce a day-to-day risk. The Articles of Confederation offered
little consolation to businessmen or politicians enraptured with the
idea of an "energetic government," one that could collect taxes and
pay off old debts. Hard cash was scarce, and the price paid for farm
products had been declining.

The first inkling of real trouble came from Massachusetts, when a
back-country riot threatened to spread. In the ensuing crisis, far more
ink was spilled than blood as men of varying shades of opinion used
the newspapers to explain why the country was going to hell in such
a hurry. "Never, it may be safely asserted, was the number of political journals so great in proportion to the population of a country as at
present in ours," the Reverend Samuel Miller boasted about 1785.
"Never were they, all things considered, so cheap, so universally
diffused, and so easy of access." [1] These easily procured newspapers,
filled with the goings-on in western Massachusetts, helped shape the
citizens' views of the postwar crisis and of the reform measures that
followed.

Daniel Shays, a veteran of the Revolution, led a taxpayer's strike
that in history became a rebellion. Shays and his neighbors, driven to
a fury by low commodity prices and high taxes, tried to stop a
sheriff's sale or two with more than gentle persuasion. There were a
few casualties, but the incident was blown out of all proportion by
men who understood the power of public opinion. From his distant
post in France, Jefferson could applaud the necessity of an uprising in
every generation to keep the wheels of democracy from rusting, but

those closer to the scene felt—or pretended to feel—the utmost horror over the Shays incident.

At first, the newspapers treated the Massachusetts outbreak as an isolated uprising. A similar incident in the Greenbrier district of western Virginia went almost unnoticed in the press. But the propaganda mills in New England began to grind anew, with Boston again the nerve center. Essayists bewailed the mockery of law and order, and the *Massachusetts Centinel* published insistent demands that guilty "Shaysites" be punished. With mixed feelings, Massachusetts assembled a punitive expedition, captured the ringleaders, but eventually pardoned them. Meanwhile, however, Benjamin Russell of the *Centinel* and his friends had found the latch string that would open the door for "energetic government."

Russell was a remarkable printer and one of the first great editors, for he was not content to stay in the back of his shop bedabbled with ink when exciting ideas were generated in the front office. He had started the *Centinel* in 1784, warmly received by the business community while he proclaimed himself a neutral in politics. Uninfluenced by Party, We Aim Only to Be Just, Russell's masthead promised. No doubt Russell was full of good intentions as he entered Boston's journalistic maze at a time when the older newspapers showed a certain decrepitness. A former apprentice of Isaiah Thomas's businesslike house, Russell exchanged his type stick for a rifle during the Revolution. After the war, he returned to Boston determined to match Thomas's enterprise. Russell was personable, and his newspaper was aggressive and well printed. Issued twice a week, it saw its circulation climb to 4,000, and Russell was making money and gathering influence in Boston's commercial circles.[2] When the Shays affair erupted, the local merchants and their lawyer friends believed that all their worst fears about postwar America had been confirmed. "Anarchy and confusion!" was their cry. Russell carried their panicky version of the Shays affair to the other states, and by the time this colored account was read on the porch at Mount Vernon, the small protest had blossomed into anarchy.

Henry Knox, the rotund Secretary of War and a particular friend of Russell's, helped spread the alarm. What Russell's *Centinel* did in the exchanges with other newspapers, Knox paralleled in private letters. To General Washington Knox forwarded a steady and distressing stream of words, all of them embellishing an "alas-we-are-undone-unless-a-firm-hand-takes-over" theme. Washington, who read more newspapers than his peace of mind allowed, soaked in all the bad news. "Light Horse Harry" Lee, a leader of the Virginia gloom-and-doom coterie, urged Washington to use his influence to set the country aright. "Influence is no government," Washington shot back. But he was impressed—mightily impressed—and when concern over the Shays tempest resulted in the Federal Convention, Washington's role was clearly staked out. By the time New England newspapers were reporting "That the Dæmon of Faction and Discord seems totally to have subsided" in the Berkshire hills, delegates from twelve states had spent an entire summer patching together a constitution.

The assemblage at Philadelphia in May 1787 quickly cut off all communication with the rest of the country. Not a whimper was heard from the printers when it was announced that the Federal Convention would deliberate in secret, although some state legislatures then had public galleries and reports of speeches were permitted. Ostensibly called to revise the Articles of Confederation, the Convention never seriously considered the possibility of admitting representatives from newspapers. Only the selection of Washington as Convention president was common knowledge, but that was promise enough to most Americans that nothing untoward would take place. "All classes seem to await with the greatest impatience the event of the Federal Convention, looking up to it as to a Fountain from which those streams of political Felicity are to flow," New Englanders read.

The news drought broke suddenly when the entire Constitution was approved on September 17 and began appearing in the local newspapers two days later. The document was conveniently brief, so that the whole plan could be printed in one or two issues of an ordinary newspaper. The result was a remarkable occurrence in American history, and perhaps in world history. Every newspaper of the period (that has survived) printed the complete Constitution. After months of silence and little speculation, the American newspaper reader was suddenly engulfed with information and allowed to make his own interpretation of it during the first days after the Convention broke up. There had been no journalistic leaks worth mentioning, so the reader was free to look upon this new constitution with only one distinctive piece of propaganda laid before him—the accompanying letter signed by Washington which skillful Gouverneur Morris used to give the coloration of the great man's endorsement. Supporters of the Constitution took extraordinary pains to disseminate the document, convinced that widespread public discussion could only benefit their cause. Significantly, those citizens favoring the Constitution as well as those committed to its defeat were eager for a general debate of the document's merits; and such skilled propagandists as Alexander Hamilton realized that most of that debate would have to take place in the newspapers.

What then followed is little short of astonishing. Within the space of thirteen months the delegates had shaped a new form of government, sent it to the people for debate, and eleven state conventions had ratified it. Nothing like it had ever happened before, and despite technological improvements nothing approaching it has occurred since. Newspapers provided a public forum, and the entire process sped along at a time when the chief means of carrying information were usually four-paged newspapers and four-legged animals.

Not only did the newspapers spontaneously provide a billboard for the Constitution, they also allowed about a month to elapse before their internal politics began to surface. Trained to believe that factionalism was akin to political suicide, editors appear to have been reluctant partners in the realignment of allegiances. Nearly every state had its country party and its seaboard-city interest, but for the first time this cleavage took on a national pattern. Supporters of the Constitution, soon to be called Federalists, hurried to gain the initiative in the brewing war of words. The bright young lawyers and the well-to-do merchants lost no time in becoming the fastest of friends with certain key printers whose newspapers became vital links in the Federalists' communications network.

Straightforward George Washington, uninterested in plotting or back-scenes maneuvering, simply thought that the new nation was in a now-or-never situation and that much depended on the conversion of printers to the Federalist cause. He prayed for a quick ratification, but knew this was unlikely. "Much will depend however upon literary abilities," Washington wrote a wartime aide, "and the recommendation of it [the Constitution] by good pens should be *openly*, I mean, publickly afforded in the Gazettes." ³

Wherever the Federalists were strongest they tried to rush things along by convening a state ratifying convention quickly and depending on the pro-Constitution press for a barrage of essays that would smother the opposition. Benjamin Russell, openly capitalizing on the power of his *Centinel*, started the Federalist bandwagon rolling in Boston. Francis Childs' *New-York Advertiser* and Andrew Browne's Philadelphia *Federal Gazette* frankly denounced the anti-Constitution forces as "wrongheads." By November it was obvious that out of about one hundred weekly newspapers then published in the United States, all but a handful were either rabidly Federalist or noticeably inclined to the Federalist cause. Only the *New-York Journal*, Philadelphia *Independent Gazetteer*, Boston *American Herald*, and nine other newspapers were determined to turn ratification into a real political contest. John Adams called the impending struggle "the greatest single effort of national deliberation that the world has ever seen," and events of the next six months proved Adams right.

With nine out of ten newspapers on their side, the Federalists should have had an easier time of it. Nonetheless, they almost overplayed their hand. The opposition, saddled with the unhappy name of "Anti-Federalists," charged that friends of the Constitution were guilty of a brazen effort to muzzle criticism. "The friends of just Lib-

erty here are astonished at the Occlusion of the Press in Boston,"
Richard Henry Lee reacted when told by Samuel Adams of Federalist tactics in his bailiwick. Lee thought the effort to suppress opposition ominous—"And in Boston too, where first the Presses pointed
America to resist attempts upon her liberty & rights." From New
York, Madison, who had once learned that the confident politician is
the easiest to defeat, looked over the situation with a furrowed brow.
"Judging from the newspapers, one would suppose that the adver-
saries were the most numerous and the most earnest," he wrote Governor Randolph of Virginia. "But there is no other evidence that it is
the fact." [4]

Even though greatly outnumbered, the Anti-Federalists caused a
great deal of trouble and would doubtless have created more had they
found an editor equipped to lead the attack. Lacking the counterpart
of a Russell, the Anti-Federalists depended on local editors who had
no particular talent for organizing a coordinated campaign. In such
circumstances, Richard Henry Lee may have been a rallying penman
for the Anti-Federalists through a series of systematic attacks on the
Constitution which were published over the pseudonym of "A Federal Farmer." [5] These strictures on republicanism, and the dangers
for it under the proposed constitution, alarmed the Federalists so that
Madison joined with Hamilton and John Jay to answer Lee—or
whoever the "Farmer" was—and reinforce Federalists' convictions.
Mainly circulated in pamphlet form, the "Farmer's" essays warned
that an extensive territory could never be a true republic with safeguards for local interests. He also echoed George Mason's lament
that civil liberties had been swept under the rug at Philadelphia. The
cry that "There is no bill of rights" stung Federalists throughout the
ratification campaign, until it was virtually conceded that one of the
first acts of the new government would be a series of safeguards, including one assuring freedom of the press.

The campaign generated more excitement than the spread-eagle
historians of a later day dared admit. Though outnumbered, the
Anti-Federalists were determined to counterattack once the earnest

business of ratification hinged on the results of state conventions in Massachusetts, Virginia, and New York. George Bryan of Philadelphia wrote as "Centinel" in the *Independent Gazetteer* and kept his identity so well concealed the Federalists rifled his father's mail for clues on their tormentor. Benjamin Workman, writing as "Philadelphiensis," had less luck. He infuriated the Federalists with his caustic essays, was ultimately discovered, and suffered dismissal from his academic post at the pro-Federalist University of Pennsylvania.[6] In New York, Colonel Eleazer Oswald, the *Gazetteer* publisher, was an old crony of Governor George Clinton and owned a part interest in Thomas Greenleaf's *New-York Journal*. Using the two newspapers with effect, the Anti-Federalists propped up the otherwise disorganized anti-Constitution effort. Considering Washington's endorsement, the Federalist phalanx of merchants and lawyers, and the heavy preponderance of Federalist newspapers, the potency of Oswald's and Greenleaf's opposition was truly remarkable.

For generations it was assumed that Jay, Hamilton, and Madison with their "Publius" signature under eighty-five essays provided overwhelming arguments on behalf of the Constitution. Historians now realize that contemporaries generally regarded these *Federalist Papers* as written above the heads of the mass audience they were intended to sway. A French diplomat who was privy to many sub rosa currents in the young Republic and who knew Hamilton was the most prolific member of the "Publius" team discounted the essays as "too learned and too long for the average men." [7] Far more important for the Federalists were such telling blows delivered in the newspaper essays of "Landholder" (Oliver Ellsworth), "A Countryman" (Roger Sherman), "One of the People" (Francis Hopkinson), and Hugh Brackenridge. Their attacks were often personal and hardly ever inclined toward a charitable view of the opposition. Old friendships were strained in many areas as partisans in the controversy employed newspapers, pamphlets, and broadsides to assail the motives of those who took a different stance. Samuel Adams, the old warhorse who was now out to pasture, could only surmise that "the Seeds of

Aristocracy began to spring even before the Conclusion of our Struggle for the natural Rights of Men, Seeds which like a Canker Worm lie at the Root of free Governments." Edward Powars, printer of the Boston *American Herald*, was pushed to the wall for his avowed Anti-Federalism. Inundated by canceled subscriptions, Powars took refuge in Worcester after a change of his newspaper's name proved a useless device that failed to halt financial reverses. Russell's *Centinel* seemed to relish Powars' plight after Powars complained that in a free country subscriptions should not be based on political leanings. Why should a Federalist patronize a "wrongheaded" newspaper? the *Centinel* asked. Such a line of reasoning, Russell thought, was simply further proof of wrongheadedness, and good riddance to Powars.

The Anti-Federalists had better luck with their makeshift campaign for a bill of rights than with the plan either to obtain a second Federal Convention or to reject the Constitution outright. Once the Massachusetts convention had ratified the Constitution in February 1788, the Federalist momentum was impossible to check. But the recommended amendments that came from the Boston meeting contained the germ of an idea that forced the Federalists to concede that once the new government went into operation, guarantees for certain civil rights (including freedom of the press) would be readily added to the Constitution. Until that time, printer Thomas Wait in the Maine district counted his *Cumberland Gazette* with the Anti-Federalists because there was "a certain darkness, duplicity and studied ambiguity of expres[s]ion running thro' the whole Constitution which renders a Bill of Rights peculiarly necessary." [8]

Before that concession was made, however grudgingly by the Federalists, they tried to avoid any tampering with the Constitution by conducting a sophisticated campaign designed to keep the opposition constantly on the defensive. Newspapers were the key to their strategy. Federalists were short-tempered with those printers who refused to switch their allegiance. Powars, the patriot-printer of the 1770s, was meant to be an example for Anti-Federalist printers who failed to perceive where their true interests lay. Thomas Greenleaf of New York joined Powars in paying dearly for his contrariness. Greenleaf's printing shop was partially destroyed by a mob after the *New-York Journal* lambasted the Federalists. In Philadelphia, Eleazer Oswald was hounded by Federalist lawyers over a libel suit filed by a pro-Constitution editor and finally was jailed for contempt of court. This brand of intimidation was a small-scale version of what the Federalists would later seek to perfect in their legislative orgy in 1798.

Printers who tried to steer a middle course found themselves caught in a crossfire between angry Federalists and their hard-shelled opponents. The well-edited Providence *United States Chronicle* recorded the dismay of intemperate subscribers who lamented the printer's efforts at impartiality. Threatened with a loss of support, printer Bennett Wheeler resented the ultimatum from local Federalists but bowed to their pressure, "Hoping that this *Mode of Procedure* may not be made a *Precedent*." William Spotswood, printer of the *Pennsylvania Herald*, told of his trials as a would-be neutral when he reported:

TO CORRESPONDENTS

NUTS for the Aristocrats to Crack, will be inserted in our next paper; but the Essay called A CHECK TO AMBITION, or the FEDERAL JUNTO DELINEATED, is inadmissible on account of its gross personality. The EDITOR takes this opportunity of informing the Public, that on the important subject now in general discussion, it is his wish to evince the strictest candor and impartiality [but] if at the same time, he rejects the effusions of party virulence and personal reflection, he hopes the justice of his readers will pronounce the HERALD to be a free, pure, and independent publication.

Spotswood found this approach pleased nobody. The Federalists accused him of being against ¬hem, and the Anti-Federalists thought Spotswood found too much room in his columns for pro-Constitution essays. By February 1788 the *Herald* had lost its tenuous hold in the Philadelphia business community. Despite a change of owners, the

Herald soon disappeared. The warning to Spotswood's brother editors was not lost.

When the Federalists' campaign seemed to lag, a private letter written by Washington was broadcast to newspapers as irrefutable proof that the country's number-one citizen was solidly pro-Constitution. Always sensitive of his dignity and the manhandling of his reputation, Washington resented the Federalists' use of his letter almost as much as the Philadelphia Anti-Federalists, who complained "that the advocates of the proposed Constitution . . . avoid all argument [about its merits], and depend principally upon the magick of Names, declamation, songs, &c."

Surely readers took much of the invective with a grain of salt. Infuriated by the charges that "an Aristocratic Junto" was behind the Constitution, South Carolina Federalists were informed by a local newspaper that "A swarm of paltry scribblers . . . are uniformly conspiring against the majesty of the people, and are this moment fabricating the most traiterous productions which human depravity can devise." Recalling the old-fashioned treatment for a libelous newspaper, the South Carolinian urged citizens to "nail them up to the most opprobrious gibbet of popular execration odium and infamy." [9]

Anti-Federalist printers thought they saw a different kind of conspiracy at work—a sinister plan to block the mail exchanges which provided their chief source of news. The Portsmouth *New Hampshire Spy* wailed that it had "rarely received a single paper from New-York or Philadelphia" for the past three months. A Philadelphia editor believed he knew why. "A certain *sublunary deity* of our own creation" had interdicted newspaper exchanges since January 1, Eleazar Oswald charged, for purely political purposes. The target of these verbal shafts was Ebenezer Hazard, the parsimonious Postmaster-General. Hazard ordered changes in the postal system that restricted the free carriage of newspapers, but he aimed at frugality rather than political reprisals. However laudatory Hazard's motive, his timing was unfortunate. Federalists and their opponents both suffered from the mail snarl, but the law of averages worked against the few Anti-Federalist printers. Oswald heaped personal abuse on Hazard and asked why newspapers critical of the Constitution were "quashed or purloined in the Post-office at New-York, while those papers which may with the strictest truth be called the vehicles of despotism, pass from place to place unmolested"?

Not the first bureaucrat to learn that public economies are rarely appreciated, Hazard tried to answer the charges in a public letter, but criticism continued. "Oswald and Bail[e]y [the Anti-Federalist printers in Philadelphia], and Oswald's Echo [Greenleaf] . . . have been pelting me at a most unmerciful rate," Hazard moaned. The din against Hazard was joined by the Winchester, Virginia, *Gazette* printer whose news flow had been dammed by Hazard's frugality. "Whatever secret views the promoters of this diabolical plan may have, we hope the guardians of our liberty and future safety, will be vigilant in frustrating so dangerous a measure." [10] Russell's *Centinel* rose to Hazard's defense, contending the mail delays had been caused partly by "the neglect of the Printers, and more to the peculation of the persons who carry the mails on horseback, between Hartford and New-York [who] take from, and sell, the newspapers directed to Printers." Russell's version was probably close to the truth, but Hazard's days as a public servant were numbered when even Washington noticed the tardiness of his newspaper deliveries.

Skepticism, an ingredient long missing in newspaper audiences, rose with the development of a genuine political cleavage in the new nation. Two rival philosophies were in contention—a phenomenon that some citizens lamented because of an old-fashioned fear of factions (based oftentimes on their reading of Roman history). Although not strictly along class lines, since most Americans were farmers in 1787, the contending groups generally split along economic-geographic lines. Professional men and merchants in the seaports pressed for that "energetic government" the farmers and planters were in no hurry to establish, as Charles A. Beard and others discerned long ago. City-based interests had newspaper voices while the farming elements usually lacked a medium of expression. The Constitution was ratified, although it was not the Federalist newspaper advantage that tipped the scale but rather the dominant posture of Washington. As Monroe noted, Washington's unseen presence was always the Federalists' trump card. "Be assured his influence carried this government," Monroe wrote Jefferson—a clear fact which no newspaper essay could deny, although the role of the press during this first great national debate was recognized. For ten months the newspapers had been filled with arguments pro and con. "Since the World began," Jefferson was told, "I believe no Question has ever been more repeatedly and strictly scrutinized or more fairly and freely argued, than this proposed Constitution."

Washington's endorsement was persuasive, and through all the raging storm over the Constitution he had been spared a word of criticism. That moratorium soon ended as partisan politics engendered in the ratification struggle spilled over again, once the Constitution was an operating political vehicle. English newspapers had long been divided into Tory and Whig factions, and now America was reaching a similar stage of political and journalistic development. Indeed, the United States was an independent power but far from free of domination by Great Britain in most aspects of its cultural and political life. The question of whether that British connection would be firmly replanted, or whether the United States had an independent destiny, was soon placed before the citizenry by the almost simultaneous establishment of the federal government and the revolutionary upheaval in France. The chief political antagonists were Alexander Hamilton and Thomas Jefferson. Both men turned to the newspapers as a means of influencing public opinion after service in Washington's Cabinet convinced each of them that the other was promoting schemes ruinous to the national interest. Jefferson, who had been abroad during the ratification fight, soon perceived what Hamilton learned in the aftermath of the Federal Convention: newspaper support was vital in the implementation of any national political program.

The vindictive partisanship of ratification journalism was latent until Jefferson found Hamilton's direction of the national economy intolerable. From the outset, Hamilton's policies had the support of John Fenno's *Gazette of the United States,* founded in New York in 1789 with Federalist backing. Fenno was one of the first editors who came into journalism with no printing experience whatever. He had taught school in Boston and contributed enough essays to the *Massachusetts Centinel* to convince Federalists that he had skills they needed. Fenno was hired to do a specific job—support Washington's Administration and at the same time laud the Hamiltonian program.

In 1790 the *Gazette* was moved to the second temporary capital at Philadelphia, where a growing band of critics began suggesting that Fenno was Hamilton's hireling. None of the powerful Treasury secretary's opponents were able to concentrate their fire, however, until Jefferson broke with Hamilton. Then Madison helped persuade his Princeton chum, Philip Freneau, to edit a newspaper frankly founded to counter the Hamiltonian influence.[11] On October 31, 1791, Freneau took over the unenviable task of editing the *National Gazette* while working for Jefferson in the State Department. The New York printer Francis Childs offered some support, and there were solicitations for subscriptions signed by Henry Lee and Madison. The list of penmen eager to attack Hamilton was long, and growing longer. In Hamilton's view, the initial issue of the *National Gazette* was the first salvo in a battle that told all knowledgeable Americans the political truce was ended. In the war of words that would follow, it was (as Jefferson once said) "the artillery of the press" that really counted—brought in votes—and swayed national policy.

Despite Jefferson's denial of complicity, there is much to suggest that he was in fact helping Freneau as an anonymous penman. In the 1792 presidential campaign, when John Adams forged ahead of Jefferson for the vice presidency, the Virginian attributed his loss to the "monarchical party." The *National Gazette* carried Jefferson's charges that the contest had ripped away the mask of Federalists "who approve the constitution merely as a 'promising essay towards a well ordered government'; that is to say, as a step towards a government of kings, Lords, and Commons." Jefferson's friends insisted that the Federalists were "devoted to the hereditary titles, orders, and balances" which plainer men abhorred "as an insult to the rights and dignity of man."

Federalists, tired of the cant over their alleged aristocratic leanings, shifted tactics to launch a scorching personal attack on Jefferson. A political crucible took form in the party newspapers where vituperative attacks on public men became commonplace in columns fed by a new breed of editor who was no printer but more than likely a former schoolmaster or ambitious young lawyer. Adams and Jefferson became the chief targets of a national party press held together not by patronage but by a common bond of distrust. To their sorrow, neither Adams nor Jefferson had the thick skin needed to shrug off the journalistic invective. Jefferson never learned to turn the other cheek to newspaper critics, while his Federalist contemporaries angered as readily as their favorite target. The pity was that neither side ever conceded any virtues to the opposition, and of good humor none was to be found.

Controversy creates excitement and interest. After Freneau attacked Hamilton's fiscal program, other Republican editors joined in the assault. For a time Washington remained above the party strife, but his vice president—pompous John Adams—took a heavy barrage from Republican editors who considered the Braintree, Massachusetts, Federalist a pseudo-monarchist. Whatever else the newspapers might have been, they were not dull, and bold editors with Jeffersonian leanings finally made Washington himself their target. The full storm broke when the Republicans, who generally sympathized with the French revolutionists, rushed to support the impudent French minister in Philadelphia, Citizen Genêt. Genêt, a most undiplomatic envoy, ignored Washington's proclamation of neutrality and prepared hundreds of blank commissions for privateers that were to be outfitted in American ports to prey on British shipping. With much energy and little finesse Genêt made insistent demands on Washington, buoyed in part by "Veritas" in the *National Gazette*. "Veritas" intimated that the president was being duped by "the aristocratic few and their contemptible minions of speculators, tories and British emissaries." His identity hidden behind the pseudonym, "Veritas" added that the American "Whigs of 1776 will not suffer French patriots of 1792 to be villified with impunity by the common enemies of both." Genêt, goaded by this kind of newspaper support, intimated that he was prepared to take his case to Congress, if necessary, to force Washington's hand.

Genêt's swashbuckling conduct forced Washington's patience to the limit. At a Cabinet meeting in August, 1793, General Knox showed the president a broadside written by Freneau headed "The Funeral Dirge of George Washington and James Wilson, King and Judge." Washington, long accustomed to Freneau's charges of monarchical pretensions, exploded. He denounced the "rascal Freneau" in terms that must have caused Jefferson to wince.[12] Before the incident was closed Jefferson had resigned, Genêt's recall had been demanded, and Hamilton was left free to run interference for a pro-British Federalist program during the remainder of Washington's tenure.

While the political storm blew over, Philadelphia was soon rocked by a news item unrelated to the factional strife. Benjamin Franklin Bache, grandson of the great man, had been trained as a printer at Passy, France, and then returned to America. With *grand-père's* aid, Bache established the *General Advertiser*. Since Bache's sympathies were French, he naturally slid into the Republican camp. The Genêt affair was still a hot coal when Bache's newspaper printed a report on the spread of yellow fever in Philadelphia. The August 28 account in Bache's paper turned alarm into panic. Business was suspended, most public offices closed, and the city was hushed as a miasma of fear seeped into the homes of the great and the poor. Before the cool winds of autumn swept the dreaded disease away, Freneau's *National Gazette* was tottering. The mosquito-borne epidemic, coupled with

Jefferson's return to Monticello, left the Republican editor hard-pressed to meet his creditors. On October 23, 1793, as the city struggled back to its feet, the *National Gazette* ceased publication.

Federalist joy at Freneau's distress was short-lived. Bache threw himself into the political fray with such zeal that before long Federalists could look back with longing on the temperate days when Freneau was the leading opposition editor. In 1794 Bache rechristened his newspaper the *Aurora,* believing a new day in political annals had dawned and that it was his mission to proclaim it.

Bache knew the printing business, of course, but he was a political figure by instinct and a printer only incidentally. Encouraged by Republican subscriptions, Bache launched a full-scale war on the Federalists that was destined to envelope the whole of American journalism. His printing office was invaded by a mob, but he would not be intimidated. Fenno tried to thrash him on a Philadelphia street, but Bache backed away from the implicit challenge. The continual source of friction was America's stance vis-à-vis Franco-British hostilities, with the Republicans favoring a pro-French policy while the dominant Federalists were seeking a détente with England. Republican newspapers were suspicious when Chief Justice John Jay was sent to London, charged with breaking the diplomatic stalemate. Jay's treaty drew a promise of British evacuation of northwestern frontier posts, but the heavy price exacted by Whitehall was bound to incense western and southern elements. Senator Stevens Thomson Mason of Virginia leaked terms of the treaty to Bache, who published an abstract in the *Aurora* on June 30, 1795.[13] An erupting volcano could hardly have caused more of an explosion.

Predictably, the Federalist newspapers defended the treaty and excoriated the *Aurora* publisher for revealing its contents while it was still being debated in the Senate. Benjamin Russell's renamed *Columbian Centinel* denounced the "Jacobin party" for embarrassing Washington's Administration, and was more dismayed when the Republicans revealed that Jay's personal expenses in England had cost the United States $52,721. No holds were barred by the contending newspapers, with Russell setting the tone for the New England hotbeds of Federalism while Bache's *Aurora* sent its Republican beams toward the South and West with attacks on Washington. A few years earlier, the president had taken a temperate view of political journalism. "From the complexion of some of our Newspapers Foreigners would be led to believe that inveterate political dissensions existed among us, and that we are on the very verge of disunion, but the fact is otherwise; the great body of the people now feel the advantages of the General Government," he then observed. But after the Jay treaty had detonated in Republican newspaper offices, Washington was weary of the personal abuse directed his way. Distressed by the rough-and-tumble politics emerging in America, Washington lamented that the Republican newspapers had alluded to him "in such exaggerated and indecent terms as could scarcely be applied to a Nero, to a notorious defaulter, or even to a common pickpocket."

Bache was not through with Washington, either. In the fall of 1795 "A Calm Observer" accused the president of overdrawing his salary by more than $25,000 and concluded "that the mask of political hypocrisy has been alike worn by a Caesar, a Cromwell and a Washington." A few days later "Calm Observer" intimated Washington had been continually overdrawn during his presidential tenure and hinted that impeachment proceedings were in order. Then "One of the People" followed these sensational charges with the flat assertion that Washington had recklessly been overdrawing on his public accounts since 1791. In the first three months of his second term, the exposé claimed, the president had received $11,200 instead of the $6,250 authorized by law.[14]

To Washington's chagrin, these charges proved to be true, and Bache had the Federalists on the run. Federalists wrung their hands in frustration because there was no way Bache could be silenced. The Bill of Rights, finally ratified in 1791, began with the plain edict that "Congress shall make no law . . . abridging freedom of speech, or of the press," and for a time they saw no way to circumvent the Constitution. Unless, of course, America went to war against France. Then the "Jacobin party" would be silent or run the risk of lending aid and comfort to an enemy of the United States. It was something to think about—and Timothy Pickering, Harrison Gray Otis, and other Federalist bigwigs must have thought about it a great deal.

Bache gave the Federalists much ammunition as he allowed his contributors to get out of hand, and never more so than in their denunciation of Washington after his Farewell Address was made public. "If ever a nation was debauched by a man, the American nation has been debauched by Washington. If ever a nation has suffered from the improper influence of a man, the American nation has suffered from the influence of Washington. If ever a nation was deceived by a man, the American nation has been deceived by Washington," the *Aurora* charged.[15] It was hyperbole, and of that kind best described as "campaign oratory," but the Federalists were too vindictive to forget such an insult. Washington smarted and burned under such attacks, all the more determined to head for Mount Vernon when his second term ended.

Meanwhile, Americans were going about their business—including the newspaper business—as the nation expanded toward the Mississippi and the great Gulf of Mexico. If it was the axe and a squirrel rifle that enabled men to push into the American wilderness, it was the printing press that signaled the shift from raw frontier to territorial status. The veneer of civilization called for a newspaper, and most frontier editors expected a printing contract from the territory to supplement their meager income. Between the patronage dispensed in postmasterships and public printing fees, enough newspapers stayed solvent to encourage other printers to try their luck in the region of the Ohio, Tennessee, and the Mississippi river systems.[16] The first pioneers were the Pittsburgh *Gazette* (1787) and *Kentucky Gazette* (1787), but before a generation had passed newspapers in some form usually trumpeted the arrival of enough settlers to transform villages into towns. The Knoxville *Gazette* (1791) and Cincinnati *Centinel of the Northwestern Territory* (1793) bore further testimony to the pioneer printer-editor's zeal. The transition from frontier to surging settlement had been dramatically accelerated from a generation to a few years as thousands of eager settlers sought cheaper, more fertile bottom lands and savannahs. Spanish New Orleans had a French *Moniteur* by 1794, and within five years the Natchez *Mississippi Gazette* told eastern exchanges that the Republic's western limits had been reached.

On the fringe of an era when political partisanship boiled over in crossroad hamlets from Maine to Georgia, newspapers were born and died with disturbing frequency. Only twenty-eight of nearly one hundred newspapers printing in 1789 were still in business in 1800. The casualties were short-lived ventures often based on high hopes and a phantom circulation. The healthy *Columbian Centinel* had 4,000 subscribers during the 1790s, but most editors were content with 800 or less.[17] Wasteful as the system seemed, fledgling editor Noah Webster bragged in 1793 that "In no other country on earth, not even in Great-Britain, are Newspapers so generally circulated among the body of the people." An English visitor who read newspapers dispatched from remote settlements soon perceived that colloquial Americanisms were already adding a distinctive flavor to the mother tongue.

> It amused us occasionally to read some of the western newspapers, whose editors being also the printers, often composed an article as they set it up. Many provincialisms were adopted as the readiest modes of expression, which, to Europeans, were not very intelligible. . . . An advertisement to the legal profession would frequently commence thus: "A gentleman of considerable experience in the law line, wishes a dependency [a 'law line' to an Englishman was a rope]." . . . It was . . . no unusual thing to read, "To be sold, part of Abraham Lawrence's neck." An announcement [such as] that might confirm some of the English people in their belief that the Americans were cannibals.[18]

Busy selling and buying necks of land, and land in all forms, most Americans had little interest in grammar or semantics. The editor who found 600 literate subscribers could break even, but it was often not the assurance of a profit so much as community pride that caused newspapers to sprout in rather arid territory. A leader of New England journalism recalled that in his Connecticut youth

> In the beginning of the year 1793, a printer . . . set up in Windham, and published a newspaper, called The Phenix, or Windham Herald. . . . [At that time] there were not more than five or six in the state, and this event was a memorable epoch in our village history. In the general opinion it seemed to add much dignity and importance to the town.[19]

Joseph Buckingham was so struck by the magic of small-town journalism that he took his vows with a type stick in Windham and rose to be one of the patriarchs of the profession.

Buckingham loved the newspaper business but after a half century he looked back on his days at the job case and editor's desk with some misgivings. "I 'hold this truth to be self-evident,' that there is no class of workingmen so poorly paid as printers," he sighed. "For *one* who makes himself rich by printing . . . *fifty* barely live above poverty, and die in possession of little more than enough to pay the joiner for a coffin and the sexton for a grave." His testimony was confirmed by the French observer Alexis de Tocqueville, who found the life of a newspaper editor no easier in the 1830s than it had been almost a century earlier. "Starting a paper being easy, anybody may take to it; but competition prevents any newspaper from hoping for large profits, and that discourages anybody with great business ability from bothering with such undertakings."

Unless a newspaper editor-printer also had outside business interests (such as book publishing or a public printing contract), his life was indeed often a race with his creditors. As long as debtor's prisons existed in America, there were printers among the inmates. Bache, for all his success as a thorn in Federalists' sides, was continually forced to plead for prompt payment of subscriptions and party contributions, yet he seems to have lost about $2,000 a year for the privilege of editing the *Aurora*. A crusading zeal sustained Republican printers when their cashboxes were nearly empty, it seems, and the Federalists were amazed at their persistence.

Making money did not seem as important to zealous printers as raising the party banner. When William Cobbett started his *Porcupine Gazette* he had no intention of losing money, but he made it clear that he was a Federalist first and businessman second. "To profess impartiality here, would be as absurd as to profess it in a war between Virtue and Vice, Good and Evil, Happiness and Misery," Cobbett declared. He loathed the Republicans for their pro-French leanings and announced that he had not launched "that cut-and-thrust weapon, a daily paper, without a resolution not only to make use of it myself, but to lend it to whomsoever is disposed to assist me."

A former editor and tutor in his native England, Cobbett believed it was the duty of newspapers to expose rascals. He found life in his homeland uncomfortable after uncovering a graft scandal in the British army, and in time wandered to Philadelphia. Cobbett quickly took to his old trade as a writer of flaming, partisan prose in his newspaper and delighted in attacking Bache. Not content with lambasting Bache personally, Cobbett dragged forth the memory of Bache's "crafty and lecherous old hypocrite of a grandfather, whose very statue seems to gloat on the wenches as they walk the State House yard." Cobbett claimed a circulation of 3,000, but his ledger never seems to have shown a profit, and when he printed a libelous attack on Dr. Benjamin Rush as "the noted blood-letting physician of Philadelphia" his career in American journalism ended abruptly. After a jury ruled against Cobbett, he fled to New York to escape a $5,000 judgment and $3,000 in court costs.

Cobbett lost his case but made a comeback through a stroke of fate and his own perseverance. The judgment against Cobbett was rendered the same day that Washington died at Mount Vernon, in part because of excessive blood-letting. In the last issue of the *Porcupine Gazette,* Cobbett attributed Washington's sudden death to scalpel-

wielding surgeons "in precise conformity to *the practice of Rush.* . . .
On that day the victory of RUSH and of DEATH was complete."
Lyman Butterfield has noted that Cobbett's death-count of the bled
and unbled during the yellow fever epidemic, which he cited as proof
of Rush's incompetence, was a valid yardstick of public health.
"Whatever his motives, Cobbett in his approach to clinical statistics
proved himself a better epidemiologist than Rush." [20] Cobbett
thought himself publicly vindicated when it was disclosed that Dr.
Elisha Dick, one of Washington's attending surgeons, was a former
student of Rush's. With tongue in cheek, Cobbett began publishing a
curious newspaper in New York, the *Rush-Light,* which was full of
brilliant satire that made the private quarrel a standing joke in the
country's two largest cities. Somewhat amazed, Cobbett reported
that the *Rush-Light* "has surpassed in circulation any publication
ever before issuing from my press." By his fourth issue, a press run of
3,000 was inadequate, and a careful historian concluded: "Rush's suit
had made Cobbett rich!" [21]

Rich or poor, Cobbett had been too much of a muck-slinger for his
Federalist cronies. "Cobbett was never encouraged and supported by
Federalists as a solid judicious writer in their cause," Benjamin Russell observed, "but was kept merely to hunt Jacobinic foxes, skunks,
and serpents." Cobbett's departure for England while the press was
unlimbering for the knockdown-dragout election campaign of 1800
robbed readers of high amusement if not solid information. No man
could have been happier to see Cobbett leave than Rush, unless it was
Jefferson, for the presidential candidate was spared jabs that might
have pushed him beyond all endurance. The Federalists were on the
defensive and Cobbett was gone. "His genius for savage journalistic
satire remains perhaps without rival in any era," Butterfield surmised.
The reeling Federalist party would miss him.

Indeed, Federalist fortunes began declining the moment Washington stepped down and John Adams up into the presidency in 1797.
French privateers retaliated for the presumed insult in Jay's treaty by
inflicting staggering losses on American shipping. Ordinary diplo-

matic channels between the United States and France became clogged, so Adams sent two special commissioners—John Marshall and Elbridge Gerry—to join Charles Cotesworth Pinckney in negotiations with the wily Talleyrand. The mission was an abject failure, but to satisfy Congress Adams sent the commissioners' report to the legislators, designating Talleyrand's agents as X, Y, and Z. The papers revealed the worst side of French diplomacy, with hints of bribes and contempt for the American envoys. Even the pro-French *Aurora* published the damning evidence as a wave of anti-French sentiment swept up and down the seaboard. Federalists, saddled with Jefferson in the vice presidency, charged the Republicans with pro-French leanings of the most subversive character. Cobbett labeled Jefferson "the head of the democratic frenchified faction," while Russell's *Centinel* reported that Adams was toasted as one who "like *Samson* [may] slay thousands of Frenchmen with the jawbone of Jefferson."

The XYZ disclosures temporarily unified the nation and gave the Federalists an excuse to speed up rearmament, particularly the outfitting of a more formidable navy. Jefferson, presiding over the Senate, thought the chief magistrate had lost his mind, but Adams was not to be hurried into war with France although some of his closest advisers panted for a declaration that would remove the fraction from what the president himself had called "the half war with France." Some Federalists looked even further and saw the anti-French hysteria as a means for throttling the obstreperous Bache and any other Republican editor or printer who continued to print a "vile incendiary paper." Instead of calming down, Bache raked the Federalists with all his editorial fire, adding personal attacks on Adams for good measure. The summer heat of Quincy, Massachusetts, had been nothing compared to the *Aurora*'s hot blasts, and the president's wife grimly recorded "we are now wonderfully popular except with Bache & Co who in his paper calls the President old, querilous, Bald, blind, crippled, Toothless Adams." [22] Abigail Adams' only comfort was her conviction that "the wrath of an insulted people will by & by break upon him."

Federalist politicians in Congress saw in Bache's excesses an opportunity to intimidate the opposition, throw Bache in jail, and discredit the rising Republican party before it capitalized on its inroads
from the 1796 campaign. Aided by Cobbett's jibes at aliens, including Swiss-born congressman Albert Gallatin, the Federalists drasti-
cally amended the 1795 Naturalization Act and pushed through alien
acts that unmistakably said to immigrants: "Go away, we don't want
you." A threat to deny the vote to naturalized aliens was pushed
back, but the xenophobic mood of Federalist legislators was apparent.
Encouraged by the president's public remarks directed at "the thousand tongues of calumny," Federalist congressmen introduced a sedition law in June 1798 that made it a crime "to oppose any measure or
measures of the government of the United States, which are or shall
be directed by proper authority, or to impede the operation of any
law of the United States."

Bache was singled out as the first target of the Sedition Act. He
had been arrested on the same day the bill had been introduced,
charged in a common-law indictment with a seditious libel against
Adams and the executive branch. Hardly a Federalist within earshot
of Philadelphia would have disagreed with Cobbett's assessment of
Bache as the "most infamous of the Jacobins . . . Printer to the
French Directory, Distributor General of the principles of Insurrection, Anarchy and Confusion, the greatest of fools, and the most
stubborn sans-culotte in the United States." [23] Not far behind Bache
in the Federalist catalog of villains was John Daly Burk, an Irish emigrant and political refugee who took over the editorship of the New
York *Time Piece* while the Alien and Sedition bills were being debated in Congress. Congressman John Allen, a high priest in the
Federalist hierarchy, soon attacked Burk "as a leading example of
perverted licentiousness," and there was much talk in pro-Adams
newspapers of tar-and-feather treatments for "frenchified editors."

Bache had been sued for libel earlier in 1798 by Secretary of State
Timothy Pickering, and he was forced to post $4,000 bond while the
common-law indictment was pressed. Thus harassed, Bache con-

tinued his attacks on the Adams Administration to the horror of Federalists who calculated that there must be no limit to Bache's temerity and credit. Then a mosquito did what the mighty Federalists had failed to do. Bache was suddenly silenced in the devastating yellow fever epidemic of September 1798. Sick one day with aching joints and fever, Bache was dead five days later. Bache was gone, but the *Aurora* was far from dead. Bache's widow turned the editorial reins over to William Duane, who lacked the late printer's volcanic style but was a more able newspaper man. Duane was so smooth and skillful, as it turned out, that the Federalists were never able to try him under the Sedition Act although they yearned for the chance.

Burk proved to be more vulnerable. The Federalists were determined to clamp down on the *Time Piece* editor—either as an undesirable alien or as a defamatory editor. The exact charges against Burk were only a matter of detail, Timothy Pickering reasoned, but the point was to make an example out of the fiery Irishman. Less than a month after Adams had signed the Sedition Act, Burk was arrested on a charge of seditiously and libelously attacking the president. A mob, probably egged on by Federalists, manhandled Burk about this same time, and he had a falling out with his business partner over editorial policy. Still, Burk attacked the Sedition Act without restraint and challenged even one of its presumably enlightened features, wherein truth was admitted as a defense. The point of the bill, Burk insisted, was to make editors into obsequious cat's-paws of the Adams party. Confronted by such a law "who dare deny that truth is both libellous and seditious?" Burk never had a chance to ask the same question in court, for his financial woes multiplied until the *Time Piece* suspended publication at about the same time Bache's funeral eliminated the other Republican scourge.[24] Once Burk's newspaper was moribund, the Federalists lost interest in his prosecution, and the president himself approved abandonment of the case on Burk's own terms—his voluntary exile.

As James Morton Smith showed in his careful study of the Sedition Act, not a single Federalist editor ever suffered from the law's enforcement while zealous Federal attorneys hounded Republican editors the length and breadth of the land. Meanwhile, the *Columbian Centinel* praised the hunting down of Republican editors who, "notwithstanding the disclosure of French wickedness and perfidy . . . continue emitting their nausea against the beloved First Magistrate of the Union," and gleefully reported the indictment of arch-rival Thomas Adams of the Boston *Independent Chronicle*. While his trial was pending, Adams asked why it was illegal to criticize the president when Federalist editors sniped at Vice President Jefferson with "the most indecent reflections"? Before his trial, Adams took to bed and, as in Bache's case, escaped a Federalist-packed jury only because of his death.

For more than a year prosecutions went on against editors, printers, windy orators, and town drunks. All the Federalists asked was that the offender be a Republican. Since the Alien and Sedition laws were set to expire in 1801 they were bound to become an election issue in the scorching Adams-Jefferson contest. The Kentucky and Virginia resolutions protesting the detested acts were not mere straws in the wind, but alarms from an aroused opposition that was gaining strength. The Federalists broke their lance on crusty Matthew Lyon, the Vermont congressman who won his reelection campaign from a jail cell, smashing the Federalist editor who ran against him to become a national hero in the rising Republican party. Instead of hastening collapse of the Republican movement and the enforced retirement of Jefferson from public life, the Alien and Sedition laws hurried their authors to political oblivion.

Perceptibly, America was moving in a new direction, but the generation that had created the Revolution remained in control. Heed was taken of Washington's farewell admonition to avoid foreign entanglements. The advice fitted the people's mood as they moved westward in great surges, with the printing press following by only a few steps. In settled townships or on the frontier, a newspaper was as much a part of community life as a church, and as an indication that secular affairs were becoming dominant, the editor was a more important man in many towns than the parson. The four columns told of epidemics, floods, fires, and funerals—but most of the fare was political. The intense partisanship of Adams' Administration was but a noisy herald of things to come. Federalists probably rued the day in 1792 when they had enacted a postal bill that fixed newspaper postage rates at one cent per copy with exchanges carried free. As Benjamin Russell noted, "the circulation of news is more certain and extensive" than ever before. The stage for a battle royal—with the presidency of the United States as the highest stake—was set. The streams swollen by the spring thaws in 1800 were nothing compared to the turgid prose about to pour forth from the Federalist and Republican presses.

4

New Light on "The Dark Age"

The year 1800 represented much more than a dawning century for the awkward young Republic. The nation's capital finally moved from Philadelphia to Washington during a stifling hot summer when new arrivals in the "ten-mile square" could not decide which was worse, the mosquitoes or the choking dust from unpaved streets. Everything seemed half-finished in the sprawling village north of the Potomac, where land speculators talked of lots and tracts as they reaped vast paper profits. The capital's disease was the nation's malady—for America seemed divided into two classes of people: those who were land rich and those who were going to be.

Few Americans thought of newspapers when they assessed the Republic's wealth in 1800. The North continued to have more journals as dozens of southern seaports became silted and once-bustling docks turned gray and rotted. Charleston, Savannah, Norfolk, and Baltimore were stacked with cotton bales and sacks of rice, but enterprising printers congregated in New York, Philadelphia, Boston, Providence, or moved to the smaller ports—New London, Salem, Portland—or west to Zanesville, Chillicothe, Lexington, and Louisville. Canals were being dug in faraway places. Turnpikes seemed to branch off in every direction. New England men sought factory sites by the Merrimack and Blackstone rivers. Restless southerners followed the Ohio or Cumberland to the Mississippi.

Americans in 1800 were busy but still had time to read newspapers. "A large part of the nation reads the Bible [but] all of it assiduously peruse the newspapers. The fathers read them aloud to their children while the mothers are preparing breakfast," Pierre Dupont de Nemours noted in 1800.[1] The number of newspapers since Washington's inauguration had doubled, with nearly two hundred editors deeply loyal to either the Federalist or Republican camps. Federalist printers seemed to outnumber their rivals as seasoned politicians exhorted followers to bestir themselves and subscribe to the local party newspaper. But with some justification an arch-Federalist in Connecticut warned ominously that Jeffersonian Republicans that summer were busy starting newspapers "in almost every town and county in the country."

Somehow this exuberant period in American history—when the number of newspapers doubled, then tripled, and finally made Americans the most well-read people on earth—has been downgraded and labeled as a blighted era. "Indeed," Frank Luther Mott surmised, "the whole period of 1801–1833 was in many respects disgraceful—a kind of 'Dark Ages' of American journalism."[2] Historians before and since Mott's day have concurred in the assessment, marking down the era as "the darkest period in American journalism." The expansive pace of American journalism in the first three decades of the nineteenth century, so the argument runs, took its toll by creating an intolerant press that left readers little choice between scurrilous Federalist newspapers or malicious Republican dailies and weeklies. There was no middle ground, the legend asserts, where a well-edited and fair-minded newspaper might have prospered.

On reexamination, this Dark Age version of 1800-to-1832 journalism is seen as an overstatement. Bitter factionalism rose in American journalism during the ratification struggle, quietly seethed until

1792, and then erupted violently in the years after 1795, with extremists calling for articles and editorials that by turns infuriated Federalists and Republicans for the next generation. Once Washington was gone, all pretense of bipartisanship evaporated. In the 1796 presidential campaign, as we have seen, Republican barbs drew such blood that the Federalist leadership ran the risk of passing laws meant to silence the most outspoken editors by either intimidation or jail. Their gamble backfired, resulting in what might better be called a Golden Age of American journalism, for never before or since have newspapers been so much a part of a national life, or more influential, or more imbued with a democratic spirit.

The late V. O. Key's comment on intensely partisan newspapers substantiates the present author's Golden Age theory.

> The significant question is what are the consequences for the role of the press in the [American] political system. In the large, the long-term changes in the treatment of political events have converted the press from a giver of cues into a common carrier. When editorial policy, often of a partisan tone, permeated the entire content of the press, the loyal reader had cues of considerable clarity. The partisan press put a degree of order into the confusing world of politics. The modern press tends to convey all its disorder; only the best informed reader who also happens to read one of the best papers can place events into a meaningful scheme.[3]

Indeed, the judgment that American journalism was in a nineteenth-century slough of defamation seems to have been a foreign judgment finally accepted as a historical truth despite much contrary evidence. Most assuredly, foreign visitors looked on journalism in the upstart Republic as highly personal, malicious, and despicable. Frederick Marryat thought the American press he viewed the world's most defamatory: "Defamation exists all over the world, but it is incredible to what extent this vice is carried in America. . . . Indeed, from the prevalence of this vice, society in America appears to be in a state of constant warfare." Although these foreign observers reported at the end, rather than the beginning of the so-called Dark Ages, they are representative and strikingly so when viewed beside the twentieth-century historians' hindsight.

What Marryat misunderstood was the lusty nature of American journalism. It was a risk-taking society and public men had to take the same risks that entrepreneurs, farmers, steamboat captains, railroad builders—nearly everybody—had to take, including the possibility of a public hiding whenever his name went on the ballots. The Scotsman Thomas Hamilton perceived none of this but typically compared American newspapers to those of Great Britain and found them "greatly inferior."

> I read newspapers from all parts of the Union, and found them utterly contemptible in point of talent, and dealing in abuse so virulent, as to excite a feeling of disgust, not only with the writers, but with the public which afforded them support. . . . The war of politics seems not the contest of opinion supported by appeal to enlightened argument . . . but the squabble of greedy and abusive partisans, appealing to the vilest passions of the populace, and utterly unscrupulous as to their instruments of attack.[4]

Hamilton found that the cause of American licentiousness rested mainly in the low price of Yankee newspapers, so cheap "that the generality even of the lowest order can afford to purchase them." This meant that workingmen could afford a newspaper, something they apparently could not do in Great Britain, and "every booby who can call names, and procure a set of types upon credit, may set up as an editor, with a fair prospect of success. In England, it is fortunately still different."

Practically all of the foreign visitors to America during the so-called Dark Era complained about the newspapers, but as Marryat indicated there was a reason for all this billingsgate. "The real source of it is to be found in the peculiarity of their [democratic] institutions," he reasoned, intending to show the depravity of the American newspapers. The defamatory press, Marryat continued, allowed every ambitious American to assert his equality as he tried "to rise above his fellows" so that "society is in a state of perpetual and disgraceful struggle. . . . How different from England, and the settled nations of the Old World, where it may be said that everything and every body is comparatively speaking in his place."

Not every foreigner agreed with Marryat, however, and one Prussian traveler admitted there was a great deal of name-calling but was far from appalled. Frederick von Raumer excused the strident brand of American journalism as the price paid by a republic which placed "no obstacle in the way of the free development of all minds. The absolute freedom of the press in America is the great lever of this development." More charitable than the British, von Raumer thought "the untrammelled presses of America show far *more* excitement, and those subject to the censorship far *less,* than really exists; and important circumstance, which is too often forgotten by those who wish to inquire into the real state of things . . . respecting American affairs." [5]

The success of political journalism in the robust Jeffersonian-Jacksonian period may be best explained by still another foreigner. In Alexis de Tocqueville's perspective, he saw that elections were won by votes, and voters turned out who were loyal to the *idée fixe.* Jefferson's supporters worked tirelessly to emplant the notion in the voters' minds that Federalists were aristocrats who adored the public debt and coveted special privileges for the few. Republican editors kept up the din until yeoman farmers, from the White Mountains of New Hampshire to the red clay hills of Alabama, believed Federalists would keep taxes high to support an expensive military force and a set of corrupt public officials. Federalist newspapers droned their message of Republican scandal and attacked Jefferson as the infidel Antichrist. "If a whole nation prefer a wicked man, it demonstrates the wickedness of the nation," dismayed Federalists reasoned. But the Federalists were talking mainly to themselves and did not speak with conviction. Bias was not a substitute for persuasion, as the majority of voters became convinced that Jefferson deserved their political trust regardless of whether he was a deist, slaveowner, or libertine. As Tocqueville discerned at a later day, "Once the American people have got an idea into their heads, be it correct or unreasonable, nothing is harder than to get it out again." The majority ignored the Federalists' newspaper cant and stuck with Jefferson.

In such circumstances, the Federalists consoled themselves with statistics. Probably more than 140 newspapers favored Federalist candidates in the 1800 elections. A few old-fashioned newspapers clung to the ancient notion of journalistic impartiality, but in Massachusetts only a dozen or so were Jeffersonian in policy, while Federalists counted 32 in their camp. In Pennsylvania the same number of Federalist newspapers prevailed numerically (but not politically) over 23 Republican editor-printers, while in North Carolina, only 3 Republican editors struggled against 11 opposition journals.[6] As a matter of local party morale, Federalists convinced themselves that the diffusion of their sentiments in local newspapers would stem the rising tide of Jeffersonian popularity. "Let the 'Hampshire Gazette' only give the word," William Cullen Bryant exorted, "which, by the by, it copies from some leading Federal paper, and every Federalist in the county has his cue, everybody knows what to think." Convinced that voters were led by an editorial halter rather than their own logic, one New England Federalist insisted that "people have not first formed their political opinions, and of course, *taken their sides,* and afterwards chosen their paper accordingly; but have formed their opinions and *derived their feelings* from their papers in the first instance." Few politicians were disposed to argue the point, and in the pitched party battles for votes, a local newspaper ally was deemed indispensable. "Public opinion governs our country, the newspapers govern *it,* and it is very possible to govern the newspapers," crusty Fisher Ames growled.[7]

No Federalist editor stood higher in his party's councils than Benjamin Russell, whose *Columbian Centinel* fanned forth from Boston to give the party faithful a glimpse of the truth. Russell's brand of Jefferson-baiting set the tone for most Federalist attacks by classifying the opposition as "the ridiculous, despicable, weak-minded, weak-hearted Jacobin[s]." One of his favorite targets was a fellow Bostonian, Benjamin Austin, Jr., whose verbal brickbats had bounced off Russell since 1787. Austin often wrote in the Boston *Gazette* as "Honestus," and he recognized in Russell the chief cause of Republican-Democratic woes in New England while the *Centinel* often dismissed Austin as "an ignorant blockhead." At a Boston town meeting their rivalry flared into gross insults and after Austin cast slurs on the *Centinel*, editor "Russell did as he threatened, spit in his face, and reproached him with virulent and abusive language." Austin's hot temper was not cooled when he sued Russell for £1,000 in damages and collected a mere 20 shillings, but he was undeterred in his attacks on Federalists.

A trivial incident which Austin chose to magnify in a newspaper screed resulted in a personal tragedy. A petty squabble over the unpaid bill for a Fourth of July celebration led a Boston lawyer to place an advertisement in the Boston *Gazette* which denounced Austin "as a COWARD, a LIAR, and a SCOUNDREL." Austin replied in kind and the same afternoon his nineteen-year-old son, Charles, sought the Federalist name-caller out on a State Street sidewalk. After hot words a pistol was drawn and young Austin fell, mortally wounded. Although the young Harvard senior had been unarmed, the Federalist was later acquitted of a murder charge. This incident, in 1806, shocked staid Boston but was the kind of direct reply increasingly favored by hotbloods offended by newspaper paragraphs.[8]

Russell never carried a gun but his *Centinel* kept up a steady fire against the Republicans, and he knew how to appeal to the voter's self-interest. During the quasi-war with France, Russell charged the "Jacobins to a man are opposed to *arming* our vessels, or fitting out a single ship of war. They well know, that owing to French *gun-boat piracies*, our mechanics and artificers are almost starving. . . . The moment the news arrives that the merchants shall have liberty to arm their vessels, not an axe, hammer, or mechanic implement will be idle. Business will assume its activity; and the music of the cunning workman will be heard on all our wharves." [9] The Boston *Gazette* tried to discredit Russell, a sure sign that he was a power in New England politics. "Mr. Russell says *arm* or *starve*—We say, STARVE you will, if you do ARM!"

Russell's *Centinel* brought nods of approval in Boston counting houses, but in the western counties the younger men were not easily frightened by newspaper salvos. Harrison Gray Otis saw the Federalist grip slipping in the autumn of 1800. "I am forcibly impressed with a belief that the tide of our politics and public affairs is changing, & that the popular current in governments like ours always sets strong & will for *a time* overflow its banks & bear down opposition," Otis confided. Otis commented on the fact that Americans were reputedly "*the most enlightened* [citizens] upon earth," but in his heart he did not believe this was true.

Newspapers, the Federalists reasoned, had to keep up party morale and win votes for men of superior talents. Russell was one of the few newspaper editors who stood well in the inner circles of the party, while lawyers and ship owners controlled the Federalist machinery when it came to making policies and implementing them. Federalists were inclined to depend on clergymen rather than newspaper editors to keep their districts safe. Federalists paralleled their party organization with the New England churches: "Its rallies took the place of religious services, its picnics became counterparts of church outings, its workers were like ministers out on call." Significantly, "one of the earliest actions of the Massachusetts Federalist Party organization was to furnish local ministers with free subscriptions to party newspapers. From an early time, the minister was made dependent upon the meager and highly partisan provincial press and, almost without knowing it, was made an adjunct of the party's general staff." [10]

Jefferson's party chiefs took a different view. They wanted newspaper support, too, but it seemed to spring up spontaneously wherever younger citizens pushed for virgin lands and more elbow room. Below the Connecticut border, Republican newspapers sprouted like mushrooms. Fisher Ames studied the election returns and concluded that "newspapers are an overmatch for any government. They will first overawe and then usurp it. This has been done, and the Jacobians owe their triumph to the unceasing use of this engine." The defeated candidate, John Adams, agreed wholeheartedly as he showed the Federalists' distrust of immigrants. "A group of foreign liars encouraged by a few ambitious native gentlemen" had combined their misguided talents to make Jefferson president.

In defeat the *Columbian Centinel* remained as the party spokesman, and what the *Centinel* was to Federalists the *National Intelligencer* became for Republicans. Published in the new capital by editor Samuel Harrison Smith, the *Intelligencer* began as a triweekly as the 1800 presidential campaign ended, and although its circulation was less than 2,000 it was to become the organ voice of the Republicans after Jefferson was finally declared the president-elect. The new president and Smith were on intimate terms. Jefferson had urged Smith to move from Philadelphia to Washington, and when official policies were staked out he left it to Smith to explain and support them. Smith was hardly a lackey for Jefferson, however. His family background and his own talents made Smith a superior editor and one of the first to sense that people wanted authentic news without bias. Smith knew how to record congressional debates in shorthand, and when Congress finally permitted reporters free access to the debate chambers in 1803, the *National Intelligencer* became an indispensable source of news for both Federalist and Republican editors.

Smith, by nature a bland scholar, printed the president's annual message to Congress as though it ranked with Mosaic utterances, and before long editors in every cranny of the Union followed Smith's lead. Smith's quiet leadership caused another Washington editor to facetiously call the *Intelligencer* "Mr. Silky Milky Smith's National Smoothing Plane," but Smith's evenhanded methods had their impact. When the telegraph lines reached St. Louis in 1848, the first message sent from Washington was Polk's annual message to Congress—a tribute to the slow-paced but comprehensive style of reporting Smith brought to American journalism by his emphasis on the political regimen between 1801 and 1828.

Smith's policies were sound enough to give the *National Intelligencer* a reputation that lived long after he and the newspaper itself were either dead or dying. Other less-temperate Republican editors who clipped his debates and official messages also kept a handy supply of political brickbats. Until felled in the famous duel with Aaron Burr, Alexander Hamilton was a favorite target for Republican editors, who never tired of reminding readers that Hamilton was born out of wedlock. They pictured Hamilton as a man who rushed "from the incestuous embraces of some deluded wife, or some public brothel," to his office, where "faithful myrmidons" carried out their master's "edicts of injustice, robbery and oppression." [11] Jefferson's opponents took to editorial columns of prodigious length to denounce him as an "infidel Jacobin" who consorted with female slaves and had tried to seduce his neighbor's wife.[12]

Possibly it was the sexual tinge of the campaign diatribes that made the era loom as a Dark Age to critics of the lusty journalism of the early Republic. To the great amusement of Federalists, James Callender had turned on his former patron and was now attacking Jefferson in the Richmond *Recorder*. A Scottish refugee, Callender had once worked for the Richmond *Examiner* and had written an Anti-Federalist pamphlet, *The Prospect Before Us*, that had led to his arrest and conviction under the Sedition Act. When he took office, Jefferson quickly took steps to wipe out all such sentences, pardoned editors imprisoned under the obnoxious act, and even helped pay Callender's fine. Freed from jail but still wretched, Callender centered all the blame for his misfortunes on the president and printed a rumor that Sally Hemings, a pretty slave who had traveled with the Jefferson family in France and returned to Monticello, had long been the president's concubine. By October 1802 the artful Joseph Dennie found a way to make political hay out of Callender's story with a bawdy ditty in his Philadelphia *Port Folio* that included one shocking stanza:

> What though she by the glands secretes;
> Must I stand shil-I-shall-I?
> Tuck'd up between a pair of sheets
> there's no perfume like Sally.

To Americans of the 1970s that may not seem so licentious, but there is no gainsaying that language of that sort left their ancestors flabbergasted. Jefferson was stung by Callender and Dennie, but the blanket judgment leveled by the Federalists seems to have carried its own antidote. No doubt many people read scurrilous accounts of Hamilton's and Jefferson's indiscretions and believed each word, but on election day the returns continued to tell their own story of Republican victory and further Federalist setbacks.

Unquestionably, Jefferson's fingers were on the pulse of the nation, and he detected an expansionist throb. He sought the Louisiana Territory and thus encouraged western settlement at a time when many Federalists still seriously considered ways and means of choking western migration. The Republican editors stridently claimed pro-British Federalists were led by pseudomonarchists and "bigoted preachers," but when the ballots were counted they tended to credit the Jeffersonian victory to Federalist bumbling rather than an altered national viewpoint. Tocqueville, detached and perceptive, glimpsed what was happening while editors themselves muddled along with flushed faces and angry editorials that probably had little actual influence on voter's behavior. What Tocqueville saw was that the newspapers reinforced the voter's judgment.

> A newspaper can only survive if it gives publicity to feelings or principles common to a large number of men. A newspaper therefore always presents an association whose members are its regular readers. This association may be more or less strictly defined, more or less closed, more or less numerous, but there must at least be the seed of it in men's minds, for otherwise the paper would not survive.[13]

This would explain what happened to the Federalists, who mistakenly believed that with a preponderance of newspapers on their side they could stem the Republican tide. They were only the first of that breed of American politicians who sat in paneled offices, looked at statistics, and won elections on paper but lost them at the polls. Our first national elections were endurance contests as well as political battles, and it often took months to learn the final outcome of a presidential race. As late as mid-December, when South Carolina's votes sealed a Republican victory, the Federalists of 1800 held a fading hope that Adams or Pinckney might win. The outcome justified the pre-election view of Jefferson that the newspaper would play a vital role in the campaign. "Our citizens may be deceived for a while, and have been deceived; but so long as the presses can be protected, we may trust to them for light," candidate Jefferson said. But Jefferson was to learn that the press can be a fickle mistress, and before long he was paying too much attention to Federalist newspapers for his own peace of mind. But most embarrassing for Jefferson as president was the attack mounted by his vindictive former ally, James Callender. Rebuffed in a bid for the Richmond postmastership, Callender turned on his one-time patron with a vengeance. Along with the scandalous charges about Jefferson's private life, he now said that Jefferson personally had paid him "for calling Washington a traitor, a robber, a perjurer." [14]

Washington had been dead but a short while, so that nothing could have angered or embarrassed Jefferson more than to have been accused of dishonorable conduct toward his fellow Virginian. Thus Jefferson, the champion of a free press, decided that there was a limit to freedom and a line beyond which only licentiousness existed. The Callender story made the rounds as Federalist newspapers reprinted it in high glee as a confirmation that Jefferson was the monstrous hypocrite they had long claimed. Democrats cheered when a common-law indictment was obtained in Republican New York to squelch the Callender smear with an exemplary prosecution. The intended victim of Jefferson's wrath was Harry Croswell, a third-rate

Federalist editing a fourth-rate newspaper, the Hudson *Wasp*. When the case came up for trial, however, it assumed classic dimensions. Alexander Hamilton, in his prime as a lawyer and still the Federalists' chief wire-puller, defended Croswell. Since Croswell had only repeated Callender's remarks, it must have been regarded as a cut-and-dried prosecution that would cause other Federalists to temper their attacks on the president. Hamilton's interest in the case changed all that, for although he agreed that an editor given to calumny was a "pest of society," Hamilton insisted that truth must be admitted as a defense. The Zenger case had made the full circle, and come to roost not far from the scene of the original prosecution. Of course Jefferson was not going to come to Hudson to testify, and without the president's testimony, who could say Callender had lied? The point was stretched pretty far and Croswell was in fact found guilty, but the case attracted so much attention that the next New York legislature rewrote the libel statute.*

Jefferson could take no solace from the way the Croswell case developed or the pyrrhic victory that resulted, and he never was politician enough to face without flinching the slings and arrows of a grueling campaign. Intuitively Jefferson saw the necessity of a free press in a republic, but as a human being he was not tough-minded enough to let a personal slur pass unnoticed. In his second inaugural address, Jefferson noted that during his first term "the artillery of the press has been levelled against us, charged with whatsoever its licentiousness could devise or dare." Such abuses of "an institution so important to freedom and science, are deeply to be regretted, inasmuch as they tend to lessen its usefulness, and to sap its safety," he continued, but "wholesome punishments" under state laws would have required valuable time of public officials that could be better spent in

---

* Mott called this a triumph for the "Hamiltonian doctrine," but James Morton Smith proved in *Freedom's Fetters* (Ithaca, N.Y., 1956) that Hamilton favored vigorous prosecutions under the Sedition Act and was instrumental in the common-law indictment of the New York *Argus* in 1800 for seditious libel.

other endeavors. "The offenders have therefore been left to find their punishment in the public indignation." Toward the end of his second term, Jefferson grew more cynical about the functions of newspapers in a free society. "Nothing can now be believed which is seen in a newspaper," he lamented. "Truth itself becomes suspicious by being put into that polluted vehicle." [15]

Jefferson overstated the case, of course. Newspapers were using the language of extremism, and men not in office were taking the vituperation in stride, voting for their self-interests—voting for Jefferson and his party—despite the ranting and ravings of the Federalist press.[16] If Jefferson had paid more attention to an analysis of voting habits and read fewer newspapers, he would have spent his presidential years in a happier frame of mind. At the very moment he was tormented by press barbs, the Federalists in New England perceived that their grasp was slipping. "The *rabies canina* of Jacobinism has gradually spread, of late years, from the cities, where it was confined to docks and mobs, to the country," Fisher Ames diagnosed. The *New England Palladium* was revived as a party organ to flush out and destroy Republican dissidents, but the only real benefactor was Federalist morale. More indicative of the trend was the Portland *Eastern Argus,* a Republican journal founded in 1804 which "immediately exploited the widespread unrest over Maine *land titles.*" Whether the *Eastern Argus* succeeded because it was an opposition newspaper, or because it gave "publicity to feelings or principles common to a large number of men" is hardly debatable, Tocqueville observed.[17] The leading Federalists clung to their small clothes, were the last to cut off their queues, and thought their newspapers ought to "whip Jacobins as a gentleman would a chimney-sweeper, at arm's length."

While political concerns consumed the attention of officeholders and office seekers in the young Republic, most Americans remained on the treadmill of daily business and farming matters. Except for the political storms brewed by election campaigns, newspapers lagged behind the rest of the country at a time when the spirit of innovation and daring was rampant. Steam-driven presses were devised but benefited only those editors of the few leading newspapers with more than 3,000 readers. Printers dreamed of a typesetting device that would replace the sixteenth-century typestick, but few new ideas emerged from newspaper offices during this era as America embarked on a binge of canal and turnpike building. Venture capital rarely found its way into a journalistic endeavor when barges and real estate seemed to make men rich with less risk, and far less work.

In only one area, but it was an important one, did newspapers along the eastern seaboard show a tendency toward change. European news still commanded a favored place in the commercial journals and it was still stale fare, but the man in charge of its selection was being alluded to more often as an editor rather than a printer. Slowly the entrepreneurial printer-editor gave way to the hired editor, a man who had never set a line of 8-point Caslon type in his life. Joseph Dennie, the Harvard-trained lawyer who accepted £110 per year to edit the *Farmer's Weekly Museum,* was of this new species. Warren Dutton, another lawyer fresh out of Yale, took over the *New England Palladium.*[18] They typified this new breed of editors, men accustomed to working with words rather than setting them in type.

Apart from political harangues, newspapers guided by these editors tried to give readers a variety of reports based upon what would be called later "the hard core" of news. There were no interviews, staged press conferences, or other devices contrived to bring notoriety to public men, while ordinary men never expected to have the events in their lives reported in a newspaper. Indeed, as historian Daniel Boorstin has pointed out, "it was a mark of solid distinction in a man or a family to keep out of the news." Weddings, funerals, and births were usually ignored unless the names involved seemed to demand some local recognition. Much of the genuine pleasantness of life was totally ignored, while the news that was reported dealt with disasters and smaller tragedies. Local crimes, runaway horses, fires, and workmen's accidents were so common they often went unnoticed by the newspaper. Editors looked with more favor on reports of

Indian massacres, bizarre murders, or accidents that involved an awesome toll of life. As steamboats began to ply the western rivers, the increasing number of boiler explosions became a regular newspaper feature. Editors favored eyewitness accounts from survivors with minutely related details of spectacular accidents. Earthquakes brought stories from terror-stricken survivors, as did accounts from areas struck by cyclones, floods, and epidemics. The dimensions of these disasters led editors to judge a news item's importance by the number of deaths or amount of property damage, but when these catastrophes were remote the size of a local pumpkin or giant hailstone seemed to deserve more space. Some editors could not resist the temptation to moralize about the community's vicissitudes, as when a young Philadelphian fell into an unlighted workmen's ditch and broke his neck. The tragic happening, a local editor warned, was proof that Philadelphians were too careless when walking down unlit thoroughfares after dark.

Every newspaper contained advertisements calling for the return of a stray cow or horse, and in the South, frequent calls were made for information on fugitive slaves. "TEN DOLLARS REWARD" and a woodcut of a black man on the run were all too familiar to southern readers as owners described rebellious slaves. The form was so fixed all the slavemaster needed to insert was the missing slave's name and physical description. "A likely negro man named NED, about 26 years of age, about four feet 8 inches high, of a yellowish complexion . . . a bricklayer by trade . . . his dress, an old rusty red coat and felt hat, and sometimes country cloth." Whatever pangs of pity these notices inspire in our time, they must have produced results in their own. An Austrian observer in the 1820s noticed the efficacy of newspaper advertisements and concluded that the "sheriff has not a surer or less expensive mode of recovering a prisoner who has escaped, or a planter of getting back his runaway slave, than [by] a public advertisement." [19] The Austrian indicated that, apart from the hope of reward, Americans relished the finding of a suspected criminal or missing slave. "It will excite no wonder that out of one hundred persons advertised in the public papers, scarcely ten escape apprehension," Karl Anton Postl concluded.

Newspapers stuck by their political alliances and would ignore the local visit of a dignitary from the opposing political party, but all journals joined to honor Lafayette during his triumphant tour of the country in 1824–1825. Editors vied with each other, during his sixteen-month visit, in recalling the nation's birthpangs and military glories, and in honoring the aged hero they paid homage to a foreign dignitary above partisanship. The deaths of great men also caused editors to forget their political loyalties as the Founding Fathers began to succumb and their passing was noted with newspaper grief, including black-bordered columns on all four pages.

Quackery was promoted by newspapers, although editors were often victimized along with readers. Good health was an overriding concern to readers during Jefferson's Administration as it was to be in Richard Nixon's. The Hartford *Connecticut Courant* broadcast the "scientific papers" of Charles F. Bartlett in 1803 for a titillated readership. Experiments with electricity convinced Bartlett that this mysterious force was "the leading or moving principle of animal life. Proceeding therefore on this idea I shall attempt to show that it is of importance first to believe electricity is the primum mobile, of all nature under God!" Bartlett modestly placed himself in the company of Franklin and Joseph Priestly, and probably kept readers attentive until he failed to deliver a promised treatise that was to prove electricity was "the first mover of muscular motion—and all the different oeconomy of the bodies of animals." Water cures, advice on the use of brimstone to clear foul air, and remedies for the bloody flux (dysentery), gout, smallpox, diphtheria, and other ills came in steady procession. The cheapness of life, reported in a front-page account of a tenement fire, would be confirmed by advertisements on page three for a 25-cent cure for cancer.

On the seaboard, the "Marine Journal" column was the most eagerly sought information in the entire newspaper. Here the first reporters established their reputation and earned their living not by writing indignant editorials but by gathering factual information from incoming ships. Probably the first great marine reporter was Henry Ingraham Blake of the *New England Palladium*. Whatever its political standing, the *Palladium* had many Republican readers simply because Blake abandoned his journeyman printer's status to seek news from newly arrived vessels in the Boston harbor. "He may be almost said to have *invented* the present *universal* mode of reporting clearances, arrivals, disasters, and the various incidents connected with the shipping interest of the country," an admiring contemporary wrote.[20] Blake kept irregular hours but relied on a sharp memory to keep *Palladium* readers informed with news that meant dollars and cents to dozens of houses along Ship and Milk streets. Most of the entries told only of ships under quarantine, coasters arrived, or clearances, but an occasional sentence spoke volumes to readers, as when the Barbary pirates raided American ships. "The Adams Frigate, passed Alicant[e] May 10, with a Convoy. There were 16 sail of American vessels at Alicant[e]." In short, a small American merchant fleet was bottled up in a Spanish harbor, awaiting the protection of the tiny United States force Jefferson had dispatched to the Mediterranean while America pondered a "Millions for defense, but not one cent of tribute" policy toward the buccaneers.

The tireless Blake in Boston was soon to have imitators in other leading American ports. The Charleston *Courier*, founded in 1803, catered to merchants eager for cotton prices from England, and it was there that James Gordon Bennett first learned the necessity for a combination of speed and accuracy in reporting. Thomas Ritchie's Richmond *Enquirer* had news from oceangoing vessels as long as ships reached nearby Bermuda Hundred, but except for Charleston and Baltimore, few southern ports could compete with a host of northern cities with deeper harbors and ready access to thriving markets. The Baltimore *American*, founded in 1799, was full of ship news as the Maryland port grew at a spectacular pace (by 1830 Baltimore was America's second largest city, behind New York but comfortably ahead of Philadelphia and Boston in population). In New York the party warfare sustained both the Republican *American Citizen* and the Federalist's *Evening Post,* but readers searching for facts and particularly transportation news looked to the old *American Minerva,* which had been rechristened the *Commercial Advertiser,* or its chief rivals, the *Mercantile Advertiser* or the *Daily Advertiser.* Allan Nevins insists that if the editor of the *Commercial Advertiser* ignored a war or an earthquake nobody minded, but if he overlooked a single ship arrival his job was in jeopardy. Reporters of Blake's perseverance or accuracy were still scarce, and the usual practice on these newspapers was to carry three pages of straight advertising matter and devote less than four columns to factual reporting. To all but the businessmen who apparently read them line for line, they must have seemed incredibly dull.

It was the public notices in these *Advertisers* that saved them from deadly dreariness, and many dealt with the recurring problems of mankind. Handyman A. S. Horton declared in the Rochester *Western New Yorker*:

> READY MADE COFFINS for sale.
> The subscriber, having long regretted the too high charges made for COFFINS and Funeral Services in this place, and at the request of many citizens, has made, and will keep on hand, a full assortment. . . . A Hearse will be in readiness at all times, and he pledges himself that his charges shall be as low as in any of the neighboring villages.

Early in the nineteenth century dockside auction sales flourished and without a newspaper buyers and sellers would have had marketing problems. Most of the advertisements fitted the modern category of "classifieds" and were brief announcements. One for

DOLLARS

A PREMIUM will be given for a few thousand DOLLARS, Spanish, at
No 27, Long-Wharf

was as typical as the South-Handley Canal Lottery notice that faced it. Nearly everybody seemed to have a lottery ticket, from the president down to the printer's devil, and whoever owned No. 216 on June 24, 1803, was entitled to $500 in hard cash. Through newspaper columns, ship captains found cargoes and merchants learned where empty holds awaited their hides and tallow. Patent medicines did not take over whole pages until mid-century, but no less a personage than Governor Jonathan Trumbull of Connecticut endorsed the testimony for Doctor Rawson's Anti-Bilious and Stomachic Bitters. Those citizens not too busy or too sick usually had the opportunity to visit exhibits or "Cabinets of Curiosity," which were displays that imitated Charles Willson Peale's natural history museum in Philadelphia. Turell's exhibit on Court Street in Boston boasted "between five and seven thousand different articles." Then there was the printer's staple, the one-dollar Bible, which he regularly reminded readers might be found at his shop.

Religion was an important part of life and one of the bitterest controversies still lingering in Jefferson's administration involved Thomas Paine's *Age of Reason*. Paine's anticlerical and deistic work appeared to have Jefferson's endorsement when the old revolutionary returned to America and released to newspapers a letter Jefferson had written in 1801 praising Paine's principles and labors. Preachers, a few of whom had read the book, took up the howl against Jefferson and in Federalist newspapers the label "Jacobin Anti-Christ" was one of the milder epithets hurled at the president. When Paine was invited to dine at the White House, the newspaper and pulpit attacks on both men were renewed. Paine tried to explain his thoughts in the *National Intelligencer,* but the Federalists simply added editor Samuel Smith to their list of iconoclasts for publishing "the poisonous shafts of infidels."

Paine was no infidel but he was hounded to his grave by a newspaper editor, James Cheetham, who had once been Jefferson's mouthpiece in New York through the *American Citizen.* Cheetham, an Englishman by birth, had a falling-out with his idol over the Embargo

Act, yet this fails to explain why he turned on Paine and strove mightily in print to destroy the old patriot's reputation. The author of *Common Sense* was demolished by charges of atheistic tendencies. Indeed only a Jefferson could have withstood repeated attacks from the press and pulpit alleging heretical conduct. For whatever reason, Jefferson saw fit to make reassuring allusions to a Supreme Being during his last year in office.

Inevitably, the denominational newspaper would come into being as evangelical churches mounted strong drives for membership, as revivals and camp meetings replaced the staid ways of the older, established churches. The steady growth of religious newspapers in nineteenth-century America has never been fully examined, but it seems safe to say that weekly denominational journals were reaching into more American homes between 1810 and 1860 than any other form of journalism. The *Presbyterian Observer, Episcopal Recorder, Methodist Advocate*, and Unitarian *Christian Register* were among the earliest and best denominational newspapers sent by the bundle to communities where other publications had sparse support. The *Christian Spectator* (founded in 1819) broke new ground for authors when it offered contributors a dollar for every page printed—a fee which soon became the standard payment. The spectacular growth of the Methodists, who had numbered fewer than 15,000 communicants in 1787, gave their *Advocate* a wide circulation edge. While other newspapers perished along the way, the *Advocate* prospered until it reached a pre-Civil War circulation of 105,000, and by 1871 was sent to 370,000 weekly subscribers—far more than any other newspaper printed in North America, if not the world.[21] Doctrinal disputes, which seemed to weaken the congregations, in fact increased interest in formal religion and helped circulation. Factional strife within a denomination led to a "vigor of expression" that one astute observer believed made "the religious press . . . fully equal to the lay and pagan press of the nation. Is this owing to the bracing air of the country? It must be so. It is robust Christianity."

No less vigorous than the American's religious indulgences were his unbounded energy and cocksureness. Jefferson had barely left the White House before his prediction that the West had "room enough for our descendants to the hundredth and thousandth generation" seemed naive. Foreign observers noted that the average American was a farmer or husbandman who thought "that nothing good is done, and that no one has any brains, except in America." The cotton gin and steamboat were cited as proof of American genius, and the farther a traveler went west the more he encountered a rambunctious, confident people who worked hard but had relatively little time for reading. Even so, before war broke out with England in June of 1812 the new state of Ohio already had several busy newspapers, and editors in Vincennes, St. Louis, Detroit, and Fort Stoddert were assuring readers that good times were as certain as the sixteen stars on Old Glory. While New Englanders cursed the Embargo Act and spoke through gritted teeth of Madison's overwhelming campaign (he received 122 electoral votes to 47 for Charles Cotesworth Pinckney), the West and South welcomed the chance to twist the British lion's tail. Far from considering the Embargo Act a calamity, some southerners saw that the law gave American manufacturers a chance to prove their mettle while competition from the British was stifled. Thomas Ritchie, editor of the Richmond *Enquirer,* was among a group of Virginians who saw what opportunities the embargo actually offered and urged southerners to begin their own textile factories. The strain between regions was showing, although an act passed in 1807 cut off all hopes of reopening the slave trade under the 1808 clause of the Constitution.

Although Jefferson considered his White House years as a "splendid misery," he found more splendor than unhappiness or he would not have wished the presidency on his devoted friend from Orange County. Before deserting Washington, the weary president believed his administration had conducted "a great experiment" to prove that honest men could not "be battered down even by the falsehoods of a licentious press. . . . I have therefore never even contradicted the thousands of calumnies so industriously propagated against myself."

Here Jefferson stretched the truth. In a letter to Washington editor Smith, Jefferson asked, "Is it worth while to contradict the barefaced falsehoods of Coleman in the 2d page 5th column of the enclosed paper [?]" Smith thought it was, for he pointed out the fallacy of the *Evening Post* article in the *National Intelligencer,* July 23, 1804.[22] When Jefferson stepped down, the opposition was temporarily bewildered because no real campaign could be mounted for the Federalist ticket despite the unpopularity in New England of the Embargo Act, which Madison had endorsed.

Madison was not the target Jefferson had been and neither Benjamin Russell or William Coleman, the lawyer-editor of the New York *Evening Post,* could whip up much fervor against the prim-and-proper Republican. During Madison's first term he encountered the usual carping from opponents but the real dissent was carried in private letters rather than in newspapers. As relations with England worsened, however, the New England Federalists decided that Madison was unfit for office and through newspaper attacks and town-meeting resolutions they condemned the man whom Washington Irving described in 1811 as "a withered little apple-John." The South and West had cause to favor Madison, for he annexed West Florida with a pen stroke and approved the Indian war climaxed at the Battle of Tippecanoe, but in New England the crisis in shipping worsened by the day. Efforts to keep American ships in international waters without offending warring Britain and France were unavailing, and expedient measures antagonized New England until Federalists declared that Madison was a more formidable enemy to commerce than either belligerent.

When war came the Federalists, with Russell in the vanguard, condemned the declaration as a device to encourage "British, Irish, and Jersey runaway sailors, to enter on board American vessels, and then to be PROTECTED, while they are underworking the native born American Seamen and Navigators. . . . This is what is called fighting for 'Sailors Rights and Free Trade.' " Russell had already made the Republicans wince with his cartoon attack on Elbridge

Gerry that gave the language a new word for rigged election districts—gerrymanders. Russell risked no danger in opposing the unpopular war around Boston, where Governor Strong had declared a public fast in denouncing hostilities against England—"the nation from which we are descended."

Antiwar sentiment, so safe in the North, proved risky in the South. In Baltimore the *Federal Republican* infuriated a mob with its taunts against the war and the commander in chief until the newspaper's office were stormed. In the melee that followed, General James Lingan and "Light Horse Harry" Lee (both Federalists) were set upon. Lingan was killed and Lee permanently crippled before slow-witted Baltimore officials squelched the mob. Federalist newspapers decried the senseless brutality as a partisan effort to shackle the press, but none was more critical than Jefferson. The retired president looked on such scenes as the *Federal Republican* fiasco and declared that "the newspapers of our country by their abandoned spirit of falsehood, have more effectively destroyed the utility of the press than all the shackles devised by Bonaparte."

Baltimore was then a vital link in New York–Washington communications, and with its good harbor a natural center for early American journalism. Thus it had been a logical location for Hezekiah Niles's news magazine, *Niles' Weekly Register*, which he founded a year before war broke out. Niles saw the imbalance caused by bitter partisanship in journalism and determined to publish a report of both sides of issues through official documents, speeches, statistics, and such reliable information as came to hand. Niles also added an innovation for his octavo-size volumes by furnishing subscribers with an index, a decision that has since brought praise from scholarly legions. Niles had a point of view—he was a Republican and became a Jacksonian Democrat—but he upheld his motto, "The Past-the Present—for the Future," and attempted to be fair and accurate. For nearly forty years his *Weekly Register* was to be one of America's most dependable news journals, more proof that the era was a far cry from any Dark Age of communication.

Not every editor during Madison's tenure was of Niles's stripe, of course. After the capture of Washington and the stagnation of commerce, Federalist editors chanted that the military farce was "Mr. Madison's War" and they wanted no part of it. Except for Perry's victory at Lake Erie, where an entire British flotilla was captured in September 1813, there was little for American jingoists to crow about. It was Niles's news magazine that told Americans of this singular event which would gain Perry a place among the nation's heroes. "We have met the enemy; and they are ours," Niles reported, and Americans thrilled to Perry's message after Yankee losses at Detroit and Stoney Creek.

The same xenophobia that Federalists had displayed in the 1798 alien laws came to the surface again during the 1812 war. Albert Gallatin, the Swiss-born presidential confidant and Secretary of the Treasury, was openly attacked as a pro-French influence in the Cabinet. After Gallatin was named a peace envoy, the Salem *Gazette* denounced Madison's choice. "Signior ABRAMA ALBERTO GALLINTINI . . . is of *foreign* extraction, came to our shores about 30 years ago, taught our citizens the French tongue, and the French doctrines of the 'holy right to insurrection,' " the *Gazette* raved. The Federalist editor charged that Gallatin had "accumulated a princely fortune from his liberal salary and by other means in which foreigners generally excel. . . . Bonaparte has his Mamelukes, and the Grand Sultan his Janizaries; so our democratic Presidents have had their Swiss and Walloon Guards."

Republican newspapers counterattacked with charges that the Federalist press consisted mainly of "Tory hirelings." The Frankfort, Kentucky, *Argus,* the Lexington *Reporter,* and other Republican journals were shocked when reports reached the West of a British fleet in Chesapeake Bay, the rout of American militia, and the burning of the White House and Capitol. The *Reporter* urged Kentuckians to enlist in the army and collected clothing and food for the troops' use. Federalist John Lowell's hare-brained scheme for reorganizing the nation regarded the western states as lost. A huge British force was headed for New Orleans, and Federalists assumed it would overwhelm the nondescript band led by Andrew Jackson. "From the moment that the British possess New Orleans, the Union is severed," Federalist Timothy Pickering gloated. Lowell's scheme called for a commercial league of the original thirteen states, with the western states left to fend for themselves. "Every Federalist paper of Boston but one promoted it as a platform for the [upcoming] Hartford Convention." The *Columbian Centinel* hailed the Lowell plan and "Crisis, No. 2," an essay published while the Federalist dissidents met at Hartford, as worthy guides for a befuddled national administration. Russell declared that the Union, "once a blessing, had become a curse under Madison," and he showed his graphic support of a secessionist plan by using woodcuts of pillars, identifying states accepting invitations to the Convention as the "Second Pillar" or "Third Pillar of a New Federal Edifice Raised." The *Centinel* device stemmed from 1787–1788, when the same illustrations recorded ratifying states for the Federal Constitution. But this time a spirited opposition turned Russell's technique into a joke. The *Boston Yankee* editor said the *Centinel* pillars resembled snuff bottles in an apothecary's window. Thereafter, Republican newspapers alluded to the Hartford gathering as "the Snuff Bottle Convention."

Events during the next few months proved that politicians in Washington, Boston, and Richmond had been too close to the scene. The Richmond *Enquirer* thundered a denunciation of the Hartford "Blue Light Federalists" and suggested that a federal army ought to be in readiness to attack New England. "The majority of states which form the Union must consent to the withdrawal of any one branch of it," the *Enquirer* counseled. "Until *that* consent has been obtained, any attempt to dissolve the *Union,* or to obstruct the efficacy of its constitutional laws, is Treason . . . to all intents & purposes." The express riders from New Orleans were carrying the first reports from the battlefield when the Hartford Convention dissolved after drafting a xenophobic, pro-New England document carrying the implicit threat of secession.

Then news of the best variety arrived from the South. The British had been soundly defeated by Jackson's ragtag army. And the knock-out blow came when word of the "Peace of Christmas Eve" arrived from Ghent. Thus Jackson's victory had been won after the war officially ended! Federalist leaders, assured in December that Madison's administration was groggy and could not last out the winter, were stunned. Russell was speechless. The three Federalist emissaries sent from Hartford to Washington to deal with a contrite administration encountered instead a gloating *National Intelligencer* and a euphoric Madison. By February 14 all the good news was shouted along Pennsylvania Avenue, almost at the moment the Federalist delegation arrived. "The little Pigmy shook in his shoes at our approach," a delegate reported in dismay because Madison had ignored their mission. Then the glorious news arrived to the great relief of the harrassed president. Republican newspapers gleefully ran a purported advertisement on the Federalist's disappointment:

MISSING

Three well-looking, respectible men, who appeared to be travelling towards Washington, disappeared from Gadsby's Hotel on Monday evening last, and have not since been heard of. They were observed to be very melancholic on hearing the news of peace, and one of them was heard to say with a sigh, "Poor Caleb Strong!" . . . The newspapers, particularly the Federalist newspapers, are requested to publish this advertisement in a conspicuous place and send in their bills to the Hartford Convention.[23]

The Boston *Independent Chronicle*, a perpetual thorn in Russell's side, was never in better form as it reported the sudden reversal in Republican fortunes with unmitigated joy. MADISON'S PEACE, a subdued running headline proclaimed, "Honorably ILLUSTRATED/REPUBLICANISM TRIUMPHANT." Federalist noses were rubbed in the Treaty of Ghent as the *Chronicle* reminded the opposition that they had long suggested a treaty would be signed by England only after Madison had resigned. "Every federal scribbler has taken this ground with the utmost assurance," and at the same time Madison's opponents "rejoiced at the success of our enemies, and even forbid us to celebrate our own victories." Earlier in the month, the *Chronicle* had warily reported the rumors drifting from New Orleans as "GLORIOUS NEWS—*if true*," with an account that made Andrew Jackson into a David facing the British Goliath.[24] Now, with the peace a reality, the Boston Republicans were ready to dish up crow for Federalists. A public notice printed after the treaty rumors gained ground told of a Victory parade that would be formed with a Grand Procession Committee consisting of "Paul Revere, J. Hunnewell, [and] Benja. Russell." Whether Russell took part personally in the Democratic victory march is both uncertain and unlikely.

Russell recovered, but only partially, for the Federalist party went downhill after Mr. Madison's war became—or so the average American thought—a great American victory. With the return of peace and the virtual dissolution of the national Federalist organization, Russell decided to turn the other cheek. In 1817 he was on the hospitality committee that welcomed President Monroe to Boston, and Russell's caption on a welcoming editorial became symbolic of the national mood: "The Era of Good Feeling." [25] Vindictive Federalists could not forgive Russell for this magnanimous conduct, since a good Federalist was also a good hater. In 1824 and 1828 Russell did much to make party amends by endorsing John Quincy Adams for the presidency. After the futile 1828 campaign Russell, perhaps the grandest Federalist of them all, sold his interest and eventually the *Centinel* was merged with its former arch-rival, the Boston *Independent Chronicle.*

The changes Russell had lived to witness indicated the quickened tempo of life during a period that modern Americans tend to consider unhurried and leisurely. As a lad of thirteen Russell had heard the news from Lexington-Concord carried by express riders, and under Isaiah Thomas's tutelage he had learned to set type and, later, to vote for the party of Washington and Adams. In the sunset of his life, America had grown to a republic that spanned the Mississippi, crisscrossed with a network of rivers and canals. Nearly 600 newspapers served a nation of 7 million people, and those journals were printed by steam-driven or hand-powered presses that were vastly more sophisticated than the cumbersome one on which Russell had learned his trade. From small sheets with two or four columns, the American newspaper had emerged as a five- or six-column sheet, larger too in the number of pages it offered readers who paid two or three copper pennies, or four dollars in advance, for their daily or weekly reading.

On the other hand, some areas of journalism were essentially unchanged. Illustrations were rarely used because they had to be cut from wood or soft metal, and as a pioneer in newspaper illustrations, Russell knew that engravers skilled in such arts were rare. The same woodcuts of sailing ships, horses, and black-faced runaways that had been used in colonial times were still the main ornaments of newspaper columns. The likenesses of public men never appeared in newspapers—it was highly unlikely that a Kentuckian knew how Jefferson looked unless he had seen him in person. Probably only the features of Washington and Franklin were well known, and that because mezzotints of these luminaries seem to have been consistent best sellers from 1785 onward—fed by handiwork from French and English engravers. The editors had taken over in city newspapers, but in the country it was still the printer-editor-proprietor who ran the entire operation and hoped desperately for a state or territorial printing contract and prompt payments from subscribers. As Tocqueville noted, "generally American journalists have a low social status, their education is only sketchy, and their thoughts are often vulgarly expressed." * With a foreigner's detachment Tocqueville saw what many Americans, including presidents, failed to perceive. "The hall-

* The Frenchman was only partly correct. It is likely that most American editors disdained an inquisitive, well-dressed foreign traveler as much as that observer was repelled by their crudeness of dress and speech.

mark of the American journalist is a direct and coarse attack" which carried "no weight with the readers. . . . What they look for in a newspaper is knowledge of facts, and it is only by altering or distorting those facts that the journalist can gain some influence for his views." [26] Russell and every other American newspaper editor before the Civil War had firsthand knowledge to confirm the Frenchman's observations. All would have agreed with his ultimate judgment that newspapers were a powerful force in American life. Whether read in a Salem coffeehouse or on a Mississippi boat landing, these newspapers rarely returned "large profits" but still made "political life circulate in every corner" of the United States.

The political tempo of American life had been rising, and the increasing number of newspapers was also a barometer of the nation's economic health. That distant echo of the January 8, 1815, battle—the Battle at New Orleans—would cause more thunderclaps before it faded. A new hero came out of the din and was to ride on a tidal wave of propaganda into the White House. By the friends he chose, Andrew Jackson clearly understood that he needed newspaper allies in order to become president. Whether they liked it or not, public men in America understood that, henceforth, journalism would be a major force in national affairs.

5

The Making of
a President:
Andrew the First

Newspapers catapulted Andrew Jackson into the White House. The high-strung beanpole of a general captured the voters' imaginations after the quiet interlude of Monroe's two terms, when so momentous a policy as the doctrine bearing his name was nearly ignored by the press.

Federalist ineptitude was a factor in Jackson's rise in national politics. The Federalists had lost touch with that part of the nation that lay outside New England. In the vacuum created by the failure of Federalist leadership, snarling party newspapers vented their wrath on local issues as the nation's main energies were turned toward internal improvements, expanding commerce, the settlement of the public domain, and away from the slavery issue. The Missouri Compromise appeared to have answered the slavery question beyond the Mississippi, and the Canadian and Florida border disputes were settled amicably. When Monroe inserted John Quincy Adams's recommendation on a Latin American policy in his 1823 annual message to Congress, newspapers printed it (as was traditional with the press by this time), but nobody foresaw that it contained an anchor clause for

American foreign policy. From the *Eastern Argus* to the New Orleans *Picayune*, Monroe's message warning European powers against further colonial adventures in the Americas was a milestone passed by, almost unnoticed. Hezekiah Niles placed the speech on the inside pages of his *Weekly Register,* after a roundup of crop reports, health items, and foreign news.

Monroe's matter-of-fact administration kept the lid on two of the three great issues facing Americans during the nineteenth century—the tariff and the United States Bank. European visitors were constantly amazed to find a Pennsylvania farmer poring over his weekly newspaper in search of information about the tariff debates or word about the bank charter. "The American attends to his newspaper not like the Germans or the French," Karl Anton Postl reported, "for the purpose of deriving a topic of conversation upon politics in which they have no concern, but for the regulation of his public and private life." The American reader took an interest in government "which would in some countries be deemed arrogance, in others a crime [yet it] is with him a point of duty. . . . The newspapers, therefore, comprehend the whole life, public and private, of the Union." [1] At the heart of the reader's interest was his concern for what the Austrian observer derided as "making money," but this preoccupation with profit was excused as a peculiar American trait. A Frenchman who crossed the country was amazed that Americans were content to read only their local newspaper, unlike literate French or English citizens who always sought out Paris and London newspapers. "The Globe and the National Intelligencer of Washington are, however, pretty generally circulated," Chevalier conceded, but he patronized American journalism by concluding that newspapers were "within the reach of all . . . consulted [merely] for the news, not for opinions." [2] It was plain to these visitors that the American reader was in no way similar to his European counterpart, who delighted in page-long essays on the minutest political disputes. The American wanted the news in small doses at a low price.

Newspapers were in such profusion that they continued to sell for pennies. An Englishman accustomed to the stamp duty in his home-land was struck by the fact that "There is no tax whatever on the press, and consequently every owner of one can print a newspaper with little risk, among a people who are all politicians." Gathering the news was not costly either, since exchanges went through the mails free. "I have often seen a printer receive as many newspapers by one mail, as would fill the room of several hundred letters," an amazed foreigner reported early in the century. By the 1820s, with presses flourishing at every crossroads or courthouse town, the num-ber of exchanges a printer handed to the postmaster must have ex-ceeded his subscription lists in scores of communities.

Meanwhile, communications in the Republic improved. A trans-portation revolution brought the Cumberland Road to the banks of the Ohio. Experiments with the new steam locomotives had bank presidents and congressmen agog with excitement. Freight rates began to tumble, land values rose fast enough for all but the greediest speculators, and such river towns as Cincinnati, Louisville, and St. Louis boomed. East and West, hard corn liquor replaced rum as the workman's favored libation (at five cents a tumbler), and New Eng-land sent missionaries to Christianize frontier Indian tribes, to the wonderment of the South and West where the persuasion of a gun barrel to a printing press was preferred in all dealings with the red men. So successful were the Yankee teachers that one gifted Indian devised an alphabet for the Cherokees and by 1828 the New Echota, Georgia, *Cherokee Phoenix* was circulated to tribesmen—the first newspaper ever printed in North America from an indigenous cul-ture with its own language.

During Monroe's second term it was apparent that he would honor the tenure limitations established by his predecessors. With the Fed-eralist party in a shambles, the various Republican regional factions began scrambling for a candidate who would—barring an unthink-able upset—become the next president. Several Cabinet members yearned for the job, Jackson's name inspired editors in some northern cities as well as in the southwest, and Henry Clay cultivated his own clique. The result was temporary confusion among many editors who preferred to wait until a definite front-runner emerged. Ambivalent journalism left the voters similarly thrown off balance, so that a free-for-all resulted that opened wounds time would never heal. As early as 1822 Jackson's followers started rolling their bandwagon when the Nashville *Whig* climbed off the candidate-straddling fence. "GREAT RACING!" the Whig announced, "The prize to be run for is the *Presidential Chair.*" Other states had entered "their nags," the *Whig* noted, so was it not time for Tennessee to "put in her stud? and if so, let it be called *Old Hickory.*" Coy at first, Jackson warmed to the idea and finally was an eager challenger. Candidates were by custom not active; however, much private work was done through the mails or in legislative halls. All the other campaign drumbeating was done in the newspapers.

Illness and opportunism finally narrowed the race to Clay, Jackson, and Adams. Ultimately, Clay's gestures made him more of a nuisance than a serious threat. The real battle was between two candidates of widely separated backgrounds, men thrown into the same political party by a variety of circumstances. Perhaps Adams's strongest ally was the *National Intelligencer,* which was powerful beyond any of Jackson's press support. Although the rough-hewn Tennessean won both the popular and electoral vote, Jackson lacked the necessary majority, with the result that the choice fell to the House of Representatives where Adams won. The Jackson men at once sensed a deal, and began shouting about a corrupt bargain when Clay was soon named by Adams as his Secretary of State (and presumed heir apparent, since all past holders of that Cabinet post, except Adams's father, had been apprenticed there for the presidency). Quickly the era of good feeling gave way to a decade of rip-snorting, predatory politics, with the Jackson crowd calling themselves Democratic Republicans and pledging to elect their man president in 1828 regardless of the cost.

As it turned out, the cost was reasonable and in large measure because of the newspapers. A definite shift of population was underway, and the Democrats expected to capitalize on new voter strength as property qualifications fell and added thousands of city dwellers to the poll lists. Adams could depend on the *National Intelligencer* and the leading Boston newspapers to hold firm, but there was a charisma about Jackson that attracted editors who knew Old Hickory only from paragraphs in the exchange. Dartmouth-trained Amos Kendall fell under Jackson's spell and made the influential Frankfort *Argus* into a vociferous advocate of the general's candidacy, located in the heart of Clay's home ground. Duff Green, a lawyer-editor from St. Louis, met Jackson on a river keel boat and became the Indian fighter's personal choice as editor for a newly established Washington journal, the *United States Telegraph*. The New York *Courier and Enquirer* was for Jackson, and its circulation of more than 4,000 copies made it the nation's largest newspaper and an anchor for the editorial war about to begin in earnest.

In every major city, supporters of Adams and Jackson either had a newspaper by 1827 or had started one. For the remainder of the nineteenth century, campaign newspapers would be spawned by zealous partisans willing to raise barely enough money to produce a four-page paper with a life tenure based solely upon the calendar. These short-lived campaign journals enlivened the contest, allowed bombastic editors to vent all their passions, and had as their chief purpose the maintenance of party morale. Usually they bore the frankest of names—*The Jacksonian* or *The Warren County Whig*—and no reader was long left in doubt as to their editorial stand. They seldom existed where the party already had a newspaper voice, and rarely outlasted the counting of the campaign's last ballot.

In the midst of prosperity and feverish political activity, the attention of some Americans fell on other matters. In upstate New York the mysterious disappearance of a Mason who had announced his intention of divulging the fraternal order's secrets led to a hysterical political movement largely supported by almost a hundred newspapers in New York and western Pennsylvania. The Anti-Masonic movement surged forward after an unidentified corpse was found floating in the Niagara River. The Chenango *Anti-Masonic Tele-*

graph was typical of papers undergoing a soul-searching between 1829 and 1835. When doubts about political loyalty were finally resolved, it became once again the Chenango *Telegraph*. Although it took no deep root, the Anti-Masonic party was a force in state politics for the next decade.

Upstate New York also was the center of unusual religious activity during the late 1820s. Charles G. Finney's Presbyterian ministry in Jefferson County resulted in a series of revival meetings that were reported in newspapers until the area's zeal against hellfire and damnation brought it the popular name of "the burned-over district." Joseph Smith's later account of his discovery of mysterious golden plates bearing a divine message set the time at 1823, in Palmyra, New York. By the decade's end, Smith had begun his battle to build a Church of Jesus Christ of Latter Day Saints from his Palmyra base. Among the older sects, one newspaper stood out as no other weekly could rival the *Christian Journal and Advocate* in circulation. The denominational paper went into 26,000 American homes in 1826.

Two newspapers that made brief appearances in the 1820s were merely a glimmer of things to come. In 1822 Benjamin Lundy started his antislavery newspaper, *The Genius of Universal Emancipation*, in Mount Pleasant, Ohio, with a subscription list of six. The early rumbles from dissatisfied laborers in New England resulted in a strike by Boston carpenters in 1825, and two years later the *Journeyman Mechanic's Advocate* appeared in New York. Lundy worried about slave labor and its effects upon a country founded on the premise that "all men are created equal," while the new Irish immigrants fought for jobs as hod carriers or shirtmakers that paid less than ten cents an hour. Lundy finally moved to Baltimore and reopened the *Genius* office, only to encounter the wrath of a slave dealer who accosted Lundy in the street and nearly killed him.

Lundy's unorthodox view of slavery invited hostility in Maryland, but other antislavery editors would know a worse fate than a street brawl. Indeed, the mood of the country became more belligerent after 1820, when the Missouri Compromise was supposed to have defused an explosive issue. Slavery was a public issue and demanded attention, but some editors indulged themselves in petty quarrels and personal vendettas that increased the hazards of newspaper publishing beyond "bloody consumption" or tightfisted subscribers. Newspaper articles had led to the shooting in Boston of Benjamin Austin, Jr., William Coleman's duel in 1803 (which brought a political rival's death), and a similar duel and murder involving the New York *Enquirer* in 1828. Most of the recorded gunplay, however, occurred in the South and came after Jackson had been elected over the protests of editors who insisted the president was one of the bloodiest duelists of all times.

The controversial, colorful Tennesseean consistently provided American newspapers with the best "copy" in the first half of the nineteenth century. Jackson had to surmount the charge that he had killed several men in duels (by true count only one) as well as a variety of other accusations. A pro-Adams broadside showed woodcuts of six black coffins, placed beneath the names of six wartime mutineers executed under Jackson's "orders," and followed these with "Some Account of some of the Bloody Deeds of GENERAL JACKSON." Infinitely worse in Jackson's eyes, as the campaign grew more heated, was the charge that his wife, Rachel, was a bigamist. The *National Intelligencer* printed evidence that the party's late founder, Jefferson, had declared Jackson unfit for the presidency. Every bit of minor gossip was dredged by the majority of America's editors to make Jackson appear as "an adulterer," a hot-tempered southerner who feared neither God nor man, and an ignoramus totally unprepared for duty in the White House. Clay's friend Charles Hammond, editor of the Cincinnati *Gazette*, raised Jackson's ire to the bursting point. "Ought a convicted adulteress and her paramour husband to be placed in the highest office of this free and Christian land?" Hammond asked. Jackson, bridling his anger, told intimate friends he would see that there was "a day of retribution [for] Mr. Clay and his tool Colonel Hammond."

Though overwhelmed by numbers, Jackson's newspaper supporters were resourceful. Adams's installation of a billiard table in the White House was offered as proof of his extravagance—and Adams finally paid the $50 bill out of his own pocket. An early instance of guilt by association was displayed in the *New-Hampshire Patriot,* which warned voters that Adams had been endorsed by prominent former Federalists including all the surviving delegates at the Hartford Convention. His appointment of Clay—"The Judas of the West"—was cited as evidence of rampant corruption in Washington. The Boston *Statesman* intimated that Adams was the darling of a Back Bay crowd eager to embrace discredited Federalism, including another version of the Alien and Sedition laws. Stung by such inferences and the repeated pejorative "Hartford Convention" din, Adams published in the *National Intelligencer* a counter-accusation that was meant to disassociate him from the Federalists by accusing them of harboring secessionist tendencies in an early day. The sensational letter alienated droves of New Englanders and made few friends for Adams elsewhere.

A sidelight of the 1828 election was the topsy-turvy battle in Boston, where Theodore Lyman, Jr., published the *Jackson Republican* as a campaign newspaper at definite odds with most of the other Beacon Hill bluebloods' predilections. A chance remark about Daniel Webster in its columns touched a tender nerve and caused the affronted senator to demand Lyman's arrest on the unusual charge of criminal libel.[3] After the expiration of the Sedition law and the Croswell case publicity, such an accusation seemed trumped-up indeed, but the case forced attention on the state's antiquated statutes. The dark-browed Webster denied an alleged association with the Hartford Convention, but the jury could not agree and the case was finally dropped. The absurdities of the situation caused the state legislature to pass a bill in 1832 outlawing common-law indictments for printed words as criminal acts and admitting truth as a defense in all libel actions. Thus, after almost one hundred years, the main contention of Zenger's lawyers had at last become fixed in law.

Jackson's triumph in 1828 was a landmark in the development of journalism as the chief arena for presidential politics. So far as we know, the popular portrait of Jackson touring the country as a speech-making campaigner is pure hokum. Jackson did as all the earlier presidential aspirants had done—he used friends to have letters written on his behalf and depended on Amos Kendall and other editors to do his public campaigning. There was no expense account to file at the end of the campaign, but if there had been it would have shown few contributions in cash and practically no outlays. Editors wrote impassioned essays out of conviction and hope. They were convinced of their candidate's worthiness and they hoped that if he won, their labors would be rewarded with a postmastership at least. Jackson's men won after five years of toil, with a preponderance of the big-city newspaper guns trained against them.

The pro-Jackson press forced Adams into a defensive position by reminding voters of Adams's Federalist antecedents and made much headway with the irrelevant but constantly mentioned Hartford Convention. Certain things were bound to backfire. The Democrats had hailed "John the Second" in derision. When the Adams Republican organization fell apart, those who picked up the pieces began writing about "King Andrew the First." At first they were known as National Republicans, but as the opponents of the king in England had been Whigs, so would they soon be. The new party thus found a name, one based solely on the American political premise that to be "agin" a candidate was in itself a political platform.

The Jackson men had built up their strength at strategic points. As early as 1823 Martin Van Buren, an ambitious local politician who had hooked his fortunes to Jackson's star, was dismayed that their campaign newspaper's editor had died. A new editor filled with zeal for Jackson had to be found at once. "Without a paper thus edited at Albany we may hang our harps on the willows," Van Buren advised fellow Democrats. "With it, the party can survive a thousand such convulsions as those which agitate and probably alarm most of those around you." Kendall's *Argus of Western America*, Charles Greene's Boston *Post*, Isaac Hill's *New-Hampshire Patriot*, and William Cullen Bryant's New York *Evening Post* constituted a whole host unto themselves and set the tone of the Jacksonian campaign. When Jackson's spelling mistakes were alluded to by a carping Federalist editor as proof of Old Hickory's crudeness and lack of qualification, the *Patriot* made friends with the multitude by replying that Washington had never won any spelling bees, nor did a man have to be an intellectual giant to be president. Honesty and a faith in his fellow man counted for more than college degrees, the *Patriot* implied. These sentiments were echoed by two leading southern pro-Jackson newspapers, the Baltimore *Republican* and the Richmond *Enquirer*. With Jackson's victory confirmed, these newspapers gained a new regional prominence, while the *National Intelligencer*, now published by Joseph Gales, Jr., and W. W. Seaton (who also published the congressional debates and other government documents), was about to fall from grace.

The newly elected Tennessean headed for his inauguration with a heavy heart, for his much-beloved and slandered wife, Rachel, died in late December. Once Jackson reached Washington there was more than the White House mob scene (including a 1,400-pound cheese offered at a public buffet) to remind citizens that a new president was in office. With his strong sense of loyalty, Jackson saw that his friends were rewarded, including a host of newspaper editors. Duff Green's *Telegraph* replaced the *Intelligencer* as the semiofficial administration newspaper. Kendall was invited to serve in the Treasury department. Editor Isaac Hill of the *New-Hampshire Patriot* was appointed Second Comptroller of the Treasury but was rejected by a recalcitrant Senate.[4] Postmaster-General William T. Barry was placed in charge of handing out favors to deserving Democratic editors, and the postmastership that had long served as a strategic sinecure for editors became a political plum to be dispensed to the party faithful.

Not all Democrats stayed with Jackson once the honeymoon phase of his first term ended. Duff Green veered away from Jackson toward a closer tie with Calhoun after a famous staring match between the president and his running mate at a Jefferson Day dinner. The two were at odds over South Carolina's nullification threat, and Green sided with the brilliant vice president in the *Telegraph* columns. The president's friends eventually decided to start another newspaper with the editorial chair filled by a Jackson man of unquestioned loyalty. Their choice was Francis P. Blair, Kendall's successor on the Frankfort *Argus*. In December 1830 Blair came to Washington as editor of the *Globe*—the editorship made more enticing by the promise of a public printing contract worth $50,000 annually. A third Kentuckian, John C. Rives, was also placed on the *Globe* payroll.

The three newspapermen were soon spoken of as Jackson's "Kitchen Cabinet"—an informal advisory body said to have been more influential with the president than the Cabinet officers.[5] "They were intimate companions of the President," Mott wrote. Jackson would stretch out on a couch, "smoke and dictate his ideas to Kendall, the scholar of the group, and then Editor Blair or Kendall would write and rewrite the paragraphs which were to crackle in the *Globe* the next day."[6] Rives was an enormous man weighing 240 pounds who liked to make jokes about his homely features. Kendall was gaunt but his appearance improved as he mellowed, and Blair was a portly gourmet whose well-stocked table and wine cellar made him one of the capital's best hosts. Blair built a mansion down the street from the White House which still stands as an official hostelry for distinguished visitors. As a team these loyal Jackson men made the *Globe* one of the leading and most profitable newspapers in the country. An order to federal officeholders who made more than $1,000 to subscribe to the *Globe* or risk dismissal doubtless had helped launch the enterprise, but Rives's sound management was also a major factor in the *Globe* success story.

Meanwhile, other important developments transforming the young Republic provided a powerful stimulus to the growth of American journalism. The Columbian, an ingenious press that worked on a lever rather than a screw principle, was invented by a

Philadelphian to ease the printer's burden while increasing his output. Further improvement came quickly, and by 1820 the "Washington" press was patented to provide printers with a rugged, lever-principle, and low-cost mechanism that would become the mainstay of small-town and frontier journalism. The Washington stood as a pigmy, however, beside the steam-driven Napier press installed in 1825 by the *New York Advertiser* that printed 2,000 copies every hour its boilers were tended. New York real estate prices leaped after the Erie Canal was finished in that same year and made the city the national center of commerce and finance, but printer's wages stayed at $8 a week and in the hinterlands nearly every newspaper had a notice plea for arrears aimed at delinquent subscribers. Although the new Napier presses cost around $5,000, it was the printer-editor who represented journalism in most communities and his capital had varied little from that of his predecessor a generation or two earlier. By the time voters were deciding between Adams and Jackson, there were more than 900 newspapers in the United States and yet fewer than a dozen papers were making over $10,000 a year in profits.

Editors seemed to have taken to journalism as they took their wives, for richer or poorer, but there was usually more excitement in a newspaper office than in the average marriage. As often happens when a strong man occupies the White House, Washington became more of a news center after 1828 than it had been since Jefferson's day. News stories radiated from the capital to the farthest hamlets and the editor was looked upon as the town's expert on political matters so that whatever the condition of his purse, his prestige in the community was uncommonly high. In the cities, ambitious printers drifted into the new calling of "reporter," a writer who assembled facts and turned them over to the editor either in a mass of notes or as a single story. The editor made changes as he saw fit, then placed the story under a brief headline (*Another Fire on DeLancey* or *A Runaway Team on Broadway*) and sent a procession of these items to "the back shop," where they were set in type and placed in a steel printer's chase after being proofread. As city journalism's pace quickened, the time between the reporter's assignment and the moment newspapers were bundled for street vendors narrowed to four or five hours. Mass production in journalism called for integrated specialties and a wary eye on the clock.

Special reporters were few in the 1820s but unlike the back-shop printer, their lives were hardly routine so that the low pay of $6 to $10 a week seemed adequate. During John Quincy Adams's Administration several New York and Philadelphia newspapers maintained regular correspondents in the capital as a press gallery was added to the halls of Congress. Beyond stenographic reporting of the great debates (including the Hayne-Webster confrontation of 1830 over tariffs and state sovereignty), however, much of the correspondents' time was spent in relating Washington gossip. The New York *Enquirer* sent James Gordon Bennett as its Potomac sentinel, a post he filled with distinction because he took the small talk around Lafayette Square and turned it into a series of reports imitative of the gossip Horace Walpole gleaned from George III's court. The travel time from New York to Washington was cut to thirty-six hours midway in Jackson's first term, and by 1832 the New York *Journal of Commerce* boasted that its special relay team of twenty-four express riders could carry a dispatch from Pennsylvania Avenue in the capital to their Manhattan offices in a breathtaking twenty hours. Two years later, the *Journal of Commerce* and *Courier and Enquirer* made a daily express service from Washington to New York into a cooperative venture, with mutual assistance needed to meet the monthly toll bill of $7,500.

Only the prosperous New York, Philadelphia, Boston, and Baltimore newspapers could afford both editors and a staff of reporters. As the country expanded, the number of newspapers increased so that more newspapers were printed in the state of Pennsylvania than in the entire domain of the Russian Czar, and although many European visitors made unflattering comments in their travel accounts of life in the United States, the variety and acceptability of newspapers continued to amaze blasé Englishmen. The acerbic Frederick Marryat somehow thought America had around 10,000 newspapers in 1837 (compared to 370 in Britain) but he hastily added "that the expense of the [London] *Times* newspaper alone, is equal to at least *five* thousand of the *Minor* papers in the United States, which are edited by people of no literary pretensions and at an expense so trifling as would appear to us not only ridiculous but impossible." [7]

For the most part, Americans shrugged off insults by foreigners because they were more interested in material rewards than compliments. The public domain, which Jefferson thought would last for several centuries, was being gobbled up at a frightening pace. Zealous printer-editors often followed behind the surveyors and lawyers when new territories were opened. By 1808 an enterprising editor had crossed the Mississippi and started the Missouri *Gazette* at St. Louis, with part of its four-page layout printed in French. When the Arkansas *Gazette* and Nacogdoches, Texas, *Republican* were founded in 1819, Natchez had already enjoyed local journalism for twenty years. Higher costs led to money-saving consolidations in the cities, but in the western territories a new breed of independent editor was coming into prominence: the booster-editor. These itinerant editors could look down a muddy ocean of a Main Street, hear the whop-whop-whop of a few hammers, and write long editorials about the city of the future with broad, tree-lined avenues in the shadows of stately buildings. "The first task of the printer in the upstart city was to bring into existence a community where the newspaper could survive," Daniel Boorstin observed. The editor-printer's enthusiasm, unlike his own personal resources, had to be unlimited. Until the 1830s the restless printer surveyed the prospects, chose a town without opposition or with no other paper of his own political persuasion, and set up his shop after some assurance from merchants or politicians of reasonable local support. The booster-editor, on the other hand, sought out seedling communities that held the promise of being another Buffalo or Chicago. Wisconsin's first newspaper, the Green-Bay *Intelligencer*, began printing in December, 1833, with the avowed purpose of "the advancement of the country west of Lake

Michigan." The founder of the Milwaukee *Advertiser* boasted of his
optimism by announcing that in all likelihood there were not 200 potential subscribers "within a circuit of fifty miles." [8] A similar faith in
the future gripped John King when he founded the Dubuque *Visitor*
in 1836. The optimistic owner of the *Western Adventurer* in Mount
Rose, Iowa, had to confess his hopes were too sanguine after two
years of disappointment and after further wanderings his type and
press were finally settled in the river town of Burlington, as the
Hawk-Eye. In league with land speculators, these editors were in step
with the spirit of the times, which was all in favor of fast profits and
high risks. If worse came to worst, a flat-bed press could always fit
onto a wagon or flatboat and a better town (or vacant townsite)
found.

Some editors moved west simply because their eastern welcome
had worn out. There was nothing typical about Matthew Lyon, the
politician-editor who was reelected to Congress while in jail under
the Sedition Act of 1798—except perhaps his peregrinations. Lyon
founded a Vermont newspaper, went to Congress, lost an election,
and moved to Kentucky to start both a town and a newspaper. Lyon
spent his last days in Arkansas, however, once again a public man as
territorial delegate to Congress. His life seemed testimony that a
moving man would find opportunity.

Frontier conditions seemed to foster a reckless derring-do, and it
was true that few printers ever starved. As the Old Northwest filled
up with settlers, new states passed quickly from frontier to farmlands,
dotted with churches and fresh-water colleges. Indiana became a territory in 1800 but was without a newspaper until 1804. Elihu Stout
brought his press to Vincennes down the Ohio and up the Wabash,
and the *Indiana Gazette* prospered with territorial printing contracts
until a fire burned out Stout's pioneering plant. By the time of state-
hood in 1816, Indiana had at least five newspapers. When Jackson
ran for a second term, he was endorsed by a majority of Indiana's
twenty-nine weeklies, most of them with printer-editors whose morale was higher than their circulation. The editor of the Bloomington

Post did not have the problem that confronted a New York editor in 1825, who accepted 1,115 new advertisements in one week and "a week later, printed 213, and stated that 23 others were left out for want of space." [9] The Bloomington editor had plenty of space available but few dollars in his cashbox as he plaintively notified readers who paid for their papers with farm products to "do so soon, or the cash will be expected. Pork, flour, corn and meal will be taken at the market prices. Also, those who expect to pay us in firewood must do so immediately—we must have our wood laid for the winter before the roads get bad."

Roads in backwoods areas were bad, but the newfangled railroads were running west from the great seaports after the momentary novelty of the belching locomotives wore off. The American-built *Best Friend of Charleston* was started on a regular run by 1831, and despite some mishaps caused by overheated boilers and stray livestock, railroads held the promise of scheduled trips in fair weather or foul. Until temporarily checked by the panic of 1837, the railroad-building mania led to the construction of more than 2,000 miles of eastern and southern tracks. The need for safety signals soon became urgent, and in the development of an electric telegraph system for railroads Samuel F. B. Morse made a revolutionary contribution that would quickly be adapted to the needs of journalism.

Before the magic of the telegraph wrought its changes on news reporting, however, ingenious editors had indulged in an exciting race for European news that probably cost more money than it was worth but demonstrated a sharp competitive spirit among metropolitan newspapers. For a time most New York dailies shared the expense of a special boat that met incoming ships from Europe and hurried bundles of foreign newspapers ashore, ahead of passengers and cargo. Once ashore, editors used scissors and paste to prepare columns of "Late Dispatches from Europe," but nearly everybody had the same material (the *Times* of London had the best foreign section, so it was a prime source of journalistic piracy). But the *Journal of Commerce* soon withdrew from the consortium and the reasons were probably altruistic, since the publisher was Arthur Tappan, an eccentric, rich dabbler in lost causes.

Tappan's current crusade was against all kinds of Sabbath-breaking activities, and he apparently had no stomach for the fight some editors waged with homing pigeons, semaphore signals, and other devices to attain a slight time advantage over rivals. Tappan sold the *Journal of Commerce* to its chief editors, who promptly acquired a sloop which was secretly outfitted. The vessel sailed out almost undetected in her first attempt to meet incoming ships off Sandy Hook, where large transatlantic vessels began trimming their sails. The subterfuge worked, the once-stodgy *Journal of Commerce* scored a notable news beat over its rivals, and brought the enlivened newspaper more public notice than all of Tappan's well-intentioned efforts "to avoid a violation of the Sabbath Day." [10] Soon the *Journal* news sloop went out nearly 100 miles to keep a vigil for inbound ships, and in a few months the rejuvenated *Journal of Commerce* was known as New York's most aggressive newspaper—though still not a paper for the average man. Like most metropolitian newspapers, it was a mercantile journal—"sniffing out the news"—but written for the businessman. [11]

The merchant, shipper, banker, or auctioneer who paid a dime for his newspaper bought four pages crammed with long, dull, and informative stories about the stock market, commodity prices, and shipping news. The business of the mercantile journals was to tell readers what was going on in the business world. The romance of the ledger sheet appeals to few men, and so the audience for the New York dailies was limited. Economic news need not be dull, however, and the banking business in the United States was about to provide the nation with some excitement. Banker Nicholas Biddle, from a long line of Philadelphia money men, was in a position to become—next to Andrew Jackson—America's man of the hour.

Besides the tariff (which southerners judged was far too high) and the ever-present slavery issue, the growing power of the government-chartered United States Bank zoomed into prominence as Jackson's second term plans took shape. The Bank—Alexander Hamilton's darling during the Federalist era—had been given a new lease on life by the "national" Republicans in 1816, when the second Bank of the United States was established under a twenty-year charter approved by Madison. From the outset of his tenure, Jackson had voiced suspicions of the Bank's constitutionality, and early in 1831 he promised to make the removal of the Bank's charter a campaign issue: No Bank and Jackson—or Bank and no Jackson. Biddle, as director of the Bank, made friendly overtures to the Jacksonians which were rebuffed. A better banker than he was politician, Biddle decided to press for an early recharter of the Bank and enlisted Henry Clay's aid.

The war of words began with the Democratic newspapers on the warpath against the twin bugbears—Biddle and his bank. No paper was behind the New York *Courier* in its condemnation of Biddle, who was depicted as an American Shylock. James Gordon Bennett, a dynamic reporter whose knowledge of Wall Street operations had made him a leading financial writer, plunged into the battle encouraged by his editor, Colonel James Watson Webb. On February 5, 1831, the *Courier* took its stand beside Jackson, declaring that the Bank was

> an Imperium in Imperia, unknown to the Constitution, defying its powers—laughing at its restrictions—scorning its principles—and pointing to its golden vaults as the weapon that will execute its behests whenever it shall be necessary to carry them into action.

Then, suddenly, the *Courier* attacks on the Bank (and Biddle) stopped. The editorial mallet had been replaced with a kid glove, but Webb's about-face was too sudden to go unnoticed. As the story began to leak out, it appeared that Biddle was neither a good banker nor clever politician.

Disclosures eventually made before a special congressional investigating committee indicated that the *Courier* was putting on a brave financial front when in fact its debts were mounting. An associate of Webb had seen Biddle concerning a $15,000 loan, and in passing mentioned that it might be possible for the *Courier* to soften its attitude toward the Bank charter. The associate got the loan, but Biddle failed to enter the transaction in his books for nine months. In August the *Courier* management obtained a second loan, this time for $20,000. Three weeks later, the newspaper reversed its earlier stand and called for "a modified recharter" of Biddle's bank. A third loan was made to the *Courier* in December 1831, making the newspaper's indebtedness to the bank total $52,975. A congressional committee got wind of these transactions and a full investigation was demanded. Webb and his partner, Mordecai M. Noah, demanded the right to testify on their behalf, and much publicity resulted for the *Courier* until the committee reported in April that the evidence of any wrongdoing by the publishers was only circumstantial. The tempest blew over and Webb persuaded Biddle to make still a fourth loan. Predictably, when the 1832 campaign was at white heat, Webb severed all past connections with the Jacksonians and switched to Henry Clay.[12]

Clay was the last candidate of the fading National Republicans, who gathered many eastern and New England editors in their fold but fell behind in the earliest balloting. Calhoun made a gesture to run as a candidate for the nullification wing of the Democratic party, but in the end left that dubious honor to John Floyd (although the Richmond *Jeffersonian* tried to make the vice president a serious contender). Jackson's tough policy on Indian removal, his spirited battle with the United States Bank, and his identification with the restless westerners were advantages no opponent could overcome. In certain areas, particularly upstate New York, the Anti-Masonic party made headway and its presidential candidate picked up seven electoral votes. More significantly, Thurlow Weed made his Albany *Evening Journal* into an important local force by exploiting the hysteria that followed prosecutions for the kidnaping-murder of William Morgan. Weed, a former printer, found political wire-pulling profitable and particularly from a newspaper office. Weed adopted William H. Seward as his protégé, and although the Anti-Masonic party faded, the *Evening Journal* prospered to become a leading anti-Democratic newspaper for the next thirty years.

Jackson had won after taking some steam out of the opposition that raved about the 1828 "Tariff of Abominations" as though the high duty measure was contrived by Satan. Old John Quincy Adams was back in politics, as a congressman from Quincy, and he helped steer a low tariff bill through the legislative halls and onto Jackson's desk in the summer of 1832. "The long debated question has been decided," Bryant's *Evening Post* assumed, "and many of the animosities to which it gave rise will now be laid asleep." Instead of a gradual calm settling over the land, however, discontent mounted. First came the South Carolina nullification convention, which threatened secession and proclaimed valid the doctrine of state sovereignty. The tariffs of 1828 and 1832 were held invalid and unenforceable in South Carolina after February 1, 1833. Any enforcement of tariffs by the federal government was to be regarded as an effort "to reduce this State to obedience" and there was a thinly veiled hint of violence. The hotheads were in command. "All appear animated, by the most thorough conviction that we are unconquerable," the Columbia, South Carolina, *Southern Times* reported.

The most outspoken southern newspaper from 1833 until the Civil War was the Charleston *Mercury*. Abrasive editorials in the *Mercury* denounced the so-called Force Bill as a Jacksonian monstrosity and counseled southerners to hold themselves in readiness for secession. The *Mercury*'s extremist position made the newspaper appear, particularly when quoted in the North, as a kind of southern spokesman. There is no evidence to suggest, however, that the newspaper had a large circulation. Indeed, the number of subscribers a newspaper served was not as important as its position. So the *Mercury* took an extreme stand and was widely quoted North and South, as an authoritative extremist voice. Soon a counterbalance appeared in the North, and between this new journal and the older *Mercury*, it was plain that

their way to cool down the smoldering fire of sectional animosity was
to throw more buckets of kerosene on it. The northern upstart was
the antislavery *Liberator.* Notoriety was editor William Lloyd Garrison's watchword. From the safe distance of Boston, Garrison promised to match the fire-eating southerners blow for blow.

A zealot with the kind of reckless courage that invited personal
disaster, Garrison flung out his challenge on January 1, 1831. "I am
in earnest," the crusader announced, *"and I will be heard."* Seemingly indifferent to how slavery must end in the United States, Garrison cared only for its complete eradication. Garrison's timing appeared perfect if he intended to inflame the South, for Nat Turner's
insurrection came that same year and seemed to confirm the evil
tendencies of northern agitation. Virginia and other slave states
reacted to the Turner uprising by passing harsher laws for controlling the slave population. Editors and politicians readily laid much of
the blame for their troubles on the antislavery newspapers and societies that gained new strength from each report of slave hangings in
the insurrection aftermath. "In the process of time, one thing is certain," Garrison predicted. Either the southerners would "give up
their slaves or the Union. The root of bitterness between the North
and the South is slavery; and, until it be removed, there can be no
sympathy between them."

What happened, of course, was that the wild accusations of the
antislavery and secessionist editors only hastened a polarization of
sectional attitudes. The extremist newspapers, instead of creating
sympathy for their ideas at the other end of the Union, antagonized
moderates and outraged conservatives. The business community was
losing control, as it had during the days after the Boston Tea Party,
when extremists carried matters beyond paper protests. In Charleston, the *Courier's* moderate tone and Unionist leanings had the merchants' blessing, but 100 miles away it was the *Mercury* that men
quoted with a shrug at first—a nod later.

Logic dictated that Charleston would be the place where Garrison
drew the most blood with his *Liberator* and there it would be, as in

Stuart England, condemned for public burning. The Charleston postmaster confiscated copies of the *Liberator* and other abolitionist literature that came to the South Carolina port on the grounds that it tended to disturb the public peace. New England editors howled that freedom of the press was being trod underfoot, but Amos Kendall had moved into Jackson's official Cabinet as Postmaster General and appeals to him were fruitless. Instead, Kendall sympathized with the Charleston fanatics and urged the president to seek legislation legalizing this backhanded censorship. Jackson went along with Kendall's recommendation, but a Senate bill authorizing postmasters to refuse antislavery literature in any state where local laws forbade their circulation was narrowly defeated. It had been a close call, however, and the New York *Evening Post*, though pro-Jackson, was relieved. "If the Government once begins to discriminate as to what is orthodox and what heterodox in opinion, what is safe and what is unsafe in its tendency, farewell, a long farewell to our freedom," editor William Leggett declared.[13]

Although there is a tendency to assume that antislavery alarms and counterblows from slave states built up for thirty years into the Civil War crescendo, the fact is that much of the worst feelings were vented by public attacks and even outright murder during the 1830s. *Niles' Weekly Register* kept a running account of mob actions and abolitionist riots, and more were tabulated in this crimson decade than in the 1840s or 1850s. Consider the anxieties of southerners as they read Garrison's call to slaves to "Alarm and shock us by the recital of your sufferings, *inflicted by a nation* of PATRIOTS and CHRISTIANS! . . . Let a mighty vent be given to your groans, that our ears may convey to our sympathetic hearts, and that the swift winds of heaven may waft them up to Him who declares—*Vengeance is mine*—I will repay!" These sentences seemed to appeal for armed insurrections, the most feared of all the nightmares haunting southerners. "Give up thy hecatombs of sable victims, murdered as beasts are murdered," Garrison roared on, "and let their voiceless tongues find utterance, that they may cry audibly—'MURDER! REVENGE!' "

Even in Boston it became risky for Garrison to venture outside his office without protection. In 1835 a mob finally caught up with Garrison and he emerged from the fray shaken but more belligerent than ever. Abolitionist newspapers in Utica, New York, Lexington, Kentucky, and Philadelphia were either intimidated or burned-out during the decade, and the first act of the drama closed as Alton, Illinois, invoked lynch law in 1837. There, on the banks of the Mississippi, the Reverend Elijah P. Lovejoy saw his presses three times ruined by mobs but still persisted in publishing his antislavery *Observer*. While Lovejoy was readying his press for a fourth try a riot broke out and he was killed. The abolitionist newspapers were outraged and for a time other editors were inclined to view the murder as the natural outcome of bullheadedness. "Died Abner as a fool dieth," the *Boston Courier* commented in dismissing Lovejoy's death as predicted by biblical warnings against the good man who went about seeking trouble.

As the country read more about Lovejoy and his martyrdom, however, it became obvious that something other than a stubborn Presbyterian minister's death was involved. As with other editors, Joseph Buckingham of the *Courier* had second thoughts.

> The time was, but it seems to have gone by, when a man had a right to set up a press and print a newspaper, and when that right was secured to him by laws, which were amply sufficient for that purpose. . . . Now, he runs the hazard of being murdered, if he should dare to exercise a privilege thus guaranteed by the highest civil authority, if he should advance a sentiment, or advocate a doctrine that should not suit every ruffian or blackguard, who can throw a brickbat or pull a trigger.[14]

Boston's council rejected a petition calling for a public meeting for a Lovejoy memorial service as a tribute to one "who fell in defence of the freedom of the press." Buckingham branded the council's action and their "alleged reasons . . . *contemptible*." The shift of public opinion toward abolitionism was not as glacial as some suspected, but other editors would see their presses smashed and their lives jeopardized before it was safe to proclaim publicly that slavery was a national abomination.

To be sure, trouble was brewing in this sprawling, boisterous land. Yet the main business of most Americans remained in their fields and their kitchens. The breeding of better livestock and the canning of more succulent preserves occupied the time of far more men and women than did all the political rallies or the tracts of abolitionist writers. To guide men of the soil who still constituted the overwhelming majority of America's population John Skinner had started his *American Farmer* at Baltimore in 1818. Soon the Albany *Plough-Boy* and *New England Farmer* were in the field, and when Jackson won the presidency his victory was noted in the newly arrived Charleston *Southern Agriculturist*. Since most of America still traveled by saddle there was always time for earnest discussion of horseflesh. The *American Turf Register* thrived from 1829 until 1844, and the *Spirit of the Times* carried racing news as well as reports on the popular (but often undercover) sport of prizefighting.

Many editors regarded news from prize rings in England and America as taboo. Few newspapers failed to note, however, the annual story of the largest watermelon or squash grown in the vicinity, or to recognize the county's canning and quilting champions among busy ladies. The *American Agriculturist*, launched in 1842, was an aggressive journal that prodded farmers to experiment with crop rotation and to improve their herds by weeding out the poorest producers among their milch cows. The readership of these farm-oriented newspapers expanded steadily. The *Agriculturist* had a subscription list of 160,000 in the 1850s, and one experienced observer "set the weekly circulations of all the agricultural press at half a million, and its readers at three millions" in the post-Civil War era.[15]

The nation was growing more food and also producing more mouths to eat it. Surpluses of wheat, cotton, and tobacco went to Europe but the population of Indiana doubled and that of Illinois tripled in the 1830s, while similar gains were noted in the border states of

Kentucky and Tennessee. Virgin timber lands in 1810 were crossed by roads and fences by 1820. In the 1830s the best lands east of the Mississippi were under cultivation and young men were restlessly seeking opportunities similar to those enjoyed by earlier generations of homesteaders and speculators. The great United States Bank was dead and wildcat banks were issuing currency as fast as it could be printed, but at the lower end of the scale some Americans still waited behind bars because of imprisonment for debt. Out of the shambles of the old National Republican party the opposition to Jackson fashioned a makeshift alliance with dissenting anti-Masonic groups, states' rights factions, and a senatorial band "held together only through its detestation of the Old Hero." [16] By 1834 these disgruntled elements had joined forces to wreck Jackson and appeared on the New York City ballot as Whigs.

The new party found its strength in the same places the old Federalists had been strongest—in New England, in the cities where banking and mercantile connections called the tune, and in fringe areas where Henry Clay's old chant for an "American System" of protectionism and internal improvements still held a natural appeal. Much of the newspaper din raised during the later stages of Jackson's tenure in the White House was based on nothing more than Old Hickory's personality. The main issue seemed to be whether a man liked Jackson or hated him. Readers of *Niles' Weekly Register* were shocked when the abuse heaped on Jackson by Duff Green's *Telegraph* and other converted Whig newspapers was the prelude to a near tragedy. On January 29, 1835, as Jackson toured the Capitol, a demented painter tried to assassinate the president by aiming a pistol from only an arm's reach away. [17] The pistol misfired, as did a second weapon the would-be killer carried. Later, Niles interviewed the president and was told that more than five hundred threatening letters had been sent to the White House. Green passed the incident off as a farce dreamed up to make Jackson a hero—Whig newspapers exonerated themselves from any guilt in the proceedings by accepting Green's premise.

Jackson was tough, but he was old. The country was moving at a pace he no longer fully comprehended. His choice as a successor was a party warhorse with a different kind of style—Martin Van Buren of New York—whom the Whig press soon lampooned as the heir apparent to "King Andrew I." Other Whig editors called Van Buren "the Red Fox of Kinderhook" or "the Little Magician" and beseeched voters to go on a national hunting party that would run the tiny "pretender to the throne" to earth. Van Buren was as short (five feet, six inches) as Jackson was tall, and even this was made out by the Whigs as a campaign liability. Lacking a cohesive party structure and disdaining a party convention, the Whigs took off at once in all directions and ran four candidates including the popular westerner William H. Harrison, with predictable results. "Little Van" triumphed and a tired Jackson returned to his Hermitage.

Jackson was weary and the economy was shaky, but the country continued—temporarily—to go forward at full throttle. Speculation in western lands was all the rage, railroad stocks were moving much faster than the dozens of corporations formed to build them, and loose banking practices encouraged men who were less than prudent to believe that the 1836 crop failure was only a temporary setback. And in the cities, tradesmen were reading about a sensational murder case involving a wealthy New Yorker and a prostitute. Indeed, there was probably more local interest in the Robinson-Jewett murder trial than in what Van Buren intended to do about the Treasury surplus. The place to find out what was on people's minds, in 1836, was in the newfangled penny press. The New York *Sun*, which began life more as a meteor in 1833, had shaken staid city journalism to its foundation by suddenly elevating accidents and petty crime into the category of newsworthy events. Neither the country nor its newspapers would ever be the same, as editorial giants began grappling over copper coins. It was to be an era much occupied over metals and money. The penny press began while financiers were worrying about the soundness of the dollar, and in time the golden calf of circulation would be worshiped by both editors and bankers.

6

The One-Cent Miracle

The most startling innovation in American journalism occurred while Jackson was still in the White House. On any weekday morning prior to September 3, 1833, New York businessmen drank their coffee and puffed cigars while poring over one of the city's nine dull daily newspapers. Patiently they read turgid accounts of market news, long columns of advertising, and news reports similar in style and content to the journalism of earlier generations. But when they awoke on this day, a new sun shone in New York. Benjamin Day's four-page, one-penny *Sun* told a not too funny story about a duel-loving soldier, reported on a Vermont boy who whistled "with astonishing shrillness" in his sleep and nearly died from it, and carried a host of steamship company ads. Day's upstart newspaper ignored the business community and appealed to those citizens who never owned a share of stock or needed cargo space on a British freighter. It was a newspaper for the man who had a spare copper and a curiosity—idle curiosity—about what was happening in the world.

Day's skimpy news sheet filled with rather unimportant information was an instantaneous success. Not only was the *Sun* priced within everybody's reach, it was also as close as the corner lamppost, for Day used dozens of boys and girls as his sidewalk salesmen. A reader no longer needed to hire a delivery boy or make a personal visit to the newspaper office to pick up a copy. The price and the corner newsboy changed the face of American journalism. Thereafter, a low-cost newspaper was a fundamental part of the nation's daily life.

Before Day's experiment, New York daily newspapers sold for six cents and subscribers were expected to pay ten dollars a year (preferably in advance) for their solid but unexciting journals. This was a sophisticated readership, mainly interested in what was happening in the money market and on the economic front generally. Day ignored this small, prosperous audience. Instead he aimed his appeal at the average literate citizen—the man who read by daylight rather than beside a whale-oil lamp—by telling him that the most interesting happenings in New York were far from Wall Street's brokerage houses. This heretofore neglected city dweller was not eager to learn the price of canal shares or know the latest word from the Paris bourse while he drank his morning pint. Day's reader wanted to know more about other average New Yorkers who could not hold their pints and who paid fifty-cent fines in the heavily trafficked police court, or spent a night in jail after some humorous jargon was exchanged with a judge. This reader was eager to learn about the wife beater on Mott Street or the overpainted prostitute on Pell Street. There was a thrill in learning that the prostitute's boy friend, a pickpocket, had been arrested. The *Sun's* readers seemed delighted to find that petty thievery was a way of life in lower Manhattan's sooty slums.

Actually, Day had borrowed his style of reporting from a popular English daily and his method of sidewalk selling from the great London circulation departments. Day sold boys and girls his *Sun* for 67 cents cash per hundred copies or 75 cents for credit. He pretty much ignored politics and business—everything the staid dailies found worthwhile—and turned to crime, humorous anecdotes, and short accounts of fires, runaway moving vans, and lesser fare. As with all successful innovations, the *Sun* rose at a moment when the public was ready to break away from traditional ideas. In the heat of the 1832 presidential campaign, the suggestion that a newspaper with no political affiliation could succeed by selling for one cent would have been considered a madman's dream. Yet Day himself had no expectation of the success about to come his way or that within a year's time the *Sun* would sell 10,000 daily copies and have a dozen imitators.

The *Sun*'s entire operation was, at the outset, simplicity itself. Day followed the doctrine of contrary opinion to wealth by stressing nearly everything the regular dailies had overlooked. In Day's success story lay the seeds of a controversy that still rages. Is a newspaper bound to report insignificant news, or must readers depend on editors for some judgment and selectivity that will give the newspaper columns a fair perspective? Day's brand of journalism was meant to produce vicarious thrills, although the *Sun* pretentiously promised to report All the News of the Day. In fact, Day gave *Sun* readers a capsuled view of the city's daily panorama of life. Even so, it proved to be enough, for it satisfied the draymen and shopkeepers who were willing to spend a penny to keep up with the life and times of the U.S.A. in 1833. Day made no effort to separate the important from the trivial because he was a businessman with a product to sell and he had no desire to educate the public. Indeed, Day had no compunction about telling an occasional lie, if that was all that was needed to turn a profit. In the summer of 1835 the *Sun* ran a series of articles purportedly from the Edinburgh *Journal of Science* dealing with a new telescope that had discerned "a distinct view of objects in the moon." Each day exciting new discoveries were revealed, and other newspapers reprinted the information as highly authentic. A team of scientists from Yale University rushed from New Haven to examine the original articles, said to have come from the pen of Sir John Herschel, son of the discoverer of the planet Uranus.

All New York was titillated by the series, and *Sun* circulation rose to 19,000 copies. Each day brought new disclosures of rotund moon fish, batmen flying around the moon, and other wonders, but mean-

while the reporter who had created the hoax visited a New York saloon with a fellow reporter from the *Journal of Commerce*. The *Sun*
reporter, his tongue loosened by ardent spirits, talked freely. With
the next day's dawn, all New York knew that Sir John's discovery
was only a *Sun* reporter's fanciful flight in fiction. Instead of demanding the reporter's scalp, however, most readers took the incident in
good humor, although other New York newspapers tried to create a
boomerang reaction. Undaunted, Day merely banked his profits and
kept printing stories of wronged seamstresses and alcoholic hod carriers. By 1837, when a financial panic hit New York and frightened
Day into selling the *Sun*, it had made as much as $20,000 a year clear
profit. Intimidated by a libel judgment and crowded by competition,
Day decided to cash in on the *Sun*'s reputation.

Most of Day's imitators lacked his business acumen, but two other
New York-based newspapermen followed in his pathway to blaze
their own trails. James Gordon Bennett, a cross-eyed Scot with a
great sense of news values, gained courage from Day's success to try
what every reporter dreamed of—owning his own newspaper. The
price was still, in 1835, within reason. With $500 and sixteen years
of experience behind him, the forty-year-old Bennett became the sole
owner, editor, reporter, business manager, circulation chief, and
prime asset of the New York *Herald*.

Success for Bennett was not immediate. Two previous attempts at
newspaper ownership had humbled without defeating him. He even
asked a local printer, Horace Greeley, to help as a partner in a journalism endeavor, but when Greeley turned Bennett down he decided
to go it alone. The *Herald* was a success by the end of its first week of
existence. Bennett's long apprenticeship as a reporter in Charleston
and New York gave his writing a distinctive flavor. To this he added
a special expertise in financial reporting that had been the envy of
other reporters when Bennett worked on the *Courier and Enquirer*.
Now his own boss, Bennett retained his Wall Street column but
added a variety of local news, including a gossipy theatrical section.
Moreover, Bennett made it clear that he was not espousing any polit-

ical cause, although he did not renounce the privilege of commenting on party affairs.

Bennett had a Scotsman's frugality—working from a desk made out of barrels and planks—yet he gave the *Herald* a flair the *Sun* had lacked. He was not afraid to spend money for reporters and recognized news as a commodity with a marketable price. When a fire burned out his printing plant, Bennett exulted that all he had lost was some bad poetry and subscription lists. Back the *Herald* bounced for a climbing readership that reached 15,000 during the summer of 1836. As the profits poured in, Bennett felt a surge of power and decided he was not spending a twenty-hour workday in vain. He proclaimed the death knell of literature, religion, and the theater. "A newspaper can send more souls to Heaven, and save more from Hell, than all the churches and chapels in New York—besides making money at the same time," Bennett crowed, then set out to prove he was right. The Robinson-Jewett murder trial certainly had the casting for a morality play when a young clerk was accused of murdering a pretty streetwalker. Bennett spared no details in the absorbing courtroom, decided Robinson was not guilty, and when the jury acquitted him the *Herald* outstripped all opponents in praise of justice. "Bennett was overjoyed," Mott chronicled, "not only at the result of the trial but at its effect on his circulation, which had tripled during the run of the story." [1] Business was so good Bennett doubled the price of the *Herald*. The readers were too loyal to balk at such effrontery, especially when prosperity permitted Bennett to increase his news coverage with a Washington bureau and flotilla of news boats for hastening European dispatches to the *Herald* pier.

Bennett's penchant for overplaying stories about love nests and eternal triangles plus his egocentrism took their toll, however. In time other New York editors banded with ministers, financiers, and some of the wealthier families that resented the *Herald*'s reporting of social functions and weddings in a crusade to bring Bennett down. His old employers on the *Courier and Enquirer* now spoke of Bennett as a newspaper man afflicted with "moral leprosy" and called for an economic boycott of the *Herald*. Bennett pretended not to be stung by a carefully planned series of attacks, but he was somewhat humbled as his circulation lists began to shrink while a host of preachers used their Sunday platforms to denounce Bennett for his ribaldry and tastelessness. They spoke of their "moral war" on the *Herald* until the chant spread to other major cities on the Atlantic seaboard, carrying with their message a certain notoriety that hurt Bennett far more than he ever cared to acknowledge. In time, Bennett was chastened by the experience and the *Herlad* columns gave less and less space to sensational stories about white slave rings and wayward women.

Innovation invariably brings imitation, so that after Bennett improved on Day's *Sun* it was certain that the *Herald* would have its own admirers. In Philadelphia and Baltimore three venturous printers combined their talents and credit to start the *Public Ledger* and *Sun* as penny newspapers. William Swain took over control of the Philadelphia operation and showed an admiration for Bennett's policies in the way he conducted the *Ledger*. His partner, Arunah S. Abell, used the same guidelines to make the Baltimore *Sun* as successful as its New York namesake and a pacesetter in its coverage of Washington news. With a third partner in Philadelphia, the trio constantly improved their presses, spent large sums for special expresses, and helped increase competition for news by stressing the freshness of their outstanding reporting. Swain was one of the incorporators of the Magnetic Telegraph Company and amassed a fortune from his one-cent newspaper, as did Abell. Their business acumen gave the *Ledger-Sun* alliance a firmness that lasted until the Great Depression, when the *Ledger* merged with the rival *Inquirer* but the *Sun* managed to stay aloof and solvent through those gloomy days.

Other penny newspapers were founded in Boston, Philadelphia, and New York, but usually they were short-lived ventures because of their shoddiness and lack of enterprise. One of the first penny-press casualties had been the New York *Morning Post*, a newspaper actually started ahead of the *Sun* but plagued by bad luck, and a short line of credit. H. D. Shepard was the *Post* editor, in partnership with a round-faced New Englander who squinted painfully as he set agate type to help defray the costs of their journalistic waif. Heavy snows had kept potential readers indoors in January 1833 so that newsboys had few takers for their two-penny *Post*, and not many more when Shepard and partner Greeley desperately cut the price to a penny. The *Post* went to oblivion, but Greeley had caught the fever and would be back. Thus the saga of America's greatest editor began during a bleak New York winter. Greeley fought the cold, poverty, and a wretched nearsightedness with a stubborn faith in his own abilities and the Whig party. Greeley's faith in himself was justified, but it was his political tie that gave him the chance of a lifetime that altered the course of his future.

Greeley had trudged into New York in 1831 with sore feet, an aching head, $10 in his pocket, "and a decent knowledge of so much of the art of printing as a boy will usually learn in the office of a country newspaper." [2] He was a high-strung, self-educated do-gooder with a country bumpkin's attachment to the Whig party born out of his Vermont background. Greeley had first known the smell of printer's ink as a gangling lad of fifteen. At twenty he ventured forth from the Green Mountains to the fleshpots of New York and was struggling for recognition when the *Morning Post* died aborning. His Whig connections gained him a printing job with the state lottery but Greeley yearned for more than a printer's life. Starting with a new partner and great faith, Greeley later recalled that the *New Yorker* started in a cubbyhole at 20 Nassau Street in March 1834, "with scarcely a dozen subscribers." Editor Greeley was still setting type, writing editorials, and enjoying the excitement of seeing the struggling newspaper gain more readers on the weekly's "paid" list. Bennett's daily *Herald* made its debut and took the city by surprise, but Greeley's weekly *New Yorker* had no startling debut. Yet somehow it kept coming out on schedule despite Greeley's partner's waywardness, until almost 9,000 copies were needed for each Saturday morning's delivery. He changed partners but found the new one no more useful. Flushed with small success, he hired Park Benjamin as literary editor and another Vermonter, Henry J. Raymond, as a reporter. Years later, after he had founded the *New York Times*, Raymond remembered those days on the *New Yorker* as valuable training. Amidst the screeching of the penny-press rivals, the *New Yorker*'s "calm, dispassionate character," Raymond recalled, "and the accuracy of its statements, won for Mr. Greeley a degree of public confidence sufficient to set up half a dozen men in any business where confidence was the main thing required." Besides being admired, the *New Yorker* was even making a tidy profit.

Greeley was then hit hard by the kind of a one-two punch that can ruin a man. His marriage in early 1836 soon turned into a heartbreaking domestic disaster which he learned to live with, but the panic of 1837 was more merciless. Greeley owned a box full of bad debts that he had once thought worth $8,000. Unemployment and poverty spread fast through the city, forcing Greeley to conclude that a dreadful winter lay in store. Editorially he advised the jobless of New York: "Fly—scatter through the land—go to the Great West. . . . The times are out of joint. . . . Let all who can, betake themselves to the country." It was the first Greeleyism of that genre that would someday be the saddened editor's trademark, "Go West, young man, go west!" This "first pronouncement of that summons . . . was written in sheer panic." [3]

Fortuitous circumstances stepped in when Greeley was almost bankrupt. Thurlow Weed, the rising Albany Whig majordomo, had heard of Greeley and was looking for an editor for a campaign weekly. He struck a bargain with Greeley, promising a salary of $1,000 for a year's part-time work in Albany and enough days left to keep the *New Yorker* going. Greeley lunged at the offer, moved to Albany, and started the *Jeffersonian* for the New York State Whig Committee. Fifteen thousand subscriptions, at fifty cents a crack, gave Greeley an appreciative audience. The Albany base also brought Greeley in contact with a man who shared his political ambitions—William H. Seward. Both Seward and Greeley became

Weed's protégés as the hard-driving Weed sought state printing contracts and other plums. Greeley enjoyed himself enormously as he hobnobbed with other enthusiastic Whigs in the capital, hurried to New York to publish his other weekly, and then dashed back to Albany for party strategy sessions. Weed was rewarded for his labors when Seward was swept into power as the governor-elect. When the loaves and fishes went out, however, Greeley was not among the blessed receivers. He chalked up one mark against Weed, but hoped the oversight would not be repeated.

A real taste of power was promised to Greeley when Weed again tapped him for the editorship of the *Log Cabin* in May 1840. Although this was the first political campaign in which a presidential aspirant actually went out on the hustings, newspaper columns filled with panegyrics and promises remained the time-honored method of drumming up enthusiasm. Greeley's task was formidable. He had the job of making a nondescript western general into the most talked-about man in America. In the process of making the nation think of "Tippecanoe and Tyler too" Greeley became something of a public figure himself. But he was still a silent partner in the political concern of Weed & Seward, although as a happy Whig warrior Greeley expected his days of privation and want were nearing an end. "I tried to make *The Log-Cabin* as effective as I could," Greeley reminisced, "with wood engravings of General Harrison's battle-scenes, music, &c., and to render it a model of its kind." [4] Greeley's success was beyond his dreams as the circulation of the *Log Cabin* rose to 80,000 copies each week, though Greeley claimed the newspaper's income barely met the printer's bill. No doubt Greeley was instrumental in securing Harrison's victory, but more disappointment was in store, for in the afterglow of victory Greeley's services were forgotten. "I doubt that General Harrison ever heard my name," Greeley recalled with some bitterness.

President Harrison died after only a month in office, with no chance to repay Greeley even if he had heard of the hard-working editor. On the day Harrison was buried, Greeley was to recall, "a leaden, funereal morning, the most inhospitable of the year, I issued the first number of THE NEW YORK TRIBUNE." Greeley remembered that he started the *Tribune* because New York needed "a journal removed alike from servile partisanship on the one hand and from gagged, mincing neutrality on the other." Several Whig supporters promised start-up loans to Greeley, but only one actually advanced any cash. With this borrowed $1,000 Greeley began publishing the *Tribune.* For the next thirty years Greeley was so thoroughly identified with the newspaper that while other editor-publishers were known as Mr. Bennett of the *Herald* or Mr. Raymond of the *Times* it was assuredly "Mr. Greeley's *Tribune.*"

Greeley's pungent paragraphs, touching a variety of interests that ranged from the virtues of unbleached flour to the inadequacies of President Tyler, soon gave the *Tribune* a daily circulation of 11,000 copies. At last, Greeley had found a way to mix politics and profit. His great coup, however, was in the weekly edition. It was started in the fall of 1841 and relentlessly promoted through premiums and discounts until it reached more than 200,000 homes, with the largest bundles bound for New England farmers and midwestern homesteads. Luckily, Greeley took Thomas McElrath into the enterprise as a partner-business manager. A careless bookkeeper himself, Greeley turned all matters of finance over to McElrath. Freed from worry, in that area Greeley proceeded to promote a series of causes that created no friends in the Whig party but spread his personal appeal. No reform scheme, however eccentric, seemed to pass him unnoticed. Greeley publicly endorsed Fourierism, Prohibition, the Brook Farm community, and vegetarianism. In time the list of *Tribune* staff writers read like a roll call of giants: Carl Schurz, Whitelaw Reid, Charles Dana, Henry James, William Dean Howells, and Margaret Fuller all took paychecks from "Uncle Horace." Abroad, Greeley signed Karl Marx as his London correspondent. When the Whig party collapsed it was Greeley who helped pull its successor, the new Republican party, together as a national organization. Yet politics only frustrated Greeley as he gained more power. His brief term in Congress (an overdue present from Weed) turned into a minor disaster as he needled other members of the House of Representatives for their petty expense accounts and considered introducing a bill which would have changed the country's name to the United States of Columbia. He wanted the governor's job in New York, but practical politicians would have none of Greeley's antibooze platform and he was denied the nomination at the state convention in Saratoga. Greeley thought Weed owed him that honor and never forgot the insult. The Greeley-Seward-Weed alliance fell in a shambles.

Mild-mannered though he was, Greeley took to carrying a pistol during his Capitol Hill days after a fellow congressman tried to knock him down. His hostility toward slavery was by then well known, and Greeley believed that on the last day of the session he could not have walked through "the Democratic side of the House at night . . . without being assaulted; and, had I resisted [would have been] beaten within an inch of my life, if not killed outright." [5]

Greeley may have overdramatized his danger, but a public beating was an occupational hazard of journalism until buggy whips became passé. Colonel Webb of the *Courier and Enquirer* was noted for his temper and stout cane, which he occasionally brought down on the head of a rival editor. Webb was verbally assaulted by Representative Cilley of Maine and quickly challenged the lawmaker to a duel. Cilley ignored Webb's card but agreed to meet Webb's intended second, and was killed. Webb successfully enticed Congressman Marshall of Kentucky into a gun battle. Arrested for breaking a state antidueling law, Webb was pardoned before a two-year sentence could be imposed.

Most of the bloody gunplay came among southern editors.* James Hagan, the first editor of the Vicksburg, Mississippi, *Sentinel*, fought

---

* Marryat inaccurately observed that most duels in America arose "principally from defamation. The law gives no redress, and there is no other way of checking slander than [by] calling the parties to account for it" (*A Diary in America*, 414).

several bloody duels in 1837 and 1838 with the local gentry, including his rival who edited the Vicksburg *Whig*. Hagan was finally shot down in cold blood on a Vicksburg street after his editorials riled political opponents beyond endurance. His successor, James Ryan, killed a critic of the *Sentinel* a year later. The bellicose *Sentinel* seemed to thrive on hot words and gunpowder, but soon Ryan was mortally wounded by another Vicksburg newspaper editor who took exception to Ryan's outspoken views on Whig principles and those who adhered to them. Walter Hickey followed Ryan and was soon drawing a bead on his editorial opponent through a gunsight. Wounded in this battle, Hickey later died in a Texas shootout. At least one more *Sentinel* editor was shot down in the Vicksburg streets.[6] In neighboring Louisiana the Baton Rouge *Gazette* editor offended a congressman in 1843, and was challenged by the enraged politician. After the fourth round of exchanged gunfire, the duel ended with a permanent vacancy on the *Gazette* staff.

The bloody roll is long and reveals the polarized conduct of the southern editors who held their personal honor indistinguishable from their journalistic endeavors. The Richmond *Enquirer* editor used a sword and pistol to finish his rival from the *Whig*, while the Richmond *Southern Opinion* editor was killed by a sniper who was later acquitted of a murder charge. One would think that after the Civil War enough blood had been needlessly spilled, but the edtior of the Warrenton, Georgia, *Clipper* was assassinated in 1869 after printing a heated column which criticized a local lodge. His assailant was promptly arrested and later lynched by a mob of Ku Klux Klansmen who forced the gunman's wife and children to witness the tragedy.

Meanwhile, mob violence was a constant threat in communities where tension over abolitionism existed. Contrary to common belief, it was usually the leading men in the community who led these attacks rather than the town ruffians.[7] "A very large and respectable meeting of the citizens of Cincinnati" in July 1836 notified James G. Birney that his antislavery *Philanthropist* was unwelcome. "We will use all lawful means to discountenance and suppress every publication in this city which advocates the modern doctrines of abolition-ism," they warned. When Birney persisted, a mob soon gathered at his newspaper office, "scattered the type into the streets, tore down the presses, and completely dismantled the office." The rioters then paraded through the town and at midnight, after a speech "by the Mayor, who had been a silent spectator of the destruction of the printing office," dispersed.

The hysteria spread to areas where once calm discussion of slave manumission and African colonizing had been possible. In Virginia an 1836 statute was enacted "to suppress the circulation of incendiary publications," and included in its penalties the public burning of any "book, pamphlet, or other writing . . . [published] to aid the pur-poses of the abolitionists or anti-slavery societies." By 1848 the Old Dominion had further evidence of repressive tendencies when a bill became law which promised punishment for "Any free person who shall write, print, or cause to be written or printed, any book, pamph-let, or other writing, with intent to advise or incite persons of col-our within this commonwealth to rebel or make insurrection." Post-masters who delivered any antislavery newspaper or pamphlet were to be fined not more than $200 and could be "dealt with according to law." Moderate voices in the South seemed muted as the Charleston *Mercury* increased the tempo of its attacks on abolitionism and cre-ated a general impression that the North as a section favored aboli-tion, which was far from the case.[8] State legislatures in the South branded Garrison an outlaw, and to display the *Liberator* in public below the Potomac was to risk great harm, if not death.

Still, some men persisted in publishing antislavery newspapers in the South, facing danger each day as though on a battlefield. William S. Bailey learned that his Newport, Kentucky, *Daily News* displeased "the leading men of Newport" who decided an abolitionist journal "was not wanted there." He found it impossible to keep printers be-cause Newport business men used John Barleycorn and other devices to keep the presses idle. The adamant Bailey then taught his six chil-dren and wife how to set type and run the press, but a midnight fire burned out the plant along with the Bailey family's clothing and bedding. A proslavery newspaper was then enticed to come to Newport, but Bailey raised $517 from friends, borrowed $1,500 more, and reopened the *News*. "My notes found their way into the hands of my opponents," Bailey recorded, and he was sued for libel by the county sheriff. One opponent gave up the fight, only to be replaced by the proslavery *Star*, which in turn gave way to the *Democratic Union*, the *Roll*, the *Garland*, and the *American Sentinel*. Bailey and his family persisted, while their opposition slowly faded. After six years on the antislavery firing line, in the most unlikely place for success, Bailey and his brood had 2,800 weekly subscribers and sold 500 daily issues. Although he set his personal loss at $17,500, a concluding sentence of Bailey's report told the whole story. "Our own family is giving from fifty to sixty dollars a week, in labour, to the cause of freedom in the United States." [9]

Bailey was regarded by the proslavery faction, of course, as a renegade fanatic. Some of the most vigorous opponents of abolitionist editors were northerners who saw that the slavery issue was hurting business. Bennett probably represented a consensus of the New York mercantile community when he denounced antislavery societies and their newspapers. "That half-a-dozen madmen should manufacture opinion for the whole community, is not to be tolerated," Bennett insisted, and there must have been plenty of nods from cotton brokers, ship owners, and mill operators who could agree that for once Bennett was right.[10] In the Middle West there was a similar distrust of what the abolitionist represented. The editor of the La Porte, Indiana, *Herald* announced early in 1840 that he did "not wish to have a single abolition[ist] subscriber" on his rolls. Editor Wilbur F. Storey regarded antislavery agitators as indolent pests who "travelled about the country . . . sponging wherever they go."

Among the motley crew of editors with antislavery leanings there was a most strange bedfellow—Mordecai Noah. Almost forgotten in the twentieth century, Noah's name was often mentioned by foreign visitors as one of the nation's outstanding editors between 1820 and

1850. Noah launched the New York *Courier* in 1826 and his pungent pro-Jackson editorials there and his later influence with *Noah's Weekly Messenger* (12,000 circulation) have been obscured by historians more intrigued with his visionary scheme for a Jewish colony in the vicinity of Niagara Falls than with Noah's journalistic career.[11] Noah used his editorial chair as a pulpit from which to denigrate slavery, to preach his newspaper sermons favoring universal suffrage for whites, and to demand the abandonment of the compulsory militia laws. A handsome, energetic man, Noah knew most of the great men over a long stretch of our early history, ranging from Thomas Paine to James K. Polk, and his acute observations were read by an influential national public. He joined with his peers in exercising a vindictive judgment on issues and office seekers, and probably reflected more opinions than he formed. He despised slavery while loathing abolitionists, which posture placed him in the company of that editor-merchant class that preferred to believe that slavery could wither away quietly rather than die of a sudden, noisy attack.

No aspect of slavery seemed as unsavory as the auction block, where black families were split asunder by the thump of an auctioneer's hammer. During the 1844 presidential contest the Whigs were prepared to broadcast a spurious story that damaged the candidacy of Democrat James K. Polk of Tennessee. A purported travel account first appeared in the Ithaca, New York, *Chronicle* with details on a slave auction in a southern city. "Forty-three of these unfortunate beings had been purchased, I am informed, of the Hon. J. K. Polk, the present speaker of the House of Representatives, the marks of the branding iron, with the initials of his name, on their shoulders." Weed reprinted this Whig-inspired report in his Albany *Evening Journal* and some damage was done before the Democratic Albany *Argus* exposed the "travel account" as a Whig hoax. Polk went on to win, nonetheless, and he took office while news columns bulged with reports on the Oregon boundary dispute with the British and the equally explosive issue of Texas annexation.

Inevitably, the Texas question began separating editors and their newspapers into polarized camps. Texas, settled after 1821 by bands of Americans with an initial blessing from Mexican authorities, had warred with Santa Anna's legions and achieved independence by 1836. Several efforts to bring Texas into the Union were turned back by northern congressmen and Whig editors bellowed that Texas was coveted by the South as a new channel for the expansion of slavery. After Texas was annexed by a joint resolution in 1845, Democratic editors took a bellicose stance toward Mexican border guards. Northern editors, however, rattled sabers when it came to the Oregon boundary question, and they seemed willing enough to risk a war with England. General Zachary Taylor helped clear the Texas air by moving an army of occupation into the disputed Texas boundary country. An exchange of shots with Mexican troops soon reverberated in Washington, and in 1846 war was formally declared. Polk kept the Oregon problem on the back burner for a while, but finally accepted a compromise that kept peace on the Canadian border and left the army free to concentrate on Mexico's former provinces in California and Texas.

In an atmosphere of mounting tension a technological breakthrough electrified the nation when Morse demonstrated his magnetic telegraph. The first telegraph line stretched from the capital to Baltimore, and in May 1844 the Baltimore *Patriot* printed the first news dispatch ever carried by the magic medium. It was a two-line announcement that full debate on the Oregon boundary problem had been thwarted by a congressional majority. Regular wire service between the capital and Baltimore, New York, and Philadelphia was commonplace by 1847. Telegraph lines paralleled the railroads that were being pushed through mountains and across prairies at a breakneck pace.

The electric miracle brought news faster but robbed the recipients of the drama provided by man's race against distance. A veteran New York editor recalled that when the first rail lines stretched from New York to Boston "the [Providence] Journal regularly expressed the New York morning papers from Danielsonville, and at first people would visit the office to see the marvel of a New York Paper in Providence the [same] day that it was printed." [12] The rapid extension of telegraph lines ended this daily race against time, but some New Englanders wondered if it was a salutary development. When Thoreau pondered the efforts to link the Union in instantaneous telegraphic communication, the Walden Pond philosopher suggested that perhaps citizens living 2,500 miles apart had nothing to say to each other. Most Americans were not so discerning, however, as speed was equated with progress on the American scale of values.

Speed had rarely seemed a vital factor in journalism as generation after generation of printers and editors leisurely clipped their exchanges and gathered reports. The industrial revolution marshaled in the railroad and steam-powered boats which greatly increased the tempo of life in America as well as any other culture it touched. Telegraph tolls were high, but in the quest for news ahead of competitors the New York dailies spent thousands of dollars until it became obvious that cooperative use of the new invention would save money and still bring news from any eastern railhead in a matter of minutes. Thus the *Herald, Tribune, Sun, Journal of Commerce*, and other leading newspapers stopped trying to outreach each other and established the Associated Press of New York, in 1848, with arrangements to send foreign dispatches on to Baltimore and Philadelphia. The era when newspapers owned their own fleet of news boats, kept homing pigeons, and devised a semaphore system to score news beats was about to close. Thenceforth, the newspaper that would outstrip competitors had to have a substantial amount of cash or good line of bank credit to pay for more presses, staggering wire tolls, and a work force of hundreds of printers, pressmen, reporters, telegraphers, teamsters, clerks, engravers, and editors. In the large cities, journalism had become something more than a service to readers and advertisers. Journalism was the dominant ally in the business community alliance where service was secondary to profits.

Like all alliances, the one binding merchants and publishers had its weakness. Although the time when businessmen decided their woes were attributable to newspaper reports cannot be fixed with certainty, the propensity of merchants to blame journalism for hard times was established by the 1850s. When the New York branch of the Ohio Life Insurance Company suspended payments in August, 1857, Bennett's *Herald* foresaw a general financial crisis. Then the predicted panic struck the money market, whereupon *Hunt's Merchants' Magazine* turned on brother journalists as the chief malefactors because newspapers had spread reports of financial ruin via the telegraph—"a still novel instrument . . . with which sensational rumors and alarms were spread [by] newspapers greedy for increased circulation." Thus have newspapers often been scapegoats for catastrophes, financial and social, which in their sweep have confused those citizens in search of simplistic cause-and-effect relationships.

Late in 1846 the *National Intelligencer* proclaimed that Americans were "the most enlightened people under the sun" on the basis of raw statistics. The nation had 19 million people and 1,250 newspapers of all varieties, only two less than the combined journalism of Western Europe. Moreover, America's newspapers were still printed on rag paper which, unlike modern wood-pulp newsprint, does not soon turn yellow or brittle. Early in the nineteenth century American paper mills ended the printer's dependence on European finished sheets, but where would the rags be found to keep them supplied? The answer, in large part, came from Europe as thousands upon thousands of bales of rags were shipped to eastern port cities from Genoa and Brest. Linen shirts from a Roman back would eventually help feed the hungry maw of American journalism. Paper came from a New England mill, ran through a rotary press at the lightning-like pace of 20,000 sheets an hour, and came to rest on a Philadelphia breakfast table for a lawyer or a drayman. Whichever, they both paid the same two cents for the newspaper that would in turn, after many readings, line the drawers of an armoire or be used to make sleeve patterns. There were many uses for a rag-content newspaper besides being read.

Most Americans devoured their newspaper with an insatiable

reading appetite. Technological advances, such as the ingenious rotating cylinder with the type locked in place with V-shaped column rules, permitted the newspapers to keep up with the demand. The output of these presses was increased by adding more cylinders, while the massive three-story machine was driven by steam-engine power. Two cents still bought an eight-page city daily, and for all his paper bills and staff salaries Bennett was sending $1,000 a week to the bank in clear profit. No wonder every stargazing reporter dreamed of being another Bennett, and success brought its band of imitators who tried to turn their newspapers into a carbon copy of the *Herald* in format, style, price, circulation, advertising, and profits. Few made the grade.

Bennett outstripped all competitors with the coming of the Mexican War, when the telegraph lines were still scarce beyond key southern points. The war was essentially a southern war, with most of the volunteers and dedicated officers coming from the South, a point not lost on northerners who deplored the expedition as a bully-picked fight to extend slavery. Greeley called Polk "the Father of Lies" who pretended "we are a meek, unoffending, ill-used people, and that Mexico has killed, cuffed, and grossly imposed [war] upon us." The fact was, Greeley went on, that "the whole world knows . . . that it is Mexico which has been robbed and imposed upon, and that our people are the robbers."

The *Herald* editor thought Greeley's editorials were nearly traitorous, but he was more concerned with facts than opinion himself and when it came to gathering news, Bennett never recoiled from the size of a telegraph bill or reporter's salary. Thus Bennett had a newsman's sense of urgency and an open-fisted entrepreneur's desire to beat the opposition with the freshest battlefield reports, casualty lists, or campaign dispatches filed from the armies of Scott and Taylor. If it meant hiring two dozen express riders and four dozen fast horses to bring the news from New Orleans to a southern telegraph point, Bennett gladly paid the price. It was a costly and cumbersome procedure, but city dwellers along the Atlantic seaboard were swept up in the excitement of a distant war and were eager for word from the conquering armies. That a thrilling dispatch might have been written ten to fourteen days before it reached New York did not seem to matter.

The American army pushed toward Mexico City by overcoming deadly attacks of measles and Mexican regulars or guerillas. Whig editors in the North clamored for an early end to hostilities—or "Polk's War," as they called it. Young men were told to avoid the recruiting depots, and a zealous Ohio newspaperman complained of the wrongs being inflicted on the Mexicans until he beseeched an avenging Providence to send American troops to "hospitable Mexican graves." Greeley did not approve of the war, but he did not lose himself in antiwar hysteria for a good reason. He was off to Albany, or checking the progress of Brook Farm, or trimming Margaret Fuller's paragraphs—more interested in helping promote the National Society of Opponents to the Death Penalty than in reporting the carnage at Cerro Gordo. What distressed Greeley about the war was the insistence of his fellow editors that a patriotic publisher could not criticize the war. " 'Our Country, Right or Wrong,' is a maxim as foolish as Heaven-daring," Greeley fumed. "If your country be wrong . . . it is madness, it is idiocy, to wish or struggle for her success in the wrong; for such success can only be more calamitous than failure, since it increases our Nation's guilt." [13]

As a good Whig, Greeley took pains to denounce the war as "unjust and rapacious . . . a curse and a source of infinite calamities," but as a political dabbler Greeley also was afraid that a Whig war hero might emerge as the party's 1848 presidential candidate. "If we nominate Taylor, we may elect him, but we [will] destroy the Whig party," he predicted.

To some editors the next election was far more important than the war, but to others the war itself was a bold opportunity for innovations in news reporting. George Wilkins Kendall led a pack of New Orleans newsmen who used the Crescent City as a jumping-off place for the battlefields. A resourceful reporter, Kendall filed eyewitness accounts that made sensational reading in the New Orleans *Picayune*. Kendall swashbuckled his way into Mexico with the American army and sent back a stream of stories that rang with authenticity, all the more so when Kendall was wounded himself in the final foray near Mexico City. There is an unproved story that Kendall spent $5,000 for a chartered steamboat that was hired to carry his dispatch from Vera Cruz to New Orleans. True or not, other anecdotes about Kendall established his reputation as the first of a new breed of reporter—the "war correspondent" who would travel with the armies, design his own uniform, and carry a privileged status as a noncombatant. Thereafter, every American war until the Vietnam struggle had its own special war reporter who was clearly distinguished by his compassionate concern for American troops, personal bravery, and sensitivity for what "the folks back home" wanted to know.* What these reporters gave the news was an element since identified as the human-interest side of history. Readers became vicarious participants in battles as war correspondents related incidents in personal terms, as this dispatch (probably from Kendall) printed in the Louisville *Courier* indicated:

> While I was stationed with our left wing . . . I saw a Mexican woman busily engaged in carrying bread and water to the wounded men of both armies. I saw this ministering angel raise the head of a wounded man, give him water and food, and then carefully bind up his wound with a handkerchief which she took from her own head. . . . As she was returning on her mission of mercy, to comfort other wounded persons, I heard the report of a gun, and saw the poor innocent creature fall dead! I think it was an accidental shot that struck her. . . . It made me sick at heart, and, turning from the scene, I involuntarily raised my eyes toward heaven, and thought, great God! and *is this war?*

* Admittedly somewhat arbitrary, the list of most-famous correspondents would include Charles Carleton Coffin (Civil War), Richard Harding Davis (Spanish-American War), Floyd Gibbons (World War I), and Ernie Pyle (World War II).

Such reports took much of the glamour out of the war and reinforced Whig feelings that it had been provoked for ulterior motives. The trenchant pen of James Russell Lowell was enlisted by the *Boston Courier* to discredit the war as a filibustering opportunity for slaveholders. Writing under the pseudonym of "Hosea Biglow," Lowell's bitter verse castigated Polk's brand of patriotism.

> They jest want this Californy
> So's to lug new slave states in
> To abuse ye, an' to scorn ye,
> An' to plunder ye like sin.

Lowell's identity became known, of course, and his *Biglow Papers* long stood as one of the most literary antiwar protests ever printed by the American press. Kendall's name never became as familiar, but he was personally credited with sending dispatches—in itself a considerable breakthrough. In time the by-line (i.e., "By George W. Kendall") became a coveted portion of a reporter's compensation—more noticed among other reporters than by the reading public, but recognition nonetheless.

When the news of Taylor's victory over Santa Anna at Buena Vista reached American newsrooms, a boom for "Our Zack" took shape in the columns of the Boston *Sentinel* and other Whig journals. Taylor's background as a native Virginian and slaveholder embarrassed some Whigs (including Greeley), but the office-poor party needed a winner. More than one editor sensed that the perennial candidate, seventy-one-year-old Henry Clay, had lost his voter appeal. Taylor seemed more glamorous than General Winfield Scott, who appeared somewhat pompous, as his nickname, "Old Fuss and Feathers," indicated. Several diehard Whig editors, including Greeley, tried to prop up the Clay candidacy for one more go at the White House. It is a tribute to Greeley's power that they came within a whisker of nominating the persistent Kentuckian on the first convention ballot. Thereafter, Clay's strength ebbed and finally Greeley had to take the military man he had long opposed in party councils.

Although Greeley was personally disappointed, the New York *Tribune* reported Taylor's nomination with lavish superlatives. In private, Greeley thought the country was in a bad way. "The War was a bad business," he soon surmised, "[and] the peace is little better." [14] The surly editor tended, as did all the Whig newspapermen, to overlook the spoils of victory. After some grumbling, they took a second look and grudgingly found certain blessings had resulted from "Mr. Polk's War." California was no longer a remote Mexican province—it was now a remote American outpost. News that would excite thousands trickled eastward from the south fork of the American River. The first report appeared in the Sacramento *Californian* on March 15, 1848. It took months for the story to wind its way across the deserts, prairies, or oceans, but the spell cast by the news far outdistanced anything produced by the Cass-Taylor presidential contest. There was a singsong magic in the headline:

GOLD MINE FOUND

In the newly made raceway of the sawmill recently erected by Captain Sutter on the American fork gold has been found in considerable quantities. One person brought thirty dollars' worth to New Helvetia, gathered there in a short time.

Soon California's other newspaper, the Monterey *California Star*, carried the same report. By May 29 the *Californian* had more details which it shared with the world: "The whole country from San Francisco to Los Angeles, and from the seashore to the base of the Sierra Nevada, resounds to the sordid cry of gold! GOLD! GOLD!! while the field is left half planted, the house half built, and everything neglected but the manufacture of shovels and pickaxes." Printers along with other gold seekers deserted their job cases as the word spread until it crashed into newsrooms off Broadway and adjacent to Pennsylvania Avenue.

The man who was known to pay the most for fresh news was

among the first in New York to hear about the gold strike in California. James Gordon Bennett received early word from the California diggings because he paid the Monterey consul to serve as a *Herald* correspondent. Skeptical because of a recent false report of gold discoveries in the South, Bennett held back Thomas Larkin's first message, but when more stories confirmed the consul's dispatch and a sample of gold dust arrived in the *Herald* office, Bennett called an assayer. The pinch of dust was judged to be "$2\frac{1}{2}$ carats fine," comparable to "the quality of English sovereigns or American eagles, and is almost ready to go to the Mint." A chastened Bennett ordered Larkin's stories printed. By the day's end, visions of wealth danced before the eyes of *Herald* readers.

America's western surge would become the great news story of 1849. Greeley, Bennett, and other great eastern editors regarded the gold rush as possibly the most exciting news of the century. Besides the intrinsic merit of the gold discovery in faraway California, the bulletin from Sutter's Mill had another element of greatness about it. The gold-rush fever would help take the country's mind off the slavery question.

7

A Guilty Generation

For sheer stubbornness and orneriness the American people between 1845 and 1865 stand as a frightening example of the misery a nation can visit upon itself. The bellicose propensity of many editors was noted earlier. The editors' volatile tempers and eagerness for horsewhipping and street-corner gunplay led to dramatic incidents with a touch of insanity about them. But a search of the files of the New York *Herald*, Washington *Globe*, Louisville *Journal*, or Richmond *Enquirer* for the period reveals that politicians, lawyers, farmers, salesmen, sailors, and a wide cross-section of American manhood often resorted to the gun or cane when they believed their pride had been injured or their pocketbooks abused. Readers of metropolitan newspapers, judging from the number of stories printed, never tired of details about the marksmanship of a disappointed member of an "eternal triangle" or a bankrupt businessman who accused a partner of ruining the firm, or a jilted lover—particularly one who tracked down a sixteen-year-old shirt factory employee and murdered her on the tenement steps.

Indeed, there was plenty of crime and violence in American life so that the problem in metropolitan newspaper offices was not how to report all the news, but how to fit a day's events into five or six columns, after the classified ads and before the patent-medicine ones. The advertisers paid most of the bills, and few publishers had Bennett's independence so that they could insist that the ads be changed often and paid for promptly. Strangely, Bennett's contemporaries were more interested in condemning his editorial practices than in imitating the soundness of the *Herald*'s business-office operations.

Looking back, there is a tendency to see slavery as the overriding issue of the whole era, when in fact most Americans probably regarded slavery as an unpleasant, possibly boring topic, and certainly one they had rather forget than read about. Abolitionist newspapers sprang up and proceeded along a rather bumpy road, but the larger, more successful dailies (the New York *Tribune* excepted) continually looked upon antislavery agitation as bad for business. When an abolitionist convention was held in New York, Bennett viewed the proceedings with considerable alarm. Full of anger, Bennett asked

> What business have all the religious lunatics of the free States to gather in this commercial city for purposes which, if carried into effect, would ruin and destroy its prosperity? . . . When free discussion does not promote the public good, it has no more right to exist than a bad government that is dangerous and oppressive to the common weal.

Bennett, no expert on freedom of expression, was wrapped up in a different kind of excitement. He was gripped with the fever caused by expanding newspaper circulation—the higher it climbed on the *Herald*'s billboards, the more Bennett wished for an even greater readership. The people who paid their two pennies seemed far more interested in a tenement fire than a burning social issue. True, large crowds turned out for antislavery lectures, but larger mobs milled outside the lecture halls muttering threats and often tossing a brickbat. Bennett spoke for the propertied men of the community when he reasoned that it was not the mob but the do-gooders inside the hall who had provoked violence by their insistence that an unpopular idea deserved a hearing.

Bennett did his best to keep the public's mind off its troubles. During the 1840 depression the *Herald* had come up with another innovation when it began reporting news from the upper echelon of New York's society set. A splendid ball at the Brevoort mansion was held at the height of the economic doldrums, with costumes that cost as much as $2,500 paraded before tables groaning with pheasant, great slabs of beef, game, and expensive wines. While thousands searched vainly for work, Bennett devoted his entire front page to the sumptuous affair and the *Herald* proclaimed the event "a greater sensation in the fashionable world than any thing of the kind since the creation of the world, or the fall of beauteous woman, or the frolic of old Noah, after he left the ark and took to wine and drinking." Shopkeepers and their wives clamored for more details from the fleshpots, and Bennett fed their curiosity. Greeley shrank from any imitation of the *Herald*'s society reports, possibly envious of the circulation they engendered but convinced there was a wide difference between what was interesting and what was significant. For the publisher or editor engrossed in the circulation battle there was no point in asking about significance, since he calculated that his unsophisticated readers were seeking entertainment and escape, not an education.

Besides his circulation triumph, Bennett was also far ahead of Greeley in gauging the public attitude toward slavery. The *Herald* editor-publisher was egocentric but he was also a realist. Bennett foresaw that turbulence would not help the slavery issue find a quiet solution, while Greeley naively assumed that slavery might be talked to death without a great national bloodletting contest. After the Compromise of 1850 cleared Congress, Greeley blasted local Whigs who fired a 100-gun salute at the New York Battery in celebration of the event (which presumably balanced California's admission as a free state with a tough fugitive slave law). Supporters of the compromise had claimed it would avert a civil war by calming the turbulence caused by sectional extremists. "All talk of forcible resistance should be treated with cool contempt," Greeley counseled.[1] To work off his own belligerence, Greeley always had the *Herald* editor as a handy whipping boy. With some glee the *Tribune* noted in 1853 that Bennett—"the low-mouthed, blatant, witless, brutal" *Herald* proprietor —had been horsewhipped nine times and suffered the indignity of having "his jaws forced open and his throat spit into."

While Bennett was content to exercise power in New York, Greeley's influence extended far beyond Manhattan because of indefatigable circulation workers who gave musical instruments, books, and cash as premiums for the *Weekly Tribune* Club. As the railroad system in the northern states expanded from a standstill in 1828 to 30,000 miles of track a generation later, the enterprising New York publishers learned to predate their weekly editions which crossed a Hudson River ferry on Tuesday or Wednesday and were delivered to Iowa and Illinois subscribers three days later, appearing with news presumably but a day or two old.

Rail lines created extravagant hopes everywhere. Chicago, a frontier outpost in 1828, took on boomtown proportions and dozens of other hamlets strove for similar growth in the 1840s. The Chicago *Weekly Democrat* was taken over by another lawyer-editor, John Wentworth, in 1836 and became a daily in 1840. The Green-Bay *Intelligencer* and Milwaukee *Advertiser* were other pioneer newspapers that lived with hard times until steam from the Iron Horse breathed new life into their communities. The Milwaukee *Sentinel* had turned into a daily by 1844, and in Iowa the Dubuque *Visitor*, Burlington *Hawk-Eye*, Davenport *News*, and Bloomington, Iowa, *Standard* kept pace with westward progress as settlements leaped the Mississippi ahead of railroad builders. A connection with a railroad was deemed vital if a would-be metropolis hoped for easy access to eastern markets, and the Cincinnati *Daily Times* warned its readers a rail connection with southern points was "a matter of life and death." A natural alliance was often formed by railroad promoters and newspaper editors who surmised that a depot in their town meant more jobs, additional advertising revenue, and that worthiest of all honors —a "courtesy pass" for the publisher from the railroad president in recognition of all past and future favors.

With so much going on everywhere (one editor insisted that NEWS was an acronym formed from the directions from which information came—north, east, west, and south) national attention shifted from politics to gold rushes and on to filibustering expeditions in Central America with scarcely a pause.[2] Greeley dispatched James McClatchy to California for direct reports from the gold fields, but McClatchy's passage was interrupted by a shipwreck off lower California. McClatchy struggled to the shore and walked to San Diego, took another ship for San Francisco, and eventually made it to the mining camps as a *Tribune* correspondent. Impressed with what he saw, McClatchy temporarily left newspapering to become an official of the new state and eventually founded the Sacramento *Bee*. Meanwhile, Greeley had found another West Coast correspondent and long before the railroads crossed the Rockies Greeley was sending a "Pacific Edition" of the New York *Tribune* west by ship and stagecoach.

America's growing pains came at the expense of national peace of mind. The Gadsden Purchase temporarily quieted criticism of American expansion in the Southwest, but the angry outbursts from southern fire-eaters at the 1850 Nashville Convention had indicated there was an obstreperous southern element that favored secession rather than peaceful accommodation. The *National Intelligencer* reported, however, that it received about three hundred southern newspapers each week in its exchanges and that only fifty carried editorials supporting the Nashville firebrand. The Richmond *Whig* counseled moderation and the *Texas Advertiser* tried to cool off the whole issue by suggesting that any congressman who brought up the slavery issue should be deprived of his seat. All thought of secession and civil war was repugnant to the Raleigh, North Carolina, *Press* editor, who told readers that the only fight they should ever consider was "for liberty . . . with the Stars and Stripes." Bennett viewed the

southern scene and decided that the fifty newspapers that had lauded
the fiery rhetoric of William Lowndes Yancey were already "backing down."

Or so it seemed, for editorial voices from Mobile, Memphis, New
Orleans, Natchez, and scores of lesser cities voiced their opposition to
the secessionists' call as chimerical. "If the *Mercury* supports a measure it is suspected from one end of the South to the other," a South
Carolina unionist surmised in 1851. Robert Barnwell Rhett and the
Mercury were discredited, he added, "and we must get rid of both." [3]
The few southern editors who continued to rave at the North appear
to have been dismissed as a lunatic fringe group with no concept of
reality and little rapport with their readers. The Columbus, Georgia,
Sentinel reacted to the 1850 Compromise by calling for an "open, unqualified, naked secession," but most southern editors agreed with the
New Orleans *Picayune*'s judgment. "We hope that the [slavery]
question is now definitely settled," that "contentions and bickerings
will cease, and harmony again be restored," the *Picayune* commented.

The hotheaded editor of the Savannah *Republican* saw matters
from another perspective and warned fellow southerners that a war
between the free and slave states could not be avoided. The Charleston *Mercury*, humbled but not silent, agreed with Rhett's analogies
between the contemporary crisis and the tension of the 1770s between England and the American colonies. Yankees in Boston were
now treating the South as their forebears had been manhandled by
the British, the *Mercury* charged, and in the end the outcome would
justify southern resistance in the same heroic mold. Temporarily rebuffed by pro-Union sentiment at home, Rhett resigned a Senate seat
but his son stayed on at the *Mercury*, and the chastening period gave a
false picture of southern calm.

Some diversion was furnished by a farfetched scheme to annex
Cuba, and whenever foreign news grew stale there was always the
West as an area for a journalist's speculations—ranging freely from
the western Mormon colony to the new state of California. Letters
from farmboys who had reached the Mokelumne River, full of re-

ports of high prices and homesickness, made good reading. Suddenly the focus of interest shifted even farther west, as Commodore Perry's visit to Japan was fully covered in the New York and Philadelphia press within six months after the American squadron dropped anchor in Tokyo Bay during 1853. The Philadelphia *Public Ledger*, still selling on Chestnut Street for a penny, informed readers on April 27, 1854, that Perry had sailed for Jeddo (Tokyo) on January 17 from a Chinese port. Other accounts told of "President" William Walker's filibustering expedition in Baja California and his later flight to Nicaragua after the fiasco. An aura of romance clung to the former New Orleans editor as Walker's foolhardy exploits were regularly chronicled in the press until "the grey-eyed man of destiny" ran out of luck before a Honduran firing squad. The settlement of the far northwest, reports of polygamy in the expectant state of Deseret, and the variegated plans for a transcontinental railroad furnished other excitement at a time when Americans presumably were preoccupied with the slavery question.

The price of a daily newspaper had stabilized at a penny or two, depending on advertising income, when Henry J. Raymond decided in 1851 that New York needed a newspaper that would become for New York what the *Times* was for London. Raymond had served his reporter's apprenticeship under Greeley, worked on the *Courier and Enquirer,* and had turned his Whig connections into a profit in an Albany investment. He raised $100,000 and on September 18, 1851, brought out his New York *Daily Times* as a challenge to the *Tribune* and *Herald.* Success came fast for Raymond's brash venture. He soon was trying to cope with a circulation of 20,000. The Whig boss, Thurlow Weed, had abandoned Greeley as a political ally and now looked with favor on Raymond's newspaper as a vehicle for party plans and favors. Besides Weed's patronage, however, the *Times* counted on a readership tired of the *Herald*'s sensationalism and the teaching cant of the *Tribune.** Raymond, a first-rate reporter himself,

---

* Greeley once printed a letter purportedly from a disenchanted Whig who blamed the party troubles on the *Tribune* editor's whims and Seward's reputation as an aboli-

stressed foreign news and straightforward local stories, using the "Thunderer of London" as his model. Despite Greeley's sneering personal attacks, Raymond shook off the *Tribune*'s vindictive remarks about the Weed alliance and won both the respect of the newspaper community and the votes of the electorate as the Whig candidate for lieutenant governor in 1854. Denounced by Greeley as "that little villain," Raymond had achieved in three years the prosperity, power, and respect that had eluded the *Tribune* editor for two decades.

The relative ease with which Raymond rose in New York journalism was a hard blow for Greeley's ego. In 1853, Weed's Albany *Journal* made it clear that the professional Whigs had finally washed their hands of Greeley. After Raymond's election, Greeley wrote a labored letter to Seward in which he recalled his party services since 1837 and admitted that he wanted the nomination Raymond had won.

> I should have hated to serve as Lieutenant-Governor, but I should have gloried in running for the post. . . . No other name could have been put upon the ticket so bitterly humbling to me as that which was selected. The nomination was given to Raymond, the fight left to me.[4]

Although Greeley claimed his allegiance to Seward was unimpaired, he had been passed over once too often. Within six years the *Tribune* was able to demonstrate to the Raymond-Weed-Seward coalition that its power was not to be despised.

There was more to mid-century journalism than the infighting of Manhattan-based editors, of course. A rising phenomenon was the foreign-language newspaper of the 1850s. The ebb and flow of great tides of immigrants to America had not, until the 1840s, disturbed

---

tionist. "Dear Sir—Our Delegate Election has just been closed, and the Whigs are shamefully beaten by the cry of [']Nigger! Nigger!! Nigger!!!' . . . [the minds of potential Whigs] are all the while poisoned with Fourierism, Anti-Rentism, Abolitionism and *Natural Reformism*." New York *Tribune*, May 9, 1846.

the basic English-Scot-Irish strain or the linguistic continuity of the Republic, despite singular exceptions of scattered German and Scandinavian settlements. But with the backwash of the Napoleonic wars and the Revolutionary movement of 1848 a new element was injected into America's blood stream that would quickly influence her journalism. Germans, with young intellectuals in the vanguard, came in hordes to the Ohio Valley and westward, making Cincinnati and St. Louis cultural outposts for thousands of new citizens who resisted efforts to anglicize their conversations or reading matter. It was a far cry from the first struggling German-language Philadelphia *Zeitung* of 1732 to the New York *Staats-Zeitung* of 1834 or the St. Louis *Westliche Post* with their wide audiences and healthy advertising columns. French, Italian, Spanish, and Yiddish weeklies eventually appeared in the cities, but it was the German-language newspapers that challenged the sedate English editions in scores of bilingual communities. Led by the *Staats-Zeitung*, the German-language press thrived so that on the eve of the Civil War, most of the three hundred foreign-language journals in the nation were printed in *Deutsche Fraktur* for readers who looked to their *Zeitungen* for enlightenment. Carl Schurz was one of the earliest German émigrés to turn to journalism in his new environment, but it was a latter-day immigrant from the Austro-Hungarian empire, a nearsighted lad named Pulitzer, who would attempt to remake all of America's newspaperdom.

German-speaking and native-born Americans alike cherished hopes that the bitterness of the Mexican War and the 1850 compromise would soon fade. James S. Pike, Greeley's Washington correspondent, viewed Franklin Pierce's inauguration with a placid detachment that represented the hopes of readers in all sections. "We expect Mr. Pierce will give us a quiet, moderate, conservative, unexceptionable, good-for-nothing kind of an Administration, to which nobody will think of making any especial objection or opposition; and that by the close of his term there will be a pretty general fusion of all parties." A new era of good feeling seemed almost at hand until Senator Stephen A. Douglas brought the Kansas-Nebraska bill out of committee in January 1854. In a quick stroke all the good will of the 1850 compromise was smashed, for instead of bringing the sectional harmony Douglas professed was his intention, the bill appeared to advance the specter of slavery into the western territories. All the old animosities came to the surface in editorial cauldrons across the nation.

How guilty editors were in deceiving their readers into believing that war might be averted, or that if war did come it would be a short fight followed by a long peace, is only conjecture. Possibly the southerners enraged by Garrison's *Liberator* were too guilt-ridden to turn the other cheek. There were other popular antislavery newspapers in the prewar decade, however, and the *National Era* published in the District of Columbia went far beyond the *Liberator* in its extremist propaganda. Mrs. Harriet Beecher Stowe, a middle-aged matron with some interest in social reforms, sent the *National Era* her serialized novel of life on a southern plantation. She called it *Uncle Tom's Cabin*. It blew the lid off the slavery issue in 1852, and just when the lid was almost back in place, Senator Douglas tipped the seething pot over again. But for emotional impact there has rarely been a series in American journalism comparable to Mrs. Stowe's innocently framed story of life in the slaveholding South. The claim that "No romance ever printed in an American newspaper attracted so much attention in the press" cannot be refuted.

Thereafter, incendiary journalism at the extremes of both sections was fanned by the slightest wind of discord. There is a possibility that while extremist newspapers continued their sham battles before 1854 the country generally grew accustomed to the tension produced by slavery and the ideological war it had fostered. To some degree, however, the Kansas-Nebraska bill upset the balanced forces by explicitly setting aside the old compromises, and by holding out the hope of slavery in territories above 36° 30′ the bill reopened the sectional issue as a gaping wound. The ensuing newspaper and legislative debate was so filled with acrimony that more than one careful historian has concluded that Douglas's bill was responsible for the Civil War.

Northern editors took their lead from Greeley, who at once denounced the bill as fraught with "measureless treachery and infamy." A tidal wave of protest poured forth from northern editorial rooms, echoing Greeley's charge that the offending bills were designed "to discomfit and humiliate the North by a surprise . . . an ambuscade surmounted by a flag of truce." When Douglas argued that his goal was popular sovereignty rather than an extension of slavery, Greeley branded the Illinois senator a forked-tongued politician. "The pretense of Douglas & Co. that not even Kansas is to be made a slave state by his bill is a gag of the first water," the *Tribune* editorialized. "What liars there are in this world! . . . Slavery won't go into Kansas! Gentlemen! Don't lie any more!" With its enormous daily and weekly circulation fanning across the northern states, the *Tribune* took up pursuit of Douglas in full cry. Protest meetings seemed to be gathering everywhere the *Tribune* looked, and were reported under a standing headline: THE VOICE OF THE NORTH. No Extension of Slavery.

The warning that Greeley voiced regarding "no more humiliation, no more truckling under," was echoed by southern fire-eaters who insisted that the South had been the loser in all the compromises and congressional deals since 1820. By their repeated claims that their sectional rivals had gained while they had lost, editors in both sections helped create a psychological powderkeg. In such circumstances old political allegiances tended to fall apart, and great attention was paid to even minor evidences of the rift. Thus when former Senator Thomas Hart Benton, demoted to the House of Representatives, denounced Douglas in a speech that brought pandemonium to the halls of Congress the incident was overplayed in the nation's newspapers.[5] The old Missouri warhorse's remarks "contained a few passages of exquisite bitterness, such as no other man but Benton can utter in the country," the Philadelphia *Public Ledger* reported. Benton's speech did not affect many congressmen, the *Public Ledger* added, but its impact on "the great mass of [northern] readers" was certain. No less objective was the New York *Tribune,* which warned its patrons that support for the Kansas-Nebraska bills by "Cotton Whig" newspapers in the South was proof that the legislation was based on "gigantic perfidies and crimes," misdeeds of a nature so heinous the reporter did not bother to spell them out. But Greeley himself left no doubt about his viewpoint as he took full measure of the brewing crisis and solemnly advised *Tribune* readers: "The conflagration it threatens is not to be extinguished by jets of rosewater." Stand firm, Greeley implored, stand firm.

Among the southern "ultra" editors the Kansas-Nebraska Act was viewed as a smoke screen used to obscure the real issue (national majority rule vs. local majority rule). In militant Charleston, the annual militia parade had been celebrated with great pomp as the Palmetto Guards, Charleston Light Dragoons, and other elite units passed in review when the news of Douglas's bill appeared in the *Mercury* and *Evening News*. "If the South shows but decent firmness, she will win in this struggle *what little* is to be won," the *Mercury* commented. Even more cynical was the Mobile *Register,* which declared that if the right of Congress to legislate on slavery was conceded, ruin lay ahead for the South. "If they do [make Nebraska a free state] and the Southern people submit to it, they will deserve to be blackened and turned into the fields, with their own slaves to make cotton and sugar for their Abolition[ist] lords," the *Register* surmised. While the *Register* and *Mercury* editors readily admitted that "God and nature" decreed that Nebraska should never have slavery, they were unwilling to concede that Congress might make the same judgment. "Not that we suppose slave States would spring up in Nebraska," the *Mercury* admitted, "but at least we should have the consolation of seeing a just principle of legislation established, and an acknowledgement of Congress that it has not the right to legislate expressly against the institutions of the South."

As the bill wound its way through Congress, inflaming the nation and providing the polarized thinkers with an excuse for inflammatory rhetoric, Greeley began taunting the South with a series of articles which purported to show that if the two great sections were split asunder, the North would invariably benefit from the division. Southern editors who received the *Tribune* were enraged. "The object of the *Tribune* was simply to intimidate the South by threats of disunion, and by false and highly-colored pictures of the consequent calamities of slavery," the Richmond *Enquirer* insisted.[6] The Virginia editor fell back on a familiar southern refrain in refuting all of Greeley's arguments. "The Union has been the instrument of Northern aggrandizement, and it would be absurd to suspect the nation of Yankee shopkeepers of anything so stupid as a design to kill the goose that lays the golden egg." While this debate raged, the New Orleans *Bee,* Charleston *Mercury,* and other southern newspapers continued to print anecdotes that buoyed their belief that black slaves were under a providential curse while all whites were singularly blessed. The *Mercury* quoted the Boston *Traveller* as proof, according to a lecture on "The Races of Man," that Caucasians had a common feature: "a noble expression of the face, above that of all other races, a mirror of the soul" indicating "the highest degree of civilization."

Bestirred by Greeley, northern Whig journals shifted the argument over the Kansas-Nebraska Act from a political squabble to a moral war. Once this had been accomplished to the editors' satisfaction, the sections were bound to collide. Sensing defeat in Congress for an abolitionist program, Greeley warned that passage of the obnoxious Kansas-Nebraska bill would place the nation's politics "on a new footing. The interposing partition of compromise being removed, Slavery and Freedom . . . will stand face to face for a desperate and deadly struggle." Southern politicians and editors read the *Tribune* with flushed faces. Greeley was rattling the sword.

"At last the enemy gives the signal for assault," the Richmond *Enquirer* snapped. "The declamation of the *Tribune* . . . will awaken the South to a just perception of its position." Earlier, the *Enquirer* had indicated that if the Kansas-Nebraska bill passed, "the federal Union is safe." But southerners had not been prepared for the northern editorial barrage which the bill touched off. Editors in the South knew that a strong element of northern Democratic newspapers looked favorably on the bill, but only rarely were these calm voices mentioned in the southern press. The propensity of the extremist southern editors was to stress their ideological conflict with the North. When the Detroit *Free Press* chided Greeley for placing the names of northern congressmen who supported the bill in a black-bordered mourning box, the Michigan newspaper also recalled that the same device was used to condemn those who had supported the Missouri Compromise, and "for years they were hunted as only the hell-hounds of abolitionism and fanaticism *can* hunt men." Perhaps southern editors were pleased to learn that a newspaper above the Potomac agreed that the abolitionists were trying to split the country into hostile camps, but the New York *Tribune* was adjudged more typical of northern opinion than the *Free Press*. The Richmond *Enquirer* perceived a change in tactics in that northern clergymen and religious newspapers, once neutrals in the slavery controversy, had come over to the abolitionists during the Kansas-Nebraska debate to become "the extremists [with] an energy in action, an exasperation of spirit, and a vindictiveness of purpose, which startle the friends of Union, and portend a coming struggle."

The good feeling spread by the Compromise of 1850 disappeared as a wispy puff of smoke. Hardly had the controversial bill been passed before an incident in Boston confirmed the South's suspicions about northern extremism. A Boston mob tried to prevent enforcement of the Fugitive Slave Act, egged on by the leading local abolitionists. A federal marshal was killed while carrying out the direct orders of President Pierce, and the South was stunned. The Boston *Advertiser* was widely quoted in the South with its report of Theodore Parker's refusal to donate to a fund to buy the fettered slave his freedom. "His reply was, 'I have nothing to subscribe but brains and bullets!,' " the *Advertiser* reported. This overt interference with a federal officer confirmed southern suspicions that there could be no compromise with abolitionists. "Such an execution of the Fugitive slave law," the Richmond *Enquirer* observed, "is a mockery and an insult . . . the blow will at last revive the ancient if not extinct courage of Southern gentlemen, and impel them to some adequate measures of resistance and revenge." The Charleston *Mercury* saw the Boston riot as proof that the Kansas-Nebraska Act had not changed the situation. "Against the delusion that the passage of this bill settles the slavery question, and forever excludes the abolition agitation from the halls of Congress, we would particularly admonish the people of the South. . . . They must not throw down their arms nor abate their vigilance in the confident expectation of peace and security," the *Mercury* warned.

From the summer of 1854 onward, sectional tensions hardly lessened as distrust was rampant, sowed in no small measure by newspaper editors who assured readers that the opposition's incendiary talk was mainly bluster, that all the threats of civil war and disunion were a gigantic bluff by their sectional opponents. Meanwhile, the Kansas-Nebraska Act hastened the death of the moribund Whig party. In the reshuffle of allegiances that followed, the new Republican party was created from the remnants of the northern Whigs, Free-Soilers, and a smattering of disillusioned Democrats. For a time a vigorous third force, the American or Know-Nothing party, rose meteorically as a nativist movement. Founded as a secret society by initiates who answered queries with a cryptic, "I know nothing," the anti-Catholic bias of the group seemed no hindrance when it surfaced as a full-fledged political party amid the dissension of the Kansas-Nebraska turmoil. Campaign newspapers sprang up under the Know-Nothing banner in every state. During the 1854 elections Know-Nothing candidates won in six northern and five southern states.

The American party successes were in part attributable to the American penchant for the novel. "Know-Nothing" candy, tea, and toothpicks were sold by merchants who exploited the craze, and a clipper ship, *The Know-Nothing*, was christened in New York harbor. Bennett's *Herald* surveyed the presidential prospects for 1856 and predicted a Know-Nothing ticket would win 140 electoral votes handily (only a few short of victory). "Even such Catholic papers as the Boston *Pilot* accepted the inevitability of a Know Nothing president after 1856," a historian of the movement noted.

Typical of the southern Know-Nothing press was the Charleston *Evening News,* edited by the obstreperous John Cunningham. Long known as a secessionist and "perfect fire-eater," Cunningham urged restrictions on immigration and curbs on the "political and property pretensions" of the Catholic church. To make matters clear, Cunningham called the Know-Nothing movement in South Carolina "the very essence of our State Rights Democracy." [7] Northern Know-Nothings also wanted to check the voting strength of German and Irish immigrants, but were silent on the states' rights matter and tried to make it appear that foreign elements were the chief threat to American unity rather than slavery. Then, after the national American party convention sidestepped the slavery issue, Cunningham helped form a splinter group in the South. Henceforth, the *Evening News* announced, the southern branch "has repudiated and holds no connection with the Northern Know-Nothings."

In the meantime, Greeley remained fearful that the Know-Nothings would attempt to take over leadership in the newly formed Republican party which had already attracted such old-time Democrats as William Cullen Bryant, editor of the New York *Evening Post.* Bryant, Samuel Bowles of the Springfield *Republican,* and a host of antislavery Democrats severed old ties and embraced the Republican party that was coalescing in all the northern population centers. One old-line Democrat stayed in the fold. James Gordon Bennett, unable to conceal his disdain for the polyglot Republican organization that assembled in 1855 at Saratoga, dismissed their platform as a wild-eyed attempt at "niggerizing." Bennett, growing richer by the day as the *Herald* prospered, viewed the extremists in both major parties with disdain and repeatedly warned that the promotion of sectional hostility was a threat to the nation's prosperity.

Bennett pretended not to see it, but violence was in the air. Greeley helped raise funds for a Kansas Immigration Society that was formed to place weapons in the hands of antislavery settlers on the western prairies. In Washington that winter, Greeley leaped at a chance to hurt the Democrats by supporting the Know-Nothing candidate for Speaker of the House. The *Tribune* editor had become a perpetual target for southern Democrats, and his rashness in appearing in the Capitol corridors was an invitation for trouble. Greeley was knocked down by an Arkansas congressman and threatened by others. "Several pistols will be bought today," Greeley advised his home office. "I will stand any chances to be horsewhipped and pistolled," the mild-mannered editor avowed. Greeley's name became a hated word in much of the South and although he gloried in the enemies he was making, Greeley's strong editorials were helping polarize the country into two hostile camps. Moreover, he seemed to delight in the results of his editorial harangues. "Let those who have chosen to commence this war take the responsibility for it," Greeley had challenged in 1854. At the extremes, *Tribune* and *Mercury* readers (along with subscribers to other firebrands) were being conditioned—"brainwashed" in bicentennial parlance—to regard the forthcoming departure of the slave states from the Union as an undisguised blessing. The detested "slavocracy" would no longer be a northern burden, Greeley averred, while the *Mercury* appeared to yearn for a quick severance of all political ties with the "Abolitionist lords."

The presidential election of 1856 fanned the flames of civil discord. Bennett's *Herald* leaned toward the Democrats, convinced that in Buchanan a moderate voice would be heard and that business-as-usual would prevail above the agitators' din. Campaign newspapers blossomed in dozens of northern communities as former President Fillmore accepted the Know-Nothing nomination, while John C. Fremont was picked by the Republicans as they chanted "Free Speech, Free Soil, Free-mont!" Southern newspapers threatened immediate secession if Fremont somehow won, but Greeley dismissed this as pure bluff. "The South plainly cannot *afford* to dissolve the Union," the *Tribune* insisted. Greeley must have believed it, as did thousands of his readers. As the presidential election grew nearer, the *Tribune* boasted a national circulation of over 220,000, with clubs in Illinois, Iowa, and Indiana sending in stacks of orders for weekly editions, intrigued by premium offers and apparently eager for advice from "Uncle Horace." "Greeley does the thinking for the whole West at $2 per year for his paper," Ralph Waldo Emerson decided after a lecture tour of the Midwest.

The West to New Englander Emerson was anything beyond the Connecticut River, but in the 1850s most easterners thought of the country beyond the Alleghenies as westerly. Dailies flourished in Cincinnati, Louisville, Pittsburgh, St. Louis, and other river towns on the Mississippi. But the Far West was something else, for California was as remote as London and far more difficult to reach. In San Francisco, the *Alta California* emerged from a hodgepodge of weeklies and dailies to resemble in format and influence Greeley's *Tribune* and its more prosperous eastern cousins. James King started the challenging San Francisco *Evening Bulletin* in 1855 which mercilessly twitted the *Alta California* and the lawlessness of the area. In his first wrap-up story of a year's carnage, King recorded that in 1855 San Francisco had witnessed 487 violent deaths, 6 hangings by the sheriff, and 46 lynchings.[8] King became a grisly statistic himself in 1856 when an offended reader assassinated him on a San Francisco street corner, but King had lived to see his *Bulletin* surpass the opposition dailies with a circulation of 6,200.

On the Pacific slope editors were busy boosting California and threatening each other, but in the East the editors continued with their political polarization. The Democratic press poked fun at the struggling Republican party as a conglomerate of northern malcontents, abolitionists, and office seekers. Stung by the half-truths in Democratic editorials and hopeful of an assist from the old-line southern Whigs, the Republicans enjoyed a brief moment when hopes were raised for giving their party national appeal. Greeley argued that factories and free white immigration could save the South. The *Tribune*'s soft answer to the southern labor problem turned away no wrath, however. Instead, southern editors sniped at the new party as "black, northern, abolitionist, and whiggified." In Buchanan the Democrats had no whirlwind campaigner, while Fremont proved to be vain, pompous, and an all-around poor choice. "I am afraid several volumes might be filled with what he don't know about the first elements of politics," Greeley confessed in private while putting up a good editorial front. If the southern editors had taken Fremont more seriously they might have made more threats, but in the circumstances they found it easier to ignore Fremont and concentrate on the North as a demoralized section headed for collapse. The North, said the Richmond *Enquirer* in 1856, was "free" all right, and as such "was everywhere starving, demoralized, infidel, insurrectionary, moribund!"

Name-calling did nothing to restore the national equilibrium, and the tendency in the most partisan newspapers was to go for the stereotypes. The New York *Herald* veered toward Buchanan as Bennett sided with the financial houses that regarded abolitionism and secessionism as equally bad for business. But the *Times, Tribune,* and a host of lesser voices cried for "bleeding Kansas" and strove mightily to create the impression that the farther south one traveled, the more familiar one became with signs of slovenly white overseers, rundown plantations, and debauched cotton grandees. To retaliate, the Charleston *Mercury,* the *North Carolina Standard,* and other newspapers painted word-pictures of the northern business community that were equally distorted. As a class, the *Standard* claimed, northerners were sordid moneygrubbers who could "be led to the devil or to an infraction of the Constitution with equal facility, *provided it costs nothing.*" [9] The New York newspapers were blamed by the New Orleans *Picayune* for much of the country's ills. The *Tribune* and other Republican journals were lumped together as "the sewers of Babylon," bent on demoralizing the South with the outpourings of "a contemptible literary squad." Before long, Raymond was lashing back in kind. The genteel southerner was gone, the *New York Times* countered, replaced by "a money-getter and a mammon-worship-

per." The result of this southern shift was that "the public press and
. . . the public men of the South" had become "more and more vulgar, barbaric and indecent."

Editorial voices became shrill and orators grew hoarse. It is safe to say that few Charlestonians were led away from their loyalties or that any number of New Yorkers suddenly decided the South was being treated unfairly. Instead, the climate of opinion grew more heated as each region developed a hard line of reasoning, impervious to logic or magnanimity. The Dred Scott Decision, the Lincoln-Douglas debates, John Brown's raid, the haunting specter of slave rebellions in the South—all flashed before the American reading public in the next four years until it seemed that the lid would have to blow off.

Editors in both sections appeared to be a good deal more bloodthirsty in print than they were in fact. Actually a mild-mannered man, Greeley took on the image of a northern savage when the *Tribune* declared that the North had a sacred duty "to send more true men, more Sharpe's rifles, and more field-pieces and howitzers to Kansas!" Faced by such an onslaught, southern newspapers tended to agree with their own extremists. For years southern moderates had turned a deaf ear on the warnings of the Rhett and Lowndes factions, but the ranks of southern Unionists grew thinner. The persistence of the Charleston *Mercury* was remarkable. In 1856 a *Mercury* editorial was disarmingly frank:

> We have an abiding conviction that it is impossible for the Union to last. . . . The South has the simple alternative of separating herself from the Union or being destroyed by it. We have faith to believe that the South will not be destroyed, but will yet live, an honored member in the great family of nations.

After Seward's "irrepressible conflict" speech in 1858 indicated a hard line was also a northern tactic, the *Mercury* reckoned "that within less than two years all true men in South Carolina or at Washington will stand together [for secession]," and the implication was that the dreadful act would come because "of the steady progress and fatal purposes of the powerful Black Republican faction."

The election battle between Douglas and Lincoln in 1858 brought the Chicago *Tribune* into the fray as a rising journalistic force from the West. Canadian-born Joseph Medill had bought an interest in the *Tribune* in 1855 and was among the original Lincoln supporters from the booming railroad center who envisioned greater things for their Springfield friend. When Greeley seemed lukewarm in his support of Lincoln against Douglas in 1858, the editor of the *Weekly Tribune* protested his loyalty although he virtually chose to ignore the famous debates between the "Little Giant" and his rail-splitting adversary. It is significant to the student of American newspapers that in the midst of this struggle Greeley overlooked the great Freeport debate but found room in his semiweekly edition for his own long speech on "The Needs of American Agriculture," and treated the last Lincoln-Douglas debate with silence while giving a full page over to reports on the prizefight between Heenan and Morrissey.

After the campaign ended in Douglas's victory, the Chicago *Press and Tribune* (the *Press* was later dropped) diagnosed Greeley's malady as plain stubbornness. Greeley's benign attitude toward Lincoln's opponent was "only to be accounted for on the belief entertained by hundreds of the friends of the N. Y. Tribune and its chief editor, that having fixed upon a policy, however visionary, he will follow it into the jaws of Tophet, rather than to admit that he was mistaken." [10] While Greeley had endorsed Douglas in a backhanded way, the southern extremists denounced the inventor of "Squatter Sovereignty." When it became obvious that Douglas was seeking the 1860 Democratic presidential nomination, Rhett's newspaper voiced the secessionist consensus. "Between Douglas and a Republican, the latter was preferable, for an intriguing, deceitful, and insinuating wretch was more dangerous than an open, candid, avowed enemy," the Charleston *Mercury* fumed.

By 1860 the country was in a strange mood indeed. Never before had so much seemed to depend on the manner of selecting the next

White House occupant, nor had there been in earlier days such an opportunity for newspaper editors to influence the course of history. If ever there had been a moment when the quiet voice of reason needed encouragement from the newspapers, 1860 was such a time. Journalists proved no more responsible than other segments of American life, however, so that the shrill cry of the demagogue only found an echo in much of the nation's press. The underlying assumption of the newspaperman was the same as the postulate of the businessman and the politician—there were many things in life far worse than a war.

Thus, in the lower South the editors and public men united in an effort "to make the ultimatum of Republican defeat or disunion the sole issue" of the forthcoming campaign.[11] Greeley dismissed the secession threats hurled by the fire-eaters in the event a Republican won the presidency as a monumental bluff. "I *know* the country is not Anti-Slavery," Greeley admitted privately. "It will only swallow a little Anti-Slavery in a great deal of sweetening . . . a Tariff, River-and-Harbor, Pacific-Railroad, Free-Homestead man, *may* succeed *although* he is Anti-Slavery." It was a pipe dream, but Greeley believed it. The mule-headed Greeley threw his editorial weight behind Edward Bates of Missouri.

So the political maneuvering went on, aided and abetted by the extremist editors whose columns seemed to lend the patina of truth to the reckless opinions. In the South, particularly, the moderates and their newspaper allies were on the defensive. John Brown's raid at Harper's Ferry had shocked the southern psyche far more than Greeley, Raymond, Medill, Samuel Bowles, or any other northern editor really understood. All the latent fears of a slave uprising boiled over, with the overt suggestion that northern conspirators—white conspirators—were thickening the plot. Typical among the converted moderate papers was the Pickens, South Carolina, *Keowee Courier*, whose reaction indicated a perceptible shift in Unionist sentiment in the average southerner. If the "cut throats at Harper's Ferry are to be sustained," the *Courier* warned, "then the sooner we get out of the Union the better." It was maddening to the southern moderates (who shared every slaveholder's fear of a slave rebellion) to read in the New York *Tribune* that Brown was only a misguided zealot who, "when American Slavery shall have passed away, mankind universally will hail . . . as a martyr." Southern editors, given it would seem to self-torture, sought out Greeley's words and quoted them at length to create in readers' minds an unshakable image of northern depravity. But a grave foreboding appeared in Washington when Representative John D. Ashmore, a heretofore moderate South Carolinian, told his colleagues that events were moving toward a shattering climax. Ashmore said of the antislavery message in Hinton R. Helper's book, *The Impending Crisis of the South*:

> If the programme marked out by Seward and his satellites; if the numerous Republican and Abolition meetings, of which I see an account in the newspaper press, be a fair index of public opinion in the North, then . . . nineteen out of every twenty of my constituents are in favor of disunion, without one hour's unnecessary delay.[12]

In such a climate of opinion, the door for compromise was about to slam shut.

It is probably a distortion of the facts to intimate that in this atmosphere of tension and distrust most Americans in 1860 arose each morning with brows furrowed by the political crisis. Much evidence suggests that thousands of newspaper readers were more excited about the rematch between the prize-ring contenders, John Heenan and John Morrissey—for the New York *Herald* had a way of giving the reading public what it wanted and that summer the *Herald* gave much front-page coverage to the boxers and the gunplay of their overheated fans. A tour of the United States by the portly Prince of Wales sent the society matrons of Cincinnati into a social whirl that was fully reported in New York and Chicago. And touring militia companies from Illinois and Georgia happened to converge upon

New York for a drill contest, apparently with little thought that the Chicago Zouaves and Savannah Republican Blues might someday have more serious business at hand. For sheer excitement in Richmond, nothing exceeded the proposed horse race between the famous Planet and Daniel Boone, with a purse of $20,000 promised the winner's owner. When far removed from the legislative halls and editors' offices, the American people in 1860 had a good deal on their minds besides slavery and officeholding.

In this climate of mock gaiety and business sobriety it was high time that something new happened in American journalism. Since the Mexican War, newspaper editors had recognized that news could be depicted in pictures as well as words. Bennett, Greeley, and other New York publishers ran maps of Mexican battlefields printed from woodcut engravings, and by 1848 these crude but timely outlines of troop movements were an accepted part of war reporting. Nothing approaching news pictures was practicable, however, even though Daguerre's picture-taking device achieved popularity in the 1850s, for there was no way that these lifelike images could be reproduced in quantity or on news presses. A breakthrough of sorts was provided by Nathaniel Currier and his partner, James M. Ives, when their lithography firm began offering prints of news events, great men, racing horses, and eventually more than 7,000 subjects of topical or timely interest. In an extraordinary way, Currier and Ives created a new dimension in American journalism by offering low-cost art related to current events and aimed at a mass market.

The Currier & Ives trademark was only three years old when the New York firm participated in the 1860 presidential campaign. Voters and other curious citizens could view and buy cartoons and campaign portraits that gave the electorate—possibly on a scale never before equaled—an accurate idea of the candidates' appearance. The beardless Lincoln portrait over a facsimile of his signature revealed a serious, intent, and rather gaunt man. In a political caricature, Currier & Ives showed the Illinois giant holding the dwarf-sized Breckinridge and Douglas on clam shells, ready for a seafood meal of soft-shell and hard-shell Democrats. In a combination of propaganda and humor, the print had the grinning Lincoln say: "These fellows have been planted so long in Washington, that they are as fat as Butter. I hardly know which to swallow first." Although a regular use of photographs by newspapers was nearly forty years away, from 1860 onward the nation was no longer in doubt about the appearance of its chief political and military figures as other lithographers rose to challenge, but never overtake, Currier & Ives' pioneer role in pictorial journalism.

Sold by agents across the land at street-corner newsstands in metropolitan areas, Currier & Ives news pictures must be regarded as an important phase of American journalism. This popular art form was the earliest signal of the menacing "Graphic Revolution" that would in time envelop the older forms of printed journalism. Currier & Ives' innovation of color in the news pictures and portraits, aided by watercolor artists hired at one cent per picture on a contract basis, touched an area where newspapers could not venture until late in the century. Moreover, even the freshest immigrant with no knowledge of English could appreciate a Currier & Ives news picture, for it required nothing of the buyer but interest and the purchase price. The line between Currier & Ives and the television coverage of President Kennedy's funeral a century later is much more direct than we have realized. This new medium would soon be exploited by the coming of war. For the moment, it was enough to know that the lithographer's crayon and the woodcut engraving had become a part of journalism. Whether he liked it or not, Lincoln's homely likeness was available at bookstalls and newsstands in a Currier & Ives colored print. Curiously, the firm failed to survive the breakthrough in newspaper illustration when actual photographs formed an entirely unique competition. Currier & Ives ceased operation in 1902 after "an average production of three subjects weekly for nearly fifty years." [13]

Early in 1860, however, the firm was in its heyday, and Greeley was probably more famous than Lincoln, when the Republicans began planning their Chicago Wigwam convention. The colorful hallway, built in part with Medill's contributions, was thought by many veteran reporters to be the first stopping place in Seward's drive for the presidency. But Greeley, denied a spot by Weed on the New York delegation, had been picked by the Oregon Republicans as a favor to the great editor. Greeley held a few trump cards and a decided grudge against the Seward-Weed alliance. Murat Halstead, the indefatigable Cincinnati *Commercial* reporter, watched Greeley in action and transported his readers to the bustling Tremont House. "The principal lions in this House are Horace Greeley and Francis Preston Blair, Sr.," Halstead reported. The aged Blair, Jackson's editor of the Washington *Globe*, was a link with the past while Greeley stalked the future. Wherever Greeley went there was "a crowd gaping at him," Halstead wrote, "and if he stops to talk a minute with some one who wishes to consult him as the oracle, the crowd becomes dense as possible, and there is the most eager desire to hear the words of wisdom that are supposed to fall on such occasions." [14] As a prophet, Greeley turned out to be somewhat less than spectacular, for Bates ran a poor fifth in the first balloting. Nevertheless, Greeley was able to settle an old score with the Weed-Seward crowd by urging delegates to switch from Seward to Lincoln, and on the third ballot the Ohio delegates did what "Uncle Horace" suggested, to make Lincoln the party's candidate.

The southern press had assumed Seward would be the nominee but had no difficulty in rejecting Kentucky-born Lincoln as a tool of northern abolitionists who had captured the Republican party. The factional split in the Democratic party led to a Douglas northern Democrat ticket and a Breckinridge southern Democrat slate, while old-time Whigs called upon John Bell to run as a Unionist. The fragmented opposition to Lincoln seemed to all but insure his victory, yet the southern newspapers followed the *Mercury* line and threatened secession if Lincoln won. To make matters worse, the *Mercury* printed long columns from the northern exchanges, quoting Yankee newspapers that derided South Carolinians' "windy bombast" and the "absurd, empty threats of secession." Raymond had reason to confirm in his *New York Times* the judgment that "the tone of the public press and of the public men of the South" had grown "more and more vulgar, barbaric and indecent."

The excitement of the election, the threats, and the remote possibility that something more than the presidency alone was at stake made Americans clamor for newspapers in unprecedented numbers. The New York *Herald* led all journals with its 75,000 daily circulation, and the New York *Sun* was close behind with 60,000 on the streets every morning. Greeley's *Tribune* combined daily, semiweekly, and Pacific Coast editions reached nearly 300,000 each week and it was probably true that after "small-town and rural subscribers . . . passed their 'Try-bunes' from hand to hand" the *Tribune* "was probably reaching . . . a total readership of over one million." [15]

Greeley was promoting a new kind of journalism, which included the news interview technique. The *Tribune* editor had tried the question-and-answer report a year earlier after his visit to Salt Lake City led to a chat with Brigham Young. The Mormon leader's replies to Greeley's questions were set down verbatim and printed in the August 20, 1859, *Tribune*. Other editors soon copied the Greeley method, but the *Nation* condemned the newfangled journalism as "the joint product of some humbug of a hack politician and another humbug of a reporter." Lincoln gave out no interviews and stood by the Chicago platform, while Greeley decided Douglas was the man to beat and began an editorial barrage on the "Little Giant." Editorials on "The Doom of Douglas," "Douglas Dumb," and "The Degradation of Douglas" splattered the *Tribune* pages. The usual campaign newspapers mushroomed into existence for the four candidates with their virtues extolled in the short-lived *Rail-Splitter, Constitutionalist, American Union,* and *State Rights Sentinel.* Nine southern states would not allow a Republican candidate on their ballots, but Lincoln's victory was made certain by the splintering of the Democratic groups that warred among each other for a prize made impossible by their frantic struggle.

A few newspapers tried to avert the crisis by reminding readers that a reckless electorate might end the current wave of prosperity. The New Orleans *Bee* noted that cotton growers were making a 100 percent profit on their 1860 crop and hoped voters would support a moderate to avoid "the gaunt and hideous spectre of Disunion." Bennett, aware that New York merchants and bankers had $150 million tied up in crop loans and advances to southerners, warned voters in the *Herald* that if Lincoln were elected "by our anti-slavery extremists" it was probable that "the pro-secessionists of the South may be numerous enough and desperate enough to light a flame of discord which will spread over the length and breadth of the land." [16] Provocation was the order of the day for an aroused band of editors who took their lead from the Charleston *Mercury*. The Newberry, South Carolina, *Conservatist* viewed "the excitement which is prevailing throughout the Southern country" as a sign of wholesome manliness. "Now is no time for delay. We must *act* at once." No less enthusiastic for secession was the ebullient editor of the Wetumpka, Alabama, *Enquirer*: "If I find a coiled rattlesnake in my path, do I wait for his 'overt act,' or do I smite him in his coil?" [17]

After the last editorial had been written and the final vote counted, the fire-eaters found themselves backed into a corner by the Republican victory. Instead of glumly reporting the results, however, the Charleston *Mercury* urged readers to embrace their destiny by calling a seceding convention together. On November 23, the British consul at Charleston reported to his home office that South Carolina "must either secede at all hazards, on or before the inauguration of Mr. Lincoln, or be content to have exhibited herself to the ridicule of the world." The ominous news from Charleston was reported by telegraph to New York, where Greeley wrote Lincoln with defiant advice. If the South asked for its walking papers, Greeley counseled the president-elect, "I should say, 'There's the door—go!' " [18]

In his own way, Greeley tried to hold back the war he was convinced would never come. He sent the able reporter Albert D. Richardson into the South in search of that Unionist sentiment which Greeley thought the fire-eaters were wilfully suppressing. So hated was the *Tribune* by this time that Richardson had to conceal his purpose and his newspaper affiliation, and in the end this honest reporter had to tell his boss that the *Tribune* was not reaching a southern audience because it was boycotted everywhere he journeyed. Any southerner caught reading the *Tribune* was flirting with as much danger as if he tried to sell *Liberator* subscriptions on a Charleston street corner. Some northern newspapers, such as the New York *Herald,* still made their way into southern hands and in some newspapers below the Mason-Dixon line the items clipped from northern journals were reprinted under the heading *Foreign Intelligence.* Since the mails continued crossing the Potomac and Ohio with curious regularity, moderate newspapers made their way into the heart of each section without interruption until the spring, when postal service between the sections was finally halted. As the wife of former Senator Chesnut of South Carolina noted, for a time there was no need for spies since everything important was printed in local newspapers and easily forwarded to the potential enemy. Federal generals, she observed, "have no need for spies: our newspapers keep no secrets hid." [19]

By February 1861, the polarization of the North and South was so complete that a clique in New York talked of a declaration of neutrality in case of a civil war. For every editor with a calm voice there was a counterpart in the other section insisting that the North (or South) would be brought to its sense only by drastic action. The United States had 387 dailies and 3,173 weekly newspapers in 1860, and a good many of them promoted an editorial policy that hinted that (1) the opposing section would in all likelihood not fight, despite the secessionists' clamor, but (2) if war came, it would be of short duration. The editors promoting these views were no longer the extremists of an earlier day, but men regarded as sober journalists respected by a cross section of the community. The flamboyant James D. B. DeBow of New Orleans, owner-editor of the influential *De-Bow's Review,* had once been a stout Unionist. He gradually swung to the far corner of secessionism under the hammer blows of Helper's incendiary book, the John Brown raid, and similar evidence (to southerners) that northern scoundrels were mostly concerned about abolishing slavery. Convinced that "the negro was created essentially to be a slave, and finds his highest development and destiny in that condition," DeBow was at last eager for a break with the North. DeBow, Edmund Ruffin, Robert B. Rhett, and other southern intellectuals repeatedly assured newspaper and magazine readers that the mercenary North would eventually rue the day the cotton states left the Union. "Cotton is King," they proclaimed. All would be well with the Confederacy, once the cotton shortage was felt in European textile markets and factories. With the mass media in the leading southern cities saturated with this palaver, it was little wonder that crossroads editors believed them and in turn counseled their readers to stand firm as the wild men of 1850 became the foremost statesmen of 1860.

Within a few days of Lincoln's election, it was apparent that America was about to turn a major corner in her short history. William Lloyd Garrison looked upon the scene in mid-November and rejoiced that "Babylon is fallen," but he of the frantic *Liberator* readily arraigned the "bloody-minded tyrants" of the South who had threatened secession with "demoniacal phrenzy." "Perhaps they will—probably they will not!" the *Liberator* reasoned. "By their bullying and raving, they have many times frightened the North into a base submission to their demands—and they expect to do it again! Shall they succeed?" Of course, Garrison doubted the fire-eaters. Stand firm, Greeley said. And all the while, the Rhetts in Charleston were praying for a Lincoln victory, to give their theories a chance. Now, everybody would have his way, and for a moment there must have been euphoria among staff zealots on the *Tribune, Liberator, Mercury, Enquirer*—every editor who had kept a chip on his shoulder through the summer and fall of 1860.

The prickly climate of 1860 had been no overnight phenomenon. The self-righteous southern editors and their morally indignant northern counterparts had converted their newspapers into propaganda mills that distorted the nation's concerns and artificially focused attention upon sectional differences until the keystone of American political life—compromise—became an impossibility. The truth was, as historian Holman Hamilton has pointed out, "that residents of [both] major sections were appallingly ignorant about each other." Their ignorance was exploited by well-intentioned, profit-minded, and overzealous editors who created offensive and shocking stereotypes. In far too many northern newspapers slavery was converted into a "fantastic caricature . . . which won wide acceptance in northern minds," while an influential group of southern editors worked overtime to create the impression "that the North would not fight successfully—if at all—in the event of secession." [20]

To say that the leading newspapers of the two great sections of the country were responsible for the coming of the Civil War is too broad an indictment. Certainly Greeley and Garrison outraged the South, and Rhett and his son did all they could to make it appear that the North was determined to bully them into vassalage; but Greeley and Garrison and R. B. Rhett, Jr., and all editors of their mold believed they were doing their duty. Yet by their willingness to bury their patriotic instincts in favor of sectional politics and thereby help provoke a great war, the powerful newspaper editors who directed American journalism between 1850 and 1860 surely deserve to be known as the opinion makers for a guilty generation.

8

"Not the Greatest Calamity"

Three weeks before the bloodiest war in American history began, one of the most perceptive reporters of that war had barely arrived in the United States and was surprised by what he saw in the New York newspapers. Urbane William Howard Russell of the London *Times* had been assigned to look into distant rumbles of war. At first he found only that James Gordon Bennett was poking fun at the new president as a bumbling "Rail Splitter" and that there were hundreds of advertisements in the *Herald* and elsewhere that the shocked British observer knew would not have been "allowed to appear in respectable English newspapers." These included notices by fortune-tellers, "Mesmeristic necromancers," and dozens of "personals," some addressed to a blue-eyed girl "who got out of the omnibus at the corner of 7th Street" or to respectable couples ready to adopt a child offered by "a lady about to be confined." A veteran of the shocking Crimean campaign, *Times* man Russell found New York dirty but interesting, cocky but unsteady, and its journalism was—well—disappointing, since it came from "the most enlightened and highly educated people on the face of the earth." [1]

True, more Americans knew how to read than in any large European country, and in statistical terms a Yankee had more choices in journalism than any literate man under the sun. In 1860 there were 387 daily newspapers with a circulation of 1,478,000. But Bennett's brand of journalism, though it gave the *Herald* a daily circulation of 77,000 (or slightly more than Russell's own standard-setter, the *Times*), was cited more for its flaws than its virtues. In fact, a Bennett critic told the British newsman, "No one minds what the man writes . . . his game is to abuse every respectable man in the country in order to take his revenge on them for his social exclusion, and at the same time to please the ignorant masses who delight in vituperation and scandal." Bennett was popular with the masses but offensive to those Americans who smoked fifty-cent cigars behind drawing room curtains. The Sunday *Herald*, which shocked prim-and-proper citizens who thought the Sabbath was not a day for newspaper reading, had the country's greatest circulation—nearly 88,000 copies were sold each Sunday as Russell walked along Manhattan's streets looking for clues as to what was happening to America.

Russell found that Americans were busy selling each other oysters, cotton bales, newspapers, sleeping car tickets, and whiskey. They were also arguing over whether secession was constitutional, how long the war would last (if it ever began), and who the rightful bare-knuckled boxing champion of the world ought to be. Confused by American journalism, Russell was eager to see what was going on for himself and dashed to Washington, where he was ushered into the White House. When the newly appointed secretary of state introduced the Briton to the president, Russell was welcomed with Lincolnesque candor. "The London 'Times' is one of the greatest powers in the world—in fact, I don't know anything which has much more power—except perhaps the Mississippi," Lincoln told Russell.[2] Certainly Lincoln was worried about the recognition of the Confederacy by England, and Russell understood what Lincoln was really saying: the United States needed the help of the *Times*. Such was Lincoln's view of the power of the press.

In March 1861 no major newspaper editor foresaw the agony ahead. Instead of a realistic appraisal of the situation, most newspapers in the North were filled with conjectures about the propriety or the legality of secession. Then, suddenly, all the speculations ceased with the firing on Fort Sumter, as Charleston crowds peered on the spectacle from verandas and church steeples. Across the land the rumors spread, telegraph wires hummed, and people asked, as they always ask when war begins, "Is it true? Is it war?" Indeed, it was war, and the newspapers lost little time in proclaiming it. Few seemed to think the actual fighting would last beyond harvest time. The glorious Charleston bombardment ended the long vigil and seemed to release pent-up emotions. A few months earlier the belligerent, pro-South *DeBow's Review* had foreseen the clash without regret.

> With all its attendant evils—with all its tragic horrors—with all its mighty retinue of sorrows, sufferings, and disasters—war—civil war—war of kindred races—is not the greatest calamity that can befall a people. . . . There is in war a sublime and awful beauty—a fearful and terrible loveliness.[3]

This kind of illogic was by no means hard to find; it was available on hundreds of street corners, North and South, and the effect of such propaganda was pervasive. The northern reader was assured that the fire-eating Southerners were in a minority—that the real majority in the South was loyal to the Union. That myth was dispelled after Sumter, when the wavering southern states fell in behind the fire-eaters. What the northern editors failed to realize, Bruce Catton discerned, was that the "average Southerner might not fight for slavery, but he would fight to the death to avert race equality." The southern mind was equally confused about what the North was capable of doing in a crisis. Lincoln's call for 75,000 volunteers startled southerners who had been told by local editors that the president was a vacillating "illiterate partisan . . . possessed only of his inveterate hatred of slavery and his openly avowed predilections of Negro equality," as the Charleston *Mercury* insisted.

In the aftermath of Sumter the demand for newspapers surpassed anything ever known to American journalism. The steam engines of the New York *Herald* throbbed as thousands of extras tumbled from the presses, while mobs waited at the front doors for more news about the mobilization Lincoln had ordered. Bennett tried to curb the war fever. "A civil war . . . what for?" the *Herald* asked. "To 'show we have a government?' . . . [this would only] widen the breach . . . and consolidate the southern Confederacy." But Greeley, hysterical as usual, told *Tribune* readers the president's call was far too modest. Instead, Lincoln was urged to bring 500,000 men under arms at once, to promptly borrow $100 million from patriotic citizens, and to order enormous numbers of rifles and fieldpieces from European weapons dealers.

Bennett wanted to avoid an all-out war, while Greeley decided the South ought to be "crushed out in blood and fire if necessary." But in the next editorial breath, Greeley promised he would "not undertake to say what the Government should do at this juncture," and proved it by advising Lincoln to proclaim martial law in the South, offer a huge reward for Jefferson Davis's arrest, and order an immediate "Advance upon Richmond and the armed holding of that city." Greeley came to regret his hard pounding on that military advice, although in the insistent editorial "Forward to Richmond!"—the *Tribune* was only reflecting northern impatience. After all, Sumter had been fired on thirty days earlier. Why was the war still all sound and no fury?

Richmond was the new capital of the Confederacy, so proclaimed when Governor Letcher led the Old Dominion out of the Union in the groundswell of sentiment caused by Sumter. In short order the Richmond newspapers—the venerable *Enquirer,* challenged by the *Examiner* and *Dispatch*—became for the Confederacy what the New York press was for northern journalism. News stories bearing a Richmond dateline were eagerly sought as carrying the latest and best information, and nearly eight hundred southern newspapers (eighty of them dailies) quickly accepted the Virginia metropolis as their political and news capital. The *Dispatch* reporter, present at the Charleston bombardment, told readers, "You cannot realize the joy, as the shouts of joy went up from thousands on the decks, wharves, houses, and steeples." When the news reached Richmond, bonfires were lit and fireworks touched off before excited, admiring mobs. The delirium of the moment swept all before it except the staid Richmond *Whig,* which had been against secession, and a few Unionist diehards. One disappointed Union man brought his cane down on the head of the *Examiner* editor and was promptly arrested for assault. Considering the circumstances, the Union sympathizer was probably lucky his life was spared.

In 1861 New Orleans was the largest southern city (168,000 population), but Richmond was strategically located 100 miles due south of Washington, D.C. Nobody could have foreseen, in May 1861, that much of the fighting during the next four years would take place on creek banks and in the woodlands between these two capitals. And as Greeley and many northern editors were infatuated with the cry of "On to Richmond!" there were other editorial-chair strategists in Charleston, Mobile, and Savannah who calculated the salutary effect of a Confederate parade down Pennsylvania Avenue.

The southern editor's strategy did not call for an immediate onslaught across the Potomac, however. The two ultrasecessionist journals, the Charleston *Mercury* and the New Orleans *Delta,* were united in the belief that European demands for raw cotton would eventually force recognition of the Confederacy. Once England, France, and other powers received Confederate diplomats, the way would be clear for vast purchases of arms in exchange for cotton. "They assume that the British crown rests on a cotton bale," Russell reported with combined truth and skepticism. To force the issue, the *Mercury* urged an immediate "embargo on Southern staples [i.e., cotton] to all countries not recognizing the Confederacy." At first the *Mercury* dismissed northern naval power as a weapon that would boomerang when European vessels headed for southern ports and clashes ensued. "Europe must be forced to choose, and quickly, be-

tween North and South." Richard B. Rhett, Sr., tried to push legislation for a cotton embargo through the provisional Confederate Congress, but he had no real support and the hostility of Jefferson Davis
meant the scheme was stillborn.

For the moment, northern editors cared little whether cotton was
king as long as the ninety-day volunteers sat idle in cantonments,
itching for a fight while wary generals parried calls for action. Egged
on by Greeley's strident demands by mid-June, other northern editors took up the call for immediate action. The *Tribune* headline set
the tone:

THE NATION'S WAR-CRY

Forward to Richmond! Forward to Richmond!
The Rebel Congress must not be allowed to
meet there on the 20th of July!
By That Date The Place Must Be
Held by the National Army! [4]

Day after day *Tribune* readers beheld the warning, and President
Lincoln was among them, so that by late June the *Tribune*'s ultimatum had become the northern battle cry. Scattered reports of skirmishes and the lack of a significant battle since Sumter gave the military situation a deceptive appearance. Privately, Greeley agonized.
While his newspaper hurled imperatives of a quick-stroke, war-end-
ing confrontation on the road to Richmond, Greeley confided to
Vice President Schuyler Colfax his fear that if the South were "not
whipped this winter, the Union is gone."

The newspapers supplied the bombast but the people in both sections were uneasy. Fratricide itself was bad enough, but nobody
wanted to talk about the possibilities of a long, bloody war. Confederate boasts that one southern rifleman was the match for ten Yankees seemed confirmed when the Petersburg *Express* reported the action at Big Bethel on the Virginia peninsula, where 4,000 Union
troops fell back after four hours of hot action with 76 men killed or

wounded, while the Confederates lost only 8 artillerymen. The easy southern victory seemed to confirm the Richmond *Enquirer's* assessment of northern military ineptitude. The Confederate army would be outnumbered, the *Enquirer* admitted, but the Union ranks were filled with "discharged operatives, street loafers, penniless adventurers, and vagrants"—clearly no match for the southerner, whose feats of marksmanship were renowned. Not to be outdone in its anti-Yankee stance, the Charleston *Mercury* said northern regiments were composed "of ignorant unemployed foreigners, loafers, criminals, and desperadoes." [5]

In such circumstances, both sides were lulled into believing that the war—which so far had the uniforms, music, and pomposity of a comic opera—would come and go without seriously disturbing either the business or the pleasure of the nation. For a time certain Democratic newspapers in the North seemed to revel in the embarrassment facing Lincoln's Administration. Until Sumter, Bennett's *Herald* reflected the abiding hope of New York's business community that somehow their southern customers had not finally, irretrievably departed. More outspoken than Bennett was Benjamin Wood of the New York *Daily News,* a thorough Democrat who seemed to think New York might even declare itself a neutral city and sit out the war as grand purveyor to both armies. Then, after Sumter fell, the businessmen resigned themselves to lost debts, and Bennett grudgingly called for full prosecution of the war. Wood kept criticizing Lincoln until the *News* was barred from the mails. Another Democrat, Manton Marble, was an able editor of the old school who took over the anemic New York *World* with support from Democratic financing in the summer of 1861. Marble was too much of a Democrat to give Lincoln unqualified support, and his aggressive journalism soon had the *World* challenging the leading New York journals. In time, Marble was recognized as a leading Peace Democrat—vitriolic critic of Lincoln's policies who insisted upon returning to the antebellum situation of "the Constitution as it is, the Union as it was."

Although it was not always apparent to the editors, reporters, and printers, their endeavors were as important as fighting on the battle lines. Morale had to be sustained when the truth about the carnage from the great collision of the two armies was revealed. Greeley's constant insistence that the war was more than an armed struggle, something more akin to a moral crusade, infuriated southerners to the point that at the notorious Libby prison a captured *Tribune* reporter was continually bypassed in the prisoner exchange. Greeley ranked only a few notches below Garrison as an arch-villain in southern public opinion, an opinion generated and kept inflamed by the southern press.

It was hot during that June and July of 1861, unseasonably hot, and perhaps the heat made matters worse. Jefferson Davis moved to Richmond and the defiant southern capital made ready for its Congress while the *Enquirer, Dispatch,* and *Examiner* boomeranged the chant from dozens of northern editors by insisting that the Confederate army should capture Washington before the Union armies could mobilize. The hottest fighting was on the newspaper front, where the Lincoln Cabinet read the editorials and interpreted them as the real voice of northern public opinion. Russell, the visiting English journalist, was struck by the manufactured quality of the military news in Washington and was even more aghast at the "excessive credulity" of northern readers. "Not a day had passed without the announcement that the Federal troops were moving, and that 'a great battle was expected' by somebody, at some place or other." Southern military leaders were also nervous. Nearly everybody around the capital seemed relieved when finally General McDowell's half-trained army moved along the very lines Greeley had decreed as the Union battle plan. The Union army started a well-publicized forward movement toward Richmond, down the road to Manassas Junction where the Confederates were fortifying a railroad line that streaked southward at a right angle to Richmond. At last, something was going to happen—someplace. All the southern commanders needed to know about the enemy's plans was available in the Washington *Star* and a score of other northern newspapers. Censorship was almost nonexistent. In a short war, who needs censors?

As McDowell's men moved down the Warrenton Pike toward Manassas, New York newspapers arrived in Washington's hotel lobbies with full accounts of the triumphant march of more than 70,000 blue-clad heroes, or about five times as many men as actually trudged along that dusty wagon-track. The inaccuracy of the accounts was a portent. The scent of victory pervaded the reports, and the mounting attack took on a festive air as congressmen and local dandies rented buggies so they could head for the battle field with picnic baskets tucked under the seats. Henry J. Raymond personally took charge of reporting for the *New York Times,* ready to cover the knockout blow that would shatter Beauregard's line of defense and leave the way to Richmond clear. Greeley sent E. H. House to file his victory report. The battle was still three days away when McDowell's plan was freely discussed by reporters, who openly speculated on its soundness. On the day of the battle, the *Times* ran a page-one headline, *The Fight at Bull's Run,* which heralded the "Undoubted Success of the movement."

Early on July 21, 1861, McDowell's advance guard moved forward. The green northern reporters mistook the Confederate regrouping for a general retreat. Messengers laden with optimistic reports were sent hurrying back to Fairfax Court House and the telegraph lines to New York. Raymond viewed the early skirmishes and telegraphed a story which appeared under the headline *Crushing Rebellion.* It appeared to be a great Union victory, Raymond noted, but he added, "the result is not certain at the moment I write." Early the next morning the sidewalks of New York were crowded with newsboys carrying the *Tribune* and *Times* with shouts of "Union victory!" "A great battle was fought yesterday at Bull's Run," the *Tribune* reported, and despite Confederate advantages the Union army had advanced on Manassas Junction. "The Rebel Batteries were ultimately silenced, and their ranks forced back inch by inch

. . . their dead on the field and the National troops undisputed victors." Raymond's first dispatches told a similar story of Confederate confusion and retreat. A sweeping victory was implied. "The Rebels Routed," the *Times* proclaimed.[6]

Then, the truth seeped back to Washington slowly. A Confederate counterattack had changed the whole picture, and in the rout that followed, censorship and confusion had combined to withhold the facts from overworked telegraph lines. Russell, the battle-wise English reporter, had sensed something was amiss when he came across a whole Pennsylvania regiment of ninety-day volunteers leaving the battlefield while the action was about to match the unbearable heat. With a veteran's eye Russell surveyed the sights and sounds of distant battle, detected the first signs of panic, and finally was caught himself in the swirl of confusion. The chaos, he reported, was "so great I could not understand what had taken place; but a soldier whom I stopped, said, 'We are pursued by their cavalry; they have cut us all to pieces.' " [7] The rout gained momentum as raw recruits joined the sight-seeing Congressmen to scurry back toward Washington in mad haste. Russell, who had seen the slaughter in the Crimea and had a natural sympathy for the Union cause, tried to calm the panicky blue-coated troops. "I spoke to the men, and asked them over and over again not to be in such a hurry. 'There's no enemy to pursue you. All the cavalry in the world could not get at you.' But I might as well have talked to stones," his readers in London learned later.

The battlefield fiasco was matched by the newspaper blunders committed that day. While newsboys hawked the victory editions of the *Tribune* and *Times* in New York, the jam of messages finally was broken and the truth hit Greeley's office like a thunderbolt. The early editions were called back as the doleful news was set for a new press run. Meanwhile, the New York *Herald* was already on the streets with the first glimmer of the truth. A young German emigrant, Henry Villard, had been sent with McDowell's army and had resisted any temptation to send an early optimistic dispatch. Villard saw that a disaster was in the making and decided to go back to Washington for an uncensored line to the *Herald* offices. Villard clattered across the Potomac bridge after midnight and at dawn handed the telegrapher his report of what had actually happened.[8] By 8 A.M., the *Herald* was preparing its first edition with the heart-sinking news about the Union disaster at Bull Run.

The news stunned Greeley, the same man who had been writing editorials a month earlier predicting "A Short War." Charles Dana, Greeley's right-hand man, wrote an editorial that placed all the guilt on Lincoln's Administration. "The 'sacred soil' of Virginia is crimson and wet with the blood of thousands of Northern men, needlessly shed." An immediate replacement of the Lincoln Cabinet was demanded. But the newspaper fraternity was not inclined to let the "Forward to Richmond!" chanters off easily. The New York press laid down a barrage against Greeley, blaming Greeley for the ill-advised attack and its tragic aftermath. None was more bitter than the *New York Times.* "Popular clamor promoted by certain reckless journals, whose senseless and incessant cry of 'Onward to Richmond' has had their [*sic*] disastrous echo," the *Times* charged. Some of the fight left Greeley, who now made a partial confession as he tried to throw the blame elsewhere:

> It is true that I hold and have urged that this war can not, must not, be a long one. . . . But the watchword, "Forward to Richmond," is not mine. . . . I wish to be distinctly understood as not seeking to be relieved from any responsibility for urging the advance of the Union grand army into Virginia. . . . I thought that that army, one hundred thousand strong, might have been in the rebel capital on or before the twentieth instant. . . . And now, if any one imagine that I, or any one connected with the *Tribune,* ever commanded or imagined such strategy as the launching of barely thirty thousand [troops] against ninety thousand rebels . . . then demonstration would be lost on his closed ear. . . . If I am needed as a scapegoat for all the military blunders of the last month, so be it.[9]

Greeley had more to say, including promises he would not keep about barring criticism of military strategy. He was deeply distraught by the Bull Run experience, however, and on July 29 he wrote the president that he had spent seven sleepless nights and was "a hopelessly broken" man. Seized with hysteria, Greeley begged Lincoln to tell him if the country was about to fall apart and to call for a long armistice if it seemed that "the Union is irrevocably gone."

Greeley slowly recovered from his acute case of "brain fever," as did the whole of the North. The worst did not happen, for the Confederate forces at Manassas were so confused and exhausted themselves that they could not pursue the stragglers back to Washington or take the capital. The jeremiads came thick and fast, however, and if Greeley was the chief target of the New York critics there was plenty of blame to spread on McDowell, Lincoln, Secretary of War Simon Cameron, and every editor who had aped the *Tribune* and called for a blitzkrieg before July 20. In the aftermath of blame and guilt, the London *Times* reporter saw matters far more clearly than most of his fellow newsmen in Washington. "Many think the contest is now over . . . ," Russell wrote, "and I, on the contrary, am persuaded this prick in the great Northern balloon will let out a quantity of poisonous gas, and rouse the people to a sense of the nature of the conflict on which they have entered."

Russell saw the coming struggle with more insight than any man who had watched the fleeing Union army at Centreville or had wondered why Beauregard had not followed through and smashed into Washington. By contrast, some southern newspapers thought the Confederate victory at Manassas confirmed all their previous predictions for a short war. The bombastic John Forsyth in his Mobile *Register,* compared the results to the English triumph over the Spanish Armada in 1588, implying that Confederate nationhood with a large place in the world community was inevitable. Confederate newspapers began their own chorus for a drive with "On to Washington!" as the theme, but the gray-clad army did not move far beyond Fairfax Court House, 17 miles from the thin line of federal outposts beyond General Robert E. Lee's commandeered home, Arlington. The year ended with disappointment widespread, generals on both sides distrusting overzealous reporters, the reporters distrusting the overcautious generals who failed to move their armies into action.

The tension was capped on the Confederate side late in December when General Joseph Johnston signed a general order that forbade all newspapermen from traveling or living with his army. Johnston fumed over the detailed reporting in some southern newspapers of his troop strength and specific information on where the Confederate army had settled in winter quarters (honoring the laudable European notion that fighting was too nasty a business for freezing weather). Union generals had the same complaint against the "specials," men hired by their newspaper to follow an army and report its day-by-day movements. More than one hundred specials traveled with the Union armies, trying to separate rumor from fact, arrange for the transmission of their stories back to the parent newspaper, and keep from antagonizing the field commanders and official censors. About the same number of reporters served the Confederate press, but many were volunteers who sent reports without the "horses, spy-glasses, writing materials," or salary furnished to regular specials. Most of the war correspondents used pseudonyms, probably for the same reason the first essayists in newspapers had noms de plume in the seventeenth century—to avoid responsibility. Peter W. Alexander, one of the best Confederate reporters, usually wrote as "P.W.A." or "Sallust," while his rival Felix Gregory de Fontaine preferred the anonymity of "Personne." Whitelaw Reid used the pen name "Agate," a self-effacing printer's term, when he started writing for the Cincinnati *Gazette* and later when a mainstay on Greeley's staff. Charles Carleton Coffin of the Boston *Journal* was a unique reporter who wrote as "Carleton," and finished the war as he began it, sloshing through battlefields and insisting that a good reporter had to be an eyewitness to the action.[10] Coffin's accounts stood far above much of the cliché-ridden hearsay printed by less enterprising and more cautious correspondents.

For their labors, the war correspondents received from $20 to $30 a week and sometimes performed near miracles in order to file their stories shortly after a battle ended. Villard switched to the New York *Tribune* and became almost legendary for his feats as an adventurous reporter. After the terrible carnage at Fredericksburg, Villard out-witted federal censors and smuggled his report of the Union disaster to New York.* Villard's facts stunned the *Tribune* staff, which re-leased the staggering news reluctantly. More than 12,000 Yankee soldiers killed or wounded in a single day's fighting—and not an inch of ground gained. The North reeled under the impact of such deadly news.

Casualty lists grew longer and were an integral part of each day's newspaper. Starved for information and fearing the worst, thousands of Americans turned to the graphic journalism that advanced the idea of news-by-picture far beyond the early, crude woodcuts that had dominated certain pages of the New York *Herald* and its eastern ri-vals for over a decade. To modern eyes the woodcuts rushed into print for *Frank Leslie's Illustrated Newspaper* and *Harper's Illustrated Weekly* have a stilted "see-one-and-you've-seen-them-all" quality that they must not have held for contemporary Americans. Apparently the fretting readers looked at the scenes painfully carved from wood blocks as authentic battle art, more to be held in awe than criticized because the "View of Action at Wilson's Creek" had a haunting similarity to "View of the Action at Stone's River Bluff." Bushy-bearded generals abounded in the columns of these highly popular news magazines and the effect of graphic portrayals of Grant, McClellan, Lee, Jefferson Davis, and Lincoln is beyond all doubt. For probably the first time in our history, dozens of public men were

---

* Villard's colorful newspaper career began in Belleville, Illinois, and included re-porting for the New York *Staats-Zeitung*. After the war he married William Lloyd Garrison's daughter and became a railroad financier. He bought the New York *Post* in 1881 and turned its management over to Horace White, E. L. Godkin, and Carl Schurz.

not mere names but were instantly associated by the reading public with these news pictures. Whatever these woodcuts lacked in realism was not apparent to a public that was only beginning to appreciate the daguerreotype and its imitators.

What was going on in the hearts and minds of citizens who bought newspapers, and read them far more intently than modern Americans can conceive, was a bad case of frustration. Criticism of Lincoln, the more partisan Republican editors insisted, was outright disloyalty. Yet something had gone wrong, and the newspapers doled out the pitiful truth in searing portions. There is no way to judge the degree of impact war news had on the common man of 1861–1865, but sufficient evidence exists to tell a story of inventive genius, confusion, profit making, heroic sacrifice, desertion, courage, industrial progress, and cowardice. The swirl was too enormous for any newspaper editor or reporter to comprehend, but there was no other source of information the people could turn to with any confidence. News became desirable because it might be good news. Sensing this, the newspapers developed a chronological style of reporting, letting a story build to its natural climax. Headlines increased, and this exhaustive kind of reporting became old-fashioned as the tempo of the war quickened. Readers wanted to know what happened—at a glance. Headline type grew in size as editors responded to the public craving for a speedier flow of information, and the capsuled "lead" (a summary opening paragraph) gained more ground with the enterprising reporters who became the editors of the next generation.

It is also likely that the war made the newspaper-reading habit more a fixture of American domestic life than ever before. On the farms, newspapers came to hand once a week, and were read in the evenings or on Sunday. But as Americans poured into cities, they moved at a different pace. Part of the attraction of the city was the ready availability of goods and services, of course. By the 1860s urban Americans reveled in the fact that everything they wanted or needed was close at hand, including a daily newspaper. "You can get anything you want in Chicago," was the highest kind of compliment a city could be paid. The urgency of the news also fitted into the city dweller's tempo. Speed in news gathering and distribution became an end in itself, so that a New York *Herald* editor could boast that far less than an hour elapsed between the time a story left a reporter's pad and its appearance in a street-corner edition. In this frenzied race for the newsstands, however, a sense of proportion was often the first casualty. It was often not the importance of a story but the constant pressure of deadlines that excited many newer editors. The leisurely trot of an early day in journalism finally disappeared in America's pell-mell cities during the Civil War.

While steam-driven presses wheezed to meet the urgent demands of circulation managers, the war took its toll in ways now familiar to a society dominated by technological development. More issues could be printed and distributed rapidly (*Harper's* circulation climbed to 100,000 during the war), but printers were conscripted, labor costs rose, paper became scarce, machinery breakdowns brought everything to a standstill, and wartime inflation pushed the penny press aside as the price rose to three, then four, then five cents a copy. In time the metropolitan press trimmed its price level back to two cents, but meanwhile the profits on the *New York Times, Herald,* Philadelphia *Ledger,* and Baltimore *Sun* were impressive. Bountiful harvests and humming factories meanwhile made the North stronger and more determined as months and years passed by, the war dragged on, the South faltered, and incompetent generals on both sides swore at reporters who carried the news of their bungling ineptness to anxious readers back home.

The Union naval blockade eventually caused the bottom to drop out of the cotton market. The Confederacy, deprived of its great source of cash, stumbled on from a conscription crisis to a currency crisis, from a munitions shortage to a food famine, and yet the leading Confederate newspapers counseled continued resistance. As the northern ring tightened, some newspapers took to flight rather than suspend publication. A notable example of the peripatetic journal was the Memphis *Appeal,* which was loaded on a flatcar by its diehard editors and published from its railroad headquarters while the enemy gave pursuit. Nicknamed by grinning southerners the "Moving Appeal," the quondam Memphis journal was issued from track-side offices in ten towns and four states before Union forces finally overran the railroad printing plant in Columbus, Georgia.[11]

Southern publishers grew accustomed to hardships. Although their numbers dwindled, they retained a wartime freedom of expression that has no modern parallel. However, the boast of a twentieth-century historian that no southern newspaper "was ever suppressed by state or Confederate authority throughout the war" gave a distorted view of the situation.[12] No Confederate troops ever occupied a newspaper office as federal platoons did briefly in Chicago, New York, and New Orleans, but when the Raleigh *North Carolina Standard* denounced the draft and insisted the war had turned into "a rich man's war and a poor man's fight" because wealthy slaveowners were exempted from conscription, the wrath of the community was felt. Editor W. W. Holden suspended publication for a time, and in 1864 the *Standard* office was ransacked by Georgia troops angered by the editor's antiwar screeds. Jefferson Davis must have regarded the Richmond *Examiner* as the journalistic cross he was forced to bear, for it was probably his sharpest critic and pummeled him unmercifully in its columns when Confederate fortunes went from bad to worse.[13]

Many newspapers in both sections of the country eschewed criticism of the war effort in the name of loyalty, but in the North as many as 150 newspapers published by the so-called Peace Democrats were intimidated by either Union soldiers (usually acting on their own, possibly after visiting a local saloon) or civilian mob action. Often labeled as the "Copperhead" press by their political opponents, most of these editors were simply outspoken opponents of Lincoln's war policies. But in the backlash of Union defeats and the skilled propaganda of the budding midwestern Republican party, innocent northern editors were occasionally jailed and their newspapers darkened until a Republican victory at the polls was assured. A most glaring example of the unofficial northern censorship occurred in Dubuque, Iowa, where Dennis Mahony edited the *Herald* with a policy that included white supremacy and admiring words for General Stonewall Jackson. In August 1862 Mahony was arrested without a warrant and whisked from Dubuque to the Old Capitol prison in Washington, then finally released after the fall elections indicated the Democrats had received the coup de grace at the Iowa polls.[14]

Despite outcries from federal officials that the Copperhead movement was a real threat, supported by dozens of disloyal newspapers, the evidence shows that only Democratic editors had their shops sacked or their newspapers suspended. Manton Marble's New York *World* was closed by federal troops in 1864 after his newspaper, the innocent victim of a hoax, printed a story that indicated Lincoln had issued a draft call for 400,000 men.[15] The faked dispatch had been written by a Brooklyn *Eagle* reporter who hoped to make a stock market killing from the temporary impact of the bad news, but in New York the spurious story fooled only Marble's staff and the *Journal,* which was also suppressed for a few days. Luckily the hoax was discovered before it created the same sensation as the 1863 draft call, which had provoked a riot that ended only after Greeley had barricaded the *Tribune* doors and twenty-two victims (many of them hapless blacks) died in the clashes between marauding bands and troops called to control the mobs.

Wartime prosperity helped Bennett amass more profits despite his openhanded policy of paying more for correspondence than any other American newspaper. But the northern editor-publisher who was not making money was rare in those days when every family had a personal stake in the outcome of battles and scanned the daily casualty lists, which grew longer after Gettysburg, the Wilderness, and Cold Harbor. Greeley, less interested in profits than in kingmaking, flirted with the idea of dumping Lincoln in 1864 and running Salmon P. Chase on the Republican ticket for president. Chase, Lincoln's secretary of the Treasury, was willing enough, and William Cullen Bryant of the *Evening Post* was inclined to join the drop-Lincoln phalanx, but suddenly the Chase boom was deflated by the home folks in his native Ohio, so Greeley and other disappointed Republicans were stuck with Lincoln. The Democratic newspapers that escaped the Copperhead epithet boomed for General George B. McClellan and made a terrible noise, but in the rising Middle West the Republican press organs took their cue from the Chicago *Tribune* and helped submerge "Little Mac" in an avalanche of Lincoln ballots.

By contrast, the South was neither prosperous nor able to afford the luxury of a wartime election. Scarcities had forced some Richmond newspapers to cut their size to two pages in 1862. After an Augusta, Georgia, paper mill burned in the spring of 1863, the paper crisis was so acute that some Confederate newspapers began using brown wrapping paper. The last issue of the Vicksburg *Citizen* was printed on wallpaper before the Union army captured the city and published its own "extra" on the fancy rolls.* When southern publishers could find it, they paid $60 for a ream (500 sheets) of news-size paper in 1864, and when Confederate currency became worthless the continued existence of a newspaper depended on the publisher's pride and his ability to swap subscriptions for corn, bacon, produce, cord wood, or items less marketable. There were about eight hundred printers in the Confederacy early in 1863, but close to five hundred of them had been drafted or had volunteered for army duty by June 1864. Cutler Andrews estimates that only twenty Confederate daily newspapers were still operating when Lee surrendered.[16] In short, two-thirds of the Confederate dailies fell victims of the war.

Before Lee's army laid down its weapons, the shrinking of the ranks of southern newspapers was not matched by a decline in newspaper criticism of the Confederate war effort. If anything, the smaller number of dailies and weeklies seemed to make more noise to make up for their loss in numbers. The lackluster Confederate Congress

---

* Facsimile editions of the 1863 *Citizen* were popular in the 1880s and like the reprints of the 1799 *Ulster County Gazette* (announcing George Washington's death) they occasionally crop up, to the dismay of museum curators and archivists.

had been fair game insofar as critical editors were concerned. The Memphis *Daily Avalanche* had complained in 1862 that "what these grovelling members lack in talent, in patriotism, and all the essentials which go to make men great, noble and trustworthy they more than make up in subserviency, in partisanship, and in all the acts of a demagogue." By the end of 1863 the more realistic southern editors began a discussion of a negotiated peace, but Jefferson Davis insisted that peace talks could not begin until the North recognized the Confederacy. Alexander Stephens, the Confederate vice president, deplored this adamant stand as he watched the manpower and resources of the South drained by battlefield casualties and disease. "With the exception of the regular partisan organ of the Administration," the Mobile *Daily Advertiser* charged in April 1864, "there is hardly a press in this city or State which does not sympathize with Mr. Stephens." Davis's influence bore down the peace-treaty advocates, however, so southerners hitched up their belts another notch and kept fighting, sustained in part by the Confederate press which made the real miseries of war seem preferable to the imagined consequences of a Union victory.

Peace talk was in the air prior to Lincoln's reelection, with Greeley playing a bumbling but well-intentioned role at Niagara Falls with some southern peace emissaries.[17] In the end, nothing came of the editor's stab at a diplomatic coup except that Lincoln finally realized that the *Tribune* editor (as a Cabinet member quoting the president recalled) "is an old shoe—good for nothing now, whatever he has been." "Has been" or not, Greeley worked hard to elect Lincoln in the race with McClellan and then resumed his editorial advice to the president on ways and means of ending the war.

After four dreary years and nearly 500,000 casualties (the names of 214,938 Union and Confederate dead appeared in the newspaper as battle casualties, but 285,000 died of other causes), the fighting finally stopped. Lee made the decision, convinced "that valor and devotion could accomplish nothing that would compensate the loss that would attend the continuation of the contest." Thus one man's decision ended a war that began in large measure because some fifty newspaper editors and politicians somehow thought earnest fighting would never occur.

The surrender news was relayed by Grant's headquarters late on the evening of April 9, 1865. Washington newsmen sent the message in all directions with telegraph dispatches, then joined in the capital's delirium and "unbent themselves in a private and exclusive jollification." A tipsy reporter remembered that two names were "on every lip, Lincoln and Grant." The weary president managed a smile at the White House demonstration—the same Lincoln who had laughed when newspaper humorist Artemus Ward (Charles F. Browne) had counted among the American Indian's blessings the fact that he had "no Congress, faro banks, Delirium tremens, or Associated Press" to deal with. Lincoln had needed Browne's jibes to help maintain his balance during the bleak days when the shocks from Gettysburg and Antietam recoiled through the North. The other funnyman in print was David R. Locke, who created a slovenly, semiliterate "Petroleum V. Nasby . . . a free-born Dimocrat" of the Copperhead persuasion who was the postmaster of "Confedrit X Roads, Kentucky." (Significantly, the number of newspaper humorists increased during the war as the reading public sought pain-killers and diversions from the terrible battlefield news.) But now sadder days were forgotten as the ringing church bells and careening celebrants told a joyful North the last shot had been fired.

The pent-up emotions released by the news from Appomatox spilled over in editorial columns when Greeley's *Tribune* proclaimed: "A new world is born and the Sun of Peace rises in splendor to send abroad over the land its rays of warmth and light! Never before had a nation so much cause for devout Thanksgiving; never before had a people so much reason for unrestrained congratulation and the very extravagance of joy." [18] The euphoria came to an abrupt end the following morning when newsboys began making their rounds and the *Tribune* headline told the whole tragic story: *Highly Important–The President Shot.*

Lincoln was dead before the sleepy pressmen had finished the first runs. Extras told the stunned nation it had lost a president. In looking back, it is also clear that America shed much of its innocence on that Good Friday, 1865.

9

As Giants Depart

Column-rules were turned upside down on America's newspapers so that black borders told readers of the Boston *Daily Advertiser*, New York *Tribune*, Chicago *Times*, Des Moines *State Register*, Salt Lake City *Deseret News*, and San Francisco *Alta California* the same message: the president was dead. As the shock wore off, dozens of reporters converged on Washington to report with painful detail the story of Booth's escape, the rumors of his whereabouts, the attempts on Cabinet members' lives, and the "dreadful conspiracy" involving pro-southern sympathizers. Woodcuts showed eager readers where Booth was finally captured and killed, and while the net was thrown out for all his abettors, reporters filed their stories of intrigue and hellish plots. Southern newspapers and southern readers were stupefied by the suddenness of the assassination and the swift reaction, but northern audiences learned that a vengeful Cabinet would seek justice and were told that the new, bewildered president was—as the *New York Times* said—"a man of courage, of sound judgment, and of a patriotism that has stood the test of the most terrible trials."

Grief over Lincoln's death almost overwhelmed the North. Reporters who piled on the funeral train, many of the hard-boiled war correspondents who had often seen man's worst side, were choked with emotion while recording the nation's reaction. The train carrying the dead president made a wide swing en route to Springfield so that most Americans would have an opportunity to glimpse the great man's final journey. Headlines told of "Buffalo's Hospitality," and "The Remains in Indiana." A New York *Tribune* reporter watched from the train window as they slowly passed through Piqua, Ohio, where he calculated that more than ten thousand people stood solemnly as they peered through the light made by bonfires at the black-draped railroad car. "Thirty-six women in white, with black sashes, are singing a plaintive tune, which we can see brings tears from many eyes." [1]

The worst carnage was over, but the newspapers had more bloodshed to report. Booth was dead by April 27, and there was the embarrassment of Mrs. Surratt and a feeble-minded accomplice; but the public was reminded by the press that Jefferson Davis and Robert E. Lee were the real criminals. Twelve days after Lincoln was buried the New York *Herald* reported that Davis had been captured ignominiously. "Davis slipped into his wife's petticoats, crinoline and dress, but in his hurry forgot to put on her stockings and shoes," New Yorkers read.[2] There were rumors that the Confederate president had been involved in Booth's plot, and for a time it seemed likely that civilian Davis would be hustled to the gallows. Soldier Lee was free, however, on parole. The press clamor to try both men along with other "war criminals" was great.

Greeley, so often a man of emotion, counseled the nation to avoid vindictiveness. Before Lincoln's death the *Tribune* had called for a general amnesty, a magnanimity the nation seemed incapable of after April 16. While troops hunted down Confederate officials and hurried them into cells, Greeley refused to join in the panic. Amid cries for drumhead courts-martial and plenty of rope, Greeley showed courageous restraint. When scores of northern editors wondered in print why Lee was still at liberty, the *Tribune* conceded that Lee had a share in the South's guilt. "During his four years of warfare on the Union, he was responsible for the worst crimes committed in the name of Rebellion," the *Tribune* admitted. To try Lee as a war criminal, however, would serve no good purpose and only prolong the agonies of the past four years. Let the verdict of history be Lee's punishment, Greeley wrote. "It will be more terrible than any which twelve good men and true impaneled to try him for treason could pronounce."

Greeley's public stand on Davis was more rash, for Davis had directed the rebellion and to many northern editors deserved a traitor's fate. But time softened Greeley's views, and within a year's time he began to call for Davis's release from Fortress Monroe on bail. In one of his few acts of consistency, Greeley finally signed the $100,000 surety bond that freed Davis—a deed that southerners could not forget or many northerners forgive when Greeley's ultimate political ambitions came to the fore.[3]

Greeley had mellowed, but most of his fellow Americans had not. The victorious North seemed to want vengeance, and vengeance it gained through the Radical Republicans in Congress who preferred punishment to reconciliation. A group of reporters traveling with Grant after Appomattox had reported southern conditions as pitiful. Worthless Confederate currency was used by joking Union soldiers to light cigars, but in truth the South was flat on its back with little gold, no cotton, no cash crops, and few of the greenbacks that were passing so freely in the North. Southerners retained only their land, so that their remaining newspapers teemed with advertisements for farms and plantations at giveaway prices. A Philadelphia *Public Ledger* reporter found that most southerners he met wanted to sell out and move away from the hunger and despair that clung to the land. Farms in the richest section of Virginia went begging at two dollars an acre, the *Ledger* noted, while good bottom land in North Carolina brought even less.[4] A New York *Tribune* reporter sent back dispatches from Atlanta telling of a thousand women besieging the courthouse where meal and corn were handed out each day to the starving. Buildings were pulled down for firewood. The barter system took over because no one seemed to have cash.

In Charleston, South Carolina, where the *Mercury* had gloried in secession and the fall of Sumter, warehouses were deserted and weeds choked the streets. The *Mercury* shut down in 1868 after a long suspension, but the *News & Courier* carried on, as did many southern newspapers buoyed more on promises than on cash payments. Merchants in many southern cities issued private bills of credit, worth a dollar or two in goods, to keep some kind of circulating medium in existence. But the number of newspapers in the South dwindled until, by December 1867, there were probably not more than twenty publishing regularly in the former Confederate states.[5] Among the casualties were the Austin, Texas, *Southern Intelligencer,* Richmond *Examiner,* and Jackson *Mississippian.*

Slowly, the paper-and-ink supplies long denied southern newspapers arrived from northern factories. Diehard editors kept alive the Richmond *Whig,* New Orleans *Times-Picayune,* and Montgomery, Alabama, *Advertiser,* and revived the Little Rock *Arkansas Gazette.* Defiant editors started the San Antonio *Express* in 1865, the Atlanta *Constitution* in 1868, the New Orleans *Democrat* in 1875, and the New Orleans *States* in 1879. In some cases, such as the brief-lived Americus, Georgia, *White Man's Paper* (1868) and Milledgeville, Georgia, *Spirit of the South* (1875), the publisher's predilections were plain. Several cities found the economy could support only a single newspaper, as in Savannah, where the competitors simply merged three struggling journals into one. Six years after the war ended such well-known newspapers as the Raleigh *Standard,* Natchez *Courier,* and Milledgeville *Union* had been forced to close. One of the hardiest southern newspapers was the Mobile *Register & Advertiser,* which learned to live with the occupying federal troops and the postwar depression. One way the *Register* stayed solvent was by giving space to the traveling shows that apparently helped keep southern morale from collapsing. The United Circus advertised a week's run in Mobile in November 1865, and was followed by the Thayer & Noyes

Circus, which soon was replaced by the arrival of the S. B. Howes Great European Circus. These allurements, plus the minstrels and acrobats at the Mobile Theater, led a young Ohio soldier enjoying his part in the occupation there to exclaim: "Lively times in Mobile." [6]

Things were lively, indeed, as the nation tried to settle down to a peacetime routine while ten states were still occupied by federal troops and politicians vied for prominence and a means for "readmission" of the renegade states. President Andrew Johnson talked tough at first, but as he discerned the Radical Republican program he showed a lack of vindictiveness that appalled those ardent northern congressmen who wanted immediate Negro suffrage and penalties levied on former Confederate officers.

Johnson had some newspaper allies, including Henry J. Raymond, who was repelled by the Radical program and sympathetic to the president's plight. Greeley, sensing a fusion of Raymond's mild Republicanism with Johnson's moderating stand toward Reconstruction, joined in the attack on the president. While New York publishers focused attention on the completion of the Atlantic cable (after numerous tries since the near-success of 1858), the Radicals in Congress saw that the president's strategy was to appeal for the election of a new Congress friendly to his soft-glove approach toward the South. When a presidential speaking tour was announced as a dramatic "swing around the circle" (but mainly through the Midwest), the Chicago *Tribune* set the tone for a vehement Radical reaction. Johnson was making the trip with the "blood of loyal men upon his garments," the *Tribune* charged. "We advise loyal citizens to avoid him as they would any other convicted criminal." Cheered by Raymond's advice that he needed to appeal to the voters "as the final judges upon the radical issue of disunion . . . the people must step in and restore the Union despite the threats and plots of Radicalism," Johnson filled a railroad car with military heroes (including General Grant) and headed for Philadelphia. There the Philadelphia *Press* warned that no self-respecting body of men would even show up at the railroad station for a presidential reception, and indeed the mayor and other officials boycotted the ceremonies as a sad omen of what was in store.

The Philadelphia snub infuriated Raymond, who denounced the *Press* while admitting the Pennsylvania newspaper had an ally "in almost every Radical sheet. Along the entire route, paltry little prints are sending forth specimens of their venom and incentives to insult; and at Chicago the big *Tribune* is trying desperately to stiffen the backs of its friends, preparatory to outrage." [7] Johnson did well enough in New York, where the *Herald, World,* and *Times* were in a strange and friendly alliance dictated by their aversion to the Radicals, but once the presidential train headed west the trouble began. At Cleveland hecklers angered the president until he indulged in a shouting match with them that embarrassed Johnson's friends and delighted the Radicals. The *Times* begged the president to preserve the dignity of his office, to concentrate on calming the fears of his critics, and to "allay their unjust apprehensions" about his moderate stand on Reconstruction. By September 8, the president's tour was relegated to the fifth page of the *Times,* but better things were expected at St. Louis. They did not happen. Most Republican newspapers derided the president's defense of what was derisively called "My Policy," and in their reporting of his speeches Johnson's remarks were often "misquoted and burlesqued by the Radicals." Johnson thought he had done well, but when his party returned to Washington on September 1 5 the gleeful Radicals believed correctly that the president had further damaged his already vulnerable reputation. The Radical press had succeeded in convincing its readership that Johnson was a drunken, untrustworthy fool.

As the New York *Tribune* observed, the North could not accept the proposition that "when Lee surrendered, reconstruction was accomplished." If that was all Reconstruction meant, Greeley's newspaper asserted, then the wartime sacrifices had been "to no purpose." After Johnson vetoed a vindictive Reconstruction bill he was headed for a showdown with the Radicals, who wanted military occupation of the South and assurances that black voters could vote for the Republican program. Perhaps Johnson was encouraged—as presidents have been before and since—to think that what people read in the newspapers was no true reflection of northern sentiment. After Johnson showed he was no pawn for relentless congressmen such as Thaddeus Stevens, the Radicals leaked stories to reporters of the president's unfitness, including a fondness for hard liquor and soft ladies. Thus a president who was hailed for his stout-heartedness in April 1865 was condemned in the Republican press two years later as totally unfit. When Johnson refused to swallow the Reconstruction bill as a Radical ultimatum, Greeley joined in the editorial din, "The Loyal Millions are at irreconcilable issue with Mr. Johnson," the *Tribune* decided.

Newspapers thereafter pressed the Radical case and created a bogeyman psychology that culminated in President Johnson's impeachment. Talk about impeaching presidents is always cheap, but early in 1867 the House Judiciary Committee was ordered to investigate the president's conduct in restoring confiscated property to southerners, in giving pardons to quondam "rebels," and other allegations. This first effort failed, but when Grant was used by the Radicals in an effort to embarrass the president, the old charges took on a new coloration. Early in the election year—1868—Johnson's impeachment passed, 126 to 47.

Newspaper readers were told that Johnson's tenure on Pennsylvania Avenue was almost over. "The trial, once begun, will be speedily ended," the New York *Independent* correspondent assured followers. But the hullabaloo over Johnson's conduct had been a political and journalistic tempest that left the public cold. General William T. Sherman viewed the proceedings from St. Louis with more perspective than the Capital Hill reporters and decided that "the people generally manifest little interest in the game going on." [8] While journals supporting Radical Republicans in their drive to unseat Johnson printed column after column of invective, the country seemed calm. The disgusted Senator Grimes of Iowa regarded the Washington press corps as "the most worthless and irresponsible creatures on the face of the earth." Greeley was away from New York on a western lecturing tour and had left John Russell Young in charge of the *Tribune*. Young backed the Radicals but found the public interest waned as weeks went by, with the president and Radical senators jousting in a spectacle that amused foreign observers but began to bore Americans. The public, even in Washington, seemed more interested in the theatrical performances of Fanny Kemble and Joseph Jefferson or the evening show at the Dan Rice Circus. The New York *Independent*'s prediction in February that Senator Benjamin Wade (the Radical choice for Johnson's successor) would soon take the presidential oath had long been dismissed as a journalistic overstatement.[9]

Johnson's opponents tried to finish him on May 16, but lacked the necessary votes. The Radical press shrieked and fumed when seven Republican senators would not budge and repeatedly voted against conviction. The New York *Herald* reported that the Willard Hotel lobby was packed and gamblers were taking bets on the outcome.[10] On May 26 the president was finally acquitted and the country settled back to other concerns, but the Radicals looked ahead to the November elections and cried "Foul!" "All we know is that money was used to secure the acquittal of the President," the *Tribune* grumbled, without mentioning any evidence of bribery. The *Nation,* glad to be rid of the impeachment nuisance, suggested that the trial be dramatized by a playwright because it was full of material "for a 'side-splitting farce.' " [11]

Not all newspapermen were convinced that the nation was preoccupied with political affairs. The New York *Herald* was making James Gordon Bennett richer by the day with a weekly circulation of over 800,000, more than 200,000 copies ahead of the nearest rival, Manton Marble's *World*. The other circulation leaders in New York, the *Tribune* and *Times,* lagged far behind. Indeed, the second largest printing plant in New York in 1868–1869 belonged to a publisher whose name is no longer found in the standard histories of the press. When Johnson was grudgingly turning his office over to Grant in

March 1869 the acknowledged leader of weekly journalism in America was Robert Bonner.

Bonner, a Scottish immigrant printer, had bought the faltering New York *Ledger* and proceeded to make it the nation's largest weekly in the post-Civil War era. Historians have shied away from Bonner and his *Ledger,* but he was among the first newspaper publishers to pay high salaries to writers, the first to advertise his newspaper in other publications, and among the first promoters of an historical preservation project. The *Ledger* columns by "Fanny Fern" won thousands of readers who doted on the platitudes that now reek of sentimentality but which thrilled our ancestors. Bonner paid $100 for Miss Fern's weekly column and also persuaded the historian George Bancroft, Henry J. Raymond, Henry Ward Beecher and his sister Harriet B. Stowe, James Gordon Bennett, and even Horace Greeley to write for his newspaper.[12] He once paid Bennett several thousand dollars to carry a single sentence of advertising repeated until it filled a whole page, and Bonner gave $27,000 for one week of similar notices in the *Herald.* When Washington's historic home at Mount Vernon was rescued from destruction by a group of ladies, Bonner paid a famous senator $10,000 for an article on the first president, with the understanding the money would be donated to help the restoration.

It is not easy to find a file of Bonner's *Ledger* today, but in 1868 the powerful American News Company bought 350,000 copies weekly for newsstand sales. Bonner paid Charles Dickens $5,000 for an original story that was to be sent on the Atlantic cable as a promotional stunt. The transmission failed but Bonner paid Dickens anyway. After Grant's election, when the financiers bulled their way into the gold market and a panic was in the offing, Bonner sent a personal letter to the president and received a public reply that helped save Grant's reputation. "I ordered the sale of gold to break the ring engaged, as I thought, in a most disreputable transaction," Grant wrote Bonner.

Unlike many of his fellow publishers, Bonner could laugh at his own mistakes. He once advertised that his showplace mansion on the Hudson was for sale. To recommend the country home, Bonner described it as perfect for anyone seeking "the fever and ague," and without knowing what caused the dreaded yellow fever of his day Bonner lightly explained that the great trees on his estate harbored hordes of mosquitoes which had not been "so much affected by the fever and ague as to prevent their biting." [13] A racing enthusiast, Bonner owned fifty horses and paid a record $41,000 for his famous Sunol. When Bonner died the *New York Times* said he had "made a great success of platitudes. He gauged his public with great accuracy." [14]

As Bonner's star was rising another New Yorker had returned to journalism and was setting a brilliant pace. Henry J. Raymond had paid a high price for his loyalty to President Johnson by falling from grace within the Republican party he had helped to found. After an abortive effort to form a third party and a break with his old friend, Thurlow Weed, Raymond forsook politics and went back to the *Times* as a full-time editor. Readers responded to his forceful writing and crusading spirit, and the *Times* began to regain ground lost during the bitter postwar years.

Unlike most of his contemporaries, Raymond was convinced that journalism had a unique mission in a democratic society. Raymond was forty-eight years old when at a banquet honoring Charles Dickens he responded to the Englishman's toast by saying that "the free press, all over the world, has but one common mission—to elevate humanity." Journalism, Raymond said, must be the champion of "the humble, the lowly, and the poor . . . against those who from mere position and power hold in their hands the destinies of the lowly and the poor." [15] Raymond set out to make the *Times* an exemplary friend of honest government and foe of crooked politicians. With Raymond at the helm the *Times* tackled the powerful Tweed machine and began to expose its sordid record of graft. Then Raymond, overworked and troubled by personal problems, suddenly collapsed and died in June 1869. Instinctively his fellow editors realized they

had lost a giant. "Nobody has done more," the *Nation* lamented,
". . . for the elevation of the profession." [16] Greeley's heartfelt eulogy was "a flat contradiction" of almost everything Raymond's first employer had been writing about him since 1851, but it was true that no other man in American journalism to 1869 had reported as brilliantly or expressed such editorial concern about his fellow man as Henry J. Raymond.

Fortunately, George Jones succeeded Raymond as the controlling voice at the *Times*. Under his leadership, the attacks on the Tammany Hall crowd stepped up until a classic battle took shape. The sniping at Boss Tweed had been going on since Raymond's day when a lucky circumstance broke one of the great news stories of the century. The *Times* persisted in its exposé until it brought down a corrupt dynasty that had robbed New Yorkers of $200 million through fake contracts, padded payrolls, and similar devices. A disgruntled Tammany worker, angered by the thought he had not been receiving a fair share of the loot, turned over to the *Times* proof that a plasterer working on the new courthouse building had been paid $50,000 a day for a month's work or $2,807,464.06 "for his season's work." [17] The money went to Tweed's "ring" for a sharing among the Tammany faithful, but when the *Times* broke this story in 1871 only the *Herald* tagged along and urged that the corrupt machine be broken. Tweed's men carried the traditional black bags to eighty-nine newspapers, and in 1874 it was revealed that at least two dozen newspapers needed Tammany bribery money to survive.

New Yorkers gasped when they learned of Tweed's arrogant thievery, then laughed when Thomas Nast, a sharp-witted cartoonist on the *Harper's Weekly* staff, began twisting the Tammany tiger's tail. Nast gave the Democratic machine its image as a striped jungle predator while characterizing Tweed and his partners as vultures. When the Tammany mayor insisted the storm whipped up by the *Times* and *Harper's* would "blow over," Nast grabbed the phrase and drew a slashing caricature of a Tweed-headed vulture perched atop the last remains of the New York city treasury, awaiting the end of a violent storm. In another famous cartoon Nast showed each of the "ring" members pointing to a neighbor under the caption: "Who stole the people's money?" On election day, 1871, Tweed was already under arrest but free on a million-dollar bond. Tammany lost the election and Tweed's gang was scattered—some to Europe as fugitives and others to the penitentiary. The exposure of Tweed by the *Times* and *Harper's* proved that newspapers and magazines could do more than inform the public. Perceptive young editors and reporters who were watching America grow at a terrible price—slums, crime, great extremes of wealth and poverty, grafting officials—did not forget the lesson.

This new social involvement of journalism was to spread slowly. For a final scene in the passing of the old school of American journalists had to be played, and it was fitting that the drama should involve the most colorful and powerful editor of the nineteenth century. Horace Greeley fell away from the scandals of Grant's Administration into the arms of the reformers who hoped, in 1872, to form a Liberal Republican party that would clean the Augean stables. Led by Carl Schurz, Henry Watterson of the Louisville *Courier*, and other journalistic powers, the dissidents gathered in Cincinnati early in 1872. At first glance it appeared they would nominate the American ambassador to England, Charles Francis Adams. Adams's diffidence and other unexpected problems threw the convention into a quandary, and before the delegates had regained their senses Greeley became their candidate.

What might have been the most exciting presidential campaign in American history turned into a bad joke, mainly because the newspaper editors refused to truckle with one of their own kind. The New York *Times* had labeled the Cincinnati meeting the "sorehead gathering" before the first gavel fell.[18] Other pro-Grant newspapers followed the same line by intimating that the Liberal Republicans were a band of disappointed office seekers in search of a hack politician. The "paltry sixteen hundred conventionists" were doomed to fail, the *New York Times* predicted on May 2 and then the bombshell burst on May 3.

GREELEY NOMINATED!

Gratz Brown Sells Out His Friends
for the Second Place

the *Times* reported, incredulously. Editorially, Greeley's bitterest foes called the final ballot "The End of a Farce," and said what may well have been true. "The first tendency of most people yesterday, when they heard that the Cincinnati Convention had nominated HORACE GREELEY for President, was to laugh. . . . If any one man could send a great nation to the dogs, that man is MR. GREELEY." [19]

When other editors stopped gaping, they too began flinging brickbats. Samuel Bowles, the respected Springfield, Massachusetts, *Republican* editor who had been a nursemaid for the Adams crowd, left Cincinnati in disgust and did nothing to help Greeley by spreading rumors that the *Tribune* editor had virtually offered his soul for the nomination. To Greeley's embarrassment, those who remembered his days of turmoil over the On to Richmond! campaign tried to revive bitter memories with the slogan, On to Cincinnati! So startled was Greeley by this abuse that he is said to have told a confidant that sometimes he was in doubt as to whether he was "running for the presidency or the penitentiary." The manner in which Greeley's brother editors turned on him went far toward establishing a tradition that newspapermen are not presidential timber. It was nearly fifty years before a major party would take a chance on another editor, and then the politicians went looking for an obscure, soft-spoken nonentity—Warren G. Harding.

Greeley was neither obscure nor soft-spoken. He was famous and he was loud—and he had been a noisemaker for thirty years on a long list of highly controversial topics ranging from Prohibition to a Confederate amnesty. In short, Greeley was the most heavily flawed candidate available.

One opposition newspaper after another treated Greeley's candidacy as a colossal joke. Nast, now the caricaturist supreme, gave readers of *Harper's Weekly* the impression that Greeley was a fugitive from a minstrel show who had somehow wandered onto the stage of national politics. Edwin L. Godkin of the influential *Nation* recorded reactions to Greeley's nomination as "a greater degree of incredulity and disappointment" than had been felt "since the news of the first battle of Bull Run." [20] The capstone of the farce was Greeley's second nomination by the Democrats assembled at Baltimore, who swallowed "Uncle Horace" out of a desperate recognition that a third candidate would assure Grant an easy victory. Old William Cullen Bryant of the New York *Evening Post* rejected Greeley while despising Grant, on the grounds that between a crook and a clown there was little reason to support a fool.

Despite his many problems, personal and political, Greeley turned out to be a hard-working, serious-minded candidate. He paid attention to the cartoonists and had his whiskers neatly trimmed, then bought some new clothes and started barnstorming the country. Huge crowds greeted him at Dayton, Louisville, Pittsburgh, and elsewhere. Dana, who learned his way in the newsroom by following Greeley's flying coattails, decided to stick with his quondam friend-employer and endorsed the "sage of Chappaqua" with headlines proclaiming the "magnificent Speeches of Dr. Horace Greeley" and "Ohio and Kentucky Boiling Over with Enthusiasm" in the *Sun*.

Greeley campaigned with such energy that he began to worry the moneybag holders supporting Grant, who was the recipient of large contributions from railroad financiers and stock-market manipulators who dreaded the thought of Greeley in the White House. In October, Greeley began to sense the hopelessness of his cause. He grew tired, and fatigue slipped into real illness as his wife's health declined and the early returns indicated Grant's victory. After his wife died on October 30 Greeley moved beyond the real world, writing friends that he was alive but wished he were dead. The returns told a story of the power of money, and of a vindictive press. Greeley, the "nigger lover" and "traitorous friend of Jefferson Davis," had lost, although 2,800,000 citizens had voted for him. The majority (Grant had 3,594,000 votes) showed that it was in no mood for a political house-cleaning despite all the scandals whirling around Grant, but the electoral vote (292 to 66) gave the impression of a crushing defeat for Greeley. Sick and confused, Greeley went back to the *Tribune* offices and soon was battling with the staff over an editorial that Greeley took as a personal insult. He fought with Whitelaw Reid, his heir-apparent, and perceived that a movement was afoot to replace him at the helm. Before any coup took place, however, Greeley had a nervous breakdown. On November 1 he had been in the running for the presidency; on November 29 the broken, dispirited exemplar of personal journalism was dead. President Grant led the parade of mourners.

Greeley's death came almost six months to the day after a third New York giant and rival editor had died, with less fanfare. James Gordon Bennett stopped worrying about the *Herald* on June 1, 1872, when his monthly profits were around $30,000. Only the London *Times* could boast more income, but probably no newspaper in the world had a larger annual circulation. After the Civil War Bennett had slowed down somewhat and given more of an editorial rein to his son, James Gordon Bennett, Jr. The younger Bennett had succeeded the newspaperman's newspaperman—Frederick Hudson—as managing editor of the *Herald* in 1866 when he was thirty-one. From the outset, young Bennett displayed a flair that made it clear he was a different breed of publisher, whatever his antecedents. Young Bennett was not content to report the news, he wanted to make it. In that spirit, he hired the explorer Henry M. Stanley as a roving reporter assigned to find the "lost missionary," David Livingstone. Stanley not only found Livingstone and gave the language a *bon mot* but the *Herald* benefited from this journalistic coup in 1871 when the discovery received coverage in the *Herald* that cynics claimed was fitting only for the Second Coming.

While Bennett had the background and training to become a great leader, he did not fill the vacuum left as the New Year's editions of 1873 carried traditional stories of the old year. Unlike Raymond, Greeley, or his father, young Bennett was more attracted to the flamboyant side of journalism and in that sense he was the forerunner of other born-to-wealth publishers. The trio of editors now missing from New York journalism had been printers or reporters who worked long hours and depended upon their writing ability to make up for capital during early years. Young Bennett spent lavishly for news reports that were, as in the Stanley expedition, really newspaper stunts—events that would not have happened had *Herald* money not supported them. This was also the case when a disastrous North Pole expedition lost an entire ship's crew on a *Herald*-financed trip to the Arctic.

Enough was going on around the country to capture readers' attention without the helping hand of journalistic entrepreneurs. The Ku Klux Klan raiders in the South were depicted as proof that the federal troops had to continue their occupation of "our conquered provinces," as lynching and terrorist activities were revealed that set back any hope of better race relations. The Chicago fire in 1871 had burned nearly 18,000 buildings, killed 250, and destroyed $200 million worth of property, yet Chicago revived, gloried in its Phoenix-like tradition, and shook off another huge fire in 1874. No wonder the Chicago *Tribune* gloated that it was astride the world's fastest-growing city, a railroad center where real estate speculation brought riches on a horde of *nouveau riche* families and catapulted the population from 110,000 in 1860 to more than 300,000 when the first holocaust came. But growth had its problems, more than the booster-spirited *Tribune* cared to admit, as boom times were emphasized while the spreading rail network was utilized to make the newspaper the largest west of the Hudson.

Indeed, city growth had its thorns, and it was the seamy side of life that made newsrooms hum as anonymous editors sent their reporters out on each day's assignment into ghettos and financial districts. In the process an integrated method of collecting and printing news evolved that still holds sway a hundred years later. The kidnapping of little Charlie Ross at Germantown, Pennsylvania, with the subsequent demand for ransom and mysterious negotiations (fruitless, as it developed) gave the new kind of reporting a full test. Such attention was focused on the boy's disappearance that the *New York Times* and other distant newspapers finally had to acknowledge public interest in the crime. The front-page report from the *Times* told the known facts after giving the dateline:

> *Philadelphia, July 4.*—The abduction of a child from his home in Germantown, on the 1st of July, continues to excite much interest here.

Readers were told, a few paragraphs later, who the boy was, where he had been kidnapped, and given other details. The first sentence told the essential facts, however, and this type of reporting came to be known as *spot-news coverage* with a summary "lead" (first paragraph). It was spot news because it had happened suddenly and without possible prearrangements (as with speeches, conventions, or elections). The summarizing first sentence-paragraph permitted the reader to skim through the entire newspaper and hurriedly scan the gist of the news. Curiously, as Americans had better lighting and more leisure, offsetting factors made the days of newspapers read carefully, column-by-column, a memory as newspapers increased to eight, then twelve or more pages.

With the flood of information it became increasingly difficult for readers to separate the significant from the trivial, and there was little in front-page makeup to help. The Associated Press, reorganized and powerful enough to keep feisty members in line, sent out a stream of dispatches from New York that gave citizens in New Haven and San Francisco the same information. The readers had the "facts" but did they have the news? The *New York Times*, well aware that Associated Press members sent out duplicates of their own stories, which were then relayed to central distribution points, complained about the power of Watterson's Louisville *Courier-Journal* and thus indicted the whole system. When a race riot was reported in Kentucky, the *Times* sent a reporter to survey the scene of carnage. From Louisville he wrote:

> All news from the news centre must have censorship at the *Courier-Journal* office before it is given the public outside of this Commonwealth. As a consequence every thing reflecting on the negroes, and every outrage that can be twisted into a negro outbreak, is sent as news matter to unsuspecting newspapers, and they comment accordingly. During the last week we have had "a war of races" at Lancaster, and now we have a "war of races" in Owen County. This kind of "stuff" is all nonsense.[21]

In such circumstances, a dispatch from Kentucky traveled across the country on telegraph wires, telling of a race riot. Yet, if the *Times* reporter was correct, it was simply a neighborhood row.

The system of distributing wire news did not change, however. Instead, the New York members continued their domination, and independent newspapers were blocked from the cooperative by the blackball privilege extended to charter members. Henry George, a California newsman who became the single-tax advocate, helped form a rival to the dominant "A.P." with a Philadelphia base. Competition in news gathering from the new American Press Association after 1871 caused the Associated Press moguls anxious moments, particularly after it began offering wire news to any client without restrictions on membership. Working with a rival telegraph company, the APA changed its name and was a distinct threat to the power structure of the Associated Press until it was virtually absorbed through secret deals with its larger competitor.

The reading public was unaware of such back-scenes maneuvers in journalism, of course. The mood of change was in the air. The old fervor was lacking in politics at the grass-roots level, particularly after more scandals came to the surface with the Whiskey Ring fraud exposé in the St. Louis *Democrat*. A sensitive *Democrat* reporter, posing as a statistician, learned that the government was losing millions of dollars on taxes that never reached the federal Treasury. Other newspapers leaped on the frauds, which exposed the Grant Administration to the point that Congress passed a short-lived "gag law" in retaliation for 238 indictments of Treasury officials and other involved persons. Most of the men with their hands in the till escaped conviction, but the "gag law" was tossed back at incumbents by the Democrats and it boomeranged in a congressional house-cleaning that showed the country was growing impatient with blindly partisan politics.

Leavening agents in the postwar news diet were the Sunday newspapers, society news, and the rise of spectator sport. In the 1840s well-intentioned Sabbath supporters had threatened not only to bring the nation's leisure activities to a halt on every seventh day, but even insisted that the carrying of mails by rail on Sunday was government-supported sin. But the movement waned under the rising tide of immigration from European countries where Sunday recreation was deemed wholesome, and the growth of urban centers where all facets of life were increasingly secular. By the end of the 1870s, only two large journals held out against the trend in New York, and over the nation about 10 percent of the 1,150 dailies published offered Sunday editions.

Since three out of every four Americans lived in rural areas in 1875, it was still the county weekly or the church newspaper that reached most homes. Patent medicine, pistols, whiskey, false teeth, corsets, shoes, spectacles, and other merchandise passed before readers' eyes in the advertising columns of these newspapers. An enterprising midwesterner, Aaron Montgomery Ward, saw the potential in this merchandising method and began a mail-order house in cooperation with the National Grange, a farmers' organization with multiple newspaper outlets in Illinois, Iowa, and adjacent states. Ward's business boomed and in 1876 he published a 150-page catalog that was a social commentary fitting into a special category of journalism.

In a way that surpassed every other medium, Ward told his audience of the vast worth of a dollar bill.

"Get Money—honestly if you can, but at any rate get money!" advised newsman Henry George as he saw the extremes of riches and poverty building up during the 1870s across the country. Other newsmen, working for $25 a week top wages, stood aghast at the displays of wealth in the booming cities. A Philadelphia editor ran a fulsome account of a local bride's honeymoon wardrobe with details on whalebone corsets "stitched with blue silk," silk stockings in "mode tints, costing $12 a pair," and enough finery to keep a hand laundry perpetually busy. "In a country like this . . . of republican institutions . . . let the respectable press . . . decry this hideous flunkeyism," he urged.[22] Grimy seamstresses read such stories more in a spirit of envy than of anger, however, and it was apparent that the vicarious thrills associated with news of the social set at Saratoga, Long Branch, and other watering places for the rich sold more newspapers than editorial denunciations of "flunkeyism."

Reports of glittering ballrooms caught the woman reader's attention, but it was spectator sport that enthralled the male audience in urban America. Baseball had been known long before the Civil War, but bored soldiers developed the game, which spread rapidly as postwar amateur leagues were organized and standings maintained. In July 1868 the New York Excelsiors challenged local teams on Brooklyn diamonds, and the pressmen on the *World* and *Tribune* staged a nine-inning thriller that the *World* won, 62 to 19. Newspapers printed box scores as professional teams were organized, so that when the National League was launched in 1876 there were reporters whose entire workday was spent covering the games and sending telegraphic reports. The New York *Sunday Mercury* claimed it had been "the father of baseball" by its innovations in reporting the national pastime.

Spectator interest in college rowing was also high during this period, as the *New York Times* indicated by running two front-page stories during the same week on the pending regatta that involved teams from Yale, Harvard, and Columbia. Collegiate track meets also required a full column in metropolitan newspapers that carried only brief notices of the newer game—football—which some newspapers dismissed as too rough and complicated to gain a hold on bewildered spectators. The size of crowds was limited by the lack of standing room at many contests, but at race tracks—probably still the largest spectator sport—it was not uncommon to have 20,000 fans in the flag-bedecked pavilions. Results were sought in newspapers as eagerly as stock-market quotations; and as one editor noted, the spectator sports had invaded the newsrooms and drawing rooms because of public demand. After prizefighting was denounced from pulpits and parlors as a degraded form of sport nurtured by newspapers, one editor replied that "If the newspapers gave voluminous reports of 'battles' for the championship between leading pugilists, they only supplied a demand; for . . . the whole people of the country began to take a more or less animated interest in the prize-ring." [23]

Promoters sensed the potential profits in sports beyond the turf and diamond when they found that people would pay to watch other humans circle a track endlessly. The New York *Sun* reported that Miss Lulu Loomer, wearing a black silk outfit complete with sky blue hose, intended to walk 750 miles in a local pavilion. Similar endurance contests were then planned at the Fifth Regiment Armory and in Cooper Hall at Jersey City. These spectacles helped rejuvenate the old *National Police Gazette,* which had been founded in 1845 and usually featured woodcuts of "snappy ladies" from the world's flesh-pots. The popularity of prizefighting crowded décolletage for space in the *Gazette* until 150,000 copies were sold each week for a wider circulation in barber shops and billiard halls.

Besides the newspaper interest in sport, there was a less wholesome journalistic effort to serve prurient tastes. Whether the *Arena, Alligator,* and similar sheets went as far as their counterparts in the 1970s is beyond proof, since we only know about these indelicate publications through allusions from contemporaries who labeled them "loathesome," "beastial," and worse. But certainly there was in the

1870s an offshoot of underground journalism which gave some readers the vicarious thrills that others found adequately supplied by
playing-field aggression. It is an interesting speculation in the 1970s
as to whether *Playboy* and far less restrained magazines will be available for research in 2076. Ribaldry in literature seems to survive only
if well bound. Otherwise, despite the size of the printing, coarse material goes from hand to hand until it finally disappears forever.
Roman artifacts and art would seem to prove that really prurient
objects, to become permanent, must involve metal and stone.

By the 1870s the times were changing and the press was taking its
share of the blame from old-timers who liked the bygone pace of life.
It seems more likely that newspapers were simply reporting on the
vicissitudes of urban living rather than helping create a different life
style. In the centennial year of 1876, when Philadelphia tried its hand
at becoming a World's Fair city, the nation counted 46 million souls;
along with the weekly medical report on live births, every ship from
Europe added to the swell. People were doing more things—killing
each other with kitchen knives or dying in buggy accidents, making
money or losing it in the stock market, escaping the heat by going to
Newport, or sweltering in the slums. By 1876 the newspapers clearly
showed less interest in politics and more in people than at any prior
time in American history. Further breaks with the past were in the
offing.

Reporters whose memory spanned whole generations could recall
the print-shop days when an editor culled the exchanges, helped set
type, and used the printer's stone for his desk. In the 1870s metropolitan newspaper staffs added reporters by the platoon, and increasingly these writers were recruited from places other than the traditional backroom printing shops. The idea of training reporters by any
method other than the apprentice system gave way slowly, but in
1869 a college president, Robert E. Lee, suggested that a course in
newspaper reporting might increase the value of an education at
Washington College. However, the idea did not catch hold until a
few years later, when Cornell University tried to live up to its pa-

tron's call by offering students a chance to learn about newspapers in the college classroom. There would be further experimentation in journalism education, and a discouraging list of failures, before the University of Missouri and Columbia University launched programs that became permanent academic fixtures. Still, the need for trained reporters was becoming more apparent. A veteran newsman's book, *Secrets of the Sanctum*, published in 1875 with guidance on writing, may have been the first journalism primer of the who-what-when-where-why type. Alonzo F. Hill drew on his experience in Philadelphia and San Francisco to give readers a "do's and don't's" list of the type still found on city room walls. "Use plain language," Hill counseled, and, "Don't go out of your way to hunt up rare words." "Never say 'insane asylum,' because, whatever may be the mental condition of the inmates, the building itself is usually in its right mind." And:

> If you speak of a dog, call it a "dog"; do not say a "mammal of the *genus canis.*" To reiterate an old precept, "call a spade a spade," not "a metallic agricultural implement for displacing and rearranging the soil."

Hill advised cub reporters to be as fair as they were skeptical. Accused persons should not be written about as though already convicted, he counseled, but only as persons "charged with" wrongdoing. Fair play and "a simple sense of justice" made such caution mandatory "even if there were no laws against libel, because many persons are suspected and charged with offences, arrested, and afterward found to be entirely innocent." [24]

Not so innocent was the Reverend Henry Ward Beecher, whose name dominated the news in 1875 after his best friend accused the famous Brooklyn preacher of seducing his wife. The reporters' ingenuity was taxed in relaying courtroom testimony fit for the pages of "a family newspaper." Details of Beecher's private life titillated the reading public, which found the minister's amorous ways infinitely more exciting than humdrum news of political corruption or even of the reported gold strikes in the Dakota hills. The trial ended with a hung jury. The third man in the triangle, Theodore Tilton, was an editor himself, but his weekly *Independent* was nearly ruined by the scandal. New York set the pace for journalism throughout the country, but it was a large city that reflected the tastes of an entire nation. Names became more and more important in big-city journalism, while in villages and on farms people generally still read about church news, animal husbandry, better ways to plant potatoes, and improvements on home canning. The low-cost *Farm Journal* built up a 200,000 circulation by giving readers homely advice on planting and cooking. Meanwhile, the Reverend Beecher betook himself to the editorship of the *Christian Union* and righteously denounced evil from its pages for seven years after his lengthy days in court.

The mortality rate for all manner of publications remained high. Except for the monster steam-driven presses in the cities, publishers still relied on less pretentious machinery, down to the faithful Washington-type hand press with its low capital requirements. The labor was back-breaking, the profits uncertain, and sometimes a country editor was forced to print advertising despite his better judgment. After a grasshopper invasion, an Algona, Iowa, publisher agreed to print an advertisement offering inducements to prospective settlers in Texas. Local indignation must have caused him to follow the notice with a letter, allegedly from a former Iowan who had bit on the Texas bait. The Texas grasshoppers were bigger than Iowa's, the sad Texan wrote, and worst of all—Texas women were notorious users of tobacco, "even snuff." [25]

Country print shops remained the same, but big-city journalism had long since transformed itself from a one-man operation. Corporation journalism was moving in on New York's Park Row, so that the leading stockholders in a newspaper enterprise could turn day-to-day operation over to an appointed editor-publisher who was their salaried employee. Deadlines for early editions (that would be rushed to the railroads for relay to points sometimes 200 miles away) required a strict routine carried on under the anxious control of a city editor. With the employment of more local reporters, the cluttered desk of a city editor became the nerve center of the newspaper. A New York *Tribune* staff member, describing a typical city room in the 1870s, said

> The walls are covered with maps. A perpendicular viaduct, for communication between the counting-, editorial-, and composing-rooms, with speaking pipes, copy-boxes, and bells, runs from the low ceiling through the center of the room. . . . A small library of books relating to city affairs leans against the viaduct. A water-pail and tin jar of ice-water occupy one corner of the room. . . . A dozen reporters are seated at a dozen small green desks.

A widely traveled fellow editor confirmed this word-picture. City rooms, he said, "are nearly the same in every large daily newspaper establishment in this country." [26] Journalistic conformity was already in full swing. If the clatter of typewriters and a carpeted floor were added to the 1870 newsroom scene, it would almost describe a healthy number of city rooms a century later. There were some things even Mr. Pulitzer could not change.

10

Cross Currents

Competition was once the lifeblood of the nation's journalism. Indeed, in no field of endeavor had what Herbert Hoover called "the emery wheel of competition" spun so relentlessly, causing weak journals to fade unlamented while furnishing the prosperous dailies in urban America with the incentive that kept their circulation and profits climbing. By an accident of history, the man who came to understand the economics of newspaper competition far better than any native-born American, however, was a Hungarian immigrant who would leave an indelible trace on the American newspaper.

Joseph Pulitzer, a discharged and forlorn Union veteran, headed for St. Louis after the Civil War in search of a livelihood and a place to improve his halting English. A trickster had advised the twenty-year-old immigrant to visit St. Louis, then a center for German-Americans who tried to re-create much of their homeland on the banks of the Mississippi, with the *Biergarten* and *Zeitungen*. Nearly as many newspapers were printed in German as in English. Newspapering was not in Pulitzer's mind when he went job-seeking, but he was young and bright and lucky enough to find a reporting job on the *Westliche Post.* In the space of a few years he became a leading political reporter, served in the state legislature, and bought an interest in the *Post.* Pulitzer then purchased the bankrupt *Staats-Zeitung,* and looked for further opportunities after making a tidy profit by selling the newspaper's chief asset—the rights to an Associated Press franchise. His luckiest break in a long series of fortunate happenings came when the St. Louis *Dispatch* went on the block for $2,500 in 1878. Pulitzer took over the broken-down *Dispatch,* and his life was thereafter dedicated to creative journalism that was so innovative and exciting that it would drastically alter the newspaper business everywhere in America.

Pulitzer saw that the stuffiness of contemporary journalism was passing thousands of readers by. Politics dominated most newspapers, as had been the case for a century, and Pulitzer himself loved a good political campaign. But readers were tired of the windy editorials and blatant prejudices that failed to convince after endless repetition. Fellow Republicans everywhere were reluctant to stop waving the "Bloody Shirt," while in St. Louis blind party loyalty had caused Pulitzer's friends to try and excuse the Whiskey Ring frauds. As Pulitzer saw it, there was a place for politics in journalism, but politicians could not remain the focal point of newspapers if those journals were to maintain wide readership. Coming from abroad, Pulitzer was peculiarly sensitive to this diffidence toward politics by an increasing segment of the people.

With the zeal of a crusader, Pulitzer hired John A. Cockerill (lately of the Cincinnati *Enquirer*) as his editor and turned the *Dispatch* into a sprightly newspaper. Wide coverage of news and a chip-on-the-shoulder stance marked its new style. Exposé campaigns ripped into a public utility that used its monopoly to extort vast sums from customers. A corrupt nest of gamblers had the spotlight turned on them by another *Dispatch* series. "What will the police do about it?" prodded the *Dispatch* after making its disclosures. An embarrassing list of local tax dodgers told readers this was no ordinary newspaper. "Pulitzer was sued repeatedly but vainly for libel." [1] The editorial help Pulitzer hired tried experiments in typography and style. The old St. Louis *Post* was absorbed, more black entries filled the ledger books, and in three years Pulitzer was making nearly $4,000 a month in profits. Crime did not pay, but crime news did.

Pulitzer realized that old-fashioned journalism was giving way to the exciting tempo of urban living. In a rural community an occasional shooting might be talked about for months, but in cities of 300,000 it was normal to have a murder a week, along with many accidental deaths, holdups, knifings, and assorted mayhem. This information which had brought such an impetus to Bennett's *Herald* in 1835 now shoved the *Post-Dispatch* ahead in St. Louis. Under Cockerill's direction Pulitzer's staff sought out the bizarre, summarized the news in shortened paragraphs, and called attention to the story through larger headline type. Crime news headed *An Adulterous Pair* or *Kissing in Church* beckoned a ready audience. Such headlines offended some priggish members of the community, but the profit ledgers told a different story about the marketplace. Early in 1881 the *Post-Dispatch* had 12,000 subscriptions, and was neck-and-neck with the *Globe Democrat* as seven other rivals in the city of 350,000 fell far behind.[2] Pulitzer's profits for the year exceeded $80,000. His reporters knew where to find news that others overlooked, and were recognized through higher salaries, while Pulitzer gave Cockerill stock in the enterprise as both a reward and an encouragement.

Although Pulitzer retained his personal interest in politics the *Post-Dispatch* caught the trend of the times by toning down partisan battles. "Political events do not affect our sales favorably," his editor frankly admitted. "Next to the assassination of President Garfield our greatest increase has been by a local hanging."[3] The power of the *Post-Dispatch* in local affairs became awesome, so that when Cockerill launched an attack on one of the city's leading lawyers during a congressional race, its outcome was to affect both Pulitzer and the future of American journalism. Cockerill called the attorney (who was Jay Gould's local lawyer) a servant of the rich and corrupt, provoking his partner to label the *Post-Dispatch* as "a blackmailing sheet." More vituperation passed between the men until the affair came to a bloody end in the *Post-Dispatch* city room, where Cockerill shot and killed the candidate's partner.

In high glee the rival **Missouri Republican** reported that Cockerill had shot the lawyer in cold blood. Public opinion was aroused and the impact on Pulitzer was unsettling. Although Cockerill was freed on a plea of self-defense, the episode proved to be a turning point in Pulitzer's life. Upset by the shooting and dismayed by the blow to his newspaper's prestige, he decided to visit Europe, but while awaiting his ship's sailing in New York Pulitzer was visited by representatives from Jay Gould's Wall Street offices. Pulitzer learned that the New York *World* might be purchased on credit. Gould, whose interests ranged from controlling railroads to (some said) presidents, had made a bad bargain when he bought the *World* and wanted out. Under Manton Marble's editorship the *World* had been a leading daily, but it had fallen on leaner days and was losing nearly $1,000 a week. The financier, impatient with a losing proposition, offered the *World* to Pulitzer for $346,000—none of it in cash.

Restless, eager to forget the St. Louis unpleasantness, and mindful of his younger brother's recent successful venture with the New York *Journal,* Pulitzer canceled his ocean voyage and agreed on the price. Albert Pulitzer had fallen out of favor with his brother, and there is no doubt but that this personal quarrel influenced Joseph Pulitzer's decision. According to Pulitzer's plan, the purchase price was to be paid out of the newspaper's profits. The man's temerity seemed boundless.

For his promissory note, Pulitzer had gained the *World's* declining reputation, an Associated Press franchise, a three-story building under lease, some worn-out presses, and a staff convinced that they worked for a dignified if starchy newspaper. At once, Pulitzer told his reporters they would have to leave the antiseptic atmosphere of the *World* city room and start prowling in the Bowery. After accepting resignations from those offended by his straight talk, Pulitzer began rebuilding the *World.* On May 11, 1883, Pulitzer announced

that the *World* would "from this day on, be under different management—different men, measures and methods—different in purpose,
policy and principle—different in objects and interests—different in
sympathies and convictions—different in head and heart." [4] Few
American newspapers ever staked out a more ambitious program and
still fewer ever pursued such a policy steadfastly. It sounded like another pretentious "statement of principles" that would become fly-
specked and frayed in a few months. Pulitzer meant every word, of
course, and from that first exciting day until a depressing one forty-
eight years later, the New York *World* set a pace that forced American journalism out of its editorial rut. Meanwhile, New York had another exciting event that somewhat overshadowed Pulitzer's debut,
for two weeks later the Brooklyn Bridge was finally opened (after
thirteen years of construction and disappointment). The *World* had
its first great news break six days after that, when panic struck pedes-
trians on the bridge's walkway after someone yelled (probably as a
prank) that the structure was about to collapse. The *World* headlines
told the tragic aftermath—twelve people crushed to death and forty
hospitalized with broken bones.

New York readers had seen a lot in their day—including the long-
remembered "horse blanket" newspapers of the 1850s, when the six-
cent *Journal of Commerce* measured 35 by 59 inches and took advantage of a poorly worded postal regulation—but they had never seen
anything like the *World*.[5] A contemporary of Bennett's said in admiration that to know the history of New York from 1835 to 1871 was
simply to scan the *Herald* files. With Pulitzer's entry into Manhattan
journalism, however, the *World* was to become the chief chronicler of
the city's life.

Lest it appear that Pulitzer's ambition and ownership were personal matters that had little effect on the people in St. Louis or New
York, the record shows a contrary picture. The pounding away at
corruption in gas company franchises and other wrongdoing in St.
Louis left the city with a legacy of progressivism. It was no happenstance that Lincoln Steffens's exposures that resulted in *The Shame of*

the Cities started with a news leak in St. Louis. In New York it is likely that *World* readers did not recognize Pulitzer's name as they had Greeley's, but they were the beneficiaries of the *World*'s presence through a more alert, compassionate reporting in all of the dailies. The methods of Pulitzer and Cockerill forced the competition to react by paying higher salaries, probing for stories in areas long neglected by the politically oriented press; and they added a vitality to life in the city by the impudent but honest tone of the *World*. Pulitzer returned the price of the paper to the prewar rate of two cents a copy, and by autumn both the *Tribune* and *Times* had to conform. The *World*'s typographic face was lifted, the editorial pages perked up, and the basic news of the day had more lilt and was in better company. The writing was condensed as the colorful side of the news was brought forward in a way other newspapers missed. Pulitzer proclaimed that the *World* was "the people's paper" and proceeded to prove it by promoting ice and coal funds for the poor, summer outings for tenement-bound youngsters, and a spectacular nickel-and-dime campaign to build a pedestal for the Statue of Liberty.

Within six months after the new *World* began making inroads on the journalism Establishment, it was clear that Pulitzer's reading of the public pulse had been unerring. Repeated disclosures of official corruption, bribery, and graft created a powerful resentment among voters. Party labels seemed meaningless when exposés showed that Republicans and Democrats often were in collusion as they ladled out spoils from public contracts or took bribes to allow gambling, prostitution, dope peddling, and other sordid activities to flourish in the underground of communities that wore the superficial appearance of staid, law-abiding righteousness.

The campaign of 1884, mixing politics and personal scandal, came during a wave of reform that the *World* rode with gusto. In terms of bitter invective the presidential contest probably marked the all-time low in such campaigns, as Grover Cleveland was pitted against the sanctimonious James G. Blaine. Pulitzer attached the *World* to

Cleveland's bandwagon, perhaps half-defiantly since Blaine was known to be a close associate of Jay Gould's.

Throughout the summer of 1884 old political loyalties were torn asunder. The New York *Evening Post* bolted to Cleveland, along with the *New York Times,* whereupon the *Tribune* blasted the latter for printing "vile scandals" about Blaine. The Buffalo *Evening Tribune* in Cleveland's home town "broke" (newspaper slang for the first revelation of a fact) a story charging the New York governor had once sired a bastard by a strumpet. The pro-Blaine Boston *Journal* leaped on this news and might have made more headway except that Cleveland wired his sweating supporters at the nominating Convention: "Whatever you say, tell the truth." Cleveland admitted he had formed "an illicit connection with a woman and a child had been born and given his name," but its paternity was uncertain. The public seemed to take this news in stride and was ready for more when the Indianapolis *Sentinel* charged that Blaine's early life also had been filled with scandal. Then a series of letters Blaine had written many years earlier, incriminating him in some shady dealings, were released to the newspapers in September. The letters seemed proof of Blaine's rapacity and several ended with his warning to the recipient to "Burn this letter." [6]

In the final days of campaigning Blaine's efforts to woo the huge Irish vote in New York and New England were damaged when an overzealous supporter told a public gathering that the Democrats were the party of "rum, Romanism, and rebellion." This slur on the Irish (not to mention whiskey drinkers and southerners) created a split in the northern vote and may have helped beat Blaine. He lost New York by 1,144 votes and with it the election. But it is possible that the remark was offset by votes from prejudiced nativists who resented the Irish immigrants. In the *New York Times* want ads printed during the campaign were over two full columns of "situation wanted" notices from women—mainly Irish and German immigrants—seeking jobs as servants, cooks, and seamstresses. Balanced against the evidence of widespread joblessness were six "help wanted" ads for domestics, and five of the parties seeking a servant specified that she be a Protestant.[7]

These classified notices along with the display advertisements from the expanding department stores furnished a considerable share of the revenues for the large-city dailies as the buying habits of the urban population underwent change. In New York the Cleveland-Blaine mudslinging had to fit between notices from R. H. Macy & Co., B. Altman, Bloomingdale's, and Lord & Taylor concerning wearing apparel, umbrellas, yard goods, and ready-made ladies' hats priced from "19 cents to 39 cents." The same tendency to consolidate many departments into one store was making Wanamaker's in Philadelphia, Marshall Field & Company in Chicago, and Jordan, Marsh & Company in Boston prime buyers of newspaper space at contract rates. More and more, readers in metropolitan areas tended to do their shopping in the newspapers rather than spend a whole day of bargain hunting on foot. Through the one- and two-column displays, a housewife could tell where nearly every family necessity could be purchased at the lowest price. Mass buying brought lower prices, and mass readers found out where they could shop for ready-made shirts, suits, and other products that had been bought at specialty shops in an earlier day. Ivory Soap, Royal Baking Powder, and an endless variety of extracts also bought their share of space to remind women that life was becoming easier at home. Ivory's slogan—It Floats—was one of the first efforts by an advertising agency to create a national market for a product through newspaper advertising claims.

One American newsman who looked at society and decided it was in need of both soap and a conscience was Jacob Riis, a Danish immigrant who worked on the New York *Tribune* for ten years and then switched to the *Sun* for another decade as a police reporter. A keen perception permitted Riis to see what postwar deflation and high immigration was doing to the inner cities. His authentic reports of conditions in overcrowded tenements, filled with evidence of human misery, awoke thoughtful citizens to the horrors that had proliferated in their midst. Riis investigated the city's water supply and proved it was carrying disease to rich and poor alike. Accompanied by a cameraman (whose plates were used by woodcutters as models for their engravings), Riis showed the despicable conditions of life in Mulberry Bend—the "foul core of New York's slums."

Politicians and landlords attacked Riis and his publishers, but his facts were unshakable. No wonder they retreated when Riis condensed twelve years of reporting into a searing indictment of landlords in *How the Other Half Lives* (1890). "So illogical is human greed," Riis wrote, that landlords justified the condition of their property by blaming "the filthy habits of the tenants . . . utterly losing sight of the fact that it was the tolerance of those habits which was the real evil, and that they . . . were alone responsible." [8] Riis exposed conditions in the sweatshops where young girls worked at least a fifty-hour week for daily wages of sixty cents. In the Hell's Kitchen area, he told readers, human derelicts rented cots for seven cents a night, paid a penny for a cup of coffee, and two cents for lunch. It was not uncommon to find a family of six living in a single room that cost them five dollars a month if white—seven dollars if black. Yet, Riis reported, Negro tenants were regarded as preferable to immigrant renters because landlords considered them cleaner and more law-abiding.

Everything Riis said was true but a portion of his readers thought his tactics were more those of a rabble-rouser than police reporter. One reader who sided with Riis was the New York police commissioner, Theodore Roosevelt, who urged Riis to organize groups that would combat poverty in the slums. Riis finally abandoned newspaper work to lecture and lead campaigns for better housing and improved living conditions for children. His belief that the poor "needed not a change but a chance" placed him in the vanguard of the reform movement that would imitate many of Riis's reporting techniques a few years later.[9]

Life in the teeming cities, declining farm prices, periodic financial panics, and severe extremes of weather were all reported in the newspapers to the post-Civil War generation, which was mainly rural in outlook. Stories of big-city crime and a scarcity of decent housing were read with satisfaction by Americans whose daily routine, garb, diet, and housing centered around farms where milk, bread, meat, and fresh vegetables were often in abundance. They seemed living proof of Jefferson's belief that agriculture was "the surest road to affluence and best preservative of morals." [10] Many farmers found the growing industrialism oftentimes merciless, however, and they banded together in cooperatives, supported inflationary Greenback movements, and urged legislators to curb avaricious railroad lords and beef trusts that absorbed profits yet took no risks on boll weevils, droughts, blizzards, or overproduction. In America's heartland, the Mississippi Valley, the Farmer's Alliance claimed it was sending its message for freight-rate regulations and eased credit through nine hundred weeklies, including the Raleigh, North Carolina, *Progressive Farmer*. Meanwhile, Henry George's single-tax idea found a journalistic supporter in the New York monthly *Spread the Light,* which urged a single-source land tax as the solution to the nation's financial woes.

When the midwesterner was not in his fields or tending flocks he could read farm journals, church newspapers, or seek the society of neighbors at corn huskings, church suppers, or Grange meetings. But for political guidance, thousands of readers between the Alleghenies and the Rockies turned to the great Chicago, Cincinnati, Cleveland, and St. Louis newspapers for advice. The great political issues of the generation appeared to be hard money and the tariff. Millions of words in print attest to what editors thought, but in general the voting habits of midwesterners indicate that farmers who needed lower tariff walls and easy credit stayed with the Republican party often enough to prevent effective change. In Iowa, the Des Moines *State Register* took advantage of the spreading rail network to become the chief proponent of Republican strategy and higher tariffs and the gold standard between Chicago and Denver. Early editions printed in Des Moines could blanket the state by 8 A.M. of the next day, a fact that turned the *Register* into a statewide newspaper of more than usual influence and a circulation far beyond that of most state capital journals.

Southwest of Iowa, the Kansas City *Star* shone in its own unique fashion under the direction of William Rockhill Nelson. The *Star* crowded into a Kansas City galaxy where four other newspapers were already serving 55,000 citizens who made a living selling each other real estate, packing meat, and switching railroad cars. Nelson offered the *Star* to subscribers for ten cents a week and hired a large staff at what one remembered as near-starvation wages. He built up circulation by tackling a streetcar franchise, urged his young reporters to peer into the folds of fat public contracts for secret corruption, and went on a one-man crusade of his own to make the sprawling cattle and rail center into a western oasis.

Nelson inspired his staff because of his honesty. William Allen White, then a young man on the make, took a job at the *Star* because it "was rated one of the dozen best and most influential newspapers in the country." White, who a generation later came to epitomize small-town journalism, recalled that Nelson was "a great hulking two-hundred-sixty-pounder, six feet tall, smooth-shaven, with a hard, dominating mouth . . . a mean jaw" and eyes that occasionally "squinted like the lightning of Job." [11] White thought Nelson had only one weakness: "His clay foot was Grover Cleveland, who could do no wrong." Nelson disliked the innovations Pulitzer introduced in New York and swore he would keep the *Star* pure by never printing any comics "and he made no concessions . . . in the way of big headlines or sensational exaggerations." [12] Living on the dividing line between the prairie and the plains, Nelson strove to make Kansas City a garden spot by promoting tree plantings, zoning ordinances, and well-planned residential districts. He carried the *Star* into battles against loan sharks, lottery frauds, quack doctors, and regarded the number of libel suits filed against the *Star* as an indication of whether his newspaper "was doing its duty." When a complaint about the *Star*'s crusading spirit was heard, the newspaper satirized the remark by listing the paved streets, playgrounds, libraries, well-designed homes, ventilated factories, reduced car fares, "and all the other things [that] have increased the cost of living and given people inflated ideas, and pretty nearly ruined the town." [13]

Between Kansas City and the Pacific Coast lay two thousand miles of terrain that periodically beckoned the get-rich-quick miner and the credit-seeking farmer in search of the dwindling public domain. A contemporary of Nelson's who had gone West looking for rare opportunities but finally took over direction of a down-at-the-heel newspaper was Harrison Gray Otis. Colonel Otis had a midwestern veteran's zeal for the Republican party as his chief asset when he purchased the Los Angeles *Times* in 1882. From his own background as a printer, Otis was friendly toward labor and tried to work out an ideal relationship with his employees as a land boom brought prosperity to southern California. Real estate promoters opened tracts for citrus groves while doctors' testimonials on the health-giving effects of the southern California climate were trumpeted throughout the nation by a well-organized boosters' club. The region around Los Angeles was said to be particularly good for chronic sufferers of consumption, or tuberculosis; but this plague of the print shop affected so many victims that the local International Typographical Union took ads in eastern labor papers explaining that there were no more jobs in southern California. Tuberculosis victims continued to pour into the area, however, so that the struggling union found it hard to keep a wage scale steady on a glutted labor market.

Otis had some of the booster virus in his veins and was determined to make Los Angeles a great transportation center. He challenged the powerful Southern Pacific Railroad over the location of a harbor and successfully located the port at San Pedro instead of the railroad's choice at Santa Monica. The awesome presence of the Southern Pacific intimidated newspapers elsewhere in California, however. As Frank Norris showed in his novel *The Octopus*, the effects of free passes for editors and advertising contracts had been persuasive in keeping protests down over most of the state. In the San Francisco *Bulletin* and Sacramento *Bee* the railroad found newspaper editors with courage enough, however, to denounce its domination of the capital and most county courthouses. Fremont Older challenged the railroad as the chief agency of corruption in his city and braved threats against his life, a kidnapping, and personal indignities while he persisted in a campaign that eventually brought jail sentences to the *Bulletin*'s local targets. The *Bee*, edited by C. K. McClatchy, noted the bribery rampant in the capitol corridors and also fought against privately owned utilities and streetcar lines. The railroad was bipartisan, choosing its senators and representatives from either party so long as their main loyalty was to the Southern Pacific. The gains made by newspaper crusaders were of brief duration until another generation passed and a reform movement, aided by Older and McClatchy, helped sweep the rascals out.

The dominant West Coast newspaper in the 1880s and 1890s remained the San Francisco *Chronicle*, which began as a throwaway theatrical program but developed into a powerful daily journal. The reform spirit of the *Chronicle* was diminished in 1880 when one of the founding partners and brothers, Charles De Young, was assassinated after a tense war of words in a local election erupted into a pitched battle. De Young wounded the Workingmen's Party candidate for mayor and was in turn gunned down by the candidate's son.[14] His brother, Michael H. De Young, was more of a regular in Republican party councils and preferred promoting San Francisco to gunfighting. Labor warfare flared on the wharves of San Francisco, Irish and Italian immigrants moved into the Bay area to fight or marry each other, and while southern California remained mostly desert it appeared that San Francisco would become to the West what New York had been to the East—a pace-setting town with six dailies. This newspaper sextet included the *Evening Examiner*, owned by Senator George Hearst. The *Bee* said Hearst was losing $250,000 a year on his newspaper, but with his fortune of $20 million made from mining and cattle Hearst seemed unperturbed. Some western newspapers had reputations for solidity both editorial and financial. The Portland

Oregonian flourished under the guidance of Harvey W. Scott, a fiercely loyal Republican lawyer turned editor. And at Salt Lake City, the *Deseret News* told faithful members of the Mormon Church all they needed to know each morning about the world beyond the Wasatch Mountains.

Across the nation American journalism was responding to the country's seam-bursting growth. Every steamship docking at an eastern port seemed full of immigrants as 5,250,000 arrived during the 1880s. The population rose from 50 million in 1880 to nearly 63 million ten years later, and daily newspapers expanded in similar fashion. While the West was losing its frontier flavor in 1890, the census showed the country had doubled its population since 1860 and now had 1,610 daily newspapers with a 3.5 million circulation—statistics that Europeans read with incomprehension. As dailies sprang up, the old weeklies disappeared. The once-mighty New York *Tribune* weekly edition that had spoken to the Midwest in oracular paragraphs finally went out of business in the 1890s along with the other outmoded weekly or semiweekly editions of the *Herald, Times,* and *World* in New York. Their revenue-producing role had been replaced by the expanding Sunday editions, which contained little hard news but a tantalizing assortment of features along with sports and society columns and ever-larger advertisements.

Printing experiments in photo reproduction had been successful at Cornell University around 1878, but only for slow-moving flatbed presses.[15] The result was that book publishers could duplicate photographs but high-speed cylindrical presses could not adapt the process. Most newspapers continued use of the woodcut engravings until the end of the century, although notable promotions such as the Boston *Journal* Sunday edition of May 6, 1894, carried more "halftones" than most dailies printed in a month. The process involved metal plates which created pictures through shadings produced by small dots—and added an engraving department to most large newspapers by 1910. The traditional "mug shot"—head and shoulders—remained a journalistic standby as photo journalism remained in its experimental stage in America when faster strides were being made abroad.

The technology of journalism after the Civil War was as sweeping as the changes occurring in the editorial rooms. Rag paper could not compete with the cheaper newsprint manufactured from wood pulp heavily impregnated with chemicals that helped hold down the price of newspapers. The Hoe Company brought out a revolutionary press in 1882 that was continuously fed by cylindrical rolls of newsprint and capable of printing 24,000 twelve-page newspapers per hour; and by the end of the decade had perfected a faster press that doubled this wondrous capacity. The presses cost as much as $80,000 each, so that any newspaper needing such speed soon became a million-dollar operation.[16] Increasing use of the telephone and typewriter changed the reportorial system, speeding the flow of local news to city rooms from newsmen assigned to "beats" who covered stories and relayed their information to rewrite men. Printers, plagued for four centuries by the indifferent handwriting that sometimes made them qualify as cryptographers, hailed the typewriter as a godsend. Only one more invention was needed before the whole system would fall into place and stand still for a century.

The printers still set their type by hand in 1884, but the near-success of a half dozen power-driven setters heralded the end of this drudgery. Several fortunes were spent developing various type-setting devices but the one machine that clearly stood above the rest for efficiency and cost was Ottmar Merganthaler's Linotype. The Linotype featured the keyboard principle, a labor-saving device for standardizing the length of all lines ("justifying" in printer's language), and automatic redistribution of the matrices after the line ("slug") had been cast from molten metal. Certain flaws in the machine were gradually eliminated through pragmatic techniques, and patent infringement suits proved troublesome. A trained operator could set three or four times as much type in an eight-hour day as four printers working with hand-set equipment. The cost of a Linotype (around

$18,000) meant it was no country-editor's toy, but a necessary device everywhere that speed and competition demanded labor-saving techniques despite the expense.

Country journalism remained important in an America where the majority of the citizens still lived on farms and in small towns. Local news of births, deaths, weddings, ladies' aid social affairs, school honor rolls, elections, shootings, and assorted misdemeanors escaped the coverage of city newspapers but were important to more than 40 million people who resisted the lure of urban life. In the final decade of the nineteenth century nearly 11,000 weeklies were operating—about 1,900 in the old South, with the rest of the thirty-three states and three territories producing some 9,000 four- and eight-page editions that told of small-community life. Henry Grady's weekly edition of the Atlanta *Constitution* was an important force in the South, but the county-seat newspapers in thousands of towns were institutions of importance and power in local affairs. Grady's editorials spoke of a new, industrialized South and the boondock editors took up the cry. Between times, however, local editors in Kentucky and Iowa shared a common bond as they dutifully reported the first arrival of a wagonload of cotton or corn, the size of the largest squash or watermelon grown that summer, and the length of a prodigious catfish pulled from the Ohio or Missouri bottoms.

New York editors bothered about cable tolls and the price of gold or Erie Railroad shares, but the important problems of runaway horses, lost livestock, and quagmire roadways had a high priority in weekly newspapers. When the editor of the Stanford, Kentucky, *Journal* broke his leg because of a treacherous sidewalk, he was quick to blame the town council for the conditions of public thoroughfares. Chances are good that Stanford's sidewalks were repaired that next week, and the same rapid response must have been true in Greensboro, North Carolina, after its *Herald* campaigned for more genteel conduct by the tobacco-chewing gentry whose aim at public spittoons was hardly perfect. More perplexing for the southern weekly editors was a stance on the ever-present racial tensions. Their attitudes ranged from the Oglethorpe, Georgia, *Echo* position that the black man "could never be a good citizen and should not be educated," to the Yorkville, South Carolina, *Enquirer*'s view that the whites owed the Negro "the opportunity to improve his condition and elevate himself above the level of absolute ignorance." [17] Perhaps as an antidote for the bitterness in race relations, the southern editors often turned to sentimental subjects shorn of all controversy. When a community needed to "simmer down" it was always safe to run an editorial on southern womanhood, as the Sparta, Georgia, *Ishmaelite* proved in 1891. A lady born and bred below the Mason-Dixon line, the *Ishmaelite* editor said, was "the strongest power in the South, that sweet-voiced, gentle, womanly creature that we call the Southern girl." [18]

Northern ladies also had a champion in Charles Dana Gibson, a beardless lad when he first took his drawings to *Life* magazine in 1887. *Life* began its existence as a humor magazine in 1883 and was then struggling for a national audience interested in contemporary art and letters along with some jibes at the social scene. Gibson's drawings of lovely girls soon captured not only *Life*'s readers but also the whole nation as the ideal concept of what a young American female ought to look like. Her thick upswept coiffure, tilted nose, sensuous lips, and perfect jaw line made her seem to step out "of *Life* into life." Rarely has a magazine illustrator had such an influence on a whole nation's attitude of what constituted the epitome of beauty, yet Gibson's girls influenced a whole generation of Americans. Along with the Gibson man, who came to be known in the advertising world as "the Arrow Collar man," the vision of loveliness first revealed in *Life* subconsciously spread to all popular art forms in America down to World War I. "Fifth Avenue looked like an endless procession of Gibsons to one contemporary, who might have made the same remark of most Main Streets." [19]

Along with an eternal interest in pretty girls, the 1890s showed some interest in faded memories of the pioneer woman in the popular weekly magazines, but more attention was focused on improving the modern woman's lot than in praising her past history. Farm-belt weeklies from Ohio through Nebraska carried columns of recipes, sewing guidance, and news of the growing woman's club movement. At county and state fairs the quilting and canning achievements of ladies were well publicized each autumn, while news of the local women's missionary society was a year-round standby. The Sunday school movement brought lists of names into the weekly newspaper columns as more than one editor was willing to forsake use of distant news items to print stories about local boys and girls. And if the *New York Times* could devote a whole column to the Yale commencement, it was only fitting that the Wabash, Indiana, *Plaindealer* should go overboard when the local college turned out its graduates in May or June.

Small-town journalism in the Missouri Valley also helped foster the cult of folk heroes with partisan coverage of the James brothers' gang. Farmers angered by low commodity prices and high railroad rates took some comfort from reports of train robberies, and the Robin Hood aura already was attached to Jesse James when he was assassinated in April 1882. The Sedalia, Missouri, *Democrat* editor collected from the exchanges a sizable list of other newspapers that joined in condemning James's murder. "Why the whole State reeks today with a double orgy, that of lust and that of murder. . . . Tear the two bears from the flag of Missouri. Put thereon in place of them as more appropriate, a thief blowing out the brains of an unarmed victim, and a brazen harlot, naked to the waist and splashed to the brows in blood." [20] In the true spirit of competition, the *Democrat* started a charity fund for Mrs. Jesse James while the rival *Bazoo* collected money for the widow of a conductor shot during a train holdup.

Politics furnished far more reliable copy for the weeklies than crime, however. The Grand Army of the Republic, a veterans' organization allied with the Republican party, held annual encampments that were fully reported as demonstrations that the Union had been preserved and the election of Grover Cleveland had been a grand fluke. For southern weekly editors, on the other hand, Cleveland was the "political messiah" who had saved America from ruin.[21] When Senator Tom Watson left the Democratic party, weekly editors from the Carolinas to Texas leveled their editorial guns at the Populist oracle who was accused of trying to wreck the opposition to Republican tariff policies.

Occasionally the press of the entire country would bury the hatchet temporarily, as at the deaths of Jefferson Davis and U. S. Grant. Grant's death in 1885, after a touching struggle against poverty and disease, had brought a similar reaction in both North and South. Davis died in 1889 and the friendly remarks in northern newspapers were reprinted throughout the South, as veterans of both sections "joined hands in grief and friendship." The campaign to build a base for the Statue of Liberty, the 225-ton bronze gift to the United States from the French government, also was presented to the people as a non-partisan affair. Promoted by the New York *World*, the base was built with $100,000 raised in a campaign where school children's nickels and dimes were welcomed along with larger contributions. When the Goddess of Liberty was unveiled in October 1886 the *World* trumpeted the achievement as another blessing personally arranged by Mr. Pulitzer.

Still, controversy could not be kept out of the papers, and everywhere social and economic unrest underlay much of the nation's news. As finishing touches were applied to the Statue in New York Harbor, printers and other workmen paid increasing attention to the movement for an eight-hour workday which seemed a distant dream to laboring men accustomed to work from ten to twelve hours, with a seventy-hour workweek not uncommon. Confronted with the Linotype machine and increased use of stereotyping (printing whole pages from a single metal casting), metropolitan printers demanded a nine-hour day and a 45-cent minimum hourly wage. Strikes occurred and labor unrest was notable in the larger cities, particularly Chicago, where an Eight-Hour Association had been organized in 1885 with support from the Knights of Labor, the Socialistic Labor party, and a sprinkling of support from tradesmen and radical anarchists. May 1 was picked as the day when a general eight-hour workday movement would commence. Most newspapers depicted the campaign as unrealistic, and even the *Knights of Labor* newspaper in Chicago "withdrew its support, holding the time was not propitious." [22]

May Day came and went with no sign of the heralded general strike. Sporadic walkouts occurred, however, and unrest was most noticeable at the McCormick Harvesting Machine Company plant, where strikebreakers went to work protected by over two hundred policemen and detectives. A witness to the attack on workers and their families by police on May 3 wrote an inflammatory handbill which was printed at the *Arbeiter-Zeitung* in German and English, ending with a plea: "To arms we call you, to arms!" The next morning Chicagoans read the Chicago *Tribune* headlines: *A Wild Mob's Work. Ten Thousand Men Storm M'Cormick's Harvester Works, Wrought up to a Frenzy by Anarchistic Harangues.* [23] At a mass meeting in Haymarket Square that night a bomb exploded near a column of policemen, followed by gunfire, screams, and widespread panic. Seven policemen and one civilian were killed or died later from wounds, while sixty-six officers and twelve other persons were badly injured.

The reaction to the Haymarket bombing was a frenzied call for punishment to the "foreign Anarchists" accused of throwing the bomb. Organized labor tried to wash the stigma from its ranks and Chicago's oldest trade union, Typographical No. 16, branded the bomb thrower "the greatest enemy the laboring man has." [24] Ten men, including the writer of the Revenge Circular and the editor of a radical newspaper, were indicted for murder, although no evidence was ever presented identifying the "bomber." All but two of the ten men were either German or of German descent. Only four of the defendants were hanged that November and the rest were either pardoned, had their sentences commuted, or escaped trial for other reasons. The incident shook public confidence in the labor movement and the conservative press long referred to the Haymarket affair as the outcropping of foreign agitation bound to end in violence and bloodshed.

When incidents arising from such tensions were not the staple of the press, lust made headlines during the 1880s when Anthony Comstock took to the warpath against printed works he believed were fomenters of crime. As the chief agent for the New York Society for the Suppression of Vice, Comstock inveighed against the "death traps" that were offered for sale in newspaper advertisements and weekly "blood-and-thunder" journals. "The eye of youth has been defiled with the scenes of lasciviousness in the weekly criminal papers, or by their offsprings, obscene books and pictures," Comstock charged, and "newspaper gossip" gave the depraved "moral monsters" a glamor that bore the odor of brimstone. Comstock lobbied for federal legislation and claimed that prior to 1882 he had pointed authorities to 22,354 newspapers "containing unlawful advertisements or obscene matter." [25] Comstock's energy and zeal kept him at constant warfare with the so-called smut-peddlers, and his definition of "lust in print" was so broad he gave anxious moments even to editors of family newspapers.

For the average American the weather still kept his interest, and newspapers in 1888–1889 never had more unleashed natural fury to report. First there was the Great Blizzard of 1888, which gripped a frozen Atlantic seaboard for four days in heavy snow and intense cold. Ill-housed victims perished from the cold while others suffered from a panic caused when food supplies ran low and fuel deliveries were cut off. A similar cold wave struck in the West decimating cattle herds and shattering the dreams of heavily mortgaged farmers. The most spectacular news of the decade came in May 1889 when heavy rains caused a dam to give way above Johnstown, Pennsylvania, unleashing a twenty-foot wall of water that shot down from Lake Conemaugh into a deep valley, engulfing four towns and drowning 2,200 victims. The magnitude of the tragedy was slowly revealed by newspapers as the toll of flood victims mounted. An unbelieving nation was stunned by the disaster, which remains the worst peacetime tragedy in American history. For almost a week the high water and debris made it impossible to tell how much damage had been done, and even the conservative *New York Times* printed early estimates of a death toll of 10,000. Flood news filled all of the *Times* front page on the day after disaster struck (except for the two-column R. H. Macy advertising) and was to claim a major share of space in most dailies until mid-June. Predictably, there was a search for the scapegoat after it was reported that cracks and leaks in the earthen dam had been noticed early in the spring but ignored by residents who lived below. While public officials, railroad executives, and angry citizens pointed accusing fingers at each other, the *Times* viewed the controversy as meaningless. What did it matter, said the *Times*, that leaks had been rumored for weeks before the dam gave way? "Men have always been willing to take these risks, and they always will." [26]

And when the excitement of natural disaster subsided, promotional extravaganzas, stimulated by knowing editors, dominated headlines. America was still talking about the Johnstown flood when John L. Sullivan fought Jake Kilrain in a seventy-five-round battle with bare knuckles at Richburg, Mississippi on July 8, 1899. The news of Sullivan's victory was carried in many newspapers as prominently as the spring disaster had been, and when "Gentleman Jim" Corbett squared off against Sullivan in New Orleans in September 1892 for a mythical heavyweight championship of the world, the Chicago *Tribune* treated the event as one of the great news stories of all time. The *Tribune* sent special correspondents to New Orleans who telegraphed a blow-by-blow description to Chicago, so that the prizering collision required the entire front page, all of page two, and part of the third page.

As Pulitzer had discovered, news no longer consisted only of those events Providence "allowed to happen." After promoting interest in politics for 125 years, the newspapers discovered that reader interest was not related to the intrinsic significance of an event as much as to the amount of newspaper space devoted to it for days and weeks in advance. The newspapers, by their constant focusing of attention on

Sulllvan, made him into a national idol and then thrilled readers vicariously by reporting every detail of what was hailed as the first-of-many battles of the century. Without a computerized study to prove what a random sample indicates, it can only be said that real battle of the century at Gettysburg received far less attention from the nation's press in 1863 than did the contrived contest of 1892.

Thus had the national scale of values been changed by the new journalism first promoted as a response to the boredom and frustration of urban life. Newspapers increasingly offered a daily fare of easily reported pseudo-events. The term *pseudo-event,* coined by historian Daniel J. Boorstin, grows out of America's journalistic experience since the Civil War as newspapers and later other media have given inordinate coverage to prearranged events. The first characteristic of a pseudo-event, Boorstin noted, is that "it is not spontaneous, but comes about because someone has planned, planted, or incited it." [27] The Corbett-Sullivan fight, probably the greatest of nineteenth-century pseudo-events, was a "battle of the century" because readers of newspapers thought the exuberant sports reporters knew what they were writing about and found the buildup of suspense more exciting than the actual outcome of the contest.

I I

Rich Man, Poor Man

William Randolph Hearst cannot be ignored in a history of American journalism although there is a strong temptation to hurry past his career as one would move swiftly by a graveyard at midnight. Not that there is anything wrong with graveyards or midnight, yet in the same way that the combination of the two causes apprehension, Hearst and newspapers together boded ill. Left to a life of dilettantism and political dabbling, Hearst would have been fairly harmless. It was the combination of Hearst and journalism that made him appear to be a formidable force in American life for nearly forty years. With more perspective it is obvious that Mr. Hearst was a self-indulgent egocentric who was rich enough to buy a number of newspapers. He inherited his wealth and proceeded to spend most of it, and his journalistic impact after 1904 was negligible.

Hearst managed to ruffle the Harvard faculty in 1885 for a college prank that in 1972 would have scarcely raised an eyebrow. He was expelled and thus left free to do what he wanted—run a newspaper. As the son of the mining and cattle king Senator George Hearst of California, the young upstart talked his father into allowing him to control the editorial policies of his family's newspaper property, the San Francisco *Examiner*. At twenty-four Hearst was enamoured with the New York *World*, and being of an eclectic rather than original bent, he set out to imitate Pulitzer by hiring a brilliant staff and turning them loose on crooked politicians, petty criminals, the Southern Pacific Railroad, and whatever else seemed a likely target for the rejuvenated San Francisco *Examiner*.[1] Readers responded by buying the *Examiner* in such numbers that its circulation doubled in 1887–1888, and would continue to climb as the tall, freehanded young publisher urged his reporters to seek out the sensational so that Bay area residents would feel culturally deprived if they did not read the *Examiner* each morning.

Hearst craved attention and power. He thought the newspaper that could outdistance the New York *World* would bring him both, and with a fortune of nearly $7 million as his stabilizer the young Californian took a calculated gamble. He hired Ambrose Bierce, a caustic but excellent reporter, and began guerrilla warfare against the mighty Southern Pacific by publicizing all of its wrecks, even the slightest derailment, as major disasters or close shaves with destiny. Bierce, who hated nearly everything anyway (his misogyny was legendary), tackled Leland Stanford as an unconscionable railroad tycoon interested only in profits. "£eland $tanford" was Bierce's way of alluding to the junior senator from California, whose crime was that he took government subsidies to build a railroad and then gave $2.5 million for a memorial university named after his only son.[2] The war against the railroad grew more heated when Collis P. Huntington revealed that the *Examiner* had been one of the so-called bribed newspapers, receiving $1,000 a month in return for "immunity from hostility in the columns of the *Examiner*" as well as a promise that Hearst's newspaper would not "seek to create hostile sentiment in the minds or the community against the Southern Pacific Company."[3] Hearst must have known of the contract because he personally turned it over to a bank as collateral during a financial pinch he suffered in 1893. Huntington revealed the bribe to prove Hearst lacked integrity—which seemed to be in short supply both at the railroad executive suite and at the *Examiner*. The upshot was that one newspaper was removed from the South Pacific's "gravy train" and Hearst chose to ignore the exposé while making new changes in other directions.

Meanwhile, Joseph Pulitzer's brother had made a great mistake in judgment and raised the price of his competitor with the *World* to two cents. The *Morning Journal* went into an immediate tailspin and had to be sold in 1895. Hearst made leaping strides in California but ached for a chance to prove his mettle in the only place that really seemed to count—New York. With the *Examiner* now prospering and his widowed mother commanding the family purse strings, Hearst learned of the *Journal's* continued plight and offered $180,000 for both the English and German-language editions of the faltering *Journal*. Hearst's goal was simple. He was going to beat the *World* at its own game by hiring good reporters and talented editors who would use the largest type possible to tell the city that a new boy was in town. Lurid crime news, feature stories appealing to the same audience that had made Bennett's *Herald* a success sixty years earlier, and large-scale illustrations soon vaulted the *Journal* into the front ranks of Manhattan journalism.

Pulitzer fought back but made a tactical error. When the *World* upset New York publishers and forced them to drastic action in 1883, they had cut their street price to a penny. Now Pulitzer (admittedly his health was not good—his nerves were on edge and his eyesight deteriorating) reacted to Hearst by cutting the *World* from two cents to one. Pulitzer made up for some of the lost income by increasing his advertising rate, but the overall effect was to tell the city that Hearst had hurt the *World*. As Pulitzer later asked, "I wonder why [I did it], in view of my experience?" [4] The rest of the New York newspapers ducked as the *World* and *Journal* scrapped for a commanding circulation lead over its rival. Hearst is said to have hired an office in the *World* building so he could pirate Pulitzer's staff more easily. As the champion of William Jennings Bryan in the 1896 election, the *Journal* stood almost alone in the metropolis where the youthful Democrat's "Cross of Gold" speech made few friends on Wall Street. Hearst delighted in the underdog role and furthered his Democratic pretensions; then his staff uncovered a public-utility swindle that seemed to prove all the *Journal's* self-praise was true. Hearst paid Mark Twain to cover Queen Victoria's Diamond Jubilee celebration in London while the Victorian attitudes of many New Yorkers caused them to blanch at the eternal-triangle murder stories or at daring artists' sketches of actresses, slain mistresses, and other wayward women.

The pace of the *Journal* was dizzy and expensive. Hearst took the profits from the *Examiner* and dipped into the family bank account to pay top-notch reporters $200 a week to leave the *World* and join in the excitement. Color presses were added, and a cartoonist left Pulitzer to draw his "Yellow Kid" for the Sunday edition as a new feature called "the funnies" spread a circulation net for the obstreperous *Journal.*[5] Indeed, the expression *yellow journalism* came from the circulation war conducted by the *World* and *Journal* as they slugged in the marketplace for the pennies of New York readers. Slowly, Hearst began to creep within striking distance of the idolized *World.* But as he did, the emphasis on sex, crime, and sensationalism caused the public to do more than talk about yellow journalism. A segment of the public, at any rate, had its fill of the newspapers' indifference to significance when there was headline type of ever-bigger dimensions for proclaiming the latest *Raid on Love Nest* or a speculative feature on whether Lizzie Borden had really killed her wealthy parents with a hatchet.

Part of the reaction to yellow journalism was the strict moral code of an era that tolerated Anthony Comstock and found it slightly indecent to talk about the legs of a piano. But there was also a part of the community that needed information that the battling giants neglected. A young entrepreneur from Chattanooga, Tennessee, saw the attrition of respectable journalism in New York with more than casual interest. He had already proved his ability to succeed in journalism by his careful resurrection of the Chattanooga *Times* from a debt-ridden journal (that cost him $250) into a prosperous newspaper. Adolph Ochs found the prestigious *New York Times* crumbling under a huge debt and loss of revenue. The asking price required only $75,000 in cash, the rest to come on profits—if ever there were any.[6] Ochs took over the *Times* while Hearst was still gloating over his triumphs in the 1896 presidential campaign. As it turned out, Ochs had the last laugh.

Ochs was a businessman, not a newspaperman. He therefore understood that he could not beat either Hearst or Pulitzer at their own game. What he needed was an innovation that would reverse the trend. The innovation was found, and Ochs called it by a simple name: good taste. The *Times* announced it would cover financial news, politics, and other affairs without stress on crimes of passion and violence. The *Times* would tell of new trends in the world of art, review the latest books, and through an exchange agreement with the London *Times* would provide worldwide coverage of important events. Ochs declared that his newspaper, unlike several he could mention, "Does Not Soil the Breakfast Cloth." Where other newspapers placed their daily circulation figures in the front page "ears" (boxes on each side of the newspaper's nameplate), the *Times* simply proclaimed it would carry "All the News That's Fit to Print." The rising middle-class readers, the financial community on Wall Street, and the department store advertising departments responded. It took two years and much patience, and one more innovation (Ochs cut the *Times*'s street-sale price to a penny). When the Spanish-American War ended, the *Times* was reaching 75,000 readers daily and making money.

Before the *Times* finally reached solid footing, the nation had fought a tiny war and there are those who say the *World* and *Journal* caused the whole mess. Frank Luther Mott, who studied the jingoism of the *World* and *Journal* for decades, concluded "that if Hearst had not challenged Pulitzer to a circulation contest at the time of the Cuba insurrection, there [probably] would have been no Spanish-

American War" [7] A search through other newspapers during the Cuban uprising of 1895 shows, on the other hand, that in New York the *Sun, Times,* and *Herald* spoke sternly about the Spanish yoke to the southward. More significantly, the *Literary Digest* in April 1895 carried an article titled "Are Americans Spoiling for War?" The prophetic magazine feature said the idea of manifest destiny, of sympathy for downtrodden Cubans, and of wartime profits might push the country into conflict with Spain.[8]

While confusing reports from the Cuban jungles trickled northward, Pulitzer cut his price to one cent with the expectation that the move would push *World* circulation to over a million copies. With the *Journal* in the vanguard, correspondents in Cuba began sending dispatches to Florida telling of atrocities committed by Spanish troops under General Valeriano Weyler. The Cuban insurgents were depicted by the *World* as assisted by beautiful Amazon guerrilla fighters with "olive complexions . . . white teeth, and dark eyes that flash out a light that when angered is terrible." [9] Hearst contributed to the legend by exploiting the imprisonment of Evangelina Cisneros, niece of the insurgent's provisional president. The *Journal* hinted at the "unspeakable fate to which Weyler has doomed an innocent girl whose only crime is that she has defended her honor against a beast in uniform." [10] With the flair of a light-opera hero, Hearst ordered one of his best reporters to Cuba with a single assignment: help Miss Cisneros escape from jail and bring her to New York. Somehow, the resourceful *Journal* reporter followed Hearst's orders and the newspaper sponsored a parade for the fugitive heroine that wound to a triumphant meeting in Union Square.

Hearst began plotting his moves as a general orders armies. His staff was keyed for action when the *Maine* blew up in Havana harbor early in 1898. Whether Hearst had once promised the bored artist Frederic Remington (after a complaint that war was not imminent), "You furnish the pictures and I'll furnish the war," is questionable. But once the *Maine* incident occurred it was only a matter of time until the country was clamoring for war. President McKinley, far from being a warmonger, had not the slightest chance of avoiding a formal declaration once the headline fever of the New York "yellows" had spread to the Boston *Herald*, Chicago *Tribune*, San Francisco *Examiner*, New Orleans *Times-Democrat*, and other leading newspapers.

McKinley's efforts to delay action after the *Maine* explosion included a request for a defense appropriation of $50 million. Most of the New York press called the president's move a "peace appropriation" or "the shortest cut to peace," but the *Journal* would have none of such milk-and-water talk. "For War! $50,000,000!" the *Journal* proclaimed.[11]

Hearst was right, of course. It was one of the few times Hearst ever hit the nail so he never forgot it, but within a month McKinley had been backed into a corner by the newspapers and a bellicose Congress. The *World* chided the president for his hesitancy in an editorial on "Mr. McKinley's Quibbles and Straddles." A month after the "peace appropriation" had been sought, the nation was on a war footing. Whether Hearst was the engineer at the throttle now seemed irrelevant, for America was highballing toward war with what the world believed to be a major land-and-naval power.

As it turned out, the war was over so fast newspapers barely had time to get reporters placed with the fleets and armies before the Spanish sued for peace. Ten weeks after the bombardment of Manila, the myth of Spanish power had been destroyed and with fewer than four hundred Americans actually killed in combat. If not the most popular war in America's history, it was assuredly the quickest, and yet it had given rise to a bundle of heroes. Colonel Theodore Roosevelt's Rough Riders were well covered by a swarm of reporters whose colorful reporting helped the New Yorker mount the stairs to the White House. Stephen Crane, Richard Harding Davis, George Kennan, Frank Norris, and a host of other reporters gained personal attention as the "by-line brigade" not only received bonuses for their exploits but much-sought-after personal recognition, ending the days of anonymous news reporting. The words "By Stephen Crane" helped sell thousands of newspapers to those who had found his *Red Badge of Courage* the best war novel from an American pen. Frederic Remington, Howard Chandler Christy, and W. A. Rogers sent back artists' sketches that carried an urgent sense of battle for readers of *Leslie's, Harper's Weekly,* and the Hearst entourage. Action photographs from the battlefronts were rarely printed, but no loss of the drama was possible with such talented artists in the field.

When the war was at its height, Hearst's ego could not be contained. "How do you like the *Journal's* war?" appeared as a slogan in several issues of his New York plaything. But as the years intervene it has become clearer that neither Hearst nor Pulitzer nor any other one man in American politics or journalism brought on the Spanish-American War. "The press could have helped bring on the war only if the people were ready for it," historian Charles H. Brown concluded in a judgment not likely to be overturned.[12]

No one enjoyed the war as had Hearst. He felt powerful indeed as the *Journal* circulation mounted ever higher in the wake of the postwar euphoria, finally reaching more than 1.5 million copies and hovering there until the fall months. But power in the pressroom was not capable of easy transfer to politics, Hearst found, when he threw the *Journal* wholeheartedly behind Bryan's second campaign in 1900 and was swamped by mild-mannered McKinley again. The Hearst newspapers had shown a notable vindictiveness in the effort to defeat McKinley by personal attacks that did no credit to either the writers or the publisher. A senseless bit of doggerel by Bierce that ran in the *Examiner* and *Journal* after a Kentucky politician had been assassinated later seemed too clairvoyant:

> The bullet that pierced Goebel's breast
> Can not be found in all the West;
> Good reason, it is speeding here
> To stretch McKinley on his bier.[13]

Shortly after McKinley's second inaugural the *Journal* made the editorial suggestion that "If bad institutions and bad men can be got rid of only by killing, then the killing must be done." [14] When McKinley was shot by an anarchist in September, the *Journal*'s intemperate words were recalled and there was even a rumor that the assassin carried a *Journal* in his coat. The public outcry against Hearst was immediate, ranging from a mob that hanged the publisher in effigy to a boycott by readers that caused a serious circulation slump. To remove some of the sting, Hearst renamed his New York property the *American and Journal* and ordered his writers to take it easy on the new president—Theodore Roosevelt.

In the reaction to McKinley's murder the "yellows" all tended to show a more sober side. And Hearst's feud with Pulitzer also lost its steam after the transplanted, mule-headed Missourian began to suffer from a variety of bodily ills. His high-strung nature had always been apparent, but by the turn of the century Pulitzer found even ordinary street-traffic noise almost unbearable and sought seclusion in soundproof hideaways while underlings took orders on *World* policy. Surely it was not Pulitzer himself who ordered the first gasoline-engine delivery truck ever used by a New York newspaper, for the backfire from one of its cylinders would have maddened him; but soon the seventy-horse *World* stable would be turned into a garage for the fleet of twenty vans that bore a million papers daily from pressrooms to street corners.

There was no letup in competition among other publishers, however. In New York, probably 2 million of the city's 3 million souls read at least one of the fifteen daily newspapers offered at newsstands. The Socialist party's weekly *Appeal to Reason* claimed over 100,000 circulation in 1899. In the whole country there were over 2,000 dailies in 1898 and close to 14,000 weeklies. Country newspapers served a large but more sedentary readership, with a format in 1898 similar to the standards of 1848. The impact of the new journalism was felt in the cities which were becoming more crowded, noisier, dirtier, and dehumanizing. Perceptive reporters who saw the changes made in the name of progress began to ask themselves and their city editors questions above the din over tariff rates, silver coinage, and other partisan issues. The social concern Riis showed in his series on slums and George W. Cable's exposé of the convict lease system left a residue on the conscience of the younger reporters who saw that the tenements were not disappearing, that sweatshops were still crammed with coughing young women, and that reform movements in city hall had a way of turning into cynical machines with only a new set of rascals in office.

Precisely when this new breed of reporter forced his way into metropolitan journalism cannot be fixed in time, but the avenue was the magazine rather than the newspaper, and one periodical over all others: *McClure's Magazine.* As S. S. McClure's staff admitted when the magazine moved into high gear as the crusading journal par excellence, their laying bare the seamy side of American life was not the result of any calculated or planned campaign. Instead, the Irish-born McClure met so many writers and made so many commitments that finally, through happenstance, he had brought together the talents of three outstanding reporters in Ida Tarbell, Lincoln Steffens, and Ray Stannard Baker. When Miss Tarbell's "History of the Standard Oil" serial appeared in the January 1903 issue of *McClure's* along with Steffens' "Shame of Minneapolis," and Barker's "The Right to Work," the magazine electrified American journalism.[15] Carefully researched articles that gave the names of corrupted men, with intimate details on their avarice and their victims, impressed a whole new generation of reporters. Miss Tarbell's digging into the Rockefeller oil empire records led to a series lasting two years. McClure claimed it cost him $50,000 but the amount was easily repaid in prestige and new readers. The spotlight of public attention focused on Standard Oil had far-reaching effects that came to a climax in 1911 with a court order to break up one of the world's largest corporations into thirty-seven separate firms.

Steffens was later and informally crowned as king of the muckrakers because he had goaded President Roosevelt into the famous remark about the Bunyan character who raked through the muck instead of looking upward to the heavens. A Californian who drifted into the newspaper business by chance, Steffens worked on the New York *Evening Post* and the *Commercial Advertiser* before joining *McClure's.* He went West looking for a story in St. Paul, lost the trail, and wound up in St. Louis where a young reformer convinced him that the leading businessmen were the city's chief sources of corruption. It became apparent that this district attorney was an honest man, appalled by the venality of big-city politics, and he was willing to talk. "Tweed Days in St. Louis" was the result of Steffens' interviews with him. Before Steffens slowed down, Minneapolis, Pittsburgh, Philadelphia, and other cities felt the lash of his investigative reporting. His articles were assembled in a book, *The Shame of the Cities,* which rocked the nation.

The distinguishing characteristic about Steffens, Miss Tarbell, and the other muckrakers was their inquisitiveness and ruthless pursuit of facts. In Steffens this dogged search for the truth about underworld links with respected businessmen grew out of his training in German universities, where he had been taught that "if you know too surely, you cannot learn; and that, for the purposes of research, you may have theories, but never, never knowledge." [16] Mark Sullivan, who was to join the muckrakers in their crusade, recalled that it was a point of honor with these eager young reporters to spend "months of investigation before printing a brief article of five or six thousand words. They investigated everything, confirmed everything." [17] *McClure's,* Hearst's *Cosmopolitan, Everybody's, Collier's,* and the other magazines where their exposures appeared hired staffs of lawyers to check the articles for libel. Predictably, the careful gathering of facts left the exposed politicians and their allies so vulnerable that instead of suing for libel they often made hurried resignations or went into early retirement.

In journalism, as in most other aspects of American life, success brought quick imitation. Hearst, whose eclectic mind saw increased opportunities for circulation building, turned his *Cosmopolitan* into a muckraking magazine when the moneymaking potential in exposés was beyond doubt. Hearst had meanwhile found a socialite wife and began casting glances toward Washington. A term in Congress only whetted his appetite for office and power, so that he ordered his newspapers and magazines to shove forward his candidacy for the Democratic presidential nomination in 1904. To prove he was a friend of labor Hearst established the Los Angeles *Examiner* as the workingman's answer to the Los Angeles *Times*, which had become vociferously antiunion. It was fashionable to denounce the trusts and live on Lafayette Square in Washington, so Hearst did both. Old-line Democrats thought Hearst too shallow and cantankerous to be considered as serious presidential timber, but the months wore on and the Democrats became desperate. The New York *Evening Post* put the matter bluntly:

> There never has been a case of a man of such slender intellectual equipment, absolutely without experience in office, impudently flaunting his wealth before the eyes of the people and saying, "Make me President." This is folly . . . [Hearst's] record would make it impossible for him to live through a Presidential campaign—such gutters would be dragged, such sewers would be laid open.[18]

No less charitable was the New York *Tribune,* which said Hearst's self-promoted candidacy was the first "open and unblushing effort of a multi-millionaire to purchase the Presidential nomination." [19]

What appeared as a joke became deadly serious when Hearst received 194 votes on the first ballot at the St. Louis convention. Judge Alton B. Parker, who eventually won the nomination, was not far ahead and for a while it appeared that Hearst's name might be opposite Roosevelt's on the November ballot. Hearst newspapers sustained morale of the faint-hearted with banner headlines: *Hearst Is Cheered for 38 Minutes,* the New York *American* exulted. Then Hearst's strength peaked at 263 votes. While Hearst newspapers were appearing on street corners with optimistic headlines, Parker finally won late in the evening of July 8. Hearst, defeated and bitter, left in St. Louis his personal presidential aspirations but clung to the idea—for another forty-four years—that he could choose the men who should hold the office that was beyond all his resources.

As an antidote to Hearst the country needed a dose of laughter and it found the needed tonic in the newspapers carrying Finley Peter Dunne's "Mr. Dooley" column. Humor in journalism had fallen on bad times in comparison to the days when Artemus Ward, David R. Locke (as Petroleum V. Nasby), and Mark Twain kept readers amused with their native brand of printed comedy. Dunne, a Chicago newspaper reporter who knew the Irish side of the booming town as did few others, began a column in 1893 based on the conversations of "Martin Dooley," a mythical son of Eire who spun his philosophy while tending bar in the Bridgeport district. Dunne's articles, featuring "Mr. Dooley's" dialect and his views on current events, reached beyond the Chicago *Sunday Post* into columns across the nation. Dunne's commentaries on the Spanish-American War "swept the country like a prairie fire," particularly his explanation of how Dewey sank the Spanish fleet at Manila. Dialect stories seem anachronistic in the 1970s, but, as the Nasby and Dooley successes proved, our forebears enjoyed material that parodied life around them. After Upton Sinclair's explosive muckraking novel *The Jungle* made thousands of citizens into temporary vegetarians because of filthy conditions exposed in meat-packing plants, Dunne turned horror into laughter with an imaginary look at the White House breakfast table.

Tiddy was toying with a light breakfast an' idly turnin' over th' pages iv th' new book with both hands. Suddenly he rose fr'm th' table, an' cryin': "I'm pizened," begun thrown' sausages out iv th' window. Th' ninth wan sthruck Sinitor Biv'ridge on th' head, an' made him a blond. It bounced off, exploded, an' blew a leg off a secret-service agent. . . . Sinitor Biv'ridge rushed in thinkin' that th' Prisidint was bein' assassynated by his devoted followers in the Sinit, an' discovered Tiddy engaged in a hand-to-hand conflict with a potted ham.[20]

Funny as Dunne's joking appraisal of *The Jungle* was, no more dramatic evidence came from the muckrakers that working conditions in food processing plants were a national disgrace. The author of *The Jungle* was the only muckraker who was not a newspaperman, but before Upton Sinclair knew it, he was counted as a member in full standing of the legion dedicated to bettering America through the printed word.

Indeed, the muckrakers had a missionary zeal and a belief that an informed public would become an aroused citizenry, demanding clean factories, honest officials, fair prices, decent wages, and social justice. Sinclair said he had aimed at America's conscience and hit its stomach, for public opinion was so stirred that the Pure Food and Drug Act finally was enacted. Later, Sinclair became disgusted with the Associated Press and wrote *The Brass Check* as an indictment of the news-gathering agency. The title implied that the "A.P." was prostituted to Big Business, particularly the Rockefeller interests, and Sinclair invited lawsuits if his evidence was faulty. As he noted in the preface to a later edition, no lawsuits were brought, but in general the newspapers began to treat Sinclair as an unsavory Socialist agitator. He learned what the full treatment might entail in 1934 when he was a gubernatorial candidate in California.

Pulitzer's voice, which might have called more newspapers into the muckraking crusade, was now only a whisper. Ill and nearly blind, the once energetic publisher of the New York *World* heard of the distant clamor from his ocean retreat, and was pleased by the exposé of insurance company finance by *World* reporter David Ferguson. During 1905, in the best muckraking tradition, Ferguson's well-documented stories told of internecine battles for control of the Equitable Life Assurance Society. Soon it was hinted that two other insurance giants—New York Life and Mutual Life—were honeycombed with officials who voted themselves outrageous salaries and then used policyholders' premium money to speculate in stocks and lands. From a European retreat Pulitzer directed the *World* via cablegrams and praised Ferguson's muckraking while offering a lesson in good writing. "Concentrate on Equitable Corruption without exaggeration, also . . . avoid superlatives, like: monstrous, traitor, anarchist, etc., as rather juvenile, feeble." [21] The old editor scented battle even from afar so that when the lid blew off on the insurance scandals, Pulitzer thought the prosecuting attorney—Charles Evans Hughes—deserved about any office a grateful people might bestow. In 1907 Pulitzer went aboard his yacht, the *Liberty,* and spent most of the last four years of his life on shipboard, sending cablegrams to the *World* city room, seeking medical advice, and thinking about his will.

Whether muckraking represented American journalism's finest hour or only the peak of Don Quixotism in print remains a moot point. Some of the best reporters began their careers as lawyers and gradually took to journalism because of their inner convictions and faith in the power of the exposé. Implicitly their motto was Revelation Will Lead to Reformation. Mark Sullivan, Ray Stannard Baker, Samuel Hopkinson Adams, David Graham Phillips, and Thomas W. Lawson became feared men through their trenchant writing and research. Most of the muckrakers came from small midwestern towns, had deep Protestant antecedents, and were still in their twenties when they glimpsed the vision of reform.[22] Readers of the exposé of patent medicines tended to remember with good-natured humor Edward Bok's revelation that Lydia Pinkham had long been in her grave while still doling out advice to disconsolate ladies.[23] Meanwhile, a compound bearing her name and a great deal of grain alcohol was available at the corner drug store and might make a Sunday school teacher into an alcoholic. "Truth will bring reform" was the muckraker's message, but as in Steffens' case, Bok and Adams found they had hit the viscera on the funny bone rather than America's conscience.

In some cases Europeans became more alarmed than Americans as the muckrakers hit their stride. In the afterglow of the "Shame of the Cities" series in *McClure's* a French publication gave readers a map of the United States with each state or territory shaded according to whether it was free from corruption, "utterly corrupt," or "partially corrupt." Only five states were judged free of political venality, while most of the country had the most somber hue, denoting widespread, unchecked graft.[24] What Steffens, Fremont Older in San Francisco, and less disillusioned newspapermen began to perceive, however, was that the American reading public had an attention span that was easily overtaxed. *McClure's* circulation hit 500,000 during 1907, a year of hard times and unemployment, but by 1908 the public was ready for other forms of excitement. The crusade of 1902–1903 had petered out, and by 1908 it was much easier to generate enthusiasm for the coming Lincoln centennial than to arouse citizens over local frauds. In fact, one magazine imitated Pulitzer's old Statue of Liberty ploy (there *really* is little that is new in journalism) by urging schoolchildren to send in pennies and nickels for a replica of the Lincoln monument to cover the possible birthplace cabin of the martyred president in Kentucky. Despite such distractions, the remarkable thing about muckraking was that it lasted so long, since it kept Americans fretting about their corrupt officeholders and dishonest businessmen for nearly six years.

Not all the journalistic excitement of the era was generated by the muckrakers. In fact, it is probable that half of the nation continued to read its weekly newspapers with slight concern for the wounded vanity of Washington politicians after Phillips' "Treason of the Senate" series appeared. In the smaller communities it was the staple news that filled columns with items that chronicled daily life in pre-1917 America.

The Epworth League pie supper will be held at the Methodist Church Friday at 6 o'clock sharp. Mrs. J. S. Smith is in charge and asks ladies to bring their baked goods wrapped in plain brown paper.

Carl Jones brought a 18-pound watermelon into the *Republican* office last Monday. Has a larger one been grown in Johnson county this year?

Mr. and Mrs. Paul Brown celebrated their 50th wedding anniversary at the family home last Sunday. They were married at Niles, Michigan, on May 15, 1855.

The friends of Mabel Jones will be glad to know that she is resting comfortably at home after a bad fall on the ice last week. Mabel had some awful bruises but Dr. Smith says there were no broken bones.

Such ordinary occurrences were the warp and woof of community journalism, and hundreds of "special correspondents" gladly left their news items at the printing office each week in return for a free subscription and a by-line. In the more settled but smaller communities of America, these chronicles of life appeared in the 1970s much as they had in the 1890s, sometimes with the same family names. But such places grow fewer each year.

There was, on the other hand, a noisier and more exciting element in the nation's journalism at the beginning of the twentieth century than country journalism indicated. Newspapermen themselves provided some headlines. In Waco, Texas, the abrasive young editor of the *Iconoclast* invited trouble by attacking the local Baptist college administration and inferred that moral standards on the campus needed bolstering. He was assassinated on a Waco street but managed to kill his murderer in a dramatic gun battle. The Columbia, South Carolina, *State* was too thorny in its approach to politics and its editor, N. G. Gonzales, was killed by an infuriated gunman. With Wintons and Oldsmobiles replacing horses, there were fewer whips around and no whipped editors of note, but injured feelings demanded retribution. One of the last federal cases of criminal libel prosecution came in 1909 when President Theodore Roosevelt smarted under the lash of news stories about Panama Canal graft in the Indianapolis *News* and New York *World*. The newspapers maintained that a member of Roosevelt's Cabinet was among the spoilsmen paid for dilapidated machinery and nebulous excavation rights. Roosevelt ramrodded his attorney general into filing a criminal prosecution against the pair for their exposés. The *World* gloried in the case and continued to ask editorially: "Who got the money?" Federal judges threw the cases out of court, reaffirming the right of newspapers to scrutinize the use of public funds, thus rebuking the federal government for its only attempt to curb journalism with a libel suit since Alien and Sedition Act days.[25]

On the West Coast, labor was furnishing newspapers with plenty of copy. The speeches of William Haywood were printed as proof that the IWW (Industrial Workers of the World) was out to take over the country. Labor strife in western mining camps led to small-scale warfare, dynamitings, and terrorized communities. Los Angeles was a growing city that had solved its major problem, a lack of pure water, by following the advice of Colonel Harrison Gray Otis and building a monumental viaduct that brought Owens River water across a huge stretch of desert to the parched city. Less than grateful, however, were the printers who thought Otis had locked them out of his *Times* with a vow never to give in to demands for a closed (all-union) shop. Hearst's *Examiner* had been founded to benefit from this confrontation but it was the *Times* that prospered and moved into a new building late in the summer of 1910. On October 1, 1910, a fiery blast ripped through the new building, killing more than a dozen *Times* employees and leaving a huge gap in the building. Immediately suspicion was pointed at the typographer's union, for an unexploded bomb had also been discovered at Otis' home. Even Hearst seemed shocked by the blast as he offered $5,000 to the mounting reward money offered for capture of the bomb planters. The union countered that the explosion had probably been caused by a gas main leak. As the death toll reached twenty-one, the union's story seemed unconvincing. Otis insisted the outrage was part of a labor plot to break every businessman who favored an open shop, and the *Times* linked the explosion to local politics where a Socialist party candidate for mayor appeared headed for victory. The sensational arrest of two labor leaders, their trial and dramatic eleventh-hour confession arranged by the ubiquitous Lincoln Steffens, dealt the western labor movement a blow that helped cripple organized labor in the area for another generation.²⁶ Thereafter, the *Times* dominated Los Angeles journalism as the entrenched voice of conservative Republican programs.

While Otis and his son-in-law laid the groundwork for what would become one of the nation's most powerful regional newspapers, the light began to flicker on an eastern beacon of journalistic power. Blessed with a staff of able editors, Joseph Pulitzer had delegated responsibility for the *World* but still kept the lead rein in his enfeebled hands. When not suffering intense pain from an increasing variety of bodily ills, Pulitzer turned his thoughts back to the *World* and to politics. "The *World* should be more powerful than the President," he told a staff member in 1910. The president was the servant of partisan politics elected to a four-year term, while the *World* "goes on year after year and is absolutely free to tell the truth." ²⁷ Pulitzer saw the potential of a New Jersey reform governor and thought Woodrow Wilson was "ten times more intellectual than Cleveland" —which was Pulitzer's way of saying he had decided on the *World's* endorsement for the 1912 presidential race. But while Pulitzer talked and dreamed of prizes to honor outstanding journalism and of a school for reporters at Columbia University he became steadily more ill. He died on a Sunday afternoon while the *Liberty* was docked at Charleston. Even in dying, Pulitzer had made the newspaperman's move, for Monday morning editions are ordinarily fairly bland because of the quiet Sabbath. But the *World* on October 30, 1911, gave over its front page to the fallen leader, with a dominating four-column illustration furnished by John Singer Sargent's penetrating portrait of Pulitzer. "A great power uniformly exerted in behalf of popular rights and human progress is ended," Pulitzer's bitterest foe wrote in the *Journal*. "Joseph Pulitzer is dead."

Telegraph lines carried the news from Charleston and Los Angeles into the East, where the death of a great innovator or the sentencing of two dynamiters probably seemed of routine consequence to news managers who controlled the wire service networks fanning out from New York. As Wall Street set the tone for the nation's business world, so did the journalistic standards set in the vicinity of Times Square serve as guides for the nation's newspapers. Aspiring young reporters such as Walter Lippmann came to New York from college campuses and small-town dailies, seeking a place at the focal point of American journalism. Lippmann was hired at *Everybody's* magazine, while Carr Van Anda brought in a whole galaxy of able young reporters at the *New York Times*. As the *Times* managing editor Van Anda breathed an excellence into his newsroom which more than any other single factor lifted the *Times* to its preeminent position by the end of World War I. Van Anda's superb ability to sense the break of a big story was never more evident than on April 14–15, 1912, when the largest steamship ever built sank while on her maiden voyage across the North Atlantic. The *Titanic* was said to be "unsinkable" because of new construction techniques. It was equipped with the newest radio equipment and safety devices. The passenger list included the foremost names from the British and American social registers. On Sunday, April 14, the *Times* ran a picture of the new luxury liner with an explanation of the *Titanic's* dimensions— four city blocks long—with passenger accommodations "among the most gorgeous of any ship ever built."

The first hint of trouble came from a Newfoundland radio signal station late that Sunday. Four hours later the news flashed into all New York city rooms, but Van Anda was on the job at the *Times*. He quickly ordered the front page revised with a new lead story and picture of the *Titanic: New Liner Titanic Hits Iceberg . . . Last Wireless at 12:27 A.M. Blurred*. The story under a Halifax dateline told of the distant distress signal picked up by the radio operator on the *Virginia*. Ships in the area were answering the call, although from midnight onward only silence answered their responses. Other New York editors inserted the bulletin, but Van Anda stuck his neck out all the way across Broadway. In the last *Times* edition at 3:30 A.M., the *Titanic* was reported as sunk. If the *Titanic* had simply lost radio contact and was limping into port the *Times* had needlessly upset the city and inexcusably violated its own tenets regarding sensationalism. White Star Line officials were reassuring, but they had received no word either.

Van Anda, showing the skepticism that is the hallmark of all great newsmen, swung his city room into action by establishing a command post near the White Star office, had four telephones installed in one room, three in another, and ordered his staff to find passenger lists, reports of other recent mishaps in the icefields, and pictures of prominent citizens known to have been aboard the stricken vessel. While other editors held back, Van Anda had the first eight pages of the April 16 edition crammed with facts about the *Titanic.* Final word from rescue ships confirmed Van Anda's hunches late that night. The next morning, New Yorkers bought for one cent one of the most dramatic news stories of all time; the headline: *Titanic Sinks Four Hours After Hitting Iceberg.* For the rest of the week, the *Times* coverage dominated that of all other newspapers or press associations.

The next three days were filled with anxious waiting for word of survivors. The passenger list included Mr. and Mrs. John Jacob Astor, Benjamin Guggenheim, J. Bruce Ismay, Mr. and Mrs. Isidor Straus, Washington Roebling (builder of the Brooklyn Bridge), Mrs. G. D. Widener, Lady Duff Gordon, and Major Archibald Butt (President Taft's military aide). A full-page feature on Major Butt had appeared in the *Sunday Times* on April 14, as had an advertisement for the scheduled April 20 return voyage of the *Titanic.* Thursday night the *Times* staff prepared exclusive rescue accounts from eyewitnesses that filled five full columns. On April 19 the *Times* devoted fifteen of its twenty-four pages to the disaster, with a banner headline: *745 Saw Titanic Sink with 1,595, Her Band Playing . . . Many Women Stayed to Perish With Their Husbands.*[28] Van Anda's achievement was known only to the newspapermen who had been scooped all week, but admiring words came from editors around the world.

What made Van Anda's expert handling of the story possible, of course, was the "Marconi Wireless Telegraph" which had been developed as a safety device but had great news reporting potential. Thereafter, wireless or radio transmissions became more commonplace in oceangoing commerce and within a decade refinements brought voice transmissions that gave journalism a new dimension through the first medium that did not rely upon a printing press.

Much of journalism remained the same, however, for although technological changes made their impact in the cities, in 1912 America was still predominantly a nation of farmers and small-town businessmen. It was the golden year of American journalism for not only had Van Anda proved how superbly news might be reported, but in sheer numbers the people probably had more choices in their quest of news, information, or entertainment than at any time in American history. There were about 2,000 daily newspapers, more than 500 semiweeklies, 12,000 weeklies, and close to 6,500 magazines. The publishers of this galaxy sold their wares for $233 million—a tenfold increase in 50 years. Leading daily newspapers cost from one to three cents, while the best weekly magazines sold for a dime. Moreover, the staid Associated Press had a vigorous new competitor in the United Press, which the patronage of E. W. Scripps supported and the young workhorse Roy Howard managed for clients who paid rates based on their market area. The United Press style was denounced as "too breezy" by the old-fashioned AP members, but slowly UP made headway with its jaunty interest in the human side of the news and well-written dispatches from Latin American capitals.

The country was on the verge of a great shift. In a few years the cities would dominate the national social and financial structure, and haylofts would disappear along with the blacksmiths who sold their shops to purveyors of Mr. Ford's Model T at $590 f.o.b. Detroit. Periodic depressions and money panics had prevented great rises in wages or prices. A ten-cent piece still bought a pound of candy or a copy of *Munsey's Magazine*. The cost of newsprint reached an all-time low in 1897—less than two cents a pound. *Munsey's* became the largest dime magazine in the 1890s with a success formula that would later bring joy to the publishers of *Esquire, Life,* and *Playboy*—dozens of pictures of "half dressed women and undressed statuary" gave *Munsey's* the circulation lift it needed to stay alive. The editors maintained their combination of bland fiction and frequent use of scantily clad females until weekly circulation hit 500,000. As Mott surmised, *Munsey's* slowly turned away from the overexposed female figure "but the reputation for naughty pictures . . . was hard to shake off." Unlike *McClure's* and the other muckraking journals, *Munsey's* eschewed controversy and instead printed a "shocking amount of mediocrity." Both *McClure's* and *Munsey's* declined after 1914 and went out of business in the Year of the Graveyard—1929.

Before America made the transition from a nation of farmers to a land of city dwellers it went on one last fling. The presidential election of 1912 split the Republican party wide open, shoved a fresh face forward at the Democratic nominating convention, and provided readers with the most exciting political news since the 1860 campaign. Theodore Roosevelt had been a newspaper reporter's delight while in the White House, and the press corps responded by giving him the most favorable treatment any president has ever received. Then Roosevelt left the White House to his heir apparent and went on an African safari that brought more headlines and pictures of a smiling, toothy, tanned former president. By 1911 Roosevelt had become disenchanted with Taft, however, and early in 1912 it was obvious that the former Rough Rider was eager for a try at the sacred No-Third-Term tradition.

During the ensuing melee, the old guard Republicans held onto control of their party but the cost was high. Colonel Otis in Los Angeles used his *Times* to brand Roosevelt as a "would-be dictator" bent on destroying his party and the country, a judgment colored by Otis' hatred of Hiram Johnson, who was the Progressive's choice for vice president. Johnson had fought the Southern Pacific to a standstill and won the governor's seat two years earlier, so he had the Los Angeles *Herald,* Sacramento *Bee,* and San Francisco *Call* in his camp. The Progressive platform builders insisted they were at work "to bridge this awful chasm that exists in our country between those who are ever growing richer, and those who are ever growing poorer." [29] Wilson, who accepted the Democratic nomination with the statement that "There is no indispensable man," had more newspaper support than any Democrat since Buchanan and went on to win the three-way contest by carrying forty states.

What Wilson's victory proved, among other things, was that the vindictive Republicans had stopped Roosevelt. The Los Angeles *Times* was only one of many Taft backers that urged voters who could not support the president to vote for Wilson as preferable to the usurper trying for a third term. "The result," said the pro-Taft Boston *Daily Advertiser*, "shows that this determination to prevent the success of the Roosevelt movement was successful beyond the imaginings of those republicans who contributed to the success of the democratic candidate." [30] No less frank was the Jacksonville, Florida, *Times-Union* in its survey of Wilson's triumph. "The Democratic party has not won a victory. The Republican party has simply committed suicide." [31]

Wilson's victory meant that for the third time since 1864 a candidate supported by the majority of the nation's newspapers had failed to win the presidency. The gains made by Socialists, Prohibitionists, and other splinter parties showed that voters were becoming more independent, however, and the ratification of the Sixteenth (income tax) and Seventeenth (direct election of senators) Amendments were symptomatic of increasing public concern over the power of wealth. The Chicago *Tribune* exposé of Senator Lorimer's purchase of his seat ultimately led to his expulsion—the kind of action Phillips had aimed for in his earlier "Treason of the Senate" series.

The editor of the Emporia, Kansas, *Gazette* had fought for Roosevelt and bolted the regular party to do it—but after the returns came in William Allen White wrote Roosevelt he had harbored no regrets "since we began the hike to Armageddon." [32] The *Gazette* dropped politics for a while and went back to printing local news and the trustworthy poetry of James Whitcomb Riley, only to be cautioned that copyrights existed on "When the Frost Is on the Pumpkin" which the *Gazette* had ignored. As White knew, nearly every country editor in the Republic reprinted Riley's poems each fall and he felt discriminated against by the implied threat of legal action. White wrote the publishers,

> I take pleasure in saying that during the first few days of every November for the past seventeen years I have printed "When the Frost is on the Pumpkin" and during the first few days of every April for the past seventeen years I have printed "When the Green Gets Back in the Trees." . . . The habit is confirmed. . . . If you desire to sue us, I am perfectly willing to go to jail and rot there for the privilege of giving my readers the benefit of these two poems."

White closed his letter by saying that if publishers' lawyers were going to become interested in country editors he would "take more interest in the candidate for sheriff and less interest in the candidate for president than I have heretofore." [33]

Small-town journalism served its readers more than poems by Riley or Eugene Field, but publishing was still a marginal operation in many if not most communities. White himself became famous as the *Gazette* owner-editor, but it was his income from novels and magazine stories that paid his grocery bills. The most hard-pressed editors used preprinted sheets or "boilerplate" forms of innocuous news to cut costs. It was not unusual during 1912 in many parts of America for newspapers to accept subscription payments in farm produce in precisely the same manner eighteenth-century printers had waived cash payments. The scarcity of dollars in farming areas prior to 1914 was a fact of life. Newspapers that charged two dollars a year for subscriptions also offered such free services as the bulletin boards that became a semiannual fixture on thousands of American Main Streets. In front of the newspaper office a large screen or blackboard would be erected for the World's Series and for local, state, and national elections. The streets were roped off, a holiday atmosphere prevailed, and telegraphic bulletins were shouted through a megaphone or flashed on a screen as a service of the newspaper and whatever merchants could be persuaded to become sponsors. The first bulletins appear to have been pasted on newspaper office windows in New York in the 1850s but the practice was refined in small-town America when baseball and election results were overriding concerns. Mr. Marconi's invention would ultimately bring an end to these old-fashioned news frolics early in the 1930s, when radio news also killed the time-honored "extra" editions.

On the eve of World War I it was still commonplace for metropolitan dailies to print at least five editions—bulldog (early or mailer), final home, late sports, late market, and street final. This replating kept the composing rooms busy and in times of sharp competition allowed city editors to assign stories gleaned from rival newspapers so that in the final edition all major events would have been "covered." Reporters were sent on beats at courthouses, city halls, or other public buildings, although the most able writers were assigned to specific stories each day. The quality of the reporters varied, though most did not deserve the spreading reputation of newspapermen as "drunkards, dead-beats, and bummers" that Harvard President Charles W. Eliot promoted in 1890. Drinking, long a problem in the composing rooms, was widespread in city rooms but perhaps no more so than in the offices of doctors, lawyers, traveling salesmen, merchants, or bank presidents. After all, Bourbon whiskey could be bought in 1912 for one dollar a quart. The newsman's day lasted from ten to twelve hours. Saloons were on every corner.

The quality of reporting was not upgraded as much by Prohibition as by higher education. Traditionally, reporters that had once come from composing rooms had after the Civil War started as *copy boys* (a generally descriptive term, unrelated to age). Copy boys were the apprentices of the "new journalism" who replaced the old printer's devils as underpaid handymen. They carried the material from reporters' desks to editors' desks, and thence to the composing room, preferably on the dead run. As one veteran city editor observed:

That Boy! In our calm moments we could not find it in our heart to give him even a cross look. He works for three dollars a week; he is here at seven in the morning, to dust things, to build a fire in the stove, when necessary, and to open exchanges and see that paste-pots and ink-stands are filled, and . . . he flies up and down those stairs one hundred and forty-six times a day; he runs out when he "must not be gone a minute," to buy us a cigar; and so his every day goes by.[34]

These tireless runners often worked themselves into the writing end of journalism, but the twentieth-century reporter was to become less and less a fugitive from the composing room and more and more a college graduate. The University of Illinois started a full-time journalism degree program in 1904, a plan quickly imitated by other midwestern state universities and nowhere more successfully than at the University of Missouri.[35] Columbia, Missouri, became the main academic spawning ground for a legion of trained reporters, and by the 1930s had become the undergraduate haven for men who would become journalistic leaders in the 1950s and beyond.

A couple of world wars, a technological breakthrough, and a social revolution would fill the interval.

12

Lost Innocence

Wars have a way of changing the course of a nation's destiny beyond all foreseeable calculations. American involvement in World War I, which seemed unthinkable in 1914, remote in 1915, unlikely in 1916, and then became a fact in 1917, was an experience which found the newspapers as innocent as were 100 million unprepared citizens. The outlook in 1913 was promising indeed. Wilson's vigorous actions as president had impressed the nation, including the conservative Republicans who controlled the largest newspapers, and the beginning of 1914 found the New Freedom program in full swing. The old political rhetoric was reinforced by Wilson's personality so that reforms long in contemplation soon became law. Antitrust statutes were reinforced, a Federal Reserve Act took the control of currency out of private banker's hands, and a child-labor act was passed. The old spark of muckraking glowed again as a Boston lawyer, Louis D. Brandeis, spoke out in *Harper's Weekly* against "The Curse of Bigness." For a time it appeared that many of the programs of agrarian reformers and social justice advocates, once considered visionary, might soon be broadly realized.

The outbreak of war in August 1914 was a remote Balkan event. Most Americans, isolated by an ocean and their instinctive feelings, believed that neutrality was the wisest policy. Wilson reflected this attitude in December when he told Congress the conflict was "a war with which we [will] have nothing to do, whose causes cannot touch us." This reassuring speech left the public secure in a belief that what happened to England or France was not America's concern. Newsman Mark Sullivan recalled that a "cigar store plebiscite" in the first days of the war would have shown more Americans sympathetic to Germany than to the Franco-Russian allies.[1]

The dream of a glorious isolation began to give way to a more partisan view once the Germans drove toward Paris and almost won the war in a quick stroke. To some degree, Americans kept their minds off European matters by watching events closer to home. The overthrow of President Diaz in Mexico and the ensuing power struggle below the Rio Grande made good newspaper copy across the nation but particularly interested southwestern and western readers, while the eastern seaboard watched the intensifying submarine warfare with growing interest. For the most part, Americans tended to favor the Central powers if they themselves had German or Irish ancestry, but a far larger element was pro-British because of a shared language, and literature and political ties. Pro-French sentiment centered around a smaller but vocal group that spoke repeatedly of Franco-American ties dating back to the War for Independence. Sentiment along the Atlantic coast was mainly for the Allies, while in the midwestern states much pro-German sympathy was evident. At the outbreak of war, America had more than 1,200 foreign-language newspapers, with nearly 500 printed in German. New York City had ten German newspapers, and two, the *Vorwarts* and *Staats-Zeitung,* had large circulations. But in the nation at large, pro-Allied sentiment was preponderant as a *Literary Digest* poll showed; 105 leading editors favored the Allies; 240 professed themselves neutral; and only 20 said they hoped for a German victory.

Early but telltale signs of eventual involvement in the war, a war in which Wilson declared Americans would be "too proud to fight," resulted from German U-boat (*Unterseeboot*) activity off the British Isles early in 1915. Although historians have made much of America's economic ties with Britain and Anglophile sentiment in Washington, German submarines were the decisive factor in leading the nation to war if one judges from the nation's newspapers. Two years before the declaration of war, eastern newspapers condemned the Imperial German order warning that enemy merchantmen would be sunk without warning. After two British steamers were torpedoed with heavy loss of civilian passengers, the New York newspapers recoiled in horror. "There can be but one opinion among right-minded men," the *Evening Post* told readers. The sinkings were "wickedness such as history will find it difficult to match." The *Times* agreed and said that Germany, "in authorizing or permitting her naval commanders to carry on war in this savage manner . . . does infinite harm to herself." The *Sun* called the sinkings "deliberate murder" beyond "the civilized code of warfare."

The British used their naval supremacy to make sure that Americans heard as little of Germany's side of the story as possible. The cable lines to Germany were cut in August 1914, and all mail between Germany and America traversed an Allied censorship network. The British began issuing a weekly newspaper for the use of the American press, and much atrocity propaganda (that subsequently proved totally false) was siphoned from Allied news sources and printed uncritically in scores of American newspapers. After the German invasion of Belgium, the most persistently circulated story was that the Kaiser's troops had wantonly cut off the hands of helpless Belgian children, had raped nurses, and had set fire to religious shrines. In time a committee of Americans, with William Allen White in the foreground, began collecting funds for Belgian relief and openly called for America's full participation in the war.

Germany tried to match Allied efforts by creating a propaganda office and by publishing a newspaper, *The Fatherland*, which sought to justify the submarine attacks and the Belgian invasion as legitimate acts of war. In general, pro-German writers were in an apologist's role that left them continually on the defensive. Worse still, the New York *World* revealed that German-supported agents were being instructed to promote strikes and organize sabotage in munitions factories with Allied contracts.[2] Few newspapers bothered to make clear distinctions as various peace movements gathered momentum with Socialist backing. By and large, German sympathizers in the midwestern river cities had few friends in the East except the Irish, who renewed their hatred of England after incidents in their homeland at Eastertime, 1916.

The European war turned into the nastiest kind of conflict, marked by enormous loss of life in pointless battles that ground down all the belligerents and left the end seeming farther away after each bloody encounter. The stalemate in trench warfare took an appalling toll of lives—on July 1, 1916, the British had suffered 57,450 casualties as the Battle of the Somme began. Before that struggle ended—without decisive movements—1,265,000 men were killed or wounded or missing on both sides. Verdun was the scene of a tragic slaughter in 1915 that killed or maimed a million combatants. Ypres became etched in the British memory as three bloody battles fought near the Belgian hamlet cost 80 percent of the British Expeditionary Force killed or wounded in the first battle, close to 50,000 in the second, and a staggering 240,000 in the last miserable maneuvering in 1917.

American readers could scarcely comprehend such carnage. They were informed of the slaughter by a crack corps of American war correspondents, but the reporting was slanted. The Anglophobic Chicago *Tribune* sent reporters in the field who saw no German atrocities, while the New York *Herald* told readers "Tourist Saw Soldier With Bagful of Ears"—Belgian ears, the eyewitness insisted.[3] Hearst had been an admirer of Kaiser Wilhelm I and frequenter of German spas, and now his newspapers seemed suspiciously pro-German to readers who were pro-Allied. Favorable stories came from the Hearst's Berlin correspondent and it was subsequently learned Wil-

liam Bayard Hale had been paid $15,000 a year by the Germans for
his services, but Hearst apparently knew nothing of this arrangement
and was more anti-British than pro-German.[4] The New York *Evening Mail* favored the German cause, a fact made clearer when secret
payments to staff members from the Kaiser's agents was disclosed.
For a time the Cincinnati *Enquirer* and Cleveland *Plain Dealer* were
also skeptical of Allied claims, but beyond a handful of midwestern
dailies by late 1915 the nation's press was pro-Allied.

In the meantime, Mexican politics maintained a tobasco-like quality and spilled over into *gringo* territory. Wilson had ordered Marine
Corps landings in Vera Cruz during 1914, but there was little real
action for the chafing American correspondents until Pancho Villa
waged civil war against his erstwhile friends. Villa's sweep across
northern Mexico attracted nationwide attention and brought Wilson's order for armed intervention when the Mexican guerrillas shot
up the border town of Columbus, New Mexico, and killed American
citizens on their home ground. General John J. Pershing was ordered
to catch and punish the Mexican leader, which he was never able to
do, but meanwhile the effort provided a score of reporters with some
harum-scarum days along the Rio Grande and brought Pershing before the American public as a tough, capable professional soldier.

The Mexican embarrassment caused Americans to look critically
at their national guard units and other defense forces. One result of
the publicity from plain-spoken reporters in the field was a nationwide call for "Preparedness Day" parades to create enthusiasm for
improved military training and weaponry. Pacifists denounced the
plan and some labor leaders were lukewarm to the movement, a circumstance that led to the immediate arrest of labor organizer Tom
Mooney after a bomb exploded at the San Francisco parade. Fremont
Older believed Mooney had been framed, but most California newsmen thought otherwise; and but for the *Bulletin* Mooney might have
been executed before it was proved that he had indeed been framed.[5]
President Wilson commuted Mooney's death sentence to life imprisonment, but Mooney's guilt or innocence and demands for his par-

don remained a volatile issue in California politics and journalism for another twenty years.

Early in 1916 Americans beyond the Alleghenies had tended to view the European war as a distasteful power struggle that was none of their business. The Republican presidential nominee, Charles Evans Hughes, pressed Wilson so hard that the Democrats found themselves desperately looking for a winning slogan and thought they had found it in He Kept Us Out of War. The strategy appeared to have failed, however, when the early returns gave Hughes a substantial lead. At midnight on November 7 the leading eastern dailies which had supported Wilson conceded Hughes' election, but at the Democratic headquarters there was a halfhearted chant of "Remember 1892." (In that earlier election, Cleveland had appeared the loser from early returns but came on in counting the next day to overtake Harrison.) The Associated Press reported from Long Branch, New Jersey, that Wilson was the only cheerful person at his vacation retreat. *Returns Indicate Election of Hughes; Democrats Do Not Concede Defeat,* the Richmond *Times-Dispatch* headlined.[6]

Then returns from the Far West began to arrive, and the Wilson supporters took heart. The New York *Tribune* predicted that the election now hinged on the California returns, as Wilson had 2 3 2 electoral votes assured to 2 3 9 for Hughes. Not until Friday was it clear that California had favored Wilson. Then the headlines proclaimed: *Wilson Re-Elected* and *Victory Assured When California Goes Democratic.*

As William Allen White discerned from his Emporia listening post, the westerners had voted for Wilson because he was pledged to peace. "The West as I read it is strongly pro-Ally, but the war is not a first-page story in the West," [7] was Allen's analysis. What made news in February 1917 was the coming baseball season and the sinking of the British liner *Laconia* in the East, the weather and Mexican banditry in the West. One of the great news breaks of the twentieth century came on February 28 to change the odds in favor of American intervention in the war. The Associated Press bureau in Washington was "leaked" (probably from the State Department, on Wilson's order or suggestion) a copy of the dispatch from the German foreign ministers to the embassy in Mexico. The note announced that unrestricted submarine warfare would soon begin and added that if the United States did not stay neutral, Mexico and Japan should be invited into an alliance with Germany. In return, Mexico was to have New Mexico, Texas, and Arizona returned to her jurisdiction after the Central Powers triumphed.[8] Whatever comic-opera ring the note had fifty years later was entirely lacking in 1917. The story seemed so incredible that the Senate at once, on the basis of the Associated Press story, asked the president to confirm the existence of such a dispatch. Wilson replied that same day through Secretary of State Lansing that the note was authentic. From that moment, the United States was committed to a war policy. In fact, the declaration of war on Good Friday, April 6, was somewhat anticlimactic.

Nonetheless, the coming of war so soon after a close election based on the peace vote caught much of America off guard. The reading public had generally believed the slogans of 1916 and reacted to the outbreak of war with a sudden arousal of superpatriotism. Almost immediately, a wave of anti-German hysteria swept westward as rumors of German secret agents at work were spread by banner headlines. A great rush toward overt patriotism saw the changing of sauerkraut to "liberty cabbage," while Wagnerian operas were considered akin to enemy propaganda.[9] Newspapers that had jubilantly hailed Wilson's election victory in 1916 as a "peace vote," seemed eager to climb on the bandwagon ladened with recruitment drives, rallies for Liberty Bond purchases, and food rationing programs aimed at realizing Wilson's call "to make the world safe for democracy."

Patriotism had its price. Indeed, the German-language newspapers were hit hard during the first weeks of the war by mobs, warrant-armed government agents, and the smothering effect of hostile public opinion. The editors' statements avowing loyalty were often to no purpose as German-Americans found it easier to stop a newspaper subscription than to explain one's views on the draft bill. Socialist newspapers in Milwaukee and other cities with large German populations were cowed by federal agents who by the Espionage Act of 1917 were armed with powerful restraints. The act made it a federal offense to "wilfully obstruct recruiting," a phrase that was interpreted to mean—in its broadest sense—any criticism of the war effort. The Sedition Act of 1918, a companion piece of legislation, made heavy fines and long prison terms the prospect for those who wrote or printed "any disloyal, profane, scurrilous, or abusive language" about the Constitution, military forces, flag, in such a way as to bring them "into contempt, scorn, contumely, or disrepute." Armed with this blunderbuss, the attorney general and postmaster-general soon were acting as official censors.

Socialists reacted angrily when their New York *Call* was denied use of the mails, along with the Milwaukee *Leader*. Victor Berger, the Austrian-born editor of the *Leader*, was twice elected to Congress (1918 and 1919) but denied his seat by the House of Representatives and instead packed off to jail for violation of the Espionage Act.[10] Berger and other Socialists and pacifists opposed American participation in the war, calling the conflict a "Wall Street" struggle arranged by an international conspiracy of capitalists. The editors of the Philadelphia *Tageblatt* went to prison for printing articles critical of the war effort, but the editors of the Socialist *Masses* escaped penitentiary terms because of a hung jury. Except in the upper Mississippi Valley and portions of the Midwest, the German-language and Socialist press was generally discredited by the spring of 1918 and never would recover its prewar standing or circulation.[11] As the hysteria spread, an Iowa newspaper reported with approval the intimidation of a local Lutheran minister who had imprudently ignored warnings to stop delivering sermons in German.

Criticism of the war was not stilled, but it was muted by the irresistible combination of government-sanctioned harassment and irrational public opinion. The *New Republic*, guided by the remnants of the now-moldy muckraking movement, denounced the heavyhanded tactics of Postmaster-General Burleson after the New York *Free-man's Journal and Catholic Register* lost its mailing privileges, in part because it was critical of America's ally, England, over the handling of the Irish revolutionaries. Pacifist Oswald Garrison Villard, son and grandson of two luminaries in journalism history, used his New York *Evening Post* to criticize the conduct of the war and the erosion of civil liberties. Several New York dailies also printed articles critical of the military supply system whereby sugar and flour denied domestic consumers was left to rot on French wharves. Most newspapers tended to cooperate with the Committee on Public Information, however, and thereby avoid any possibility of either damaging gossip or government action. "Report the man who spreads pessimistic stories," the CPI director admonished citizens, and the threat had its effect on the city rooms.*

Coverage of the actual fighting produced its crop of heroes, led by Floyd Gibbons, who as a passenger on the *Laconia* had filed one of the war's great eyewitness stories. Richard Harding Davis had covered the first part of the war, and in typical fashion had been arrested as a suspected spy by the Germans, but he died before the American Expeditionary Force reached Europe. Frank Norris and Stephen Crane were gone, and the new breed of war correspondent was more workmanlike and less inclined toward literary artistry. Paris became a rendezvous for American reporters covering all phases of the great struggle, and at the sidewalk cafés the journalistic careers of Heywood Broun, Ring Lardner, and Walter Duranty seemed to improve. The AEF newspaper, *The Stars and Stripes* (published from a Parisian base with a khaki-clad staff that included Harold Ross, Alexander Wolcott, and Grantland Rice), kept the million American troops in Europe informed of news from other fronts and back home.[12] Soldiers and sailors also were mailed special sections clipped

---

* George Creel, the former newsman who headed the wartime Committee on Public Information, later ran for the Democratic gubernatorial nomination in California against the muckraking Upton Sinclair, lost, and endorsed the Republican candidate.

from hometown newspapers containing digests of local news, although a few newspapers printed special editions for service men, including the Baltimore *Sun* Overseas Edition which carried news across the Atlantic to Maryland men in the AEF.

At home, editors were inclined to write editorials about the kind of world that would emerge after the war. Wilson's announcement of a fourteen-point peacetime program after "the war to end all wars" convinced his supporters that the president would find a phoenix in the ashes of European battlefields. Editor White, a Republican who backed Wilson because he was leading the country in "a righteous war," told the chairman of the Republican National Committee that a speech delivered to the Indiana newspaper editors' convention was on the wrong track. The American people were not interested, White warned, in the Republicans who were "forever harping on the fact that after the war we are going back to the good old days." The *Literary Digest* directed its editorial thrusts toward the questions on readers' minds in such articles as "Why We Are Fighting Germany," and "How to Secure Permanent Peace." Thus the reading public was prepared for Wilson's idea for a League of Nations, which was at first hailed by the mass media as a brilliant plan that would prevent repetition of the current slaughter. Wilson presented the plan at a hastily called joint session of Congress, and the press was more inclined to speculation upon the reasons for the extraordinary meeting than on such specific proposals as that for "a general association of nations." Moreover, editors saw in the Fourteen Points what they wanted to see, as the Jacksonville, Florida, *Times-Union* demonstrated by judging Wilson's purpose to be (among other things) a check on its favorite whipping boy—the protective tariff.

Increasingly, American readers were told the war was being fought to stay the barbarian's hand and to help spread the gospel of democracy. Among the few newspapers occasionally at odds with the majority view were Hearst's New York *Journal* and his California properties. Hearst harbored a latent fear that the real threat to Western civilization was the "yellow peril" created by the rise of Japan.

Thus Hearst was regretful that Japan had joined the Allies, nor could he trust British intentions after years of courting Irish-American voters by twisting the British lion's tail. No less unfriendly toward the British was the Chicago *Tribune,* a bow perhaps toward the Irish and German immigrants who formed a substantial part of the *Tribune*'s readership.

Most American editors, however, strained to convince subscribers of the valor and sacrifice of America's wartime partners. In the midst of war the editorial writers hinted repeatedly that the promised land of peace was within sight. In such circumstances it was natural that organized morality would temporarily capture the nation's sympathies if not its full attention. Thus the Women's Christian Temperance Union gained friends in the legislatures of farming states until the clamor for a Prohibition amendment to the Constitution could no longer be dismissed as a practical joke. "I used to laugh at th' Pro-hybitionists," Mr. Dooley confessed, "I used to laugh them to scorn. But I laugh no more; they've got us on the run." [13]

Gradually, Americans realized from the news dispatches and the state of their pocketbooks that wars are costly in terms of more than human life. Newspapers bowed to inflationary pressures and raised their prices from one to two cents, then three cents or a nickel, and before the Armistice some were forced to ask readers for a dime per copy. Labor costs mounted, along with the price of machinery, paper, ink, and cable tolls. The *New York Times* had transatlantic messages coming in at such a prodigious rate that its weekly toll bill ran as high as $15,000. Young reporters volunteered for military service or were drafted, leaving to older men extra burdens that were sometimes placed (without great enthusiasm) on women anxious to prove that sex was no deterrent to the practice of good reporting.

There were other costs of a more subtle variety. The marginal newspapers were in no position to pay higher salaries or larger paper bills. Advertising rates historically run behind the rise of other prices, so that newspapers oftentimes are the last to participate in a general inflationary expansion of the economy. In 1917–1918 old machinery wore out and could not be replaced because of defense factory commitments. Publishers knew that when the war ended, the cost of replacing worn equipment would probably not fall back to prewar levels. One result of the combined circumstances of labor, paper, and machinery cost increases was that the crest of American journalism, reached in 1912–1914, had begun to recede at an accelerated pace. Hardest hit was the foreign-language press, already reeling from governmental sanctions. By the war's end, the loss of almost 2,500 dailies and weeklies had been noted in the authoritative Ayer's *Directory of Newspapers,* with the definite turn coming in the 1917 edition that showed 1,043 new journalistic enterprises balanced against the suspension of 1,659 newspapers.

Magazines had some wartime readjustments to make, but on the whole the news and opinion journals became entrenched while the popular fiction groups suffered. The *Saturday Evening Post* and *Collier's* reached into America's parlors through a varied bill of fare that intertwined wartime romance with articles on Prohibition, women's rights, and safety on the growing network of highways. The *Post* had long since passed the million mark in circulation. *McClure's, Everybody's,* and *Munsey's* all tended to live on their past reputations. Their demise in postwar America was clearly predictable by the autumn of 1918.

Through much of the summer of 1918 there were rumors of a German peace overture, leading the aggressive United Press finally to stumble into one of the biggest journalistic blunders of all time. Roy Howard, the UP general manager, believed a high naval official who told him on November 7, 1918, that the Allies and Germany had formally agreed to stop the fighting. Howard and the UP French bureau chief signed a cable which, through a combination of strange circumstances, went directly to the UP New York headquarters. "Urgent Armistice Allies Germany Signed Eleven Smorning Hostilities ceased two safternoon," was the pertinent part, written in "cablese" to save tolls. UP wires quickly dispatched the story by telegraph across the nation, which jubilantly accepted what it heard. Extras proclaimed the war's end until Howard's "kill" message came through several hours later, but the country had already launched a binge with mobs in the streets, factory whistles blasting, and hoarded stocks of liquor opened for the long-awaited occasion. Howard's embarrassment led him to launch an investigation and concluded that the false armistice story was planted by a German agent who hoped the fake story would afford the Germany army a brief respite from its "disastrous retreat." [14]

The war helped afternoon newspapers because stories filed in Europe would still reach America and be printed the same day, provided they came over the Atlantic before noon in New York. News of the real armistice came early on November 11, and after some hesitation because of the false alarm, the crowds in cities surpassed anything in man's memory. *Nation Wild Over War's End,* the Philadelphia *Inquirer* headline said, on November 12, 1918, buttressed by an eight-column picture of a cheering mob in South Penn Square *Gathered to Celebrate the Victory of Democracy Over Autocracy.* Discerning readers began to see that morning newspapers carried the same dispatches they had read the day before in the "P.M. Blue Streak," "Five-Star Final," and other afternoon editions. The coming peace negotiations and reopening of bureaus throughout Europe helped the afternoon newspapers hold an edge in transatlantic reporting for another few years, until the radio reporters made all printed journalism into a secondary accounting.

America required a few days to recover from the Armistice celebration, but there were other concerns. A devastating epidemic of what the newspapers called Spanish Influenza (and finally shortened into "flu") struck that winter and was killing more soldiers at home than had German bullets in France. Editorials urged careful citizens to wear protective gauze masks and shun public places. The advance of medical science in the past decade permitted reporters to explain the harm that coughing and exposure could bring to those readers still in good health.[15] In most farming states, the legalized sale of whiskey had ended before the war started, but the metropolitan centers resisted change until the Eighteenth Amendment finally passed Congress in January 1919. With most of the nation's attention centered on peace negotiations and the president's dramatic trip to Europe, the full impact of the Prohibitionists' victory escaped editorial writers and their insouciant readers. News of the Prohibition amendment was sandwiched between items on Wilson's Paris talks and the influenza epidemic, until mid-January 1919 when the Associated Press belatedly realized that seventeen states had ratified the Eighteenth Amendment. The news acted as a prod on usually dilatory state legislatures and before the week was out—on January 16, 1919—Nebraska won the race to become the necessary thirty-sixth ratifying state. *Entire Nation Rides On the Water Wagon,* an Atlanta *Journal* banner headline announced. A side story revealed that the revivalist Billy Sunday called the amendment "the best news since the signing of the Armistice." At Washington, the Anti-Saloon League of America announced it was not going out of business now that its objective had been achieved, but would carry its crusade abroad in an effort "to make the world bone dry." [16]

Closed liquor counters did not appear to threaten Americans as much as the wave of strikes that hit the postwar economy in 1919–1920. Meanwhile, Russia had been through one successful counter-revolution and an Allied expeditionary force had been sent to make threatening gestures. At first editorial writers were inclined to sympathize with the Czarist overthrow, but the bloody purges, followed by ouster of the moderate Kerensky clique, boded ill for the hopes of a truly democratic Russian government. Ultimately the emergence of a powerful dictator in Lenin was deemed a grave threat to international stability by the State Department, a judgment readily accepted by editors and publishers. The government's refusal to give official recognition to the USSR was in keeping with the climate of opinion, fostered by the mass media, which regarded strikers as promoters of anarchy. The rabid antilabor Los Angeles *Times* implied that there was little real difference between a striking union leader and "a godless Bolshevist." A wave of criminal syndicalism laws passed state legislatures in a reaction to the news from Russia, with implications for freedom of the press that were mainly ignored by the newspapers as their intent was praised by the publishers. The laws permitted prosecution of any person who advocated the overthrow of organized government by violence. One prosecution in New York State against the distributor of a Communist leaflet resulted in the Supreme Court's classic doctrine that while the right of free speech or a free press was not unlimited, there had to be proof of "a clear and present danger" before the government could interfere.[17]

Postwar America was so unlike the sleepy nation of 1913 that an aroused Rip Van Winkle would have been lost indeed. Along with other signs of change, the press corps in Washington had been vastly expanded. During the war Wilson had discontinued his regular press conferences but he understood that public opinion was still a powerful force, and editorial opinion was regarded as the chief weathervane on public issues. Preoccupied with the League of Nations, Wilson was dismayed by the Republican stance on what he regarded as the foremost issue in American politics since the Civil War. A Kansas editor who had seen the crowds cheer Wilson in Paris returned to his home town and reported that "Sixty per cent of the Kansas people are against the League today, possibly more." [18] The great New York dailies favored American participation in the League, but the farther West one went the harder it became to find pro-League newspapers. Blocked by the Senate, Wilson decided to carry his battle to the people and over the heads of Republican publishers and editors who were enthralled with Senator Lodge's rhetoric. Somewhat in the manner of Andrew Johnson, Wilson started making a swing through the nation, and as with Johnson the result was disappointing. The tour halted after Wilson had a sudden seizure. A *New York Times* headline reported, *President Suffers Nervous Breakdown, Tour Canceled,* but a reporter explained that the president's physician termed Wilson's condition "not alarming." The *Times* also carried a front-page feature, "Strain of Years Tells on Wilson," which gave a full account of Wilson's punishing schedule since 1916. The Associated Press story quoted Dr. Grayson but left the impression that Wilson's ailment was acute indigestion, not a paralytic stroke.[19]

Wilson had tried to be friendly with reporters traveling on the presidential special train, and perhaps they were trying to protect him from further disappointment. For whatever reason, the reading public was not well informed about Wilson's health unless the *New York Times* came to its desk or doorstep. *Doctors in Consultation Call Wilson "A Very Sick Man,"* a *Times* headline revealed on October 3. The Senate killed all hope of American participation in the League, and Wilson was too ill to appeal to the nation for a revival of the issue. Before he became incapacitated, Wilson reportedly said that autumn that he was growing tired of newsmen. "They ask me such foolish questions." [20] Now there were no questions and no answers. A sick, defeated and outgoing president was not "good copy," editors reasoned. Normalcy became the key word in newsrooms as the ailing president faded from the front pages.

"Normalcy" seemed far away in 1919–1920 as news columns told of a wave of new strikes, high prices, bathtub gin, and a nostalgic longing for "the good old days." Republican chieftains hoped to capitalize on the public's impatience with soaring costs, labor unrest, the so-called Bolshevist threat, and a resurgence of racism in metropolitan areas that led to bloody race incidents in Tulsa, Omaha, and Chicago. Tension between white and black workers in the packing plants helped account for the bloody Omaha and Chicago disturbances. The *New York Times* quoted Nebraska Governor McKelvie as saying, "One of the most alarming features of the situation is the extent to which young boys were engaged in the destruction of property and the violence that characterized the riot." [21] The public seemed to want to get its mind off its troubles, which was what the newspapers were rammed with—through five editions. The editor of the Iola, Kansas, *Register,* asked a colleague the direct question: "Is the country going to hell?" The Emporia editor sidestepped a direct answer but observed that America was suffering from "the worst case of social bellyache that it has been my misfortune ever to see or hear about." Thousands of federal agents began enforcing the Eighteenth Amendment on January 16, 1919, and the *New York Times* reporter decided that "the interest in a general celebration in farewell to liquor" was hardly discernible as the last "wet" day faded. As saloon doors were padlocked, the *Times* noted, a government official was speculating that complete "bone-dry conditions" would probably not prevail until 1926. However, a start had been made, and public attention quickly but temporarily swung to reports from the Marconi laboratory that indicated that the inventor of radio had picked up "mysterious signals" that might have come from Mars or "other worlds." [22]

Meanwhile, the dollar bought less and less. For newspapers with high fixed costs and low profit margins, the inflationary spiral touched off by the war could lead in only one direction. Mergers of weak newspapers in Chicago between 1914 and 1918 left the nation's second largest city with only two morning newspapers in the postwar era. Similar consolidations took place in Pittsburgh, New Orleans, Cleveland, and elsewhere as some of the most respected names in American journalism fell victims to hard times. The New York *Sun* acquired the *Press* (both bought by Munsey), and on January 15, 1920, the *Herald*'s sale by the James Gordon Bennett, Jr., estate was announced. Munsey had merged the *Herald* with the *Sun*, but vowed that as long as he lived the venerable king of the old penny press would live on. The younger Bennett had spent much time in Paris and the *Herald* had been drained by his high living, so that Munsey was to find he had bought a great name along with some wornout equipment. Paper costs continued to rise and the relentless demands of the expensive presses kept many publishers continually indebted to paper mill owners. There were rumors that even the New York *Tribune* was in trouble. Munsey, convinced he could make money in metropolitan journalism as he had with his magazine, tried to talk the Reid family into selling its *Tribune* interests so he could merge the *Herald* with the *Tribune*.[23] The Reids said they were not interested.

Hearst no longer had open presidential ambitions but he was at a pinnacle of sorts in 1920. He owned a string of newspapers stretching from Manhattan through Baltimore and the Midwest to Seattle, along with a group of magazines, a budding newsreel company, a cattle ranch of gigantic proportions, mineral interests, and the Cosmopolitan film studios, where he could order the production of feature motion pictures starring Miss Marion Davies. Hearst's publications had orders to give Miss Davies' pictures generous space and it was well known in journalism circles that Miss Davies and Hearst had formed a liaison that could not be discussed in print but would furnish much gossip at press-club bars. The word *American* again became prominent in the Hearst vocabulary as occasional editorials routed from the pleasure dome at San Simeon in California to Hearst properties spoke of the "yellow peril" created by the Japanese navy and growing industrialism in Asia.

In retrospect the 1920s proved a time of great trial for New York journalism. A technological breakthrough made voice transmissions possible by radio, and the 1920 election returns broadcast from a makeshift station atop a Pittsburgh building presaged a fundamental change in news reporting. Even before that change became unmistakable, however, the personality of certain newspapers was changing as able editors died or retired, new publishers took over, and the devastating effects of inflation became obvious. The New York *World* under Frank Cobb and Walter Lippmann was a good newspaper with thoughtful editorials and above-average reporters, but it was fighting on the street corners for the same readership that the *New York Times* also sought. The *Tribune* continued to lose money.

An upstart newcomer, the New York *Daily News,* made its inroads with a less thoughtful readership in a spectacular way. The *Daily News* was founded by Joseph Medill Patterson, partial heir to the great Medill-McCormick fortune in Chicago, on the premise that what worked in London would work in New York. He modeled the *Daily News* along the lines of the successful London *Daily Mirror,* a tabloid (four-column, or half-size) newspaper that stressed sex, violence, and pictures. After a slow start, the *Daily News* staff began experimenting with the English language so that a headline—*Killer's Gat Found*—intrigued the crowds rushing toward subway stations. In August 1919 the *Daily News* had a 26,636 circulation. Patterson, supported by a plentiful family treasury, could afford to wait for the success that came by 1921. What people in the cities seemed to want—most people—was the same kind of "Gee whiz!" journalism Hearst had developed in imitation of Pulitzer. Newspapers found more readers as they featured information and ways of conveying it that did not require great thought. The average American newspaper reader in the 1920s may not have been the "booby unmatchable" H. L. Mencken of *Smart Set* and the *American Mercury* said he was, but he did not want to read long stories about the German war debt or international trade agreements.[24]

Thus, Jazz Age journalism grew out of the postwar reaction to heavy news that taxed the reader who preferred to be entertained. In one sense, it was 1835 all over again, for Bennett's experiment in sensational journalism needed no fresh confirmation. What had happened was that photo journalism had added another dimension to the reporter's story, and a considerable shift in social customs and mores permitted newspapers to print details of crimes and gossip about public figures in a way that would have provoked duels, horsewhippings, and crowded dockets of libel cases prior to 1900.

13

Headlines
and Breadlines

The nation's heroes between the 1920 presidential election and the Great Depression were men who became famous for hitting a baseball or killing thugs or safely flying airplanes across the ocean or taking a pratfall in front of a motion picture camera. This shifting of the spotlight from public men, and particularly presidents, to another kind of hero was something entirely new in American history. The rise of the sports figure, gangster, aviator, or movie star in public esteem was in direct proportion to newspaper coverage of every phase of the lives of these new folk heroes.

High expectations left Americans disappointed in 1919 and 1920 when it became apparent that the Great War had not been the last one, as Wilson had implied, but only the most recent one. There were troubles in the Balkans, in Asia Minor, in Germany, in Russia —where was that elusive peace that had seemed so near in November 1918?

Symptomatic of the nation's response to tiresome wartime restrictions and bewildering foreign involvement was the professional politicians' search for candidates from the midwest of 100-proof mediocrity. Governor James M. Cox, publisher of the Springfield, Ohio, *Press-Republic*, emerged from the Democratic convention as a lackluster but safe nominee. Fellow publishers in the GOP ranks quickly dismissed Cox as incapable of national leadership. No wonder the reading public was pleased to see the handsome features of the Republican nominee, Warren G. Harding, on front pages above promises of a return to "normalcy." The publisher of the Marion, Ohio, *Star* had been in the newspaper game for thirty-five years while Cox also published papers in Dayton and Canton. The Ohio Associated Dailies organization kept a foot in both camps by endorsing the two candidates as "practical publishers and brilliant Ohioans." Editors elsewhere were not always as charitable, and there were also barbs for the second man on the ticket. "As for Franklin D. Roosevelt, the Democratic nominee for Vice-President," the Los Angeles *Times* of July 6, 1920, commented, "he adds no merit to the ticket. He is a radical of unsafe tendencies."

Taking his lead from another successful Ohio campaigner, Harding conducted a front-porch campaign, trounced Cox, and to his credit began holding regularly scheduled press conferences after he took residence in the White House. But, as happens frequently with presidents after their honeymoon with the press ends, Harding ultimately grew impatient with reporters on the presidential beat.

Finally, when Harding was accused of attempting to "muzzle the press," he began lecturing reporters on their functions. *Editor & Publisher* was quick to remind Harding that the publisher of the Marion *Star* could ill afford "to tell the press of America what is and what is not news from the Presidential standpoint." Whatever Harding's faults, he was an affable man and popular with reporters as well as with their bosses. Yet, only a month after Harding told the American Society of Newspaper Editors convention in 1923 that he would hold on to the *Star* "because I would rather be a newspaper publisher than anything else in the world," he had sold the Marion journal to an Ohio chain. The inconsistency did not pass unnoticed, except that it seemed the president had simply been showing the rest of the country how to succeed in business. He had purchased the *Star* at a sheriff's sale in 1887, and sold it for $550,000.

Nobody faulted Harding for making a neat profit, but he was criticized that same spring of 1923 for having been too loyal to men in his administration who had difficulty separating their own best interests from the public good. The president's popularity was manifest and newsmen who sensed trouble in his administration kept a truce with the White House. The stock market appeared healthy. Baseball season was in full swing, and the promise that the country would soon be "back to normal" did not seem unattainable.

The census figures indicated otherwise. By 1920, census compilations revealed, America had pulled up its agrarian roots and moved into town. For the first time in history, most Americans no longer lived on farms. The automobile had helped bring about the transformation and some perceptive Americans, including a *New Republic* reporter, saw that the "normalcy" people wanted had nothing to do with the American past. What concerned people most, a nationwide questionnaire of businessmen indicated, was not the Bolshevist threat or high taxes or labor strife. The *New Republic* printed a Portland, Oregon, businessman's candid answer—that the average man's attention was "devoted principally to motion pictures, baseball, prize fights, automobiles, dress, murder, and divorce." Only the newspaper gave every member of the family a chance to be informed about these topics. If the natural flow of events lagged, there was that new division of the larger newspapers to be consulted—the promotion department—where pseudo-sports events competed with the growing popularity of collegiate or professional sport for attention. Bathing-beauty contests, automobile races, air circuses, and similar events were staged by newspapers seeking more circulation and identification with growing public interest in mammoth outdoor spectacles.

Baseball had long held the attention of the American male newspaper reader, but the rise of college football in sports pages of the 1920s was breathtaking. Grantland Rice and John Kieran, two sports writers with a scholarly bent, looked back on the era and were unable to decide whether newspaper publicity had thrust college football into the public spotlight or whether the public was only finding what was demanded by an urban society intensely bored by office and factory work. Machinists and manicurists thrilled as they read of the exploits of Harold "Red" Grange at the University of Illinois. Grange's fame grew as testified by a newspaperman's nickname, for "The Galloping Ghost" was hailed as a folk hero in headlines across the land. The winning streak of the Coach Knute Rockne at Notre Dame created thousands of "subway alumni" for the Indiana university in Manhattan and on Chicago's Loop. Fifty years later, residents of Louisville still recalled with warmth that on October 29, 1921, little Centre College had defeated Harvard, 6 to 0, in a football upset that deserved a double banner headline in the *Courier-Journal* and public rejoicing. The Chicago *Tribune* began building a network of small-town correspondents who telephoned results of high school games to the metropolis. The University of Michigan built a stadium for nearly 100,000 spectators who learned the details about their team from sports pages that devoted more space to the Michigan-Notre Dame games than to the combined coverage of the League of Nations and congressional proceedings.

Not that baseball was neglected by the newspapers. After the bad taste of the scandalous 1919 World Series had dissolved in a new wave of publicity for the 1920 season, the heroic struggles of the teams of John McGraw, Connie Mack, and Miller Huggins demanded reams of copy from pounding typewriters at Shibe Park or the Polo Grounds. Christy Matthewson, the New York Giant pitcher, shared a hold on the public's attention in prewar days with presidents and senators; but the shouting fans of the 1920s had one hero who stood ahead of any public man: Babe Ruth. The New York Yankee outfielder's batting prowess, along with his offfield interests, were duly reported to the nation from March through October. Ruth was as popular as President Harding and far more visible.

Harding, suffering from self-doubts and Cabinet troubles, left Washington in the summer of 1923 for an Alaskan hegira. While on the West Coast the president confided to several reporters his feeling that key members of his administration had betrayed his confidence, but the scandals that later rocked Washington were still locked in filing drawers when the distraught president died suddenly in a San Francisco hotel. The nation paused to mourn, decently and hurriedly, then switched its attention back to the thrilling pennant race between the Pirates, Reds, and Giants for the 1923 National League championship. Newspapers assigned whole batteries of reporters to cover training camps and regular season games, so that one newsman might spend eight months of each year devoting his entire workday to descriptions of a rookie's curve ball or the nuances of a squeeze-bunt play.

A similar journalistic interest in all facets of organized sport was apparent. The exploits of the racehorse Man o' War led the wire services to carry minute details of the thoroughbred's ancestry, track records, and total winnings. The dashing triumphs of "Big Bill" Tilden in tennis, Bobby Jones in golf, and both Jack Dempsey and Gene Tunney in prizefighting created reading habits in the American male that were not easily broken. Even a chief justice of the Supreme Court admitted that he turned first to the sports pages in the newspapers because "that's where the good news is."

It was not in sports alone, readers found, that Americans won and lost. While the names of Mary Pickford, Clara Bow, and Rudolph Valentino titillated readers of the New York tabloids, in the Midwest and South a frightful phenomena began capturing the headlines. By 1924 more than 2 million Americans were members of the Ku Klux Klan, a semisecret society modeled on the post-Civil War bands that had terrorized southern Negroes. In its newer garb the Klan was fiercely Protestant, anti-Semitic, anti-Negro, anti-Catholic, and full of busybodies who took delight in burning wooden crosses or tarring and feathering "uppity" blacks. The New York *World* took notice of the Klan's spread in the fall of 1921 by publishing an exposé of the Klan's founders and its violence. Then the New York *Journal-American* snapped at the Klan's heels with a series of articles on the financial sleight-of-hand practiced by officials at the national headquarters. But despite the syndicated *World* series and other exposés with details of whippings, arson, and torture, the Klan during the early 1920s found more friends than enemies in small-town America. Indeed, the publicity from newspaper stories seemed to spread the Klan's gospel.

Newspaper reaction to the Klan varied, ranging from brave criticism in the Sacramento *Bee,* Norfolk *Virginian-Pilot,* and Emporia *Gazette,* to an ostrichlike open tolerance—particularly in the lower South. The Richmond *Times-Dispatch* and *News Leader* tried to ignore the Klan as it gained converts in the state's rural areas, vainly hoping a news blackout would stifle the movement. In Texas, the Amarillo *News* and Wichita Falls *Times* were occasional supporters of Klan activities, but Kansan William Allen White's *Gazette* castigated Klansmen as "moral idiots" and carried their membership rolls on page one. The militant Sacramento *Bee* editor, a Catholic stalwart with a long record of campaigns for public betterment, was upbraided by the city hall crowd which reinstated Klansmen who had been fired from the police and fire departments.[1] *Bee* publisher C. K. McClatchy printed a Protestant minister's statement that "Nearly all the bawdy houses, bootleg joints, and other dives [in Sacramento] *are* owned or controlled by Romanists." McClatchy persevered in his exposures and eventually the local Klan foundered on a rock of internal dissension over money matters. Finally, the Klan movement spent itself, but in the national election of 1928 there were lingering overtones of bigotry after the Democrats nominated Alfred E. Smith, a New York Catholic, for the presidency.

Although several newspapers consistently reported Klan activities and the Indianapolis *Times* won a Pulitzer prize for its exposés, a historian of the KKK concluded that in general, newspapers told their readers of Klan vigilantism only "partially and poorly, and often not at all." Indeed, David Chalmers concluded that publicity for the KKK helped swell its membership rolls in its earliest days, and it was a matter of record that the Indiana Republican Editorial Association reprimanded a Vincennes editor who had revealed the seamy side of

Klan affairs. The official KKK newspaper in Oklahoma, the *Fiery Cross*, went into 100,000 homes and helped split Democrats in 1924 so bitterly that a Republican nonentity won the Senate race over an avowed Klan enemy.[2]

Far more widespread than the Klan was the bootlegger of the 1920s who ranged from the powerful gangster kingpin in Chicago—Al Capone—to hill-country farmers who operated a still in time-honored fashion. The Prohibition amendment had barely been in force when an increase in violent crimes was noted in the larger cities where organized gangs began staking out territories for the illicit sale of smuggled whiskey, wine, and beer. Chicagoans witnessed a variety of wars as the *Tribune* circulation crews fought Hearst's *American* truck drivers, while rival rum-running crews battled for the patronage of speakeasies. The reading public grew cynical as crime seemed to dominate life in all big cities, but particularly in Chicago. Small-town readers shook their heads when they read that seven Chicago policemen had been killed or wounded during three days in April 1925. The *New York Times* quoted the Chicago chief of police as saying after four murders in one day, "I am tempted to issue an order allowing policemen to shoot all suspected criminals at sight." [3]

Crime was not limited to metropolitan America, of course, but the high stakes in illegal whiskey sales made New York, Chicago, Philadelphia, and St. Louis appear to have been evenly balanced between criminal elements and sober citizens. In rural America there were criminal folk heroes who matched Capone, however, as the exploits of "Ma" Kate Barker, her four sons, and lesser "stick-up" men were fully covered by the small-town newspapers, with the stories often taking on a romantic tinge. The tendency in much of the South was to shift attention from local petty crimes or the occasional lynching of a black lad accused of rape, by pointing to northern gangland slayings. The Albany, Georgia, *Herald* was in the minority of southern newspapers that insisted there was nothing to be gained by playing down lynchings and other local outcroppings of violence, but the Albany *Morning News* made an editorial plea that gangster murders be classed in the same category with southern lynchings to balance the ledger of violence.[4]

The South took its share of ribbing, much of it tongue-in-cheek, when a Dayton, Tennessee, schoolteacher was tried for violating the state's antievolution laws. John T. Scopes was charged with teaching Darwinian theories to a biology class. William Jennings Bryan offered to prosecute Scopes on behalf of the people of Tennessee and a nation of churchgoers, while Clarence Darrow was brought into the crossroads village as Scopes' defender. Scores of reporters descended on Dayton and sent wire reports to the wire services and metropolitan newspapers full of colorful descriptions of the courtroom dialogue and local reaction to the trial. Bryan won the case but Scopes was later freed on a technicality. Darrow's scathing remarks left Bryan an easy target for reporters who barely remembered that the old man's "Cross of Gold" speech had once struck sparks of hope in the downtrodden. Amidst the circuslike atmosphere at the end of the trial, Bryan suffered a stroke and died five days later. Editorials paid tribute to the stamina of "The Great Commoner," but between the lines of many eulogies there was implicit recognition that a Bible-thumping politician was a boring anachronism in 1925. As the fledgling *Time* magazine noted, Bryan was "dead on the scene of his last combat . . . with his last great speech unmade." [5]

Brash and bouncy, *Time* was in 1925 a healthy two-year-old that had survived despite predictions that circulatory anemia would soon send the upstart into bankruptcy. Briton Hadden and Henry Luce, Yale classmates with a smattering of newspaper experience on metropolitan dailies, nourished their dream for a different kind of magazine until the first issue appeared on March 3, 1923. *Time* was not too different from the successful *Literary Digest,* but it had a certain special cockiness and brevity that appealed to the man-in-a-hurry, who was becoming accustomed to condensation in his news as in other facets of American life.[6] What better name for a magazine in a country where time was always at a premium? By 1927, *Time* was guaranteeing a circulation of 135,000 to a growing number of advertisers.

For those who could spare only a monthly glance at a magazine, the *Reader's Digest* had been founded, a year ahead of *Time,* basically on the same premise as the newsmagazine and tabloids: everybody is in a hurry. The purpose of condensed news and features, as *Reader's Digest* pointed out, was "to please the reader, to give him the nub of the matter in the new faster-moving world of the 1920s." [7] Increasingly, editors assumed readers had too many demands on their time to permit leisurely reading. Newspapers of more than 24 pages looked bulky, and *Time* itself kept to a slim 40-page average in 1927. Even so, New York wits continued to make clever remarks about the growing *New York Times* Sunday edition—a heavy 274 pages on April 1, 1928. The delivered price: one nickel.

Whether Americans were working less and playing more could not be flatly asserted. But whatever postwar Americans did, they did intensely. Radio, which started as a hobby for amateur wireless operators, had grown rapidly from a tiny experiment into a full-blown industry with enormous potential. The public quickly passed from the crystal-set stage to demand large receivers with cavernous speakers. Some newspaper publishers entered the radio field as a hedge against the new medium's threat to printed journalism, but other publishers loathed the very call letters of their local station (from WEAF to KHJ). Thus news was handed out parsimoniously as "bulletins," and even that slender fare was too much for the old-timers who controlled the Associated Press. The bulletins were intended to serve as "teasers to stimulate readership for the station owner's newspaper enterprise." [8] Since the AP was essentially antiradio, it was predictable that on a vote the nation's largest newsgathering agency would deny use of its news wire to the mushrooming radio industry—a roadblock that may have shoved radio into the entertainment channel with more abandon than was probably justified. The exception was that occasional special broadcast in which a football game was sent on a weak signal to distant fans, or the 1924 Davis-Coolidge broadcasts on the evening before the election. Radio officials consoled themselves by saying that there was no profit to be made in newscasting anyway, a judgment that long hung over the electronic medium to hamper the training of capable radio reporters.

Except for the distant threat of radio, America's newspaper publishers were a smug lot during the 1920s. Advertising revenues had risen steadily since 1917, and a businessman was in the White House pledged to rivet prosperity on the economy. No longer was 1600 Pennsylvania Avenue the bustling news center it had been in Teddy Roosevelt's day. Reporters had no entrée to the executive offices during Coolidge's tenure, and he never permitted newsmen to quote him directly. Saddened early in his term by the loss of a fourteen-year-old son, Coolidge was by nature a taciturn New Englander who was determined to live out his philosophy of near-silence. "Four-fifths of all our troubles in this life would disappear," Coolidge once petulantly remarked, "if we would only sit down and keep still." [9] By keeping quiet himself, Coolidge left the country in the hands of headstrong congressmen and their friends who controlled the largest industries.

Election returns in 1924 indicated that the voters approved of this policy, apparently strongly enough to offset the breath of scandal as the 1924 elections approached. Although the Teapot Dome exposé was still under investigation, Harding's Administration was already under a cloud. One side effect of that episode, wherein oil drilling concessions had been lavished on a favored few with such stealth and bribery that a Cabinet officer finally went to jail, directly concerned Rocky Mountain journalism. Fred G. Bonfils, a part-owner of the supersensational Denver *Post*, was implicated in the plot when it was revealed that the *Post* had suppressed information on the Teapot Dome scandal after making a lucrative deal with the oil operators. The *Post* series of revelations had halted all too suddenly, a coincidence that later caused the American Society of Newspaper Editors ethics committee to ask for Bonfils' expulsion. Other Denver newspapermen became involved in the oil scandals, and when Bonfils attacked the *Rocky Mountain News* in a circulation war the whole area was nearly drenched in petroleum. The *Post* offered want-ad purchasers free gasoline, leading the *News* to make a counter-offer of five free gallons with each classified ad it sold (for 2 5 cents). "All Denver was riding on free gasoline," Mott noted, while "the Sunday papers went to over 100 pages, stuffed with classified advertising, and the *Post* and *News* lost money like drunken sailors." [10] Finally, a truce was arranged that gave the *Post* a clear morning field in Denver while the *News* took exclusive rights to afternoon circulation. As Denver citizens surmised about most *Post* promotions—the emphasis was not on news but on fun.

If Americans were not having fun in 1927 it was hardly the fault of the nation's press. The New York *Daily News* had won a signal mark of success in 1924 when Hearst—the great imitator—started his *Daily Mirror* tabloid and Bernarr MacFadden risked his millions on the *Daily Graphic*. A flood of stories in 1927 were tailor-made for the tabloids, starting with the bedroom romps of "Daddy" Browning and his nymph, "Peaches," that were fully explained in a lengthy court action. The three tabloids chased each other through a series of alternative horrors and heroism until the reading public was limp. In the process, tabloids gained an unsavory reputation as their city editors approved the use of faked photographs and sent out rude reporters who understood no rules of privacy. A low-water mark was reached when the competing tabloids let no detail escape during the trial that recounted the homicidal saga of once-obscure Ruth Snyder and her corset salesman-lover. Jaded New Yorkers began to speak of the *Graphic* as the "Daily Pornographic" at newsstands, and when the axe of the Depression fell it was the first tabloid to collapse. But the Jazz Age journalism it supposedly symbolized left a mark on the cultural scene. The Broadway hit play *The Front Page*, still periodically revived with success, was patterned after a composite of *Graphic-News-Mirror* reporters who played poker incessantly, drank enormous quantities of "booze," and worked for a tyrannical managing editor whose first loyalty was to a newspaper devoid of ethical standards.

To a greater degree than at any time in the nation's history, the public's attention in the 1920s wavered between the significant and the trivial as both were accorded equal coverage by a growing band of "beat"-assigned reporters and rewrite men.

While the convicted immigrants Sacco and Vanzetti waited on death row amid the world debate over their innocence or guilt, Jack Dempsey signed a contract for a rematch with Gene Tunney in a prizefight that produced reams of copy and brought in one million dollars in ticket sales. Crackling radio loudspeakers carried the story of this latest version of "the fight of the century" to listeners whose interest had been whipped to a frenzied pitch. Awed sports editors proclaimed that the slugging match was only slightly less significant than the David-Goliath contest of biblical times, reckoning that Dempsey would earn $5,000 a minute for his night's work and regain his lost title. If radio sets had not cost almost as much as a Willys or Essex automobile, more people would have been listening to the fight instead of waiting at the telegraph offices or outside newspaper city rooms to learn of Tunney's second victory.

The biggest news story of 1927 centered around a new figure—a perfect hero. A slender twenty-five-year-old airplane pilot from the Midwest collected enough money to equip an airplane for a solo flight to Paris in quest of a $25,000 cash prize. No man had ever crossed the Atlantic alone in a nonstop flight, but plenty of daring fliers had drowned or injured themselves in the attempt. Contrary to later conceptions of the event, Charles A. Lindbergh did not arrange his flight or depart for France in secrecy. His plans were widely pub-licized by oil companies, bearing manufacturers, and other commer-cial interests gambling that the young pilot might have the guts and luck to make the flight successfully. The idea that a gangling freckle-faced youth might go aloft in his *Spirit of St. Louis* in New York and reappear in Paris seemed to reporters to rank with Columbus's voy-age in its confident daring. "A sluggish gray monoplane lurched its way down Roosevelt Field yesterday morning, slowly gathering mo-mentum," the *New York Times* reported. "Inside sat a tall youngster, eyes glued to an instrument board or darting head for swift glances, at the runway. . . . Death lay but a few seconds ahead of him if his skill failed or his courage faltered." [11] When the first reports were full of bad news, the suspense mounted. *Encounters Fogs in Early Hours of Hop; Close to Disaster Starting,* the Richmond *News Leader* headline read.[12] Throughout the next day, a Saturday, the nation's attention was focused on Lindbergh's progress. Lindbergh carried five sandwiches but no radio, so contact had been lost once the ocean fog engulfed his airplane beyond Newfoundland. Extras told of nothing really new, but the pictures grew larger. The suspense in city rooms mounted higher as copy boys and city editors hovered around the wire machines. The *New York Times* on Saturday morning gave most of its first six pages to details of the aircraft, Lindbergh's early life, the flight plan, and Atlantic weather information.

Then the telephones and teletype machine bells began ringing in a wild scene of relief and joy. *Lindbergh Does It! To Paris in 33½ Hours,* the *New York Times* proclaimed. The story broke on Saturday afternoon and only a hermit would have been unaware of the Lindbergh triumph by Sunday morning, as the nation was delirious with excitement all the next day. No gift the nation might then have bestowed would have been beyond Lindbergh's reach, so widespread was his popularity. The drama continued to unfold as Lindbergh gave his story to the *New York Times* for syndication. Editors gushed with pent-up sentiment. "He had the right sort of mother, to start with," said the Richmond *News Leader*, "as nearly every man has who amounts to any thing." [13] Political cartoonists forgot their local battles and turned to the vision unleashed by the flight. One popular drawing showed the silhouette of Lindbergh's airplane passing over a packet labeled "1957—New York to Paris Passenger Service." The nation was still agog when the hero returned to New York for a ticker-tape parade that was broadcast by the new National Broadcasting Company network of fifty stations. Perhaps George Seldes was right when he claimed that Lindbergh "flew the Atlantic for the

Times," but once "Lindy" returned the mass media embraced Lindbergh as no other man has ever been courted.[14] Lindbergh's shyness and modesty only brought forth more stories.

Newspapers gave Lindbergh's flight, return reception, and countless triumphant airport visits across the country (financed by a foundation to promote aviation) saturation coverage in what was to be remembered as the last of the great newspaper stories. To be sure, bravery as well as cowardice and corruption alongside sacrifice was still important news whenever reported, but the printed word was no longer an exclusive journalistic monopoly.

Newspaper publishers were of two minds about radio. One group decided to treat radio as a competitor whom a prudent businessman would ignore, hence their newspapers refused to print radio station programs or discuss developments in the rival medium. Radio stations in these communities were forced to buy advertising space to print their daily fare. Other publishers decided to make prudent investments in radio stations, such as the 5-watt station at Fresno owned by the Sacramento *Bee,* and await developments. The more conservative group had dominated the Associated Press from the outset, so that from 1922 onward members were under strict orders not to share their dispatches with radio stations, even those owned by such powerful franchise holders as the Detroit *News* and Kansas City *Star.* It was one thing to make the rules and quite another to police the airwaves, so that Lindbergh's flight and landing were common knowledge in the cities before extras hit the streets. Newspapers could supply details of an important story, but by 1927 the urban public was becoming accustomed to the idea of broadcast bulletins. A year later the three major news services (Hearst's International News service included) entered a consortium to carry two brief newscasts on their wires daily—more for public information and to scare off competitors than to develop responsible radio journalism. Thus the final rejection of pleas for Sacco and Vanzetti left newscasters unmoved at a time when world indignation was aroused by their execution in August 1927. "I wanted the news [about the convicted men], though the news would do no good," a listener recalled, "but the air was full of jazz." [15] Far more interesting for both radio and newspapers had been President Coolidge's typewritten note handed that same month to the White House reporters: "I do not choose to run for President in nineteen twenty-eight." Coolidge's announcement killed all the speculative stories about a possible attempt to break the third-term tradition, and threw the news spotlight on Herbert Hoover. Fewer men have ever been more uncomfortable then Coolidge's successor.

Led by the *New York Times*, the nation's press assumed from the outset that Hoover would easily win the Republican nomination. "White House Spokesman's Slip Makes It 'President Hoover,' " the *Times* reported of a humorous incident that soon became rare (the "spokesman" was doubtless Coolidge himself).[16] The Democrats held a rousing convention in Houston and adopted a "dry" platform but chose "wet" Governor Alfred E. Smith of New York as their presidential nominee. Smith, a big-city Catholic with an unmistakable East Side accent, was soon assailed in a whispering campaign mainly based on his religious affiliation. Even the Democrats' dependable "Solid South" seemed shaky, and southern editors sensed the rebellion brewing over Smith's Catholicism. "Those alleged Democrats who are staging a fight against the national ticket are doing nothing more than staging a fight for the Republican party," a Lynchburg, Virginia, newspaper warned.[17] The Memphis *Commercial Appeal* endorsed Smith but printed damaging letters to the editor from Protestant ministers and laymen who denounced him. "Any man, who recognizes a foreign potentate as his 'infallible guide,' " a Memphis Presbyterian letter writer said, "we feel it dangerous to entrust with our chief magistracy." [18]

Will Rogers, an Oklahoma cowboy who became a Ziegfeld Follies star by twirling a rope and commenting on politics and society, took to newspapering with a syndicated column that over one hundred newspapers printed daily, usually on the front page. "This campaign ends Tuesday," Rogers noted, "but it will take two generations to sweep up the dirt." New Yorkers seemed more interested in the theater than in the election; Mae West's arrest along with the entire cast of her naughty play *Pleasure Man* deserved front-page space only a few weeks before the election. The Associated Press began offering clients a daily radio listing of regional programs, but with radio sets still selling for $155 (while a Chevrolet was $585) most Americans expected to watch the results daubed on billboards outside newspaper offices, or on the new electric billboards operating in the larger cities. In Lynchburg, Virginia, the *Daily Advance* invited readers who could not find standing room at its downtown bulletin board to watch the returns "from the Morse wire" at the local football stadium. This would be the last election for such spectacles. RCA stock was selling for 209¾ on October 2, 1928, a gain of over 100 points since February; and three national networks would provide the competition that soon included regular daily news programs. The time when news came over the radio set as a special feature limited to the World's Series, championship prizefights, or presidential elections was nearly ended.

Hoover's victory in 1928 was devastating. Smith lost such Democratic strongholds as Virginia, Texas, Florida, Oklahoma, Kentucky, Missouri, North Carolina, and Tennessee. Newspapers also noted the surge on Wall Street the next day. The "Hoover Market" was hailed as stock prices of some shares went ahead as much as $10 in a postelection rally. RCA stock rose to 400. Reporters had found Hoover a hard man to talk with, and the strong hint was that, in contrast to the garrulous Smith, the nation had chosen another tight-lipped chief executive. What bothered a few editors, however, was the rationale behind the choice. "It is inescapable that Al Smith's religion played a prominent part in the defeat," a Virginia editor lamented. "Smith's Catholic background played a most prominent part in giving his opponent several southern states. . . . It is no tribute to our broadmindedness."

For the next eleven months the newspapers stressed dispatches on European unrest and domestic prosperity. The contrast between European instability and American solidity must have impressed newspaper readers, although the *Wall Street Journal,* a well-edited daily managed by Clarence W. Barron, also told of the nation's mounting per capita debt as the average wage earner bought automobiles, radio sets, refrigerators, and homes on the installment plan, and Wall Street speculators bought stocks with a 10 percent cash margin. A late summer rally sent stock prices to all-time highs. While the newspapers featured "Back to School" sales and sports pages teemed with reports of coming gridiron matches, a Detroit industrialist was quoted by the Associated Press as maintaining that America had reached "a permanent level of prosperity." Mr. Hoover accepted an invitation to watch the Philadelphia Athletics play the Chicago Cubs in the World's Series. In Memphis, a chic new real estate development at "Chickasaw Gardens" opened—one of many realtor's promotions then sweeping the country. A minor stock market drop in September was discounted as a technical correction. Most Americans owned no stock anyway, but it was generally conceded that the nation's economic health had no better barometer than the Wall Street daily averages—and they were at an all-time high again in October 1928.

Unexplainably, the market began a dramatic reversal from its previous upward trend in mid-October. Newspapers that had never carried stock market reports began running front-page stock stories. RCA stock fell 72 points in one day, rallied, and had split its shares five-for-one in the summer of 1929. The new shares sold for 83 early in October, but fell 8½ points during four bad sell-offs. *True Story* magazine bought a full-page ad in the *New York Times* to help bolster confidence. The blame for the market's uneasiness was generally placed on the buying habits of the American consumer, but *True Story* defended the sharp rise in personal indebtedness. Indeed, the advertisement explained, there was much sound evidence that a high national average of personal debt was beneficial to an economy. "We find a constant *lightening* of the economic pressure as this personal credit goes *deeper down* into the mass. They seemed to be *buoyed up* by the very thing that is supposed *to bear them down*." [19]

Despite all kinds of assurances, the market continued to drop, with the selling finally reaching panic proportions on October 24. Every segment of the Establishment tried to restore confidence in the nation's economy. Hoover made reassuring statements to the White House reporters on the essential soundness of the business community. A consortium of brokers and bankers sought to bolster the price of the bellwether United States Steel shares. Newspaper editors were not immune to the pressure that is nearly always exerted by businessmen in times of stress. Chambers of Commerce and individual merchants are never pleased by news of an economic downtrend, and they freely offer opinions to editors and publishers whose interests they share. The Memphis *Commercial Appeal* ran a typical front-page story after the heavy selling wave: "Wall Street Fights Back Out of Disaster." Businessmen were frightened by the uncertainty of the preceding three weeks, and the newspapers tried to calm readers with reassuring stories based on hope rather than fact. "Powerful Support Thrown Into Market," the *Commercial Appeal* added, with much "soundness evidenced" by the rally that sent prices "from $2 to $21 higher."

The next week, however, confidence collapsed on a broad front. RCA stock reached a new low of $38\frac{1}{2}$ by the end of October, and other issues were similarly battered. Still, financial editors wrote their columns with lighthearted confidence. "The essential fact established by yesterday's stock market was that panicky liquidation had been checked," the *New York Times* observed on October 31. "All such hysterical declines as those of the present week are certain to end eventually with an upward rebound of prices." Two years later, RCA stock sold for 5 and United States Steel had fallen from 257 to 31.

In the two-year interval, journalism recorded the deepest depressions in American history and was itself sucked into the vortex of a financial crisis that deepened each day as stock brokers continued to insist, "the market is so low, it can't go any lower." A *New York Times* headline—*Broker Still Missing*—noted after the first heavy selling—was a tragic forecast often repeated as financial failures and bankruptcies became all too frequent on business news pages. Despairing merchants snapped at city editors, "Why don't you print some good news for a change?" Except for the society pages, where marriages and parties were still reported, and in the sports sections where somebody still won games or tried to win them, there simply wasn't any good news to report.

The depression hit the Establishment, of course, but like a bear in hibernation there was much fat to be lost before the publishers, news executives, stockholders, and other powers in journalism felt a real bellyache. Weaker newspapers suffered most because they had pressing paper bills and weekly salary rolls that in a few cases proved to be the last straw. The Pulitzer heirs found lawyers who broke their father's will and sold the *World* in 1931, but most of the silver-spoon publishers found ways and means of staying in journalism. The Ochs-Sulzberger-Dryfoos dynasty was the most solidly entrenched, and the Hearst empire was among the weakest, but the tenacity of second- and third-generation publishers in Chicago, Los Angeles, Des Moines, San Diego, and elsewhere was reminiscent of medieval primogeniture. The antilabor prejudices of many of these family-owned newspapers were evident to the point that their well-controlled national news agency, the Associated Press, showed apparent bias in its stories. One vocal AP member found this hard to take. "It is so easy for a reporter, copy-reader, the city editor, and the staff of our prosperous papers to take the Country Club attitude, the boss's slant, toward those who for one reason or another are whacking the established order," William Allen White told the AP general manager. "But the easy thing must be avoided, if we retain any value as a news agency except . . . as may come to us as a purveyor of journalistic fodder for contented cows." [20]

Reporters' salaries plunged along with everybody else's, until a newsroom veteran was willing to take $15 a week for work that had brought $75 in 1928. Attempts by reporters to organize a labor union resulted in the formation of the American Newspaper Guild and a bitter fight with the Associated Press that finally went to the Supreme Court before the ANG won bargaining rights. As their line of credit ran out, publishers began to seek alternatives. Cash was in such scarce supply that those with money or a credit source made purchases of newspaper properties at rock-bottom prices. One of Iowa's oldest daily newspapers, established in a thriving riverfront town in the 1840s, changed hands when the despairing owner took a $17,000 note for the two-story building, presses, linotype machines, and all other assets of the venerable but bankrupt journal. Weekly publishers joined in cutting their prices. New York dailies dropped to two cents, and weeklies offered subscribers a full year for a dollar, in cash or produce. Circulation departments hired agents who rigged poultry coops on Model T Fords and ranged through the county in search of chickens, eggs, and butter worth the price of a subscription. "Situation Wanted" advertisements in the classified sections helped make up only slightly for the declining revenues in the display accounts of advertising departments.

A sense of humor was hard to maintain, but the newspapers searched for a way to make unemployment and uncertainty bearable. In the regular comic sections readers of all ages saw their troubles light compared to those of the ageless "Little Orphan Annie" or smiled at the nonsense in "Toonerville Trolley" or "Mr. Milquetoast." Dialect humor was sickly but not yet dead, and J. P. Alley's "Hambone's Meditation" had a large syndicated following in the South and Midwest, where the daily sayings of an overall-clad, corncob-smoking black man were not thus regarded as racist. "Folks is lak Automobuls—if dey got *quality* in 'em, a l'il dus' on de outside ain' gwine hurt 'em!" But no other newspaper humorist had the appeal of Will Rogers, whose public grew larger as the depression deepened. Rogers' daily delight was in pinpricking the pretentious. When the police chief in Chicago announced that the city was rid of gangsters, Rogers was skeptical: "Well, they run all the racketeers out of Chicago, and they had no more than got them out till the Rotarians' convention got in. Now they are talking about letting the crooks come back." [21]

Bank failures continued to destroy savings accounts. Government statisticians reported what the people already knew—unemployment had reached dimensions that few could fully comprehend: 8 million, then 10, and finally 12 million former wage earners were out of work. Farmers sold their equipment and shot cattle that were easier to kill than feed and later sell below feed costs. Commodity prices plunged, bales of cotton stood unwanted in gin sheds, and crude petroleum in 55-gallon barrels briefly scraped a bottom price of $2\frac{1}{2}$ cents in east Texas oilfields.[22]

Readers wanted to know how this collapse had come about, and the news media tried to explain in ways that never carried much satisfaction but helped consume time. The bustling American slowed down by working crossword puzzles, jigsaw puzzles, and playing "screeno" at the movies. The *Nation* told readers that the depression started because of "a failure of the purchasing power of consumers to keep pace with the increasing power of production in . . . industry and agriculture." [23] The Senate began an investigation of stock trading and particularly of the "short sales" by bearish speculators.

Families with shriveling incomes read that the World War I debt of America's allies had been suspended, and with the Hearst newspapers in the vanguard pressure was brought on President Hoover to see that the next installment of $270 million was paid when due in 1933. Colonel Robert R. McCormick, publisher of the Chicago *Tribune*, thought that many of the nation's ills were traceable to Washington. The federal budget for fiscal 1933 came to nearly $4 billion, a sum McCormick condemned as so staggering that he declared taxpayers "must tear these weasels [in Washington] from the throat of the nation." [24] President Hoover told a press conference he was at work on a balanced budget. "It is the very keystone of recovery," the president said. "Without it the Depression will be prolonged indefinitely." [25]

Editorial writers still labored to explain and recommend, but it was clear that long, unsigned editorials were no longer read by most readers. Research surveys confirmed this truth, which editors had resisted when the devotees of *Editor & Publisher* were loath to admit that readers wanted information on jobs and security rather than political advice. Increasingly the personal columnist took on stature as the local editorial writer declined. Mark Sullivan had been a syndicated columnist for the New York *Herald-Tribune* since 1923, but it was the depression that gave political columnists their great forward push. After the *World* was sold out from under him, Walter Lippmann began writing in 1931 on the nation's ills for an expanding audience of over 160 newspapers. Lippmann's clear prose and persuasive style brought imitators into the field, but his diagnosis of the national problem and the solution stood out:

> There is no use looking into the blank future for some new and fancy revelation. . . . The revelation has been made. By it man conquered the jungle about him and the barbarian within him. The elementary principles of work and sacrifice and duty—and the transcendent criteria of truth, justice, and righteousness, and the grace of love and charity—are the things which have made men free. . . . These are the terms stipulated in the nature of things for the salvation of men on this earth.

In the coming decade Boake Carter, Marquis Childs, Raymond Clapper, Hugh S. Johnson, Raymond Moley, Westbrook Pegler, and Thomas Stokes would send their syndicated wisdom to scores of newspapers where the editorial-page format hardened into three local editorials, a political cartoon, and four syndicated columns. Political gossip and an occasional exposé came from the "Washington Merry-Go-Round" column syndicated by Drew Pearson and Robert S. Allen, which in time led all other syndicated columns in reader coverage and brought Pearson such notoriety that he was publicly singled out by a president as "that s.o.b." [26]

As in a Greek drama where the hero is stalked by tragedy, Charles

A. Lindbergh was back in the news in March 1932, when his infant
son and namesake was kidnapped from the famous flier's New Jersey
home. A note demanding a $50,000 ransom was left pinned to the
nursery windowsill. The news electrified the nation for over two
months as extras and radio bulletins told of rumors that the child had
been seen in Mexico, in Cuba, or in Virginia. Negotiations with the
kidnapper were carried on secretly. Other kidnappings were reported and public indignation was reflected in the introduction of
federal legislation making abductions a capital crime. When the
Lindbergh baby's body was found in underbrush near the family
home it was clear that the child had been killed almost immediately
after he had been taken from his crib. Public interest stretched over
four years as the mystery deepened when clues led to dead ends,
minor figures involved died or committed suicide, and the Lind-
berghs were so harassed by reporters and curious sightseers that they
shunned all public appearances. Finally a German immigrant carpen-
ter was arrested in September 1934 on suspicion of possessing a part
of the ransom. More headlines and extras revived interest in the bizarre case, which furnished front-page stories through the accused
man's trial, conviction, and finally his execution in April 1936. Unquestionably, Lindbergh had figured in two of the most sensational
news events of the twentieth century—at first adored by the nation
for his heroism and then pitied as the agony caused by the kidnapping and murder became apparent.[27] The Lindbergh "extras" in the
spring of 1932 were probably the last special editions in the old
classic tradition, where newsboys on street corners were surrounded
by excited crowds. By 1933, radio bulletins made the extra edition
superfluous.

Even before the Lindbergh kidnapping, radio had been on the
verge of breaking news barriers as the production price of receivers
tumbled along with everything else, while the public craving for
news increased. Network executives conceived of radio as primarily
an entertainment medium and doted on audience ratings for "Amos
'n' Andy," but it was apparent that what radio had already achieved

in sports reporting might be done with equal skill on other kinds of news. Graham McNamee was well identified in the public mind as a rapid-talking describer of baseball games and prizefights, while the Chicago *Tribune*'s WGN's ("World's Greatest Newspaper) rival WJZ in New York had Ted Husing as a $45-a-week sports broadcaster.[28] United Press sold radio stations its regular news wire but the style was stilted when read on the air and usually required extensive rewriting. The Associated Press, dominated by publishers resentful of the competition from radio for advertising dollars, still refused to permit radio stations to join its news-sharing society. The biggest national advertisers were now the tobacco, soap, and automobile companies, with an hour-long national broadcast on NBC costing Lucky Strike or Lux sponsors about $175 a minute for airtime alone. RCA, Philco, Zenith, and other manufacturers soon were producing cheap sets technically far advanced beyond those that had cost $175 only a few years earlier.

With the 1932 election, campaign radio news came of age. H. V. Kaltenborn, a Brooklyn *Daily Eagle* reporter in 1921, had built a local reputation as a news analyst with New York's WEAF audiences. His radio appeal had been proved in 1924 when Kaltenborn's critical comment on the coldness shown by the State Department toward recognizing the USSR offended Washington bureaucrats. WEAF threatened to clip the *Eagle* reporter's wings, but when irate listeners responded with a deluge of favorable mail Kaltenborn stayed on to become the most experienced and knowledgeable newsman in radio. But in 1930, Kaltenborn was fired by the *Eagle* and he moved to the newest broadcasting network—the Columbia Broadcasting System—as a "sustaining" (unsponsored) weekly commentator.

When the 1932 conventions were fully covered by both NBC and its rival, CBS, newspaper editors themselves listened to the proceedings and then wrote headlines for stories that were oftentimes stale when delivered on neighborhood porches. Broadcast in the interest of "the public service," the 1932 conventions were dramatic testimony to the impact of radio journalism. Listeners knew that they were hearing Hoover at the same time his convention audience heard his voice over convention hall loudspeakers. The listener was a participant in the news because candidates were also addressing themselves to a nationwide audience of voters. Here was unedited news, "hard-core" news that was the closest journalism had ever come to making millions of citizens eyewitnesses to events. Commentators could give colorful descriptions of the crowds and rallies, but the speeches themselves needed little analysis or embellishment.

As it turned out, the 1932 Democratic convention was also Hearst's last serious involvement as a pretended kingmaker. Hearst had become enamored of Speaker John Nance Garner of Texas, and his California properties swung hard for Garner in the presidential preferential primary that spring. With the added Texas and Illinois delegations, Garner stood behind Smith and his erstwhile friend, Governor Franklin D. Roosevelt, in the race for the nomination at Chicago. Hearst had helped topple Smith in 1928 by making the Democratic candidate appear to be "a boozer and tenderloin tough," and in 1932 Hearst was willing to use the Garner votes to stop Smith again. A "stop Roosevelt" movement on the floor boomeranged when Hearst persuaded the Texas and California delegations to swing to Roosevelt. A bandwagon psychology soon developed, and a Roosevelt-Garner ticket resulted. The Hearst organization supported Roosevelt in the campaign but the alliance was tenuous, and dissolved completely when the New Deal began its pump-priming policies a year later. Then Hearst denounced the Roosevelt cortège as a "communistic" and "socialist" Brain Trust.[29]

Both Hoover and Roosevelt spoke to national radio audiences during the ensuing campaign, which was marred by the "Bonus March" on Washington and the erection of a tarpaper-shack shanty town in sight of the national capitol. From around the nation, veterans of World War I had assembled to demand action by Congress on legislation providing a lump-sum payment for military service in 1917–1919. The reader's view of the episode depended on where he read about it. The Sioux Falls, South Dakota, *Argus-Leader* had been featuring the area's blistering heat wave and the AP's grasping-for-straws reports of a business recovery when Hoover ordered federal troops directed by General Douglas MacArthur to disperse the veterans. A riot followed. *Police Fire on Vets, One Slain*, the *Argus-Leader* headline read. On an inside page the next day an editorial blamed the violence on lawless elements among the veterans. The Chattanooga *Times*, looking similar to its first cousin the *New York Times*, gave nearly all of its front page to the clash, including a list of the fifty injured veterans and a romanesque "mug shot" of MacArthur: *Routs Bonus Army*. "One of the blackest pages in American history was written yesterday when veterans of the Bonus Expeditionary Force . . . and . . . constituted authority clashed," a *Times* editorial asserted. The cause of the battle, which news photographers covered with considerable skill, was sheer demagoguery to the *Argus-Leader*, but the *Times* laid the blame on the doorsteps of "Congressmen playing politics with the bonus." News photographs of the burning shanty village with the Capitol dome in the distance were widely printed alongside views of bayonet-wielding troops moving through a teargas barrage toward fleeing veterans.

The sight did not inspire confidence that America had "turned the corner" on its troubles, and after a merciful adjournment midwestern congressmen went home to find farmer's strikes gripping parts of Iowa, Nebraska, South Dakota, and Illinois. Milk prices slid below a nickel a quart, causing angry farmers to dump thousands of gallons onto roadways in full view of news photographers. The Des Moines *Register* reported that fourteen farmers attending a mass meeting at the Cherokee courthouse had been wounded by an unseen gunman. The Omaha *World-Herald* found itself in a beleaguered city when the farmer's strike spread to the stockyards.

Mother Nature also seemed in rebellion as the thermometer hovered around 100 degrees in the prairie and plains states. Huge billows of dust formed and swept eastward from New Mexico and west Texas, choking livestock and sending fine sand into the cracks of tightly closed windows, into the workman's sandwiches, and the schoolchildren's lunch pails. The city editor of the Tulsa *Tribune* decided to run a front-page box to remind readers of the number of rainless, over-100 degree days through which the city had suffered. After one day, a merchants' committee made a visit to the publisher and the box was removed. "Somehow they blamed me instead of God," the editor recalled.

Publishers bowed to businessmen, who were their mainstays in times good or bad, and tried to stay solvent by staff reductions and lower wages for reporters and editors. Those printers protected by the ITU were dismayed by the hard lot of the editorial side, but were often more inclined to thankfulness for union rules than charity for low-salaried rewrite men. In the midst of retrenchment in the newspaper business, radio networks became one of the few profitable endeavors of the depression.[30] Radio advertising revenues doubled between 1930 and 1933 as soap and cigarette companies embraced the new medium, while newspaper advertising income dipped 45 percent. NBC had a 1932 profit of $1 million, and CBS made over $1.6 million. Gradually, NBC left the news commentaries to its rival and concentrated on the more profitable entertainment side of radio.[31] CBS formed a news staff headed by a former United Press executive and added Lowell Thomas, Boake Carter, and Edwin C. Hill to its evening news and special events staff. "The March of Time" program on CBS began in 1933, sponsored by *Time* magazine, and quickly captured a wide audience as it carried dramatized versions of current events with a deep-throated commentary by Westbrook van Voorhis. Newspaper publishers may have winced when van Voorhis signed off in his doomsday voice, "Time Marches On!" for their profits were in full retreat while the arch-rival radio flourished.

In the midst of evident envy, the publishers took solace from the fact that newspapers remained sacrosanct when the federal government began to involve itself in the communications business. Regulation of the radio stations began, however, only after managers and investors came begging to the federal government for strict licensing procedures that would end airwave jamming, which was causing some chaos in the most populated areas while remote regions had no radio contact whatever. As a result, it was in the public interest that the Federal Radio Act of 1927 was amended and the Federal Communications Commission created in 1934 to give the federal government implicit control over program content, with guidelines on the amount of time that should be devoted to the public interest. In fact, the government moved into the area of media regulation with tenderness. Except for the now-overturned "fairness doctrine" of equal time for political candidates and public issues, the airlanes have been as free from outside control as the most ardent civil libertarian could wish.

Meanwhile, NBC opened, with much fanfare, its new studios in Rockefeller Center (an enterprise conceived to help provide architectural standards and steady jobs) and the lesson was not lost on some newspaper executives. James Stahlman, publisher of the Nashville *Banner,* sounded a warning. "Newspaper publishers had better wake up or newspapers will be nothing but a memory on a tablet at Radio City," he told a convention of southern newsmen. Publishers with cash and foresight continued to buy their own radio stations, so that by the time Roosevelt was inaugurated in 1933 nearly one hundred newspapers also had a radio affiliate, ranging from the *New York Times* to the *Daily Oklahoman.*[32] Convinced of the truth of the if-you-can't-lick-'em-join-'em philosophy, the merger of newspapers with radio stations during the 1930s accelerated until nearly one-third of the nation's air outlets were owned by corporate newspapers.

14

The Brat Grows Up

While Americans waited in 1933 for Roosevelt to lift their spirits, the nation's attention was diverted to events in Germany. Newsreels in 1932 showed a band of brown-shirted followers of Adolf Hitler strutting down the streets of Munich. By early 1933 Hitler had become the German chancellor and was reviewing troops of a supposedly disarmed country, but Americans were too preoccupied with domestic problems to share European fears over rising German militarism. Network radio carried broadcasts direct from the Reichstag with commentators providing translations of Hitler's promises and threats. In New York, where the city's large Jewish population was anxious over the latent anti-Semitism of Hitler's menacing gestures, newspapers covered the rise of the Austrian-born *Führer* with more space than the rest of the country seemed to require. *Time* magazine discerned a marked difference between the statements of Japanese diplomats and the manuevers of the Japanese army, and also told readers how 500,000 Berliners had turned out for a state funeral ordered by Hitler for a murdered Nazi hoodlum.

On inauguration day, March 4, 1933, Franklin D. Roosevelt told a nationwide radio audience that they had nothing to fear but fear itself. The country's ills, Roosevelt said, were numerous but "They concern, thank God, only material things." He appealed to listeners to show the resolve that had always been the nation's greatest source of strength, and promised action. Roosevelt immediately took command and for the next one hundred days newsmen in Washington sent out more copy than they probably had prepared during all of the Hoover years. Directives, legislation, and proposals bombarded Capitol Hill in a fervent effort to end the depression. Where Hoover had reluctantly spent time discussing the national debt and taxes with reporters, Roosevelt held two press conferences each week at which crowds of reporters were urged to fire questions directly at the chief executive. Roosevelt held more press conferences during his first month in office than Hoover had granted reporters between June and mid-September in the campaign year of 1932, and eventually would set a neck-breaking pace.* Roosevelt appeared to enjoy the give and take of these lively sessions, and the reporters responded by filing stories that were hardly objective, except for those representing what the president himself called "the Tory press." Roosevelt abandoned the old ground rules about written questions submitted in advance and spoke with wit and directness to the two hundred reporters. He drew the line only at questions based on hypothetical situations. "The 'if' questions" he knew were often a trap for the unwary politician, "and I never answer them."

During these exciting days the two cents that metropolitan readers spent on their newspapers brought a daily tonic for the spirit and also the introduction of a new vocabulary. The administration, labeled the New Deal, was calling in "Brain Trusters" who helped write legislation for the NRA, AAA, NYA, PWA and scores of other public agencies. A seasoned observer guessed that 90 percent of the Washington press corps was enraptured with the New Deal and headline

* Roosevelt's total of 998 press conferences between 1932 and 1945 will never be broken by an elected president unless the twenty-second Amendment is repealed.

writers gaily adopted the shorter form of the president's name—FDR—not only because it fit better but because it was somehow a warm way of alluding to this genial newsmaker. Except for the newspapers from the Republican heartland (notably the Chicago *Tribune*) the stories carried overtones of the optimism Roosevelt exuded in these meetings. A bank moratorium stopped the dreadful rise of failures. Real action was scarce, but the president talked constantly of jobs, projects, and ringing cash registers. Congress responded and passed bills for fair trade codes, farm parity price-supports, public works, collective bargaining, bank deposit insurance, and conservation programs. If Roosevelt did not seem preoccupied with the $6 billion federal debt, he also did not verbally commit himself to abandonment of the parsimony that had marked the Coolidge-Hoover years. Meanwhile, in the *New Republic* and elsewhere, Roosevelt was told that the national debt was no great curse. The gross national product had fallen to $40 billion in 1932, writer George Soule observed, and *that* was the nation's difficult statistic.[1] As a follow-up, the *New Republic* began a series on "Panaceas for the Depression," but by April 1933 the New Deal was well on its way, with a whole bundle of nostrums, palliatives, and cures that managed to keep readers and listeners hopeful, if not fully recovered.

Less than a week before the New Deal settled on the national scene, news wires from Germany told of a suspicious fire that had razed the Reichstag building during the fervent German election campaign. American correspondents filed stories of a reign of terror that had quickly seized Berlin and then spread across the German countryside in some organized way that was not altogether clear. Americans read of "Socialist mayors deposed and beaten to death, of Jewish rabbis left dying in the gutter, of Communists shot 'while trying to escape,' " and similar atrocities that seemed filed from some faraway and medieval nation rather than a modern industrial, constitutional power. A flood of dispatches from Germany competed with news from Washington, and indeed, veteran reporters could not recall when such excitement was evident in newsrooms as bulletins came in profusion on both the foreign wire and trunk lines out of New York and Washington.

Foreign news now crowded the New Deal for space on front pages, and headline writers added a new word to the understandable jargon of the day: Nazi. Here in America, the shortened name for Hitler's National Socialist Worker's Party soon had brutal connotations. *Time* featured the German chancellor's portrait on its cover and told of the 92 percent rise in Nazi voting strength in the most recent elections. The news objectivity approach taught at journalism schools a decade earlier found no support in *Time*'s columns, where there was a viewpoint of no uncertain dimensions. "Today most Germans are agreed that Hitlerism . . . would have swept their country years ago had not Germans been lulled by a false, post-war prosperity induced in the Fatherland by a flood of U.S. loans."

As the *Time* editors said, their stories were meant to set an event in perspective, so that readers could assess the meaning of events intelligently. This view was reinforced in a shift of journalism schools toward subjectivity, a movement thrust forward by Curtis Mac-Dougall's persuasive textbook *Interpretative Reporting* (retitled in 1938; it had first been published as *Reporting for Beginners* in 1932). College professors were persuaded that future reporters needed a great deal of background knowledge and the means of relaying this information to readers in crisply written "think pieces." Teachers of journalism either flocked to MacDougall's banner or flung barbs at it, but there was no mistaking a reaction against the older objectivity which held that "the only safe thing in a newspaper . . . was a fact. The reporter's duty was to supply his readers with the cold, hard[,] barren details of what had happened—and with nothing more." [2] Instead of this fetish for fact, MacDougall's disciples accepted the premise that Americans had been dumbfounded by the outbreak of World War I because of the sterile reporting of foreign news, and that the stock market crash had hit an uninformed, naive public in 1929. The rise of *Time* and its rival *Newsweek* was explained by a public craving for interpretive stories that crossed far beyond the old guidelines of the five *W*'s—Who, What, When, Where, and Why. Elmer Davis, a former *New York Times* reporter turned radio commentator, concluded that old-fashioned objectivity "often leans over backward so far that it makes the news business merely a transmission belt for pretentious phonies," but critics of the new reporting insisted that the fine line between opinion and interpretation often led newsmen into a "treacherous no-man's land." [3]

What seemed to worry the reporters and editors reared in the five *W*'s school was the subtle infusion of a writer's ideas so that the story could take on the appearance of straight news when in fact it was heavily slanted. A *Time* report during the waning days of Hoover's Administration carried an example. In a round-up story on "Radicals," the *Time* story said: "Most thoughtful observers agree that the U.S. is now undergoing a tremendous socialistic revolution which will leave its imprint on the nation long after the Depression has passed." [4] Old-fashioned newsmen were horrified by this kind of journalistic swashbuckling, and wanted to know who these "thoughtful observers" were, and how they had been polled, and what exactly was this "socialistic revolution" occurring under Hoover's nose? The battle over newsroom philosophy, thus touched off in 1933, was still raging in the 1970s.

Readers and listeners were not privy to these professional undercurrents, however. Roosevelt's dramatic inaugural address, his first intimate chat with perhaps 20 million people on radio a short time later, and the direct broadcasts from Germany and Italy where chants of *"Sieg Heil!"* and *"Duce! Duce!"* needed no translation—these events told Americans they were participating in historic events through a new electronic medium. While political cartoonists in newspapers made Hitler appear to be a comic parody on Charlie Chaplin, the commentaries of eyewitnesses in Berlin and Rome told a different story. Increasingly, Americans turned to their radios for news summaries, and distressed publishers began to react. In May 1933 the Associated Press tried to curb the use of news on the air by limiting members to thirty-word "pony" bulletins on sustaining programs. No news was to be broadcast on sponsored programs, and to reinforce its decision a suit was filed against KSOO, a Sioux Falls, South Dakota, station the AP claimed was improperly using its dispatches.[5] When CBS formed its own full-time news staff the Washington *Star* dropped all free listings of that network's daily programs on the ground that CBS was now a full-fledged competitor. Undaunted, CBS under Paul White's leadership hired "stringers" across the country but still employed only two dozen regular reporters. Faced with declining advertising revenues and circulation, the press Establishment insisted in *Editor & Publisher* that radio reporting was so limited in scope it was "detracting interest from the legitimate newspaper service, and creating confused, incomplete thought and intensified ignorance on public matters." An Indiana prison break, reported with embarrassing inaccuracies by the local CBS affiliate, seemed to confirm the newspapermen's judgment. Fearing interference by the federal government if the newspaper publishers continued their attacks, CBS agreed to disband its own newsgathering service in March, 1934. Irate H. V. Kaltenborn commented: "The only saving grace of this agreement is that it will not work." [6]

Kaltenborn was right, because the public had a direct pipeline to the news from the White House as President Roosevelt took to his homely "fireside chats" whenever he wanted to speak directly with the electorate. Radio sets could now be purchased for $15 and high antennas were no longer needed. Even on farms, wind-driven generators gave the current for radios far in advance of the government's Rural Electrification Program, for only one farm in five had regular electricity service. As Roosevelt discerned the turn of the publishers against his program (some even feared newsboys might fall under wage-and-hour laws), he found the radio an effective means of circumventing the mounting indignation of the Chicago *Tribune* and Los Angeles *Times,* two of his earliest and most outspoken critics. Cartoonists on the *Tribune* staff pictured the president (who was actually quite crippled) as a marauding soothsayer whose chief attribute was an ability to spend taxpayers' money foolishly. The Los Angeles

Times could not stomach the New Deal labor program, particularly the fourty-hour week. Most workers, a *Times* editorial noted, were incapable of spending their spare time except in "the only diversions they know—pool, poker, drinking and petty agitation over [a] fancied grievance." Thus the fourty-hour week, instead of creating more jobs, would only provide leisure time "that nobody would know what to do with." [7]

By 1934, most daily newspapers were safely back in the Republican fold when the fall elections were held, a fact that little bothered Roosevelt since his program was endorsed by voters resoundingly. Radio stations now scrupulously avoided any kind of editorial comment, fearful of losing their federal licenses, but it seemed that the facts were all the people wanted anyway. Perhaps more voters went to the polls than would ordinarily have turned out because the authoritative *Literary Digest* poll had indicated national sentiment on Roosevelt's policies was about evenly divided—50.97 of the polled group was favorable, while 49.03 disapproved of the New Deal.[8] The election results generally proved these soundings were highly inaccurate, except in California where the old muckraker Upton Sinclair ran for governor and promised to end poverty in California. Leading newspapers in Los Angeles and San Francisco attacked Democratic nominee Sinclair as a communistic-socialistic atheist and printed photographs purportedly showing boxcar loads of tramps arriving to await Sinclair's election victory. Later evidence indicated extras at film studios had been hired as models for the rigged pictures. Sinclair lost and the Los Angeles *Times* was exultant.

Obviously, political endorsements by newspapers in national elections were no longer an important barometer of voter sentiment. As the *New Republic* observed, for decades it had been easy to "sense the drift of popular sentiment" by talking to a few bankers, checking with business community leaders, and then perusing the "editorials in the established city dailies and country weeklies." [9] Radio and a fresh spirit of political independence had wrought a change. The old farm bloc was fragmented, while urban voters tended to identify with the

Democrats, and the city dweller was accustomed to the purchase of a newspaper not because of its politics, but in spite of them. The Chicago *Tribune* was a prime example of this reader loyalty, for a Peoria truck driver who consistently voted for Roosevelt could enjoy the *Tribune* sports and comic sections without regard for the vitriolic Orr cartoons or the McCormick-inspired editorial attacks on the New Deal.

After the president found that through his fireside chats he could circumvent the opposition press, the pace of those broadcasts increased. Before Roosevelt's day, a single mailman handled all incoming White House letters; but after the radio talks began the president's mail grew to mountainous proportions. On the other hand, newspaper circulation fell to a daily total of 37 million in 1933, down 5 million from 1929. Radio was embraced by the larger advertisers, who favored dramatic presentations and daytime serials (*soap-opera* came into the language), but CBS continued to expand its news staff with the hiring of such promising newcomers as Edward R. Murrow.[10] Farm and home news programs became popular, reporting crop conditions and market prices on powerful clear-channel stations to an audience dependent upon cream and eggs for much of its cash income. Then in 1935 the United Press offered its exclusive radio news wire which led to the "rip-and-read" type of newscast—where inexperienced announcers sometimes faltered in pronouncing the names of such faraway places and people as Addis Ababa, Guadalajara, or Haile Selassie.

Germany stormed out of the League of Nations, Italy invaded underdeveloped Ethiopia, and Russia was shaken by the failure of its food and industrial programs. Americans learned of these events while listening to the radio during suppertime. At home, drought plagued the Great Plains area until newspapers began to write about a sobering "Dust Bowl" where the disenchanted left the land for migrant-labor camps or city relief rolls. In the midst of want there was talk of a "technocracy" where all men would have productive work, and in electronic laboratories research continued on television sets that displayed a studio image two inches high and three inches wide at the Chicago "Century of Progress" World's Fair.

The shortwave broadcast of Edward VIII's abdication speech when the British monarch decided to give up his throne in order to marry an American divorcée caused Americans to miss daytime serials as they heard an emotional king speak of "the woman I love."

Mainly because of the radio coverage from Europe, which supported the newspaper coverage in the *Christian Science Monitor,* Chicago *Daily News, New York Times,* and New York *Herald-Tribune,* it could not be said that Americans were left ignorant of the seething state of European politics. Kaltenborn covered the Spanish Civil War by visiting the battlefronts and then returning to France for an uncensored view of the carnage that involved German, Italian, Russian, and Portuguese troops alongside the fratricidal native veterans. Increasingly there was editorial speculation that Spain was the proving ground for weapons that would be used in World War II. Arch-conservative publishers were embarrassed by the Spanish fighting because their preference was for a victory by the Franco-led Rebels, who had Nazi support. In the press, Loyalists were usually identified with left-wing backers. Hence the Abraham Lincoln Brigade, formed in the Loyalist army by American volunteers, was accorded little newspaper space. The reading public learned more about the group later, from Ernest Hemingway's fiction, than from contemporary accounts of the brigade's lost-cause endeavors.

One cause that seemed definitely lost in the autumn of 1936 was Franklin D. Roosevelt's reelection—at least the *Literary Digest* poll gave this impression a week before the actual balloting. The magazine was proud of a record that had "for nearly a quarter century . . . been right in every Poll," and quoted the Democratic national chairman as proof of the poll's accuracy in 1932. The final *Digest* prediction was for a Republican victory that would make Alfred M. Landon president. Landon, a candidate William Randolph Hearst thought he had personally "discovered" in Topeka, had been warmly embraced by anti-Roosevelt publishers and editors as the Republicans' forlorn hope. The *Literary Digest* told them they fought no losing battle however, for the key states of California, New York, Ohio, and Pennsylvania were all placed safely in the Landon column. The New York *Daily News* stood out as a wayward seer after it predicted a Roosevelt victory, although the newly formed Gallup poll and the Baltimore *Sun* syndicate made similar prognostications. Estimates of the number of daily newspapers endorsing Landon varied from 63 to 80 percent, so that except in the South and the larger cities, the editorials people read hailed the day when the New Deal would be turned out.

Roosevelt's devastating victory stunned most publishers. Landon carried only Maine and Vermont, and gleeful Alexander Wolcott and other critics of the press cited the forty-six-state sweep "as evidence that newspapers have lost their influence with the people." [11] The mortified *Literary Digest* tried to explain "What Went Wrong with the Polls?" Despite some good-natured kidding, the magazine's prestige was seriously damaged. Long a circulation pacesetter, the *Digest* began to falter and finally sank into oblivion early in 1938.

While an old-timer was suffering from embarrassment and financial strain, a brash newcomer leaped into the journalistic puddle in November 1936 with all the fanfare the Luce organization could muster. *Life* magazine was born anew, taking the old title of a humor magazine and creating a new style of innovative pictorial journalism. *Life* copied early success stories, such as *Munsey's* and *Esquire,* and printed a plethora of undraped female forms for a circulation "teaser." Luce gambled that readers would buy a magazine they could scan rather than read with care. Action pictures from the world's battlefronts, coverage of the nation's many and changing fads, and a breezy style that already characterized *Time* soon shot *Life* into circulation leadership as secondhand copies sold for ten times the dime charged at newsstands, where supplies rapidly disappeared. Margaret Bourke-White's gripping photographic coverage of the Spanish Civil War soon showed *Life* readers the potential of the camera as a journalistic medium. Imitation was sure to follow soon.

Look, Peek, and a host of lesser photomagazines proved that once again Luce had shown that entrepreneurial flair was not dead in journalism. The public apparently never tired of learning more about the Dionne quintuplets, whose five pretty faces had been pictured in millions of press releases since their birth in 1934, always with photographs supplied by one syndicate. World interest in the young Canadian sisters was so widespread that when a new, exclusive picture contract was negotiated late in 1936, the NEA service proudly admitted it had outbid the opposition for another exclusive contract by offering "an amount more than 12 times the original contract figure." [12]

Interest in every form of pictorial journalism during 1936 also led the industry into crystal-ball gazing about the future of the recently developed facsimile newspaper. Through use of the photoelectric cell, which had been adapted to send news pictures by an electronic beam of light, it was confidently said in 1936, the day was not far away when the family newspaper would be carried into homes—not by a newsboy but by a living room receiving set. Teletype machines had eliminated the last newspaper office telegraphers by 1935, and the head of RCA predicted that electronic recording devices would make older systems of news transmission "as outmoded as the pony express." [13] The cost was still high, but experiments were to continue; and since Americans already had $3 billion invested in radio sets, the expense of the first facsimile recorders or television sets did not deter RCA, Zenith, Philco, and other firms from continuing their research.

The running battle between Roosevelt and the publishers led to some interesting sidelights. The most significant probably was the antitrust suit against the Associated Press monopoly, which went to the Supreme Court and finally ended the historic blackball privileges of AP members (thus saving the pro-New Deal Chicago *Sun* $334,250 in waiver rights). To insiders, the poll conducted by Leo Rosten for his notable study on 154 Washington correspondents was considered highly revealing. Rosten asked newsmen working in the nation's capital in 1936, "What is the most fair and reliable newspaper in America?" Most reporters ignored their own newspaper and voted for the *New York Times* (747 points in Rosten's system), with the Baltimore *Sun* (284 points) second and the *Christian Science Monitor* third (90 points). The reporters were also asked to name the newspapers in America that were "the least fair and reliable" and threw their onus on the Hearst newspapers (714 points), Chicago *Tribune* (455 points), and Los Angles *Times* (103 points).[14]

At the beginning of 1937 newspapers dutifully published editorials noting the sesquicentennial of the Constitution, and much lip service was paid to the parchment recently enshrined in the National Archives. Soon it seemed that a test of that hallowed document was in the making as Roosevelt, buoyed by the huge plurality over Landon, showed his pique with a recalcitrant Supreme Court and announced a plan to increase the number of justices from nine to fifteen. This was one of Roosevelt's few political blunders, as editorial pages quickly indicated. Opposition newspapers denounced the "court-packing plan" as the act of a power-mad president angered because the High Court had nullified several key New Deal programs. Even newspapers friendly to the New Deal turned cautious.

Soon it was apparent that Roosevelt had miscalculated the public reaction to his plan, which had been presented with more than the usual White House flair. Seven of the New York *Herald Tribune's* eight columns on page one gave every detail of the proposal. As columnist Raymond Clapper discerned, Roosevelt was tampering with the one thing Americans really revered—the Supreme Court—and the average man was a little suspicious of his hero.[15] During a "fireside chat" in March Roosevelt insisted he was not trying to fill the bench with "spineless puppets," but this did not dispel the distrust, and when the Supreme Court upheld the controversial Wagner Act (on labor arbitration) much of Roosevelt's support faltered. At the press conference that next morning, the president joked with reporters. "I haven't read the Washington *Post*, and I haven't got the Chicago *Tribune* yet. Or the Boston *Herald*. Today is a very, very happy day."

In truth, Roosevelt was vexed but finally had to give up his Court plan, although he was no happier with the newspapers. "As you know," he wrote an American diplomat, "all the fat-cat newspapers —85% of the whole—have been utterly opposed to everything the Administration is seeking. . . . However, the voters are with us today just as they were last fall." [16]

The voters were busy with more than politics in 1937. The Hollywood columnists—mainly Hedda Hopper and Louella Parsons—told readers of backlot gossip from the film studios as much attention was focused on the death of the platinum blonde Jean Harlow. Preparations for filming the best-selling novel *Gone With the Wind* included a studio search for the feminine lead (Scarlett O'Hara) that received more attention in the tabloids than any legislative proposal. In certain circles, a person became a celebrity if he was mentioned by columnist Walter Winchell's daily Broadway report, which was syndicated nationally by the Hearst organization. Meanwhile, the depression had caused cracks in the Hearst financial foundations and the strain became so great that "the Chief" had to transfer control over the twenty-five newspapers, magazines, and other properties to a holding company. Although 1937 marked Hearst's fiftieth year in journalism, he was, at seventy-four, an anachronism from a bygone era. Still, Hearst was not absolutely powerless. He continued to barrage his editors with memorandums on his pet schemes, such as an antivivisection league, and his loathing for Roosevelt and the growing power of organized labor was evident.

Despite the financial strain, which lost Hearst $1 million annually on the New York *American* alone, the *New York Times* was making money, along with such older journalistic institutions as the Kansas City *Star* and Milwaukee *Journal*. The *Star* had been bought by its employees in the late 1920s after W. R. Nelson's heir died, and by 1939 the staff was able to burn its $8.5 million mortgage two years early.[17] The *Journal's* founder, Lucius W. Nieman, died in 1935 and a year later his widow's death permitted the creation of a stock trust that eventually turned full ownership over to employees in a plan similar to the *Star's*. Steadfast employees on these newspapers found that in time their stock dividends and shareholdings afforded them an income that equaled or exceeded their salaries as reporters and editors.

In retrospect, 1937 was the last year when Americans were permitted the luxury of an isolationist existence, wherein the local news often concerned a controversial mural painted in the post office by a WPA artist or the comparative merits of a V-8 Ford or a Packard sedan. In October the president went out of his way, while speaking at a bridge dedication in Chicago, to make what was later called the "Quarantine Speech." Japan had reinvaded China despite a pledge of nonagression. Hitler and Mussolini had all but concluded a military alliance of "Axis Powers," following the German reoccupation of the Rhineland and other adjacent territories in violations of solemn postwar treaties. Roosevelt denounced unnamed powers "which today are creating a state of international anarchy and instability from which there is no escape through mere isolation or neutrality." The speech was greeted with outspoken reactions. Colonel Frank Knox, publisher of the Chicago *Daily News* and Landon's 1936 running mate, hailed Roosevelt's speech as "magnificent." The *New York Times* and *Washington Post* printed a letter from former Secretary of State Henry Stimson in which the speech was praised as an indication of "a new birth of American courage." But isolationist elements denounced the speech as intemperate and dangerous. "Stop Foreign Meddling; America Wants Peace," the *Wall Street Journal's* front-page editorial observed. Hugh Johnson, the former New Dealer who had turned newspaper columnist, was equally upset. "Well, here we are again, taking sides in a War." [18]

Whether Roosevelt's radio speech was saber rattling or not depended on what newspaper a citizen read. The Chicago *Tribune's* attacks on Roosevelt made the president appear as history's greatest spendthrift, bent on using foreign entanglements to cover up domestic blunders, but the Los Angeles *Daily News* took the same facts and concluded Roosevelt was that rare statesman who was not intimidated by Hitler's tactics or a $15 billion national debt.

While public opinion in America was thus divided on the need for strong language about international bandits, the rush of events overtook cautious Europeans. Edward R. Murrow had been sent to Berlin as the CBS European news manager. Working with William L. Shirer, the two American reporters formed a team to cover the *Anschluss* of March 1938—when Hitler's troops occupied Austria. "This is Edward Murrow speaking from Vienna," the young CBS executive began his first report. ". . . Young storm troopers are riding about the streets, riding in trucks and vehicles of all sorts, singing and tossing oranges out to the crowd." American listeners learned to recognize the voice and respect it, as Murrow spoke "with dramatic understatement." [19] With Shirer joining the report from London, Pierre Huss from Berlin, and other CBS staff members commenting in the New York studios, the radio "news round-up" had been born. CBS added to its staff and was not challenged by NBC when the world seemed on the brink of war during the Munich crisis. Americans heard on their radio sets (more than 31 million were in use) Hitler's speeches in Nuremberg demanding the Sudetenland, the screams of a frenzied crowd in the swastika-fringed Berlin *Sportpalast*, and descriptions of the two dramatic airplane trips of British Prime Minister Neville Chamberlain to Hitler's headquarters. Finally, at Munich, France and Britain met Germany's terms so that Chamberlain could return to London and announce on the radio that the results guaranteed "peace in our time." Kaltenborn's descriptions on CBS (which carried 151 shortwave pickups during the crisis) were called "the greatest show yet heard on American radio." The other media stood in awe. "For the first time, history has been made in the hearing of its pawns," the *Nation* said in admiration.[20]

Although CBS maintained its initiative as the leading newscasting network, competitors were forced to supplement their entertainment fare with more attention to current events. Raymond Graham Swing, Quincy Howe, H. R. Baukage, Elmer Davis, and Robert Trout became newscasters whose commentaries helped citizens try to understand what was going on in the world. In sports, Ted Husing, Clem McCarthy, and Bill Stern rose as announcers who took millions vicariously to Churchill Downs, Madison Square Garden, and the Rose Bowl. Increasingly, newspapers became the promoters of sports events in which the climactic contest would be carried directly to fans over the air. While the Chicago *Tribune* threw page-one editorial barbs at Roosevelt, its astute sports editor, Arch Ward, entrenched reader loyalty by initiating the all-star baseball game and the college all-star football contest as *Tribune*-sponsored events which gave Chicago the appearance of a spectacular sports center. The exploits of baseball pitcher Carl Hubbell, boxer Joe Louis, and the racehorse War Admiral reassured citizens buffeted by the depression and foreign threats that life was not totally ominous. Louis's smashing first-round victory over the German heavyweight champion made up for previous defeat by Max Schmeling and may have helped race relations when the black American proved the hollowness of Nazi racial dogma.

If Americans had been surprised by events in the autumn of 1914, the coming of World War II was by contrast repeatedly foretold by newspaper columnists after the German occupation of Czechoslovakia in March 1939. The Richmond *Times-Dispatch* printed a photograph on page one, where the banner headline told of Hitler's coup, of two unlikely animal playmates. "The Lamb Meekly Follows the Lion," the caption read; "The Picture Was Taken in Hollywood, But the Idea Is Mittell Europa." [21] *Life* magazine, still following its frothy pictorial approach with an emphasis on bosoms and bareness, carried a cover that same week featuring two nude statues prepared for the coming New York World's Fair. The magazine's combined street-and-mail circulation reached 2 million copies, exploiting the oldest of man's interests that same week with a sin-and-sex feature from Germany captioned "Hitler Gives Germany Its Cue to Have

Fun." [22] After the *Wehrmacht* occupied Prague, however, *Life* gave the takeover adequate coverage but fell back on its nebulous attributions in an attempt to explain Western surprise at Hitler's continued audacity. "Some observers found the explanation in the desperate internal condition of Nazi Germany," *Life* hinted, with a guess that Germany needed some $92 million in gold from Czechoslovakia, now annexed to the Third Reich. [23] *Time* gave the "rape of Czechoslovakia" five pages and included a column headed "Time Table" to emphasize the precision of Hitler's conquests. *Time* concluded with a report that German storm troopers had entered Bohemia singing "Today we own Germany, tomorrow the whole world." [24]

Radio commentators took a more sober tone. Roosevelt sent Hitler a request that Germany guarantee the territorial sovereignty of a list of thirty-one nations. Hitler read the list to the Reichstag in an ironic voice that was carried to Americans by radio and newsreels. The German dictator made the president's list sound like an enormous joke, and finished reading it amid laughter and applause. The isolationist press took smug satisfaction from the boomerang effect of Roosevelt's message, and Senator Gerald Nye summed up their indictment of the president's rebuff for "meddling in European affairs" tersely: "He asked for it." [25]

Many Americans apparently believed that the Neutrality Act of 1935 isolated the nation from European troubles. The *New York Times, Washington Post* (bought in 1933 by Eugene Meyer and slowly revitalized), and a scattering of eastern newspapers were lumped as the "internationalist" press by the midwestern isolationists, who began an "America First" movement aimed on rigorous enforcement of the neutrality laws. Clearly, as the Gallup poll showed soon after a general European war finally broke out in September 1939, the American people were afraid of being dragged into the fight. When Germany invaded Poland the swift movement of events brought on a showdown and war with Great Britain and France. The American Institute of Public Opinion soon took a poll on whether the United States "should do everything possible to help

England and France win the war, even at the risk of getting into the war ourselves?" [26] Sixty-six percent of the polled Americans said no.

Journalism went into the business of reporting World War II with its belt tightened. Mergers and consolidations had eliminated some of the weakest Hearst holdings, while the Scripps-Howard chain had lopped off such losing properties as the *Oklahoma News* and added the profitable Memphis *Commercial Appeal* to its national empire. The Minneapolis *Star*, founded as a cooperative enterprise in 1920, had rapidly fallen into financial chaos and was bought in 1935 by the Cowles family, which then merged it in 1939 with the *Journal*. Before the war ended, the Cowles' *Star-Tribune* combination was serving over 500,000 readers. These newspapers, added to the Des Moines *Register*, the nucleus of the Cowles chain, gave the family a powerful role in midwestern journalism. Rising costs for paper and machinery forced many once-bitter rivals to consolidate their printing operations while continuing a separate editorial identity, as in the partial merger of the Tulsa *World* and Tulsa *Tribune*. Critics who feared that these combinations would eventually deny readers a broad view of public questions were answered by publishers who pointed to anemic balance sheets, insisting that corporate journalism meant no lessening of concern over high editorial standards.[27] They could point to the *New York Times*, which was still far below the *Daily News* in circulation but steadily advancing by its plowback method of profit reinvestment in better equipment and expanded news facilities.

The war brought some shuffling of the radio personalities who had become celebrities in their own right. H. V. Kaltenborn, chafing under mild pressures from CBS executives to tone down his subjectivity, switched to NBC as the 1940 election campaign began to warm. *Time* and *Life* made little effort to conceal their publisher's desire that Roosevelt honor the third-term tradition. Publisher Luce surveyed the field of Republican candidates after it was clear that Roosevelt would try for a third term, and found all of them wanting until an Indiana-born lawyer showed tremendous appeal after a radio appearance on *Information Please*. Wendell Willkie's name began appearing in *Time, Life,* and *Fortune* with more frequency, and Luce threw his support behind the new face in other ways as well. When Willkie won the Republican presidential nomination, in a whirlwind finish that left party regulars gasping, several reporters claimed they had first spotted him as a dark horse but "for the first time in the memory of living man, William Randolph Hearst had nothing whatever to do with nominating a candidate." [28] When a letter to the editor congratulated *Time* for Willkie's sudden rise and nomination, the editors modestly sidestepped the bouquet and gave credit to "the normal operation of a free and alert press."* Summing up the story of Willkie's nomination, *Time* said: "For the first time since Teddy Roosevelt, the Republicans had a man they could yell for and mean it." [29] Colorful radio coverage of the Philadelphia convention improved Willkie's chances as the summer polls indicated a nip-and-tuck battle lay ahead.

Radio also kept the news spotlight shifting back and forth across the Atlantic. The gravity of the European crisis was obvious after France fell and Britain turned desperately to Winston Churchill for guidance. Murrow's broadcasts from the bomb-pitted British capital always began with a plaintive fact. "This is London," Murrow would say, and then launch into a description of British fortitude, hardship, and death. As CBS chief in Europe, Murrow added Eric Sevareid to the staff and teamed with William L. Shirer to describe the might of Germany's armies and air force. Newspaper coverage of the war was hampered by censorship, but the use of action pictures and maps gave readers a more precise view of what the German armies had accomplished with a devastating blitzkrieg. The fear that this conflict would be a repetition of the trench warfare of 1914–1918 was replaced by anxieties that the war would soon end in Nazi Germany's complete domination of Europe. Faced with this possibility, a committee was

---

* Letters to the editor have been known to appear in print when, in fact, the writer was a staff member of *Time* or the *Washington Post* or an equally vocal opponent of "managed news."

formed under the chairmanship of William Allen White "to Defend America by Aiding the Allies." The Emporia editor was brought in to give the group a more national aspect, and in late July it had purchased full-page ads in the major newspapers headed, "Between Us and Hitler Stands the *British* Fleet!" A bewildered public read in August that Charles A. Lindbergh, who had left retirement to speak for isolationism, was warning Americans that Hitler might win the war and suggesting that an accommodation with Germany was preferable to the horrors of war. Shocked by widespread support for Lindbergh's plea, the Kansas editor pronounced the hero of 1927 as "blind" to the choice between Britain's survival or living "beside Hitler's world enslaved." [30]   If the public was confused, the publishers were not. Three out of every four daily newspapers, including the *New York Times,* endorsed Willkie's candidacy. The Chicago *Tribune* cartoons portrayed Roosevelt as a monarch with insatiable ambitions for a third term, then a fourth, and perhaps more. Roosevelt fell back to radio in his final weeks of campaigning, jested with reporters who wrote in their dispatches of the relaxed chief executive, and nursed a secret grudge against the Chicago press dynasty. Roosevelt won Illinois by 102,000 votes out of over 4 million ballots cast, and easily defeated Willkie to the dismay of the Luce, Gannett, Scripps-Howard, Hearst, Copley, Pulliam, Cowles, and smaller publishing groups across the country.

As Roosevelt directed the nation toward a warlike stance he was infuriated by the published report in the Chicago *Tribune* that told of America's contingency plans for mobilization in case war broke out with Japan. The top secret documents, of the kind usually kept by general staffs for standby purposes, had been leaked to the *Tribune* reporter by a bitter Roosevelt foe. The incident was allowed to pass officially unnoticed, although publisher Robert McCormick of the *Tribune* cited the military blueprints as further proof of Roosevelt's duplicity. The Administration's tolerance of the *Tribune* was strained again, this time beyond endurance, when a report of the naval victory at the Battle of Midway all but gave away the vital knowledge that the United States Navy had broken the Japanese secret code. Fortunately, no Japanese agent read the *Tribune* and the government eventually dropped a plan to prosecute the *Tribune* for endangering the national security.[31]

The president's displeasure over the imagined power of the Chicago *Tribune* had not been lost on Marshall Field III, a department-store heir with liberal leanings and White House support. Field first helped finance the New York experimental newspaper *PM* in 1940, an idealistic attempt to publish profitably by street sales alone without any advertising revenue. *PM* had some of the old muckraking spirit infused in its staff and by exposés of income tax and other scandals showed a zest lacking in the established New York dailies. It struggled along through the war and finally went broke (as the rechristened New York *Star*) in 1946. Meanwhile, Field focused his attention on journalism in his hometown base and began assembling the staff for a morning challenger to the *Tribune*. On December 4, 1941, the Chicago *Sun* sold 896,000 copies of its debut two-cent edition. A million copies were printed for the Sunday, December 7, edition.

Chicagoans who were reading "Terry and the Pirates" or New Yorkers tuned in to the Philharmonic broadcast on that Sunday afternoon were among the millions who stayed close to their radios after a terse "We interrupt this program" bulletin. The wire service teletypes struck a seven-bell FLASH. Pearl Harbor was being bombed by Japanese aircraft. Then a curtain of censorship fell as fragmentary reports continued to reach the West Coast. As work around the nation stood suspended the next day, Americans heard a sparse account of the damage in the president's war message to Congress. For the next forty-five months they would hear and read the fullest possible account of the most massive military undertaking in American history.

As in all past wars, labor soon became scarce and paper prices shot up from $50 to $68 a ton before controls were employed. Publishers voluntarily cut back on the size of newspapers but metropolitan prices rose to five cents a copy for a wartime edition. Newsprint famines were rare, but certain economies had to be practiced, and in notable instances newspapers refused to print several pages of advertising to hold down paper demands. The New Orleans *Item* finally omitted advertising from its editions for a full week in 1945.[32] Staff problems were often acute but not desperate as more women took regular reporting assignments in the news and even the once-sacrosanct male strongholds—the sports departments.

Radio supplied listeners with bulletins from a galaxy of war fronts as Americans became aware of tiny Pacific beaches where Americans fought savagely against a well-trained, determined enemy. Combat correspondents with the Marine Corps battalions sent home factual accounts of agonizing hours in a beachhead hospital. Ernie Pyle, an Indiana-born columnist, relayed in his column personal interviews with infantrymen in North Africa and Italy that carried a universal message of homesickness and fear. Bill Mauldin, a soldier-cartoonist with the 45th Division in the Mediterranean campaigns, created two bewhiskered "GI Joes" (one named Willie) who spoke plainly and humorously of small tragedies and large sacrifices. *Yank* magazine, prepared by military reporters for servicemen in every theater of the war, sent out over 2 million copies each week crammed with cartoons, stateside reports, "Sad Sack," and dozens of photographs of smiling, long-legged American girls in bathing suits. Around 1,900 dailies had survived the depression and were now turning a profit and printing a column on "Our Men in the Service" that told of the meanderings of almost 12 million Americans in uniform.

Elmer Davis took over the Office of War Information but the difference between 1914 and 1941 insofar as journalism was concerned was the comparison between a hurricane and a kite-raising wind. By 1941 the only minority group that could have been worrisome to Americans was the Japanese nisei on the West Coast, and in an ill-advised maneuver (almost universally applauded at the time, by newsmen ranging from Lippmann to Winchell) relocation camps were established for thousands of loyal Americans who were of Japanese ancestry. The few Japanese-language newspapers published in California were banned, but the country had learned a few lessons and, more important, there was hardly a serious note of dissent about America's war aims. The nation was united in its conviction that Nazi Germany and Japan had to be defeated and subscribed to the Allies' terms of "unconditional surrender."

Radio brought listeners into the heart of battle with shortwave broadcasts from bombers on missions over Europe or minesweepers in the English channel. Radio and newspaper correspondents followed troops at the landings in Normandy in June 1944, and a host of American reporters (including the ubiquitous Ernest Hemingway) were among the early arrivals in liberated Paris. "Pool" reporters sometimes carried special assignments for all the media when a single correspondent might be allowed on a dangerous mission. The presidential campaign of 1944 was a sideshow to the real action. At least 796 daily newspapers endorsed Thomas E. Dewey, while Roosevelt's fourth-term bid was approved by 291, but a combination of "stateside" and servicemen's absentee ballots gave Roosevelt another easy victory. Roosevelt's death in April 1945 transformed a stunned Vice President Truman into the commander in chief of forces hurtling toward final victories on two fronts. Then, as in 1918, an over-zealous reporter sent the country on a celebrating binge as an Associated Press war correspondent filed a premature story on a German military collapse. As part of a "pool" sent to witness the German surrender, the AP reporter decided to send his story without an official release. He was rebuked by angry colleagues and AP was briefly suspended from its reporting privileges, but the story which broke in New York at 9:35 A.M. on May 7 was never authenticated. Unperturbed, the publishers printed extra editions and radio newscasters interrupted programs with the "flash from Supreme Allied headquarters." President Truman's official announcement on May 8 "was less an anti-climax than a happy confirmation." [33]

America still had to win the war in the Pacific, and it took three more months and the explosion of two atomic bombs to accomplish final victory. Curiously, the public often learned of events in the Pacific from monitored Japanese broadcasts rather than from official

American reports. The first bombing of Tokyo by General Doolittle's raiders was announced in an English-language broadcast from the Japanese capital, and a skeptical public learned that there was a frankness about the Japanese propaganda agencies that was in contrast to the hysterical mendacity that marked similar broadcasts from Germany in 1941–1945. Characteristically, the United Press almost filed a premature announcement of the Japanese surrender on August 12, 1945. A false report with a Washington dateline had been carried through to the New York UP headquarters but a hurried telephone call "killed" the message before it was sent to press rooms. A $5,000 reward for information on the hoax went unclaimed.

Nobody knows how many listeners heard the news on their 56 million radio sets, when the official news came on August 15, 1945, of the Japanese surrender. Those who witnessed the public's reaction to the news could only remember that the word spread rapidly. In Oklahoma City, a movie audience watching *Gone with the Wind* suddenly saw a blank screen as a loudspeaker voice reported, "The radio has just announced that Japan has surrendered. The war is over!" The screen remained blank and everybody filed out into the street. The Armed Forces Radio station on Okinawa announced the surrender and servicemen began firing their weapons in the air and down tent-lined streets. Seven American soldiers and sailors died that night on Okinawa celebrating the war they had helped end, while a mile to the west, on the tiny island of Ie Shima, the dirt was still fresh on Ernie Pyle's grave. He had died while trying to give readers back in Indiana and Florida some news about their boys.

15

Seeing It Now

The generation of Americans born after World War II ended grew to maturity in a world that regarded many past institutions as museum pieces of doubtful value. The far-reaching effects of television on journalism stood out as the kind of technological advancement that had somehow crept up on the nation and clobbered it. In 1941 a *Fortune* poll indicated that nearly one-half of the American people learned of the world about them from newspapers alone, while one-third both read and listened to the radio news. By 1951 television viewing appeared to be a national preoccupation. The new electronic medium moved down the old path trod by radio pioneers who thought of their mechanism as an entertainment device, but the spectacular potential of remote television coverage made it impossible for 14-inch screens to become simply Hollywood-in-your-home. Even Greeley and Pulitzer understood that reading and comprehending were two different things, but with television the mere act of turning a knob brought on a flood of ideas, information, and sometimes—regrettably—misinformation. In a sense, the trail begun in a

German printing shop had come to an end, perhaps a dead end, in a broadcasting studio.

Still it would be unfair to name television as the villain when chronicling the vicissitudes of American journalism in the post-World War II era. Countries without millions of television sets also were confronted with rising crime rates, family disintegration, and conspicuous overindulgence. But television did make vast numbers of Americans aware of the wide disparity between their expectations and the realities. Concerned citizens who saw the U-2 photographs, the 1968 Democratic convention confrontations, or the Mylai incident realized that mendacity either was or had become a part of the American political picture. The sobering coverage of the Kennedy assassination, the Watts riots, and the drawn look of Lyndon Johnson as he withdrew from the 1968 campaign left an impact on viewers that newspaper stories could not convey. Television had added a misty dimension to news coverage—with every man his own viewer and interpreter of events—that was not easily comprehended by even veteran reporters. If the American moon walk was not (as the president declared) the greatest event in history, it was still a startling fact that had only recently been a Jules Verne fancy.

There was an unreal quality to space explorations and the paraphernalia of astronauts for many Americans, although the V-2 missiles hurled on London in the last stages of the war had an ominous familiarity to the generation that had known the cartoon-strip antics of Buck Rogers and Flash Gordon. Before Americans' thoughts turned to rocket research, however, there had been much unfinished business left from the war. Research had provided mankind with new medicines, new building materials, and other discoveries that pointed to the postwar era as one of a long and good life.

"Research" seemed the key to man's age-old problems, yet few newspapers or magazines showed much interest in research that was not conducted to increase product lines and profit. To the credit of the *Wall Street Journal, New York Times,* and *Time-Life* it could be said that they generously supported postwar efforts to enlarge knowledge of the communicating process. Henry Luce persuaded Chancellor Robert M. Hutchins of the University of Chicago to form a commission to study freedom of the press in 1942, and distinguished scholars joined the group, which finally reported in 1947. Newspaper publishers quickly noted that their numbers had been ignored in forming the commission, and tended to dismiss the commission's critics as invalid. Law professor Zechariah Chafee's hand was evident in the 139-page report, which reaffirmed the Supreme Court findings in the 1931 *Near v. Minnesota* case. "Many a lying, venal, and scoundrelly public expression must continue to find shelter under a 'freedom of the press' built for widely different purposes, for to impair the legal right even when the moral right is gone may easily be a cure worse than the disease," the commission noted.[1] The report also observed that the press was notably hypersensitive to criticism, and "By a kind of unwritten law the press ignores the errors and misrepresentations, the lies and scandals, of which its members are guilty."[2] Except for A. J. Leibling's "The Wayward Press" columns in the *New Yorker* magazine, one of the nation's most important industries was without a watchdog and apparently liked it that way.

Editors showed little patience with most of the commission's report, which included recommendations that the press should serve the public "as [a] responsible critic, gadfly, and source of [social] incentive." Instead of regarding the carefully worded report as a challenge, the reaction in *Editor & Publisher* showed widespread dismay. *Commission Alleges: "Press Fails to Meet Needs of Society,"* the newsmen's house journal headline read. A week later *Editor & Publisher* noted, *Commission Report Under Fire Generally,* with the biggest blast coming from the Chicago *Tribune*. The *Tribune* story on the report was headed, *A Free Press (Hitler Style) Sought for U.S.,* with much space devoted to "a determined group of totalitarian thinkers" who wished to see all newspapers end "effective criticism of New Deal socialism, the one-world doctrine, and internationalism." With tongue in cheek, the Chicago *Sun* pointed to the *Tribune* account as "conclusive documentation of the Commission's charge of bias and irresponsibility of the press."

Obviously the publishers were in no soul-searching mood in 1947. They were reacting in the same way that doctors, lawyers, schoolteachers, and social workers react when told that their house is not in perfect order. Moreover, the economic prognosticators from 1944 onward had scared the publishers (along with much of the business community) by articles and speeches on an ominous postwar depression. "Back to 1929?" the *Christian Century* asked in August 1946, and it was easy to find a dispirited answer in any daily newspaper. Still, "We Can Prevent the Next Big Bust," the ever-optimistic *Reader's Digest* insisted early in 1947. Publishers were wary, and to add to their anxiety there was the newest threat to newspapers moving rapidly from the experimental stage—television. Technology had run amok, and costs were mounting. The publisher who installed a color-run press often figured he had made the ultimate step in progressive journalism. No doubt many delegates to the 1947 American Newspaper Publisher's Association convention were inwardly cheered upon learning that television, unlike radio, had one great drawback—it could not be easily transmitted over natural obstacles.

Technology forced men to accept new marvels, but there was still a human side to the news of the 1940s and 1950s. The presidential election of 1948 was a dramatic case in point. President Truman, dismissed by all the major polling agencies as a cumbersome albatross clinging to the Democratic party, was opposed by 771 dailies and supported by 182 publishers, yet reporters aboard his campaign train were optimistic. Most assured of all, however, was the Chicago *Tribune* editor who ordered an early printing of an election night edition with the headline *Dewey Defeats Truman* before any substantial number of reports had reached the city room. This boner edition was waved jubilantly from a train platform by Truman the next morning after his victory had been confirmed. The Los Angeles *Herald Express* headline, *Dewey Victory Seen as Vote Lead Grows*, also had a wan look, but other dailies had been more prudent. Columnists were dumbfounded by the Truman triumph. With hindsight, Arthur Krock of the *New York Times* concluded that he and other newspapermen had failed to concern themselves "as we used to, with the facts. We accepted the polls, unconsciously." The company was good—Krock, Lippmann, Marquis Childs, James Reston—but the reporters' and pollsters' prognosis was bad.

Upsets make great news stories, but Truman was perhaps the last of his breed. Television barely carried the conventions beyond the largest cities in 1948, so that it was Truman's midwestern twang that brought the message of "a good-for-nothing, do-nothing Eightieth Congress" to voters over radio during the waning days of October. Thereafter, it became important to have another attribute in the new journalism about to take over. The "image" was a metaphor that covered both projected personality and the public man's appearance. By 1950, when the coaxial cable first was creeping and then leaping westward, the first important newscasts on network television came when Senator Estes Kefauver called underworld characters to testify before his committee investigating crime. The lanky Tennessean became a national figure in a matter of days as the television screen brought details of crime without punishment into homes, bars, laundromats, business offices, and campus "Union" corners. Edward R. Murrow, projecting his own image as a handsome chain-smoker, successfully moved to the new medium and at the 1952 conventions provided commentaries alongside old colleagues and a host of new ones, including Walter Cronkite and John Daly. The election of Dwight Eisenhower in November came after charges from Adlai Stevenson that the nation was dominated by a "one-party press," buttressed by some impressive statistics on newspaper editorial endorsements. *Editor & Publisher* found that 67 percent of the reporting dailies favored "Ike," 14 percent endorsed Stevenson, and 18 percent remained aloof. The real difference was in the circulation figures. Eisenhower's backers claimed 80 percent of the total national circulation, and in the key states of Illinois, New York, and Pennsylvania the Republican nominee was favored by 206 dailies (12,478,000 circulation) while Stevenson had the backing of 16 (1,400,000 circulation).

Eisenhower's image of honest strength was so fixed on the American voter's mind that the articulate and witty Stevenson faced an impossible task and yet made friends when he lost by recalling a Lincoln anecdote. A radio reporter thrust a microphone at the loser and asked the all-purpose question which inept reporters seem to hold in readiness for such occasions: "How does it feel?"

"Well," Stevenson said, "I guess I feel like Mr. Lincoln did when he lost an election and somebody asked him the same kind of a question. 'It hurts too much to laugh, and I'm too old to cry.' "

How much the nearly unanimous press endorsement of Ike had added to Stevenson's distress was only conjecture.

During the campaign, Eisenhower had appeared on the platform with Joseph McCarthy, a Wisconsin senator with a reputation as an outspoken anti-Communist. What bothered McCarthy's critics was the senator's shoot-from-the-hip tendency that damaged reputations while McCarthy was protected by congressional immunity from libel or slander suits. Eisenhower mildly rebuked this kind of demagoguery in a television speech seen by perhaps 38 million viewers and heard by another 20 million citizens in 1953, but McCarthy rushed on unabashed. His investigative techniques during a hearing on "coddling of Communists" in the Department of the Army were widely televised and provoked much polarized press comment. The *Times* of London told Englishmen: "Senator McCarthy this afternoon achieved what General Burgoyne and General Cornwallis never achieved—the surrender of the American Army." [3] Increasingly, most newspapers grew cautious as McCarthy's search broadened, but the *New York Times, Washington Post,* and *Time* magazine continued their criticism of the senator's tactics. Some of the more timid newspapers allowed McCarthy's friends and enemies to go at it in their letters-to-the-editor column while preserving a seemingly impartial stance.

What the newspaper could not do, television did when Murrow

and his partner, Fred W. Friendly, ran a two-part "See It Now" series on McCarthy that placed the senator's record on a half-shell, with little commentary from Murrow. Now McCarthy had been challenged—by his own words and actions on film. What the viewing public saw was a senator acting like a bully. Thereafter, it was easier to question the sincerity of McCarthy's anti-Communist crusade, and reporters who had reported all of McCarthy's charges as prima facie facts became more skeptical. By midsummer the situation had gone so far that there was talk among his senate colleagues of censuring McCarthy, a humiliating step which in fact took place before the year ended.

As McCarthy's image of white-charger Americanism faded, the public was suddenly confronted with a historic Supreme Court decision that would reveal the thinness of civilization's veneer in many regions. The court rejected an 1896 doctrine that Negroes and whites could be segregated by "separate but equal" facilities and held that no American child could constitutionally be denied his place in a public schoolroom because of his color. In short, the decision seemed pointed at the South, where de jure segregation had been under attack by NAACP lawyers since 1947. The court held that in the twenty states practicing segregation in their public schools, the separation was "inherently unequal" and had to be ended by integration methods pursued with "all deliberate speed." Southern newspapers reacted with more sublety than the fire-eating politicians. Governor Tallmadge of Georgia called the decision "a scrap of paper," predicted integration would never take place in his state, and recommended the abolition of the state's public school system.[4] Southern senators Harry F. Byrd and Richard Russell denounced the decision as "dangerous" and "outrageous," but the leading Virginia newspapers counseled a period of calm study of the court order. The Richmond *Times-Dispatch* called the decision "the most momentous . . . in the interracial field since the DRED SCOTT case of 1857," and asked the public "to avoid threats and hysteria." The Atlanta *Journal* declared that the white majority in the South was against integration.

"Nothing can change their feeling overnight," the *Journal* said in an implicit plea for time to carry out the sweeping judicial order.

What the court meant by "all deliberate speed" was to some southerners the key to the question. Before the issue was settled by an integration of classes in most of the South, the boiling point was reached in a scattering of cities and in the case of Little Rock despite calm, low-key press coverage. The moderate *Arkansas Gazette* could not assure public acceptance of integration in the state capital, where national guardsmen finally were mustered on a presidential order to help restore calm at the central high school. Television cameras recorded the indignities heaped on a lonely black girl as she walked to school under a verbal barrage from white adults. A hundred years of improving race relations seemed to melt away as concealed gunmen fired at young Negroes in Arkansas, Alabama, and Mississippi. Where men carried no guns but spoke of supporting "massive resistance" to the Court order, the air was also tense. Despite a surplus of political rhetoric and editorial alarums in such newspapers as the Jackson, Mississippi, *Clarion-Ledger,* the affected states slowly fell into line with integration plans of either token or real proportions.

The exception came in a southern Virginia farming community, in Prince Edward County, where the Farmville *Herald* had long ignored demands for better schools for the blacks. A month after the Supreme Court decision had been announced, the *Herald* declared the high court had forced Virginia to abolish public education. *Herald* editorials bolstered the community leadership that was prepared for a drastic answer to the Court order, and even the Richmond *News Leader* approved the idea of "freedom of choice" in education (that is, let private schools operate with state subsidies). Two years after the Court ruling, the *Herald* announced that "Prince Edward has no plans for integrating its schools." The result of this newspaper-led defiance of the law was that for four years (1959–1963) the public schools in Prince Edward County were shut tight. The *Herald* was triumphant, but not exemplary, as the press Establishment often can be in local affairs. No other southern county took such extreme steps.[5]

At the national end, newspaper journalism in the 1950s strengthened the convictions of those inclined to believe that the rich get richer while the poor go to potter's field. The Los Angeles *Daily News,* one of the few liberal voices in southern California journalism, closed its creaky front door in 1955 while the scion of the Oakland *Tribune,* conservative Senator William Knowland, stood at a pinnacle of popularity. Suddenly the political winds shifted. At the reactionary Los Angeles *Times,* deaths and staff changes rapidly brought an objectivity to the *Times'* local and national reporting that the burgeoning desert metropolis had never known before. Still anti-union by tradition, the *Times* improved substantially to make a *New York Times* venture in a West Coast edition prove abortive and costly. The *Wall Street Journal,* long the financier's daily almanac, similarly expanded its news and feature sections until its excellence justified a series of regional printing plants with overnight transmissions of duplicate editions for every major urban area. As the Los Angeles *Times* forsook its reactionary provincialism and the *Wall Street Journal* was sought by readers who had little interest in the stock market, it was apparent that quality brought rewards in the American marketplace, despite the inroads television had made on news-reading habits. A research survey indicated that the average American adult probably spent less than thirty minutes a day reading but might sit as much as two and a half hours in front of a television set.

Predictably, the shift in public taste brought profit strains to the weaker newspaper and magazine properties. As Oswald Garrison Villard had predicted in 1923, the future trend was strongly running toward the time when one-newspaper cities would become the rule.[6] By 1960, New York still had ten daily newspapers but sixty-six cities with a population of over 100,000 had only one choice. Indeed, in only ten metropolitan areas were there more than two competitive newspapers. The nation's total daily circulation had risen from 1.5

million newspapers in Lincoln's day to reach 60 million copies. But careful research teams found that the average reader of these newspapers had a twelve-year-old's view of the news. Those stories written by reporters with Ph.D. degrees were being read by a tiny part of the total audience. Moreover, as the author of *The Fading American Newspaper* said, "A man no longer needs to read a daily newspaper in order to be well-informed." Hourly news round-ups on radio, the network news programs, and the torrent of paper issuing from the presses of *Life, Look, Time, Newsweek,* and *U.S. News and World Report* were competing for the citizen's precious eight hours when he was not working or resting.

Understandably, the newspapermen who balked at the lumping of all the mass media under the heading of *journalism* were troubled by the development in the late 1950s of shoppers' or "throwaway" weeklies that were essentially advertising vehicles for supermarkets, suburban shopping centers, and classified sections. Not true weeklies in the old sense, these new sources of income were portable billboards with only the look of a newspaper. Much of the news copy was carried over from syndicated material or from publicity handouts, set in type merely to give the whole package the appearance of a bona fide newspaper. As a marketing device these weeklies helped saturate bedroom communities surrounding large metropolitan areas, but they were often compiled, rather than written, by a single employee whose main admonition from his boss was that he print nothing controversial. Thus the new weeklies profaned an honorable calling and produced the antithesis of Pulitzer's charge that the main business of a newspaper was "to comfort the afflicted and afflict the comfortable."

If newspapers were not performing spectacularly in the public interest, television was equally disappointing to those who lamented the ineptitude of broadcast journalism. Radio and television news directors squirmed when Murrow told their national convention in 1958 that their "responsibility is amplified to the degree where it reaches from one end of the country to the other [yet] does not confer upon you greater wisdom or understanding than you possessed when your voice reached only from one end of the bar to the other." In a sober, self-critical mood, Murrow said that "if there are any historians about fifty or a hundred years from now, and there should be preserved the kinescopes for one week of all three networks, they will there find recorded in black and white, or color, evidence of decadence, escapism and insulation from the realities of the world in which we live." Murrow lashed out at the newsroom attitude that "we must at all costs shield the sensitive citizens from anything that is unpleasant." He concluded with a plea for newsmen to treat controversial subjects fairly so that the viewing public could recognize good reporting "for what it is—an effort to illuminate rather than agitate." [7]

Murrow's plea was eloquent but generally overlooked as much public attention was focused during the late 1950s on comfort and beauty as legitimate ends of life. The newspapers supported this view by adding beauty-hint and health columns, while radio and television stressed conspicuous consumption in their entertainment programs. Professional football took a sudden spurt in public interest, aided by blanket coverage from the local media, as tournament golf and other competitive sports reported by remote-unit television were embraced by eager sponsors. Except in boxing, where television rights were excluded, no major sports event went unreported by camera crews from the major networks, leaving newspaper reporters with only the post-contest diagnosis of second-half surges or faltering in the home stretch. Perceptive John S. Knight, owner of a newspaper chain stretching from the Detroit *Free Press* to the Tallahassee *Democrat,* looked at sports sections and concluded they were filled with "interesting, uninhibited writing with a weakness for hero worship." Knight believed sports editors were too uncritical and not concerned with "digging into the big-time sports rackets [or] promoters who exploit young athletes." Except for the likes of Grantland Rice, John Kieran, and "Red" Smith—Knight's comments amounted to a nationwide bill of particulars on sports writers and editors.

For a time, the life of the political reporter was almost sedentary.

President Eisenhower's heart and ileitis attacks left the public sympathetic toward his desire for more time for resting, a situation made possible by the increasingly important role of presidential press secretary James Hagerty. As a buffer between his boss and the press, the former newsman sometimes showed more adeptness than the White House press corps appreciated. Perhaps they had been spoiled by memories of Roosevelt's record of 998 presidential press conferences, or Truman's banter through eight tiring years with more than 320 press sessions. Hagerty was able to hold the average of Eisenhower's press meetings to about one a month, although the innovation of presenting these before the television cameras brought viewers into the ringside of Capital Hill politics.

Two remarkable incidents during Eisehower's second term showed that the president's attitude toward public questions was not formed by a careful weighing of the alternatives. When the Soviet Union launched its first earth satellite in October 1957, the president was not immediately available for a comment on an event that clearly stunned the nation. The postwar years of complacency toward military might and space exploration dissolved on an October Saturday which the president spent on a Gettysburg golf course. Pressed for an official reaction to "Sputnik," press secretary Hagerty told reporters the Russian scientific feat was "no surprise," and that the president had sent the Soviet Union a congratulatory message in a spirit of good sportsmanship.[8] "The White House, in the person of Mr. Hagerty, may not be impressed," Edward R. Murrow said the next evening, "but the rest of the world is." In this same period, Hagerty told reporters he and the president were "outspokenly angry" over a broadcast dealing with the Little Rock school crisis, which the presidential aide termed "junk."

Nonetheless, it was the president himself who apologized to the Soviet Union in May 1960 after a United States reconnaissance airplane was shot down by the Russians on the eve of a Paris "summit conference." Early dispatches said the aircraft had been reported missing from a Turkish airbase while on a weather reconnaissance mission, but when the Russians produced not only the U-2 plane wreckage but the American pilot, the State Department (in what *Time* called "manly candor") announced that the plane had been on an espionage photographic mission. "America's latest intelligence fiasco," the *New York Times* said, had given the Soviet Union extraordinary opportunities to gain public sympathy owing to "the absurd lying and confused explanations on behalf of the United States." [9] *Times* columnist James Reston said the incident proved that America had swung from the "personalized Presidency" of Jackson, Lincoln, Wilson, and the two Roosevelts to the "institutionalized Presidency" of Eisenhower that left "the world, the nation, and the President himself in a state of uncertainty about who is doing what." The Paris peace conference of the heads of state collapsed, but somehow Eisenhower emerged with no damage to his popularity. Indeed, several days before he left for the ill-fated Paris talks, Eisenhower told a press conference, "No one wants another Pearl Harbor." Public opinion quickly confirmed that the people as much as the generals and admirals were still thinking about 1941, although Walter Lippmann seemed to wince as he wrote that the president's frankness "put everybody on the spot." [10]

The U-2 incident helped generate campaign issues during 1960 as the handsome young senator from Massachusetts began his climb to succeed Eisenhower. From the New Hampshire primaries on through to the Los Angeles convention, tousle-haired John F. Kennedy moved so fast the news cameramen and reporters found it hard to keep up the pace. After both conventions had named nominees, the television networks sent a joint invitation for a series of "Great Debates" to begin in September. Kennedy leaped at the chance while his Republican counterpart, Richard M. Nixon, was reluctant to give his lesser-known opponent such public attention, but finally he also seemed eager for the telecasts that were spoken of as more significant than the Lincoln-Douglas debates. In the first debate Kennedy appeared tanned and refreshed, while Nixon was haggard and testy. What was important apparently was that the debates on radio seemed a standoff, but viewers believed Kennedy was self-assured and confident in the face of Nixon's hostility and hollow-eyed look. Neither man had used television makeup for that first debate, a mistake that Nixon remedied later but a device the well-tanned Kennedy thought unnecessary. Nixon looked and sounded better in the remaining three debates, but polls after the television programs ended showed that Kennedy had made a more favorable impression on the voting public, which had seen the senator in a new perspective. An average of 67 million viewers watched the debate.[11]

Since Kennedy won by the narrowest of margins, it is inescapable that he was the first president clearly elected because of a favorable television image. The endorsement of newspapers, an anachronism in the light of a generation of experience, confirmed this judgment. Nixon had been supported by 694 newspapers, while Kennedy was favored by 194—a bare nudge above Stevenson's 189 backers in his second losing race in 1956. Perhaps the kind of support Kennedy received said more than the numbers, since he was endorsed by the *New York Times* and four other New York dailies; the Denver *Post* also came out for Kennedy, thus supporting its first Democratic presidential choice since Woodrow Wilson.

The Kennedy family in the White House gave the mass media all the qualities needed for an orgy of overreporting. Foreign correspondents showed an unparalleled interest in the presidency, too, as the Kennedys elegantly refurbished the official residence, brought a pony back to the White House lawn (for the first time since Theodore Roosevelt's day), and gave soirées for renowned artists, authors, musicians, businessmen, and other citizens with a flair that was breathtaking to viewers and readers.

Yet a highly publicized summit meeting between Kennedy and Khrushchev in Vienna was reported as a glamorous event rather than the sobering experience it really was. Cuba, under Fidel Castro, turned from friend to enemy with shocking suddenness. The *New York Times* reporter in Miami heard rumors that a counterrevolutionary force was being trained to invade Castro's Cuba, supported by sub-rosa American aid. White House reporters were tipped by friends at the State Department that something involving Castro's hold on Cuba was underway. Karl Meyer of the *Washington Post* wrote an article for the *New Republic* that was full of details on a projected Cuban invasion. The article was in galley form when the *New Republic* publisher brought it by the White House. Kennedy read it and asked Gilbert Harrison not to print it. The president also was told that a *New York Times* article on an imminent Cuba landing was ready for publication. After a call from Washington, *Times* officials finally decided to submerge the main point in the interests of national policy. Arthur Schlesinger, Jr., who saw the drama unfold, later surmised that the press had failed in its function to keep the people informed. "In retrospect I have wondered whether, if the press had behaved irresponsibly, it would not have spared the country a disaster." [12] A CBS story hinting at the coming invasion drew quick official denials.[13]

The CIA-sponsored invasion turned into a tragic fiasco, and as in the U-2 incident, it became apparent that the United States Government could lie when mendacity seemed dictated by "the national interest." Ambassador Stevenson was shown at the United Nations denying that the United States was in any way involved in the Cuban landings on April 15, 1961. Stevenson's indignant denial, telecast around the nation, was framed by CIA personnel who deliberately misled the ambassador. Presidential press secretary Pierre Salinger was quoted as saying, "All we know about Cuba is what we read on the wire services." It was a profound shock for Americans to learn that they had been misled by the whole machinery of government with the aid of the media which, by silence or cooperation, kept the public ignorant of truth concerning the damaging incident.

Kennedy had a way of bouncing back. His "live" telecast press conferences set attendance records for accredited reporters, and were marked by an urbanity and wit rarely seen in a public man but now visible to 40 million people at the moment Kennedy spoke. During his thirty-four months in office Kennedy held sixty-four regular meetings with the press, along with countless informal chats with friendly reporters and editors. His wife also conducted the public through a White House tour telecast at "prime viewing time," and public opinion polls showed Kennedy to be almost as popular as Eisenhower. Much of the fare on the NBC Huntley-Brinkley evening news program or from the CBS Cronkite-Reasoner report focused on the White House and its dynamic occupant.

The press continued to work with Kennedy, charmed, it seemed, by the man's vitality and sense of purpose. In October 1962 a presidential trip to Chicago was suddenly canceled because it was reported that Kennedy was suffering from a slight cold. What was really troubling the president was a series of aerial photographs of Russian missile sites in Cuba. Kennedy chose to share this information with the American people in a telecast on October 22, 1962, that in effect laid an ultimatum before Russia to withdraw the missiles. Days of tension followed, with the country prepared, with resignation, for the kind of nuclear war Kennedy held in prospect if the Soviet Union did not take immediate action to "eliminate this clandestine, reckless, and provocative threat to world peace." The cloak-and-dagger aspect grew when the Soviet embassy in Washington chose to use ABC reporter John Scali to carry Russian terms for a settlement to the White House. After an anxious week, the president accepted Khrushchev's assurances and soon television sets in Tacoma and Topeka showed Russian freighters homeward bound with the dismantled missiles on their decks. The tightest censorship since World War II prevailed and all information to the press came channeled through government sources. The brevity of the incident resulted in a minimum of complaint over censorship, and, moreover, there seemed to be no other responsible way of informing the people that a nuclear war might break out before nightfall. Nonetheless, the "managed news" aspect clung to the Kennedy press team, and as the Los Angeles *Times* warned, "You can't both con the press and count on it."

The fall elections in 1962 were somewhat overshadowed by the

Cuba missile crisis, but the unsuccessful bid of Richard Nixon for the California governor's seat caused some ripples in the press corps. After Nixon lost the race he called a special press conference and for seventeen minutes told the reporters what he thought of them. A poor prognosticator, Nixon concluded: "You won't have Nixon to kick around any more, because, gentlemen, this is my last press conference. . . ." [14]

With a hammered-and-sickled Cuba twice in the news it seemed that the 1960s had started full of violence and revolution, and the country turned to domestic problems with some sense of relief. Little came, however, as a Mississippi civil rights worker was murdered and Martin Luther King led a huge parade of black and white supporters for equal rights to the Lincoln Memorial in Washington. Television cameras covered King's speech as he said, "I have a dream. It is a dream . . . that one day this nation will rise up and live out the true meaning of its creed: 'We hold these truths to be self-evident, that all men are created equal.' " News documentary films on television told viewers of King's progress as a civil rights leader and a South Carolina senator accused the network of "following the NAACP line." [15] Increasingly, conservative and reactionary groups found the Kennedy family a ready target for their verbal assaults, since the president's brother was the attorney general active in the civil rights ferment.

The Dallas *Morning News* carried a full-page advertisement on November 22, 1963, as the president and his wife flew to the Texas city for a motorcade and speech in an effort to enlarge his political base. *Welcome Mr. Kennedy to Dallas,* the advertisement read in mock hospitality. The message charged that the president had ignored the Constitution and predicted he would lose Dallas in 1964 as he had in 1960; it also asked a number of questions, including "WHY have you scrapped the Monroe Doctrine in favor of the 'Spirit of Moscow'?" Kennedy undoubtedly never saw this advertisement for he was shot shortly after noon on a Dallas street by a sniper. The UPI sent out the FLASH at 12:30: KENNEDY SERIOUSLY WOUNDED PERHAPS

SERIOUSLY PERHAPS FATALLY BY ASSASSINS BULLET. By radio and television the word spread across the nation. An hour later, it was clear that Kennedy was dead and that Lyndon Johnson was the new president.

Thereafter, no detail escaped the press or radio-television reporters as the nation learned of the suspected murderer and millions in turn saw him murdered before an NBC camera covering the Dallas jail. Air Force One carried the president's body back to Washington and those Americans who wished to stay in front of a television set for the next three days witnessed all the tragedy ordinarily crowded into one lifetime. "America wept tonight, not alone for its dead young President, but for itself," James Reston observed in the *New York Times.* "The grief was general, for somehow the worst in the nation had prevailed over the best." The *Times* gave the Dallas events an unprecedented coverage—the first sixteen pages were completely filled with news about the assassination.[16] All sponsored programs were dropped by television networks as the funeral dirge continued on, hour after hour.

The nation pulled itself together, but without the confident air of the past. The mass media joined in a reexamination of American society that was still continuing when Lyndon B. Johnson became that rarest of rarities—a Democratic president endorsed by most of the nation's dailies. In 1964 Johnson was supported by 440 newspapers with a circulation of 27 million, while Barry Goldwater drew the favor of 359 dailies (but their circulation was only 9 million).[17] Johnson won handily, promising to go slow in Vietnam. Besides the war, the newspapers seemed to be filled with stories about increasing crime problems in the cities, and arguments raged in all the media over the effects of marijuana on college campuses from Harvard to Berkeley. As Eric Sevareid observed on CBS, "The biggest big business in America is not steel, automobiles or television. It is the manufacture, refinement and distribution of anxiety." "If the nineteenth century was the age of the editorial chair," Marshall McLuhan noted, "ours is the century of the psychiatrist's couch."

The public slowly recovered from one tragedy, only to learn of another. Martin Luther King was assassinated in Memphis. Then a fanatic killed Robert F. Kennedy, who was in Los Angeles campaigning for the Democratic nomination his brother had won eight years earlier in the same city. The puddle-type war in Vietnam deepened into a quagmire. The press spoke of a "credibility gap" between the White House and reporters. Los Angeles police gunned down Black Panthers, and Black Panthers shot each other in internecine power struggles. The media attempted to chronicle these events with objectivity, yet they all seemed to fit a pattern of distrust. The great voices that had helped reassure were missing—Elmer Davis, Murrow, Kaltenborn—they were dead, as were the men of good humor who in earlier times helped restore the nation's sense of balance. There was no Artemus Ward, no "Mr. Dooley," no Will Rogers to help ease the pain.

The depth of America's wounds in the 1960s were nowhere probed with more attention or less solution than in black communities. "Distrust and dislike of the media among ghetto Negroes encompass all the media," the Kerner Commission surmised, "though in general, the newspapers are mistrusted more than the television." [18] The commission report on urban riots indicted the mass media for their failure "to report adequately on the causes and consequences of civil disorders and the underlying problems of race relations." The chief flaw in reporting about black citizens was that the press coverage had mainly been by white men, about white men, and for white men. Still, since Frederick Douglass' day Negroes have published their own newspapers in a reaction to the Caucasian bias of the press. Beginning with Douglass' *North Star*, the black press has been a viable carrier of information and the chief local medium for the Negroes who needed an avenue for both protest and social continuity. The Baltimore *Afro-American,* founded in 1892, has had a wide influence in the East, along with the Harlem district's *Amsterdam News* (founded 1909), the Pittsburgh *Courier* (in several regional editions), and the newer Chicago *Daily Defender.* Although white readers have barely been aware of the existence of these news-papers, the eastern black press helped establish the Negro identity in the American cultural stream and trained able reporters for the general media. Some Negro editors, such as John Dungee of the Oklahoma City *Black Dispatch,* were community leaders who worked for solutions to the problems that beset segregated urban centers. The rise of black journalism as a force in the lives of 20 million Americans was undeniable, as the growth of *Ebony* magazine (to a circulation of 1,239,000 in 1971 from its 1945 beginnings) proved. Moreover, black journalism by the 1970s was assertive, critical to a more pronounced degree than it had been in the prewar years, when the Swedish observer Gunnar Myrdal had noted that "the Negro press serves as a safety-valve for the boiling Negro protest." [19]

Simultaneous with improvement in limited areas, the newspaper world of both black and white America continued to experience fundamental economic troubles. The conglomerate built of straw from the once-great *Herald, Tribune, Sun, World,* and lesser lights made a brief stab at holding on in New York before a final collapse. A city of 7 million people had only three major daily newspapers left. (The Spanish-language tabloid, *El Diario La Prensa,* serving blacks and whites, claimed 80,000 daily circulation.) Hearst's *Mirror* had fallen along the way, leaving a bewildered Walter Winchell to ask, "How can a newspaper with 850,000 circulation go broke?" The complex answer centered around the economics of newspaper publishing, which had long ago abandoned circulation as a goal in favor of lucrative advertising contracts and moneymaking, weighty Sunday classified sections. These and other hard lessons had been learned by survivors in the publishing world who paid their newsprint bills on time. In San Francisco, Los Angeles, and other metropolitan areas, strikes and consolidations narrowed the choices left to urban readers, but the old notion that competition produced a better product had been discarded after the tabloid wars in New York simply led to gutter-level journalism. Moreover, surveys indicated that more Americans were turning to television for their daily news diet. In a poll on credibility —"Can you believe what you see?"—television was regarded as twice as reliable as newspapers. The poll also revealed that in many Negro homes, a daily newspaper was a rarity while the television set was the families' sole source of news.

Elsewhere the content rather than the economics of American journalism was profoundly disturbing. Riots following Martin Luther King's assassination closed a part of the national capital as marauding bands of youths tossed firebombs into stores a mile from the White House. The police in Detroit, Los Angeles, Chicago, New York— nearly every large city with a black ghetto—were accused of brutality. As the media reported on these events, it appeared that society was becoming more polarized by the minute. President Johnson's decision not to run for reelection, or even to attend the Democratic convention in Chicago in August 1968, was a precedent-shattering fact that said much about the state of the nation's anxieties. Television cameramen converged on Chicago and presented viewers with scenes of club-swinging policemen, goaded on by publicity-seeking demonstrators who were among the thousands of sincere protesters of the Vietnam war picketing the convention. Violence spread to the convention floor, and confused policemen arrested a CBS reporter in one melee. Hubert Humphrey was nominated to oppose the resurrected Richard Nixon, who was picked at a smoothly functioning Miami convention. The difference between the embattled Chicago meeting and the serenity at Miami was brought into sharp focus by the saturation news coverage of both affairs.[20] The two parties spent over $40 million on advertising, most of it for television time, but voter apathy was widespread (except in the Deep South where George Wallace appealed to the blue-collar white vote and came close to throwing the final election into the House of Representatives). Nixon won the endorsement contest of daily newspapers, 634 to 146, but more significant was the fact that in ten states Humphrey had not a single daily newspaper in his corner.[21] Nixon shied away from another "Great Debate," remembering his problems with television in 1960. Repeatedly, Nixon promised to end the highly unpopular war in Vietnam.

Nothing caused such resentment in America in the late 1960s as the Vietnam war. Never before had a nation stood and watched—almost as a spectator sport—a war being fought. In the past, war reporting was of tactical movements or personal accounts of individual heroism. In Vietnam remote camera units took a viewer to the front and allowed him to see the misery firsthand. The brutality of this experience left some viewers—particularly younger people who had been born since World War II—numb.[22] Atrocity stories came to light. American soldiers were accused of murdering at Mylai a whole village of civilians in their relentless pursuit of Viet Cong enemies. The older wars had been perceived as battles between the forces of good and evil. In Vietnam the American allies were considered unsavory, while young protesters praised the North Vietnamese premier, Ho Chi Minh, and carried that Communist country's flag in campus demonstrations and public rallies. Whether the American people wanted to know it or not, they were being force-fed the brutal story of American participation in Vietnam. The reporter in 1969 who reminded the public that more Americans died in traffic accidents that year than in five years of Vietnam fighting found his perception unappreciated. Whatever the costs in Vietnam, the media reflected a national consensus by 1969 that the price for victory was too high.

In these circumstances, the mass media mercifully shifted national attention from Vietnam to the moon that summer. "The greatest show in the history of television begins when Armstrong starts down the nine-rung ladder leading from the Eagle's hatch to the [moon] surface," the New York *Daily News* predicted. In a world where telephones went dead and trash was not picked up, it was miraculous to behold the American astronauts reaching the distant planet exactly as planned. The television relays of the moon walk were viewed by probably the largest global audience in history. Here was the ultimate staged news event, so perfectly timed that newspapers found it superfluous to report the historic mission in too much detail. Everybody had seen it—both the original and the video replay.

The costs of the moon trip had been staggering—over $50 billion had been spent since 1955 on the space program. *Underground newspapers*, a term coined to show complete divorcement from regular journalism, came from mimeograph machines and presses stretching from Greenwich Village to Berkeley, asking searching questions about national priorities. Obscene passages in the Los Angeles *Free Press* or *Berkeley Barb* shocked the Establishment publishers who were more concerned about the verbal behavior of the young than the implications of their questions. As the brainchild of an alienated section of the nation's youth, the underground press emerged from the so-called hippie culture shortly after President Kennedy's assassination, when the distress of the time seemed to confirm many of the young people's suspicions of established American institutions—including the mass media. The underground press sprang from no single motive, but from bored or angry young minds, and from people with enough credit or money to find a press and enough intelligence to learn how to use the printed word.[23] A *Newsweek* reporter also discerned that the underground press came about "because enough readers, young, poor, and black, want to read the other, not official, version of police-hippie or police-Muslim clashes." The simple process of producing a newspaper led to the proliferated underground press, but the absence of an underground radio or television station stems from the lack of sophisticated knowledge, expensive equipment, and a federal license. Above ground, but also critical of the press performance in metropolitan areas, were a number of new metropolitan magazines that were partially or wholly devoted to journalistic criticism at the local level.

Indeed, the underground press broke through the "four-letter word" barrier with a vengeance that soon left side effects on all journalism and art, and with long-range effects that will not be measured for another generation. As *Look* magazine, with over 7 million readers, closed its doors in 1971, the renegade press claimed that the ten leading underground newspapers had a circulation of between 400,000 and 500,000. Still the general public was unsympathetic toward any movement that tolerated or encouraged the use of "mind-blowing" drugs, sexual promiscuity (or freedom, depending on where one stood), and communal living that eschewed the mores of mature Americans. Thus the underground press might be poised at the edge of a dangerous precipice or resting on a solid foundation—depending on the trend of American thought between 1972 and 1980.

The future was not foreseeable, but the past had been too full of hope. This implicit message at the beginning of the decade assailed viewers of 60 million television sets and readers of 1,780 daily newspapers who either witnessed from parlor chairs or breakfast seats the killings at Kent State and Jackson in May 1970. These campus trage-dies were covered in depth—so that it was possible to behold National Guardsmen aiming and firing at unarmed fellow Americans. Whether a major stock market break later that same month was completely unconnected with these shocking incidents could not be discerned by the press, which shared the general sense of frustration.

Grave doubts concerning the truth of news from Vietnam was heightened when the *New York Times* and *Washington Post* began printing classified material about the Vietnam war in June 1971. After one day, there was an effort by the attorney general to prevent further revelations by halting further publication of the so-called Pentagon Papers. Within two weeks the Supreme Court held that the government could not exercise prior restraint—in short, it could not stop newspapers from printing material although the publisher-editor might be liable later for any breach of the law. It was a reaffir-mation of good eighteenth-century law, straight out of Blackstone, that left some lawyers and editors disquieted. As a *National Observer* reporter pointed out, the Supreme Court gave the Justice Depart-ment more time to show why the articles ought to be suppressed. Al-though the Court finally ruled that the government had not proved its case, the temporary restraining order "remained intact as a legal precedent."

The upshot of the Pentagon Papers incident was a demonstration of the old truth that the battle lines where a free press was continually in the thick of controversy stretched all the way from 1735 to 1971. "The possibility of future attempts by the government to suppress the news is not good for the country and is a prospect with which the nation's press cannot easily live," a *New York Times* executive said as the controversy waned. Beyond all the lawyers' rhetoric about "lack of prior restraint" and exhortations to preserve the national security, there was no alarm bell in the night calling good and free men to do their duty. There was only the tinkling memory of a distant battle over the same issues with protagonists somewhat more renowned. In 1799, when the Sedition laws were stifling the press, James Madison's views gave heart to men who saw that perfect solutions to human problems were not likely to be found. The right to print criticism of the government had cost many lives, and Madison admitted mistakes had been made in pursuit of the truth. No freedom was "more deeply impressed on the public mind than the liberty of the press," yet that liberty was sometimes "carried to excess," and "sometimes degenerated into licentiousness . . . *but the remedy has not yet been discovered"* whereby the one could be stopped without shutting off the other.[24] *"Perhaps it is an evil inseparable from the good with which it is allied; perhaps it is a shoot which cannot be stripped from the stalk without wounding vitally the plant from which it is torn. However desirable those measures might be which might correct without enslaving the press, they have never yet been devised in America."*

Whether these views from a Founding Father will be widely shared by America's public men in the coming decades will be crucial to America's future and the test of its leadership. Willingness to accept criticism is rare indeed, and the mass media have been under heavy attack by officials, scholars, and the journalistic profession itself. Most publishers, disturbed by the uncertainties that lay before them in the 1970s, regarded the critic more as a deadly enemy than as an honest friend. But the health of American journalism is tied to willingness to accept criticism, and both the profession and the nation at large are likely to prosper in the future in proportion to their ability to subject themselves to probing self-analysis. A great deal of research has been done on the reading habits of various age groups, and publishers willingly support this work because they expect that the results will inflate their profits. But many publishers would resent any effort to explain why most newspapers since 1800 have hewed to the Federalist-Whig-Republican line during presidential elections. Nor are publishers worried because the printing process remains a fifteenth-century breakthrough still being practiced in the twentieth. Indeed, automation is helping eliminate most of the laboring non-printers who have a propensity to strike, but as the Louisville *Courier-Journal* publisher noted:

> Newspapers are the heralds of change in a volatile world. Isn't it strange, then, that we ourselves have been so resistant to change in our own operations? We report new techniques in every line of business, but we are reluctant to adopt them in our own profession.[25]

When the vice president of the United States leveled charges against the media early in the 1970s, wails of protest reached ear-splitting proportions. Internal criticism by thoughtful men was more easily ignored. "The fact that no more dogs are biting men should be bigger news than 'Man bites dog,'" a discerning newsman observed. But this view of what prevails in American journalism, and what ought to prevail, ignores the short attention span of the American people. They are easily bored.

Perhaps, in their eagerness to increase their circulation and power, editors and publishers have helped mislead Americans. Newspapers might have pointed out that for too long Americans had rushed to novelty and been preoccupied with broad technological change until the two became confused with progress. In the midst of mounting tension over the slavery issue more than a century ago, Henry David Thoreau thought that both the publishers and readers of newspapers labored under fundamental misconceptions. Thoreau was one of the few who regarded the telegraph as no miraculous invention. When Greeley and Bennett outdid each other in proclaiming the dawn of a new era, Thoreau quietly suggested that most of the messages transmitted on the new device would be energy wasted. "We are in great haste to construct a magnetic telegraph from Maine to Texas; but Maine and Texas, it may be, have nothing important to communicate," he suggested.[26] Already, the routine reporting in newspapers bored a man of Thoreau's bent, for he claimed "never [to have] read any memorable news in a newspaper." One report of a murder, robbery, or train wreck blended into another, Thoreau noticed, and "One is enough."

Thoreau's observations still made sense 130 years later. Thus one challenge to the mass media is to revise its priorities, giving a lower one to the means of gathering or transmitting news, and assigning the highest to improvement of the quality of information it delivers each day. More attention should be paid to the content and less to the package. By pandering to the lowest levels of the American's taste since 1833 the mass media have surely helped citizens lose their identity and intensified "their moral isolation from each other, from reality and from themselves," as Ernest van den Haag has noted.[27] Although the point is overstated, McLuhan's observation that classified ads and stock-market quotations "are the bedrock of the press" ought to incite the press to more soul-searching.[28] For as McLuhan suggests, if an inexpensive, easily distributed alternative "to such diverse daily information [could] be found, the press will fold. Radio and TV can handle the sports, news, comics, and pictures. The editorial . . . has been ignored for many years, unless put in the form of news or paid advertisements."

If emphasis on the Jeffersonian ideal that "the earth belongs to the living" becomes paramount during the 1970s, it is evident that the quality of American journalism will be rigorously scrutinized before 1976, and a crisis may arise when the public studies the profit sheets of the larger newspaper chains and finds that the most exemplary dailies are suffering from economic malnutrition while some of the most innocuous, bland, and poorly edited journals are among the biggest money-makers. What lesson, for example, can be drawn from the dwindling revenues of the *New York Times* in late 1971, or the large losses reported by the *National Observer* and *Washington Post?*

The response of the mass media to the dangers latent in absolute freedom of expression will also make exciting news in the Bicentennial decade. For balanced against the Pentagon Papers incident is the complete lack of restraint in the underground press, which reflected a social revolution well underway by 1965. The dollar gap between the well-edited, financially secure *Wall Street Journal* and the hand-to-mouth existence of the *Chicano* or *Black America* widened. Reporters of the protest movement interviewed a variety of participants and observers, ranging from Walter Lippmann to Abbie Hoffman, in search of answers to the agonizing questions confronting society. How distant seemed that day in 1945, when the nation seemed preoccupied only with finding jobs for 12 million servicemen who would soon be mustered out into the labor force. Ponderous television commentaries and piles of magazine and newspaper articles on the future of America only seemed to bring more confusion. "We accustom ourselves to what we see," the Cardinal de Retz once noted, but Americans in the 1970s read and watched and were dismayed. A *New Yorker* cartoonist diagnosed the problem by depicting a bewildered, middle-aged man on the doctor's examining table, listening to the physician's finding: "You're suffering from too much media intake." An observer of the effects of technology on the nation put it another way: "Americans watch television too much." [29]

No one could prove, for all the media choices available to Americans in 1972, that Americans were a wiser and freer people than their forebears who had shaken off that imperial yoke almost two centuries earlier. Perhaps the mass media had fallen far short of the ideals of the Founding Fathers, who expected that a free press would make Americans the most enlightened and happiest men on earth. Or was the picture painted too black? After all, the Constitution still survived although in 1787 it had been fashioned out of some motley compromises and came forth as an emergency measure. Over the years the emergency passed and new ones arose, but the Constitution was flexible enough to keep the country from falling apart, even though on occasion it came close to the brink.

And then there was the First Amendment, which had been adopted to keep Congress from making a fool of itself and ruining the nation in the process. How to keep publishers, editors, writers and reporters careful and responsible was beyond the Constitution's scope. Indeed, American journalism since 1690 had displayed great flaws as well as immense strengths; and in relative terms the nation's mass media have probably performed better than any in the world. The first guideline was well drawn. The Republic, Jefferson reasserted in the last month of his life, guaranteed its citizens "the free right to the unbounded exercise of reason and freedom of opinion." From 1776 until 1972 each subsequent generation has substantially upheld that ideal. This has been no small task.

As the nation goes into its third century of existence, however, the old criteria are under fire. The bicentennial era seemed the era of bad feeling, but perhaps in retrospect it will only appear to have been a time of extraordinary affluence—and affluence obviously breeds as much anxiety as did the poverty of the 1830s or the 1930s. Tensions once confined to a section reached every nook of the Union, but one sign of the nation's strength was the unquestioned freedom of expression prevailing. Despite occasional carping over "managed news" or complaints from newsmen that public sources were uncooperative, the hard-working reporters were still producing discomfiting information and the citizen was left to make a judgment. Oftentimes a reporter would attempt to shield a news source as a highly confidential matter, much in the professional manner of a doctor or lawyer. How-

ever, the courts have not been sympathetic to such claims by reporters.

Before the purveying of information becomes a lost art, the newsmongers must accept the fact that the real test of professionalism is
not whether one can protect sources or hang out a shingle but how
well one performs a task that is vital to society. By telling the American citizenry the whole truth, the newsmongers of the future can
vindicate their professionalism. To tell the truth is still the highest
calling in politics, in medicine, in law, and above all, in journalism.

–30–

Notes

CHAPTER 1: DARING MEN AND
THEIR PRINTING MACHINES

1. Frederick S. Siebert, *Freedom of the Press in England, 1476–1776* (Urbana, Ill., 1952), 21, passim.

2. Lawrence Wroth, *The Colonial Printer* (New York, 1931), 157.

3. Isaiah Thomas, *The History of Printing in America* (2 vols.; Worcester, Mass., 1810), II, 270, 272, 292, 362, 367. C. S. Brigham, *Journals and Journeymen* (Philadelphia, 1950) lists 36 widows who became publishers, 72–73.

4. M. L. E. Moreau de St. Méry, *American Journey [Voyage aux Etats-Unis de l'Amerique, 1793–1798]*, Kenneth and Anna M. Roberts, trans. and eds. (New York, 1947), 282.

5. Frank Luther Mott, *American Journalism, A History: 1690–1960* (3rd. ed., New York, 1962), 18.

6. Leonard W. Labaree et al., eds., *The Autobiography of Benjamin Franklin* (New Haven, 1964), 163–64.

7. Philip Davidson, *Propaganda and the American Revolution 1763–1783* (Chapel Hill, 1941), 228.

8. Arthur M. Schlesinger, *Prelude to Independence, The Newspaper War on Britain 1764–1776* (New York, 1958), 41.

9. Samuel Briggs, comp., *The Essays, Humor, and Poems of Nathaniel Ames, Father and Son, . . . from their Almanacks 1726–1775* (Cleveland, 1891), 47–51, passim.

10. Davidson, *Propaganda and the American Revolution*, 223. Italics added.

11. Schlesinger, *Prelude to Independence*, 44.

12. Josiah Tucker, *Four Tracts on Political and Commercial Subjects* (3rd ed., Gloucester, 1776), 161–62.

13. The effect on American readers of *Cato's Letters*, which were first printed in the *London Journal* starting in 1720 and then placed in book form, can hardly be overestimated. See Bernard Bailyn, ed., *Pamphlets of the American Revolution 1750–1776* (Cambridge, Mass., 1965), 30–31, 34. John Trenchard and Thomas Gordon were the authors of these essays, which were "a searing indictment of eighteenth-century English politics and society."

14. Leonard W. Labaree et al., eds., *The Papers of Benjamin Franklin* (13 vols. to date; New Haven, 1959–   ), I, 13.

CHAPTER 2:
INK-STAINED REVOLUTIONARIES

1. See Stanley Nider Katz, ed., *A Brief Narrative of the Case and Trial of John Peter Zenger* (Cambridge, Mass., 1963), 3–35.

2. Both Katz and Leonard W. Levy take a more narrow view of the Zenger case and its impact on history. "The Zenger case in 1735 gave the press freedom to print as far as the truth carried and a jury's emotions might be sympathetically swayed, if the truth was directed away from the House [local legislature]." Levy, *The Legacy of Suppression, Freedom of Speech and the Press in Early American History* (Cambridge, Mass., 1960), 44.

3. Williamsburg *Virginia Gazette* (Purdie & Dixon), 2 June 1774.

4. See Clyde A. Duniway, *The Development of Freedom of the Press in Massachusetts* (Cambridge, Mass., 1906).

5. Advertisement in the *New-York Weekly Post-Boy*, quoted in James Melvin Lee, *History of American Journalism* (New York, 1917), 74.

6. Annapolis, Maryland, *Gazette*, 8, 15, 22 September 1774, quoted in the "Trivia," *William and Mary Quarterly*, 3d. ser., XXIX (1972), 159–60.

7. Davidson, *Propaganda and the American Revolution*, 102.

8. Peter Oliver, *Origin and Progress of the American Revolution*, Douglass Adair and John A. Schutz, eds. (San Marino, 1961), 148.

9. Robert A. Rutland, ed., *The Papers of George Mason* (3 vols.; Chapel Hill, 1970), I, 435.

10. Schlesinger, *Prelude to Independence*, 69.

11. John C. Miller, *Sam Adams: Pioneer in Propaganda* (Stanford, Calif., 1960), 57.

12. Rutland, ed., *Papers of George Mason*, I, 65–72.

13. John Dickinson, "Letters from a Farmer in Pennsylvania, No. II," in Samuel Eliot Morison, *Sources and Documents Illustrating the American Revolution 1764–1788* (Oxford, 1948).

14. George Mason [of Boston] to ?, 11 November 1769 (Ms., Houghton Library, Harvard University).

15. David Ramsay, *The History of the American Revolution* (2 vols.; Philadelphia, 1789), I, 115.

16. A. H. Smyth, *The Writings of Benjamin Franklin* (10 vols.; New York, 1905–1907), II, 172–79.

17. Quoted in Richard B. Morris, *The Emerging Nations and the American Revolution* (New York, 1970), 14.

18. The pamphlet Inglis printed was *The Deceiver Unmasked; or, Loyalty and Interest United . . . By a Loyal American.* See Thomas Adams, *American Independence* (Providence, R.I., 1965), 157.

19. Thomas, *History of Printing*, I, 308. See also Catherine Snell Crary, "The Tory and the Spy: the Double Life of James Rivington," *William and Mary Quarterly*, 3d. ser., XIII (1959), 61–72.

20. Thomas, *History of Printing*, I, 412.

21. Rush to Elias Boudinot, 2 August 1783, quoted in Lyman H. Butterfield, ed., *The Letters of Benjamin Rush* (2 vols.; Princeton, 1951), I, 307.

22. Humphreys to Alexander Hamilton, 16 September, 1787, in Frank L. Humphreys, *The Life and Times of David Humphreys* (2 vols.; New York, 1917), I, 423.

23. Nicholas B. Wainwright, *The History of the Philadelphia Inquirer* (supplement to the Philadelphia *Inquirer*, 16 September 1962).

CHAPTER 3: "THE DÆMON OF
FACTION" TRIUMPHANT

1. Quoted in Daniel J. Boorstin, *The Americans: the Colonial Experience* (New York, 1959), 327.

2. Brigham, *Journals and Journeymen*, 21.

3. Washington to David Humphreys, 10 October 1787. Max Farrand, ed., *The Records of the Federal Convention of 1787* (4 vols.; New Haven, 1911–1937), III, 104.

4. Galliard Hunt, ed., *The Writings of James Madison* (9 vols.; New York, 1900–1910), V, 16.

5. Lee's essays first appeared in pamphlet form, and were then printed in various newspapers including the Poughkeepsie *Country Journal* between 14 November 1787 and 2 January 1788.

6. Philadelphia *Independent Gazetteer*, 11, 14, 26 March 1788; 1, 3, 15 April 1788.

7. "Liste des Membres et Officiers du Congrés. 1788." Farrand, *Records of the Federal Convention*, III, 234.

8. Thomas B. Waite to George Thatcher, 8 January 1788. Samuel B. Harding, *The Contest Over the Ratification of the Federal Constitution in the State of Massachusetts* (New York, 1896), 39.

9. Charleston *South-Carolina Weekly Chronicle*, 9 October 1787.

10. Quoted in the Boston *American Herald*, 28 April 1788.

11. Donald H. Stewart, *The Opposition Press of the Federalist Period* (Albany, N.Y., 1969), 9–12.

12. Dumas Malone, *Jefferson and the Ordeal of Liberty* (Boston, 1962), 90–131.

13. James Morton Smith, *Freedom's Fetters, the Alien and Sedition Laws and American Civil Liberties* (Ithaca, N.Y., 1956), 189–90.

14. Stewart, *Opposition Press of Federalist Period*, 528–29.

15. Philadelphia *Aurora*, 26 December 1796.

16. Rollo G. Silver, *The American Printer 1787–1825* (Charlottesville, Va., 1967), 66–70.

17. Brigham, *Journals and Journeymen*, 22.

18. John Bernard, *Retrospections of America, 1797–1811* (New York, 1969), 194.

19. Joseph T. Buckingham, *Personal Memoirs and Recollections of Editorial Life* (2 vols.; Boston, 1852), I, 21.

20. Butterfield, *Letters of Benjamin Rush*, II, 1217.

21. Ibid.

22. Smith, *Freedom's Fetters*, 9.

23. From Cobbett's *Porcupine's Gazette*, quoted in ibid., 190.

24. Ibid., 216.

CHAPTER 4: NEW LIGHT ON
THE "DARK AGE"

1. Stewart, *Opposition Press of the Federalist Period*, 630.

2. Mott, *American Journalism*, 169. In all likelihood, Mott was following a false path first trod in this century by Willard G. Bleyer and James Melvin Lee, who appear to have been the twentieth-century historians first enunciating the idea that the 1800–1830 era was the "period of black journalism" (Lee, *History of American Journalism*, 143).

3. V. O. Key, Jr., *Public Opinion and American Democracy* (New York, 1961), 393.

4. Thomas Hamilton, *Men and Manners in America* (London, 1843 [1968 reprint]), 444–45.

5. F. von Raumer, *America and the American People*, W. W. Turner, trans. (New York, 1845), 301.

6. Stewart listed 92 American newspapers in 1790 and 242 a decade later. See the Appendix in his *Opposition Press of the Federalist Period*, 868–93, which gives an editor's political leanings.

7. James M. Banner, *To the Hartford Convention: The Federalists and the Origins of Party Politics in Massachusetts 1789–1815* (New York, 1970), 134.

8. Joseph T. Buckingham, *Specimens of Newspaper Literature* (2 vols.; Boston, 1850), I, 276–80.

9. Ibid. II, 69.

10. Banner, *To the Hartford Convention*, 162–63.

11. Stewart, *Opposition Press of the Federalist Period*, 553.

12. Mott, *American Journalism*, 169.

13. Alexis de Tocqueville, *Democracy in America*, George Lawrence, trans. (New York, 1969), 519–20.

14. Mott, *American Journalism*, 169–70.

15. Jefferson to John Norvell, 11 June 1807. Adrienne Koch and William Peden, eds., *The Life and Selected Writings of Thomas Jefferson* (New York, 1944), 581.

16. Jefferson's appearance as a champion of civil liberties and his own feelings about newspaper defamation lead to a double image of the third president. Whether this makes Jefferson into a hypocrite or merely an oversensitive politician is debatable. See Leonard W. Levy, *Jefferson and Civil Liberties, the Darker Side* (Cambridge, Mass., 1963), 158–76.

17. Tocqueville, *Democracy in America*, 519.

18. Buckingham, *Specimens of Newspaper Literature*, II, 160, 175.

19. Charles Sealsfield [Karl Anton Postl], *The United States of North America As They Are* (London, 1828 [1970 reprint]), 114–15.

20. Buckingham, *Specimens of Newspaper Literature*, II, 169–71.

21. Fredric Hudson, *Journalism in the United States from 1690 to 1872* (New York, 1873), 305.

22. Jefferson to Samuel Harrison Smith, 19 July 1804 (Smith Papers, Library of Congress).

23. Lee, *History of American Journalism*, 142.

24. Boston *Independent Chronicle*, 2 February 1815.

25. Thomas, *History of Printing*, II, 96.

26. Tocqueville, *Democracy in America*, 185–86.

CHAPTER 5: THE MAKING OF
A PRESIDENT: ANDREW THE FIRST

1. Sealsfield [Postl], *United States . . . As They Are,* 113–14.

2. Michael Chevalier, *Society, Manners and Politics in the United States* (Boston, 1839), 452.

3. Josiah H. Benton, Jr., *A Notable Libel Case, The Criminal Prosecution of Theodore Lyman Jr. by Daniel Webster* (Boston, 1904), 34, passim.

4. Hudson, *Journalism in the United States,* 272–73. Hudson blamed Hill's rejection upon "the hostility of Tyler, Iredell, and a few other Jackson senators to the appointment of editors to office."

5. Leonard D. White, *The Jacksonians* (New York, 1959), 263–264; Arthur M. Schlesinger, Jr., *The Age of Jackson* (Boston, 1953) has details of Jackson's newspaper ties, as does James E. Pollard, *The Presidents and the Press* (New York, 1947), 147–181.

6. Mott, *American Journalism,* 180.

7. Frederick Marryat, *A Diary in America,* Sydney Jackman, ed. (New York, 1962), 406.

8. Daniel J. Boorstin, *The Americans, The National Experience* (New York, 1965), 125–28.

9. Frank Freidel, *The Golden Age of American History* (New York, 1959), 366.

10. Hudson, *Journalism in the United States,* 365.

11. Edwin Emery, *The Press in America: An Interpretative History of Journalism* (Englewood Cliffs, N.J., 1962), 251.

12. James L. Crouthamel, *James Watson Webb, A Biography* (Middletown, Conn., 1969), 34–47.

13. Leggett was an editorial writer for Bryant. The remark was a warning to the Democrats that went unheeded. Nelson M. Blake, *A Short History of American Life* (New York, 1952), 245.

14. Buckingham, *Personal Memoirs and Recollections of Editorial Life,* II, 107–108.

15. Hudson, *Journalism in the United States,* 333.

16. G. G. Van Deusen, *Horace Greeley, Nineteenth Century Crusader* (Philadelphia, 1953), 87.

17. Niles's report of the assassination attempt is proof that the expression "Stop the press!" is a vintage cry. "We stopped the press last Saturday when all except 6 or 700 of our papers for the mails had been worked-off, to get in a paragraph noticing the assault on the president of the United States, in the east portico of the capitol. . . ." *Niles' Weekly Register,* 7 February 1835.

CHAPTER 6: THE ONE-CENT MIRACLE

1. Mott, *American Journalism,* 233.

2. Horace Greeley, *Recollections of a Busy Life* (New York, 1868), 84.

3. William Harlan Hale, *Horace Greeley: Voice of the People* (New York, 1950), 41.

4. Greeley, *Recollections of a Busy Life,* 133–34.

5. Ibid., 233. Greeley had managed to offend other congressmen on a variety of counts, but he believed that his brusqueness and sharp tongue had little to do with his personal safety. "I was obnoxious only because I was presumed earnestly hostile to Slavery," he recalled.

6. Hudson, *Journalism in the United States,* 762–63.

7. Mob opposition to the abolitionists was often furnished by the extremes of wealth and poverty in many communities. See Leonard L. Richards, *Gentlemen of Property and Standing: Anti-Abolition Mobs in Jacksonian America* (New York, 1970).

8. Emery, *The Press and America,* 274–77.

9. From the *National Anti-Slavery Standard,* 16 August 1856, quoted in Harold N. Nelson, ed., *Freedom of the Press from Hamilton to the Warren Court* (Indianapolis, 1966), 210.

10. Vernon L. Parrington, *Main Currents in American Thought* (3 vols. in one; New York, 1945), II, 357.

11. Bernard A. Weisberger, *The American Newspaperman* (Chicago, 1961), 72.

12. Hudson, *Journalism in the United States,* 321.

13. New York *Tribune,* 20 May 1846.

14. New York *Tribune,* 27 July 1848.

CHAPTER 7: A GUILTY GENERATION

1. Van Deusen, *Horace Greeley,* 142.

2. The term *news* as an acronym appeared as early as 1784. "In the first place as news comes from all quarters of the terraqueous globe, so the very word itself points out to us, viz. N. North, E. East, W. West, S. South; so that, I believe no language in the world can furnish us with a title more expressive." *Virginia Journal & Alexandria Advertiser,* 18 March 1784.

3. Laura Amanda White, *Robert Barnwell Rhett, Father of Secession* (Gloucester, Mass., 1965), 124.

4. Greeley to Seward, 11 November 1854. Greeley, *Recollections of a Busy Life,* 315–20.

5. Philadelphia *Public Ledger,* 27 April 1854. "After Col. Benton had spoken, the hammer came down, and then a scene of confusion ensued which beggars description." The reporter—"Observer"—went on to say speech "was marked by great moderation . . . though it contained a few passages of exquisite bitterness, such as no other man but Benton can utter in this country."

6. Richmond *Enquirer,* 24 May 1854.

7. Harold S. Schultz, *Nationalism and Sectionalism* (Durham, N.C., 1950), 79–80.

8. John Bruce, *Gaudy Century: The Story of San Francisco's Hundred Years of Robust Journalism* (New York, 1948), 41–42.

9. Henry H. Simms, *A Decade of Sectional Controversy* (Chapel Hill, N.C., 1942), 160.

10. Harlon Hoyt Horner, *Lincoln and Greeley* (Urbana, Ill., 1953), 160.

11. Schultz, *Nationalism and Sectionalism,* 187.

12. Ibid., 208. Ashmore spoke on 1 March 1860.

13. Colin Simkin, ed., *Currier & Ives' America* (New York, 1955), 4.

14. Murat Halstead, *Caucuses of 1860: A History of the National Political Conventions . . .* (Columbus, Ohio, 1860), 121.

15. Hale, *Greeley, Voice of the People,* 227.

16. New York *Herald,* 30 September 1860.

17. Quoted in Donald E. Reynolds, *Editors Make War, Southern Newspapers in the Secession Crisis* (Nashville, Tenn., 1970), 142.

18. When he reviewed the era Greeley admitted that he had been complacent about the threat of southern secession, but explained that in his judgment he had been joined by most of the intelligensia and men of wealth in the North. Greeley, *Recollections of a Busy Life,* 395.

19. Mary B. Chesnut, *A Diary from Dixie* (New York, 1929), 80–81.

20. Holman Hamilton, *Prologue to Conflict, the Crisis and Compromise of 1850* (New York, 1966), 190.

CHAPTER 8:
"NOT THE GREATEST CALAMITY"

1. William Howard Russell, *My Diary North and South* (Boston, 1863), 27.

2. Ibid., 39.

3. Quoted in John W. Tebbel, *The American Magazine: A Compact History* (New York, 1969), 97.

4. New York *Tribune,* 26 June 1861.

5. Charleston *Mercury,* 26 April 1861, quoted in James Ford Rhodes, *History of the United States from the Compromise of 1850* (7 vols.; New York, 1893–1906), III, 288n.

6. *New York Times,* 22 July 1861.

7. Russell, *My Diary North and South,* 452.

8. J. Cutler Andrews, *The North Reports the Civil War* (Pittsburgh, 1955), 94.

9. New York *Tribune,* 24 July 1861.

10. Andrews, *The North Reports the Civil War,* 82–84, 634–35.

11. Mott, *American Journalism,* 364.

12. E. M. Coulter, *The Confederate States of America, 1861–1865* (Baton Rouge, 1950), 503.

13. J. Culter Andrews, *The South Reports the Civil War* (Princeton, 1970), 383.

14. Frank L. Klement, *The Copperheads in the Middle West* (Chicago, 1960), 100–102.

15. Hudson, *Journalism in the United States,* 671–74.

16. Andrews, *The South Reports the Civil War,* 478–505.

17. Horner, *Lincoln and Greeley,* 297–310.

18. New York *Tribune,* 14 April 1865.

CHAPTER 9: AS GIANTS DEPART

1. New York *Tribune,* 1 May 1865.

2. New York *Herald,* 16 May 1865.

3. Van Deusen, *Horace Greeley,* 353–54.

4. Quoted in John B. McMaster, *History of the People of the United States During Lincoln's Administration* (New York, 1927), 636–37.

5. Andrews, *The South Reports the Civil War,* 44.

6. F. N. Boney, ed., *A Union Soldier in the Land of the Vanquished* (University, Ala., 1969), 64 and 64n.

7. *New York Times,* 30 August 1866.

8. Quoted in Claude G. Bowers, *The Tragic Era, the Revolution After Lincoln* (Cambridge, Mass., 1929), 179.

9. Quoted in George F. Milton, *The Age of Hate, Andrew Johnson and the Radicals* (New York, 1930), 515.

10. New York *Herald,* 12 May 1868.

11. *Nation,* 21 May 1868, quoted in Bowers, *The Tragic Era,* 197.

12. Hudson, *Journalism in the United States,* 648.

13. Ibid., 652.

14. *New York Times,* 7 July 1899.

15. Hudson, *Journalism in the United States,* 663.

16. *Nation,* 24 June 1869, quoted in *The Dictionary of American Biography,* XV, 411.

17. Mott, *American Journalism,* 383.

18. *New York Times,* 27 April 1872.

19. *New York Times,* 4 May 1872.

20. Hale, *Greeley, Voice of the People,* 337.

21. *New York Times,* 29 August 1874.

22. Alonzo F. Hill, *Secrets of the Sanctum, an Inside View of an Editor's Life* (Philadelphia, 1875), 63–64.

23. Ibid., 47–48.

24. Ibid., 27–28.

25. Ray Ginger, *The Age of Excess* (New York, 1965), 5.

26. Hill, *Secrets of the Sanctum,* 30–31.

CHAPTER 10: Cross Currents

1. W. A. Swanberg, *Pulitzer* (New York, 1967), 69.

2. S. N. D. North, *History and Present Condition of the Newspaper and Periodical Press of the United States* (Misc. Docs., 47th Cong., 2d Sess.; Washington, 1884), 77.

3. Swanberg, *Pulitzer,* 71.

4. Mott, *American Journalism,* 434.

5. North, *History and Present Condition of the Press,* 89, 141.

6. *New York Times,* 15 September 1884.

7. Ibid., 1 October 1884.

8. Jacob Riis, *How the Other Half Lives* (New York, 1890), 8–9.

9. John Haynes Holmes, "Jacob August Riis," *Dictionary of American Biography,* XV, 606–608.

10. Julian P. Boyd, ed., *The Papers of Thomas Jefferson* (18 vols. to date: Princeton, 1950–   ), XII, 28.

11. William Allen White, *Autobiography* (New York, 1946), 230.

12. Staff of the Kansas City *Star, William R. Nelson* (Cambridge, Mass., 1915), 22.

13. Kansas City *Star,* 1 October 1913, quoted in Mott, *American Journalism,* 472.

14. Bruce, *Gaudy Century,* 174–76.

15. Mott, *American Journalism,* 501.

16. Ibid., 498.

17. Thomas D. Clark, *The Southern Country Editor* (Indianapolis, 1948), 190–91.

18. Ibid., 96.

19. Fairfax Downey, *Portrait of an Era as Drawn by Charles Dana Gibson* (New York, 1936), 1; Frank Luther Mott, *History of American Magazines* (5 vols.; Cambridge, Mass., 1966–70), IV, 564.

20. Quoted in William A. Settle, Jr., *Jesse James Was His Name* (Columbia, Mo., 1966), 120–21.

21. Clark, *Southern Country Editor*, 299.

22. Bessie L. Pierce, *A History of Chicago* (3 vols.; New York, 1937–57), III, 273.

23. Chicago *Tribune*, 4 May 1888, as quoted in ibid., III, 278.

24. Ibid., III, 280.

25. Nelson, ed., *Freedom of the Press from Hamilton to the Warren Court*, 274–77.

26. *New York Times*, 2 June 1889.

27. Daniel J. Boorstin, *The Image, or What Happened to the American Dream* (New York, 1962), 11–12.

CHAPTER 11: RICH MAN, POOR MAN

1. Emery, *The Press and America*, 416–18.

2. Swanberg, *Citizen Hearst* (New York, 1961), 50.

3. Ibid, 95.

4. Mott, *American Journalism*, 521.

5. Swanberg, *Pulitzer*, 238.

6. Meyer Berger, *The Story of the New York Times 1851–1951* (New York, 1951), 105.

7. Mott, *American Journalism*, 527.

8. Charles H. Brown, *The Correspondents' War: Journalists in the Spanish-American War* (New York, 1967), 4.

9. New York *World*, 5 April 1896, quoted in ibid., 36.

10. New York *Journal*, 16 August 1897, quoted in Mott, *American Journalism*, 530.

11. New York *Journal*, quoted in Brown, *Correspondents' War*, 142.

12. Ibid., 443.

13. New York *Journal*, 4 February 1901, quoted in Emery, *The Press and America*, 460.

14. New York *Journal*, 10 April 1901, quoted in Mott, *American Journalism*, 541.

15. Harold S. Wilson, *McClure's Magazine and the Muckrakers* (Princeton, 1970), 129–48.

16. Lincoln Steffens, *Autobiography* (New York, 1931), 375.

17. Mark Sullivan, *Our Times; the United States 1900–1925* (6 vols.; New York, 1926–35), II, 478n.

18. New York Evening *Post*, 1 March 1904, quoted in Swanberg, *Citizen Hearst,* 211.

19. New York *Tribune*, 12 May 1904, quoted in ibid., 215.

20. Elmer Ellis, *Mr. Dooley's America* (New York, 1941), 217.

21. Swanberg, *Pulitzer*, 363.

22. David Graham Phillips, *The Treason of the Senate,* George Mowry and Judson Grenier, eds. (Chicago, 1964), 10.

23. Louis Filler, *Crusaders for American Liberalism: The Story of the Muckrakers* (New York, 1961), 152.

24. Sullivan, *Our Times,* II, 327.

25. Mott, *American Journalism,* 605–606.

26. Steffens, *Autobiography,* 660–89.

27. Swanberg, *Pulitzer,* 443.

28. *New York Times,* 14–19 April 1912; Berger, *Story of the New York Times,* 193–201.

29. San Francisco *Bulletin,* 31 August 1912, quoted in George Mowry, *The California Progressives* (Berkeley, 1951), 192.

30. Boston *Daily Advertiser,* 6 November 1912.

31. Jacksonville, Florida, *Times-Union,* 16 November 1912.

32. Walter Johnson, ed., *Selected Letters of William Allen White* (New York, 1947), 139.

33. Ibid., 140.

34. Hill, *Secrets of the Sanctum,* 75.

35. Mott, *American Journalism,* 604.

CHAPTER 12: LOST INNOCENCE

1. Sullivan, *Our Times,* V, 52–53.

2. Henry B. Parkes, *Recent America* (New York, 1943), 300–301.

3. Sullivan, *Our Times,* V, 79.

4. Ferdinand Lundberg, *Imperial Hearst* (New York, 1936), 238–39. Lundberg was not an admirer of Hearst's and the account is biased. Swanberg, *Citizen Hearst,* 295, insists that Hearst's alleged pro-German sentiments cannot be supported by the facts.

5. Fremont Older, *My Own Story* (New York, 1926), 336–38.

6. Richmond *Times-Dispatch,* 8 November 1916.

7. Johnson, ed., *Letters of William Allen White,* 176.

8. Harvey Wish, *Contemporary America* (New York, 1966), 211–12.

9. Carl Wittke, *The German-Language Press in America* (Lexington, Ky., 1957), 269.

10. Oscar Ameringer, *If You Don't Weaken* (New York, 1940), 340–43.

11. Wittke, *German-Language Press in America,* 274.

12. Mott, *American Journalism*, 628.

13. Sullivan, *Our Times*, V, 636.

14. Mott, *American Journalism*, 631.

15. Sullivan, *Our Times*, V, 654.

16. Atlanta *Journal*, 17 January 1919.

17. Gitlow v. New York, 268 U. S. 652 (1925).

18. Johnson, ed., *Letters of William Allen White*, 200.

19. Pollard, *The Presidents and the Press*, 674–88.

20. Gene Smith, *When the Cheering Stopped* (New York, 1964), 61.

21. *New York Times*, 1 October 1919.

22. Ibid., 29 January 1920.

23. John W. Tebbel, *The Compact History of the American Newspaper* (New York, 1963), 220.

24. Henry L. Mencken, *Mencken Chrestomathy* (New York, 1949), 8.

CHAPTER 13:
HEADLINES AND BREADLINES

1. David Chalmers, *Hooded Americanism: The First Century of the Ku Klux Klan 1865–1965* (New York, 1965), 35–36, 123, 146, 203.

2. Charles C. Alexander, *The Ku Klux Klan in the Southwest* (Lexington, Ky., 1965), 199–205.

3. *New York Times*, 21 April 1925.

4. Louis T. Griffith and John E. Talmadge, *Georgia Journalism 1763–1950* (Athens, Ga., 1951), 148.

5. *Time*, 3 August 1925.

6. In their propectus the *Time* publishers said they planned to stress brief reports of "Every Happening of Importance" and promised that their magazine would be unlike the *Literary Digest*, which "treats at great length a few subjects selected more or less arbitrarily from week to week." Robert T. Elson, *Time Inc.* (New York, 1968), 8.

7. Quoted in Boorstin, *The Image*, 135.

8. Erik Barnouw, *A History of Broadcasting in the United States* (3 vols.; New York, 1966–70), I, 138.

9. George Mowry, *The Urban Nation* (New York, 1965), 45.

10. Mott, *American Journalism*, 570.

11. *New York Times*, 21 May 1927.

12. Richmond *News Leader*, 20 May 1927.

13. Ibid., 23 May 1927.

14. George Seldes, *Lords of the Press* (New York, 1938), 287.

15. Leon Whipple, in *Survey,* 15 October 1927.

16. *New York Times,* 1 February 1928.

17. Lynchburg *Daily Advance,* 7 July 1928.

18. Memphis *Commercial Appeal,* 16 September 1928.

19. *New York Times,* 21 October 1929.

20. Johnson, ed., *Letters of William Allen White,* 326.

21. Atlanta *Journal,* 24 June 1930.

22. George B. Tindall, *The Emergence of the New South 1913–1945* (Baton Rouge, La., 1967), 363.

23. *Nation,* 20 July 1932.

24. *Time,* 18 April 1932.

25. Ibid., 4 April 1932.

26. Mott, *American Journalism,* 691–92.

27. *New York Times,* 2–7 March, 13 May 1932; 21 September 1934; 5 February 1935; 1–6 April 1936.

28. Barnouw, *History of Broadcasting,* I, 167.

29. Lundberg, *Imperial Hearst,* 274, 281.

30. Llewellyn White, *The American Radio* (Chicago, 1947), 54–55.

31. In 1933 NBC scheduled 76 percent music and drama, 7 percent "talks and discussions," and 2 percent news. CBS was about the same. By 1939, however, NBC had 77 percent music and drama and 3.8 percent news while CBS logged 62 percent music and drama and 11 percent news. White, *The American Radio,* 66.

32. Ibid., 238.

CHAPTER 14: THE BRAT GROWS UP

1. *New Republic,* 22 March 1933.

2. Newbold Noyes, Jr. of the Washington *Star,* quoted in Curtis MacDougall, *Interpretative Reporting* (New York, 1957), 8.

3. Ibid., 17, 21.

4. *Time,* 9 January 1933.

5. *Editor & Publisher,* 4 March 1933.

6. Quoted in *Harpers,* September 1934.

7. Seldes, *Lords of the Press,* 73.

8. *Literary Digest,* 20 October 1934.

9. *New Republic,* 7 November 1933.

10. White, *The American Radio,* 55.

11. *Editor & Publisher,* 7 November 1936.

12. Ibid., 28 November 1936.

13. *Literary Digest,* 4 July 1936.

14. Leo C. Rosten, *The Washington Correspondents* (New York, 1937), 195–96.

15. James MacGregor Burns, *Roosevelt: The Lion and the Fox* (New York, 1956), 298.

16. Ibid., 317.

17. Mott, *American Journalism,* 652.

18. *Time,* 11 October 1937.

19. Barnouw, *History of Broadcasting,* II, 78.

20. Ibid., 80, 83.

21. Richmond *Times-Dispatch,* 16 March 1939.

22. *Life,* 20 March 1939.

23. Ibid., 27 March 1939.

24. *Time,* 27 March 1939.

25. Burns, *Roosevelt: The Lion and the Fox,* 391–92.

26. Barnouw, *History of Broadcasting,* II, 134.

27. Herbert Brucker, "Can Printed News Save a Free Society?" *Saturday Review of Literature,* 10 October 1970, 52–53.

28. *Time,* 8 July 1940.

29. Ibid., 8 July 1940.

30. Walter Johnson, *William Allen White's America* (New York, 1947), 535.

31. Joseph Alsop column, *Washington Post,* 4 July 1971.

32. Mott, *American Journalism,* 783.

33. Ibid., 785.

CHAPTER 15: SEEING IT NOW

1. *A Free and Responsible Press* (Chicago, 1947), 11. The study commission that produced the report was headed by Robert M. Hutchins so that the findings and recommendations were generally referred to as the Hutchins Report.

2. Ibid., 65.

3. *New York Times,* 25 February 1954.

4. Norfolk *Ledger Dispatch,* 17 May 1954; Atlanta *Journal,* 18 May 1954.

5. Bob Smith, *They Closed Their Schools* (Chapel Hill, 1965), 23, 33–34, passim.

6. Oswald Garrison Villard, *Some Newspapers and Newspaper-Men* (New York, 1923 [1933 ed.]), vii–viii. Villard had one thing in his favor—his ancestral credentials were outstanding. The grandson of William Lloyd Garrison and son of Henry Villard, he inherited the wealth of one and the contrariness of the other, and for a genera-

tion said irrevent things about fellow publishers while he guided the New York *Evening Post* and later the *Nation*. Villard was a silver-spoon newspaper man himself, but he had no liking for his peers who had also inherited their properties and used them for glorified profit-and-loss sheets. Villard retained some of his grandfather's altruism— enough at least to lament the decline and fall of journalism between 1900 and 1935.

7. John J. O'Connor, "What Made Murrow So Special?" *New York Times*, 16 January 1972.

8. Los Angeles *Times*, 6 October 1957.

9. *New York Times*, 11 May 1960.

10. *Time*, 16 May 1960.

11. *Broadcasting*, 7 November 1960, quoted in Barnouw, *History of Broadcasting*, III, 164n.

12. Arthur M. Schlesinger, Jr., *A Thousand Days: John F. Kennedy in the White House* (Boston, 1965), 261.

13. Barnouw, *History of Broadcasting*, III, 187.

14. *Time*, 16 November 1962.

15. Barnouw, *History of Broadcasting*, III, 224.

16. New York Times, 23 November 1963.

17. *Editor & Publisher*, 31 October 1964.

18. *Report of the National Advisory Commission on Civil Disorders* (New York, 1968), 374. The commission was headed by Governor Otto Kerner and hence alluded to as the Kerner Report.

19. Gunnar Myrdal, *The American Dilemma* (New York, 1944), 910.

20. William Small, *To Kill a Messenger: Television News and the Real World* (New York, 1970), 203–17.

21. *Editor & Publisher*, 2 November 1968.

22. Small, *To Kill a Messenger*, 129.

23. Robert J. Glessing, *The Underground Press in America* (Bloomington, Ind., 1970), 11–38.

24. Hunt, ed., *The Writings of James Madison*, VI, 336. Madison was quoting with approval from the XYZ ministers' reply to Talleyrand.

25. Barry Bingham, Jr., "Does the American Press Deserve to Survive?" *Quill*, January 1971.

26. Henry David Thoreau, *Walden and Other Writings*, Brooks Atkinson, ed. (New York, 1937), 47.

27. Ernest van den Haag, "Of Happiness and of Despair We Have No Measure," in *Mass Media and Mass Man*, Alan Casty, comp. (New York, 1968), 5.

28. H. Marshall McLuhan, *Understanding Media* (New York, 1964), 207–208.

29. Small, *To Kill a Messenger*, 1.

Acknowledgments

Whatever merit these pages hold is mainly owing to the perceptive comments of Leonard W. Levy, Grace Shaw, James R. Short, and particularly Paul H. Smith. Help at vital times also came from Hodding Carter III, Steven Hochman, Lallé Hoffman, Donald Jackson, and the staff of the Alderman Library of the University of Virginia. Conversations with Joseph A. Brandt, the late Fayette Copeland, Sr., William Weber Johnson, Jack Lyle, Hugh Patterson, Ed Tribble and dozens of students at UCLA (Martin Cooper, Robert Davenport, and Robert O. Young were particularly keen) also contributed to the nature of the book.

Index

Abell, Arunah S., 143
Adams, Abigail, 77
Adams, Charles Francis, 226
Adams, John, 59, 80; anger over
defeat, 90; attacked by Bache,
79; dispatches XYZ envoys, 77;
elected president, 76; elected
vice president, 67, 68; intense
partisanship, 81
Adams, John Quincy, 109, 112,
115, 119, 120, 123, 124
Adams, Samuel, 39–40, 41–42, 60,
61; writes as "Vindex," 45
Adams, Samuel Hopkinson, 277
Adams, Thomas, 80
Advertisements: by department
stores, 247; early "classified,"
97; "help-wanted," 246; national
campaigns, 247; "quack-medi-
cine" ads, 98; rates behind general economy, 300
Agricultural journalism, 135
Albany, Ga.: *Herald*, 315; *Morning News*, 315
Albany, N.Y.: *Argus*, 152; *Evening
Journal*, 130–131, 152; *Jefferson-*

ian, edited by Greeley, 145;
Ploughboy, 135
Alexander VI (pope), 5
Alexander, James, 47–48; defends
Zenger, 28–30
Alexander, Peter W., 205
Alien and Sedition act (1798), 78,
91; aimed at political opponents,
79–81
Allen, John: leading Federalist,
78
Allen, Robert S., 330
Alley, J. P., 328
Almanacs: influence during 18th
century, 19–20
Alton, Ill., *Observer*, 134
Amarillo, Tex., *News*, 314
American Agriculturalist, 135
American Expeditionary Force
(AEF), 299; published *Stars and
Stripes*, 298
American News Company, 223
American Newspaper Guild: seeks
bargaining rights, 327
American Newspaper Publishers'
Assn.: fear of television, 364

The most striking aspect of American journalism since 1776 has been the tremendous technological progress in gathering and distributing news to a mass audience, maintains Robert A. Rutland in this trenchant, panoramic view of U.S. journalism from colonial times to the present. Despite these amazing technological advances, he holds, "the basic product only costs more, with a negligible improvement in quality."

An unconventional history of American journalism, *The Newsmongers* reveals the profit-making instinct that has often smothered the social reformers and achieved goals opposite from those sought by the founding fathers. The hopes of 1776–1791 were that free men would make an intelligent choice if given full information on public issues. *The Newsmongers* tells of the close liaison between the business community and journalism, with newspaper editors often expected or willing to use their newspapers as vehicles for keeping society quiet rather than progressive. With some impatience, Rutland examines the irresponsibility of Northern and Southern editors in the decade preceding the Civil War, as well as the editorial routes America followed toward more recent wars. Rutland delves into the precolonial roots of our journalism, the town crier, broadsides, almanacs; how a newspaper with nearly a million copies sold each day can go bankrupt; and why a gangster can become a national hero. The relationship of Presidents—strong and weak—to the press is also examined, along with charges of "one-party journalism" during Presidential election years.